TERMS OF EXCHANGE

the
LIFE
OF
IDEAS

SERIES EDITOR

Darrin McMahon, *Dartmouth College*

After a period of some eclipse, the study of intellectual history has enjoyed a broad resurgence in recent years. The Life of Ideas contributes to this revitalization through the study of ideas as they are produced, disseminated, received, and practiced in different historical contexts. The series aims to embed ideas—those that endured, and those once persuasive but now forgotten—in rich and readable cultural histories. Books in this series draw on the latest methods and theories of intellectual history while being written with elegance and élan for a broad audience of readers.

Terms of Exchange

Brazilian Intellectuals and the French Social Sciences

IAN MERKEL

The University of Chicago Press
Chicago and London

The University of Chicago Press, Chicago 60637
The University of Chicago Press, Ltd., London
© 2022 by The University of Chicago
Published 2022
Printed in the United States of America

31 30 29 28 27 26 25 24 23 22   1 2 3 4 5

ISBN-13: 978-0-226-81936-5 (cloth)
ISBN-13: 978-0-226-81979-2 (paper)
ISBN-13: 978-0-226-81937-2 (e-book)
DOI: https://doi.org/10.7208/chicago/9780226819372.001.0001

Publication of this work was supported by a grant from the
Société des Américanistes.

SOCIÉTÉ DES
AMÉRICANISTES

Library of Congress Cataloging-in-Publication Data

Names: Merkel, Ian, author.
Title: Terms of exchange : Brazilian intellectuals and the French social sciences /
    Ian Merkel.
Other titles: Life of ideas.
Description: Chicago : University of Chicago Press, 2022. | Series: The life of
    ideas | Includes bibliographical references and index.
Identifiers: LCCN 2021042919 | ISBN 9780226819365 (cloth) | ISBN 9780226819792
    (paperback) | ISBN 9780226819372 (ebook)
Subjects: LCSH: Universidade de São Paulo. | Social sciences—Brazil—
    São Paulo—History. | Social sciences—France—History. | Intellectuals—
    Brazil—São Paulo.
Classification: LCC H53.B6 M47 2022 | DDC 300.981/61—dc23
LC record available at https://lccn.loc.gov/2021042919

⊗ This paper meets the requirements of ANSI/NISO Z39.48-1992
(Permanence of Paper).

For Mariella and Antonina, with love

Contents

Figures

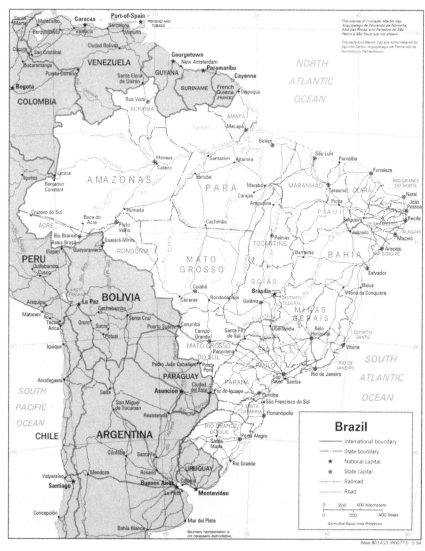

FRONTISPIECE Map of Brazil, 1981. Perry-Castañeda Library Map Collection, The University of Texas at Austin.

Introduction

Fernand Braudel, one of the most eminent historians of the twentieth century, once declared, "It was in Brazil that I became intelligent."[1] Claude Lévi-Strauss, the father of structural anthropology, claimed to have "made his first weapons" in São Paulo.[2] Roger Bastide, a pioneer of Afro-Brazilian studies, human geographer Pierre Monbeig, and a number of other prominent social scientists also spent their formative years in Brazil, where they combined fieldwork with new methodological approaches that would prove foundational for scholarly conversations about the global economy, temporality, syncretism, race, and social structure. This book makes the case that Brazilian intellectuals such as Mário de Andrade, Caio Prado Jr., Arthur Ramos, Gilberto Freyre, and Florestan Fernandes were crucial partners in framing these conversations—and indeed, in making them possible.

Well before Braudel was synonymous with the Annales school or the *longue durée*, he, like many other French scholars, began his university career in Brazil.[3] In 1934, the year before his arrival, São Paulo inaugurated Brazil's first full-scale university, the University of São Paulo (USP). In its second year, USP called upon younger, less-established figures to join its faculty. Braudel, for example, had been teaching secondary school for ten years in Algeria. He had yet to complete his ambitious study of the history and geography of the Mediterranean—or really start writing it, for that matter—when he first encountered Caio Prado Jr.

Prado hailed from the very planter and commercial elite that founded

USP and gave French scholars such as Braudel the opportunity to teach and research. He had already published two books: the first, a historical analysis of Brazil's political evolution; the second, a favorable account of the "new world" of the USSR.[4] Prior to Braudel's arrival, Prado had helped to initiate the Associação dos Geógrafos Brasileiros (Association of Brazilian Geographers)—an innovative, interdisciplinary organization in which Braudel would actively participate during his time in Brazil. Because of his political involvement with the leftist Aliança Nacional Libertadora, however, Prado was imprisoned and ultimately exiled shortly after his encounter with Braudel. This would delay more extensive conversations between the two until Braudel's return to France.

After two years teaching at USP, Braudel landed his first job in Paris. Hired as a Hispanist at the École Pratique des Hautes Études in 1937, he taught courses on topics such as the "Iberian expansion in America."[5] During the years 1937–39, he saw Prado frequently at the Bibliothèque Nationale, where they discussed transatlantic trade, the relationship between history and geography, multiple temporalities, and other ideas that would be central to their subsequent scholarship and highly influential for generations to come.[6]

During those years, Prado was in the midst of researching what would become his most significant work. *Formação do Brasil contemporâneo*, published in 1942, offered a new understanding of colonial Brazil that examined the structures of unequal trade and peripheral capitalist accumulation.[7] As such, *Formação* became a forerunner in Brazilian historiography as well as in what is commonly known as dependency theory.[8] It also anticipated some of the geographic and economic aspects of what Peter Burke has called the "French Historical Revolution."[9]

Well after Prado's return to Brazil in 1939 and into World War II, he and Braudel continued to correspond. Just before the outbreak of combat between France and Germany, Braudel wrote Prado: "I think about our conversations of yesterday—let us hope there will be those of tomorrow."[10] Shortly after the war, he reviewed Prado's work as he prepared his magnum opus *The Mediterranean and the Mediterranean World in the Age of Philip II* for publication.[11] As I demonstrate in chapter 4, the young Braudel's exchanges with and readings of Prado influenced his conception of the Mediterranean in at least two ways. They encouraged Braudel to consider the Atlantic as the geographical extension of the inner Mediterranean Sea and as the temporal starting point for its secular decline.

Braudel's Brazilian "intelligence" is illustrative of a much broader pattern of exchange. Mário de Andrade, for example, helped to mount Lévi-Strauss's expeditions into the Brazilian interior that made him famous. Others, such as Gilberto Freyre and Arthur Ramos, proved invaluable interlocutors for Roger Bastide and crucial for postwar thinking about race relations more generally.

Brazil and Brazilians, whether as objects of study, sources of institutional support, or a properly intellectual network, came to feature prominently in the French social sciences. This is the story of both how this came to be and how it largely came to be forgotten, until now.

In São Paulo in particular, the founders of the new university modeled it almost entirely on the French system and recruited French scholars to professionalize intellectual activities that had until then largely taken place in private institutes and libraries.[12] Although to a lesser extent than at USP, such a French presence was also felt in Rio de Janeiro, at the University of the Federal District and the University of Brazil, and in Rio Grande do Sul, at the University of Porto Alegre. All in all, in the period between 1934 and 1945, some thirty-seven French professors went to launch Brazil's first universities.[13] There, they exercised disproportionate influence on the development of the social sciences—much more so than Italians and Germans, considered too compromised by fascism for the ostensibly more ideological disciplines, or Americans, who, with the exception of the Escola Livre de Sociologia e Política (Free School of Sociology and Politics), or in applied areas such as public health, were relatively absent from university life until much later.[14]

Although numerically small by today's standards, these professors were among the first to be employed as philosophers, historians, sociologists, geographers, and anthropologists in Brazil, and they trained the first generation of university-based Brazilian academics. It is therefore of little surprise that Brazilian social scientists themselves have long grappled with the importance of France in their intellectual genealogy.[15] This book argues that the reverse is also true: namely, that what we think of as the French social sciences were profoundly marked by the story of USP and of Brazilian universities more generally.[16]

In Brazil, the period between the 1920s and the 1960s saw the end of the First Republic, with the Revolution of 1930; the rise of Getúlio Vargas's Estado Novo; and the postwar democratic experiment that would last until the military seized power, in 1964. In terms of culture and intellectual life, these years saw the rise of modernism, the consolidation of national social thought, and the institutionalization of the social sciences.[17] This study uses the French university missions to Brazil to offer a new story of international exchange across this all-important period in Brazilian and French intellectual history traversed by fascism, war, and decolonization. The military coup of 1964 and the subsequent agreements between the Brazilian Ministry of Education and USAID would ultimately displace France from the social-scientific landscape in favor of heightened exchange with the United States, developmentalism, and national-modernizing tendencies.[18] Nonetheless, as I show, "Americanization" was neither as ubiquitous nor as early as is sometimes suggested.[19]

Terms of Exchange furthers diplomatic historians' analysis of soft power and cultural politics, emphasizing the importance of international relations for the social sciences and intellectual history more broadly.[20] As a "transnational history of the social sciences," it uses institutions such as the Sociedade de Etnografia e Folclore, the Associação dos Geógrafos Brasileiros, and UNESCO to examine the construction of the Annales school, human geography in pioneer zones, creolization in the New World, and racial democracy.[21] Above all, I propose to connect histories and scholarship that have remained fragmented for linguistic and institutional reasons, and, sometimes, due to the assumption that certain places are unable to contribute to theory because of their position in the political economy of knowledge.[22]

New works in English posit Latin America as a source of ideas and practices relevant well beyond the region.[23] At least in principle, the Eurocentric and diffusionist theories of yore seem to have been put to rest.[24] Nonetheless, there remains a great deal of work to be done in bringing Latin American scholarship to bear on the relationship between history and theory: to "move the intellectuals of the periphery into the core of our discussion," as Steve Stern wrote some thirty years ago.[25] This is especially the case in global history and global intellectual history, where Latin America continues to play a minor role when compared to other world regions.[26]

By highlighting the role of Brazil and Brazilians in the French social sciences, this book reveals connections that help to rethink the history of modern social thought. Empirically, it examines understudied institutions—the University of São Paulo first and foremost—and an extensive corpus of correspondence, much of which has only recently become available in private archives. Theoretically, it considers Brazil's importance for broader questions such as race relations and even the concept of "structure" that pervaded post–World War II academic life, moving beyond the alleged incommensurability between *longue durée* and structuralist approaches.

Terms of Exchange builds upon scholarship that has demonstrated that intellectual works—and those of social scientists arguably more than others—are always a collective undertaking inseparable from place and social relations.[27] Informed by sociology, such a constructivist approach aims not to reduce intellectual works to their context, but instead to enrich our understandings of their genesis and meaning.[28] When I analyze Lévi-Strauss's "rebellion" against Durkheim or the emergence of structuralism, I draw upon Pierre Bourdieu's courses on the painter Édouard Manet.[29] Just as Manet depended on fellow painters, artists, and writers in homologous positions to enact the aesthetic revolution for which he is so well known, Lévi-Strauss depended on his colleagues and friends whose work complemented and sometimes provided the foundations for his own.

While later chapters consider the autonomous nature of thought—that is, its distance from immediate social circumstances—the first three chapters in particular examine international partnerships and institutions. As I show, the agreements between Brazilian governments and the cultural wing of the French Ministry of Foreign Affairs made this story possible, giving France a central place in the Brazilian social sciences. This, in turn, transformed the life trajectories of the French professors who went to Brazil, along with those of their Brazilian peers and students. The Service des Oeuvres Françaises à l'Étranger (Service for French Works Abroad), which worked to diffuse French culture and educational institutions abroad, secured positions at Brazilian universities, recruited French professors to fill them, and paid for their transportation. Brazilian governments, state and federal, covered salaries and additional expenses.

This book focuses on these scholars who came of age professionally in Brazil, many of whom were taking up their first university teaching position there. It sheds light both on how their teaching and research influenced Brazil, and on how the time they spent in Brazil and the relationships they forged with Brazilian intellectuals shaped their thought. While a broad range of people appear in what follows, the argument centers upon the "cluster" around Claude Lévi-Strauss, Fernand Braudel, Roger Bastide, and Pierre Monbeig.[30] These intellectuals all overlapped at USP, they were all profoundly influenced by their time in Brazil, and they all have archives that demonstrate a rich correspondence not only with Brazilians but also with one another.[31] By weaving their stories and oeuvres together, I hope to reveal patterns that would not be visible or legible within the context of a single life or a single discipline.[32]

This collective subject offers a different scale than most intellectual histories—often based on a single institution, group of scholars, or discipline—and therefore neutralizes certain kinds of biases. As private archives and memoirs continue to proliferate, Brazilian historian Angela de Castro Gomes has warned of a new "fetishism" of historians for individual biographies.[33] While this book uses private archives extensively, it reads them with and against one another—for example, using the archive of Paulo Duarte as a window into Lévi-Strauss's time in New York rather than taking the latter's own archive at its word.

This is all the more important for the tumultuous years between the 1930s and 1960s, traversed by revolution, World War II, and dictatorship. All the protagonists of this story had their lives upended by extensive travel, domestic and international politics, and even exile. Their archives, therefore, are uneven—most complete in the postwar period once they had settled. Beyond published sources, therefore, it is at times difficult to know what the French scholars were reading during their time in Brazil, especially in the 1930s; much of their correspondence from this period, too, has since disappeared.

By examining a larger collective and a much broader source base than more textual or "internalist" forms of intellectual history, this book fills in and makes connections across preexisting scholarship.[34] Furthermore, in its analysis of how exchange takes places across disciplines, it is more than a history of individual disciplines, of history, of anthropology, of sociology, or of geography.[35] As calls for interdisciplinarity become so ubiquitous, this book brings us back to a period when the boundaries between disciplines were relatively porous if they existed at all, therefore reminding us that the present fragmentation in the humanistic social sciences is far from natural or inevitable.[36]

TERMS OF EXCHANGE

At a basic level, this book should familiarize English-language scholarship with the wealth of intellectual exchanges between France and Brazil. Its function, however, is more than documentary. As its title suggests, this book examines the "terms of exchange" between French and Brazilian intellectuals: terms that were and largely continue to be unequal.[37]

The fact that the Brazilians looked to European professors to inaugurate their universities and train students already says a great deal. Historian Fernando Novais joked that the French sought to "catechize the natives" (their students); Carlos Guilherme Mota recounted the rumor of Braudel calling his students imbeciles for not having read Proust.[38] Such hierarchies were less pronounced when it was the Brazilians who were the senior scholars, having published more extensively or with important networks abroad. Still, even the most privileged of Brazilians faced significant disadvantages. Portuguese remained a minor if not subaltern language in a world dominated by English, German, and French, and, at least at the beginning of the twentieth century, few considered their country to have much to offer as an object of study.[39] As Dain Borges writes, "Brazilian thinkers listened to Europeans, but were rarely heard by them."[40]

Nonetheless, different from in other areas of knowledge and culture, Brazilians, I argue, were crucial partners in remaking the French social sciences beginning with the founding of Brazilian universities and through the postwar period. French thinkers such as Claude Lévi-Strauss, Fernand Braudel, Roger Bastide, and Pierre Monbeig not only read the work of their Brazilian counterparts; these thinkers defined their disciplines, conducted fieldwork, built innovative and interdisciplinary institutions, and even developed theory together with them. As I will demonstrate, the collaboration that ensued would follow them throughout their careers and influence their understandings of settler colonialism, religious syncretism, the global economy, and the foundations of social structures more generally. If the book's title, *Terms of Exchange*, highlights the inequalities between French and Brazilian social scientists, the subtitle looks to rethink, rather than reify, the kinds of exchange that took place. *Brazilian Intellectuals and the French Social Sciences* understands the Brazilians of this story as actors with significant agency.

Until recently, the historiography of intellectual and scientific exchanges between Europe and Latin America in the modern period has been largely unidirectional. Reproducing the colonial order of things, scholars have assumed that the producers of knowledge were based in Europe—or, by extension, North America—and that Latin America has been and likely always will be a receptacle of the knowledge, practices, and ideas coming from the center. Well after decolonization, this "hyperreal Europe" continues to shape modern imaginaries through its symbolic and discursive forms of hegemony, as Dipesh Chakrabarty wrote in *Provincializing Europe*.[41]

Europe not only benefited from unequal exchange with much of the rest of the world in the past: both European and non-European intellectuals have tended to further reify these inequalities in their understandings of how the world came to be in their present. In other words, the intellectual structures left in place by the colonial order of things have made it so that those outside imperial and capitalist centers are constrained in their choices. In Partha Chatterjee's typology, either they can mimic the discourse, form, style, or agenda of the colonizer, or they can withdraw into the domestic—and in doing so, become at best exotic and at worst voiceless in global intellectual life.[42]

Throughout the nineteenth century, a significant portion of elite Brazilians saw France as the pinnacle of modernity and civilization. Brazil's newly independent royal court was shaped by French artists and architects, becoming what Kirsten Schultz has called a "Tropical Versailles."[43] Rio de Janeiro's urban reforms, like those undertaken elsewhere in Latin America, used Paris as their explicit model.[44] And during Brazil's First Republic, Brazilian positivists, inspired by Auguste Comte, inscribed "Order and Progress" on the Brazilian flag, where it remains to this day.[45]

By the 1920s such attempts at imitation had become an object of ridicule. Modernist Oswald de Andrade, for example, mocked Bahian statesman Ruy Barbosa in racialized language as a "top hat in Senegambia."[46] He used Barbosa as a metonym for out-of-place assimilation to European norms, whereas he and his fellow modernists sought to "cannibalize" European forms and transform them into something authentically Brazilian. For example, paraphrasing Shakespeare but replacing "to be" with the name of the "Tupi" Amerindians, Oswald opened his "Manifesto of Anthropophagy" ("Manifesto antropófago") with "Tupi, or not tupi, that is the question." In other words, Brazil would be either Indian or nothing at all.

Despite his nationalist rhetoric, Oswald remained deeply influenced by European thinkers. He and his wife, the famed painter Tarsila do Amaral, who had launched the anthropophagist movement, spent a considerable amount of time in Paris.[47] The Swiss-French author Blaise Cendrars, who came to Brazil upon their invitation, waxed ironic about the fact that their "independence" from Europe depended on his presence. Cendrars claimed, "They hated Europe, but couldn't manage to live an hour without the model of its poetry. They wanted to be inside, the proof being that they invited me."[48]

Just like the modernist artists and writers that preceded them, the Brazilian universities at the center of this book could not completely escape the charge of mimicry. Especially in more traditionally "French" disciplines such as philosophy, one can even find instances of almost colonial mimicry.[49] Thirty years after USP's founding, Paulo Arantes went so far as to call his own academic unit "an overseas department," playing with the French administrative term *département d'outre-mer*.[50] The overseas departments of Martinique, Guadeloupe, Guyane, and Réunion decolonized through assimilation to metropolitan France—a process the likes of which Martinican Frantz Fanon decried in *Black Skin, White Masks*.[51] However, the social sciences, as compared to better-established disciplines such as philosophy that could be transplanted elsewhere, proved more original, in part because they were new just about everywhere.

The Brazilians who make up this story served both as intellectuals in their own right and as intermediaries for those who came into their midst.[52] Living in "complex societies," these largely urban, bourgeois, and highly literate thinkers also served as the "native informants" so dear to anthropology.[53] Informed by the work of anthropologists that has sought to write certain people back into the production of knowledge, this study highlights both the practical and cognitive contributions of Brazilian intellectuals across the humanistic social sciences.[54]

Micol Seigel's work on Brazilian musicians, journalists, and more organic intellectuals than those analyzed here argues for "the power of non-elite subjects to see very far afield; to understand the world as well as anybody can; and to influence people, institutions, and ideas that seem unyieldingly more powerful than they are."[55] If qualitatively different from the largely Afro-descendant protagonists that Seigel and others write about, the Brazilian intellectuals of this story share a homologous relation to power.[56] In spite of the linguistic, geographical, and at times social inequalities they suffered, they changed the course of the social sciences—at times more than they themselves recognized.

Instead of looking to uncover original sources of a given kind of thought or to study their dissemination and reception, this book builds upon recent work in intellectual history that examines how ideas and concepts emerge within the context of labor arrangements, modes of production, and political economy more generally. In particular, I look to further Andrew Sartori's criticism of "diffusionism"—that is, the unidirectional transfer of ideas and concepts from one society to another—by recasting the discussions of the origins of social-scientific research interests, methodologies, and institutions in a transnational and transregional frame.[57] The global nature of such a project lies not in its pretention to cover the span of the globe, but instead in its exploration of the significant connections between phenomena otherwise fragmented geographically or culturally.[58]

My point here is not to insist that Latin Americans did something before Europeans or North Americans, although important examples of this abound. (Did you know that the Brazilian Alberto Santos Dumont was the first person to make a verified flight in an airplane—not the Wright brothers?) It is instead to say that Latin American intellectuals were an integral part of the global production of knowledge, at times preceding their European and North American counterparts, at others serving as crucial collaborators in their projects, and always living as their contemporaries.

Rather than obsess about originality and who was copying whom, Roberto Schwarz encourages us to think of cultural production as "an infinite sequence of transformations, with no beginning or end, no first or last, no worse or better."[59] If, as Sebastian Conrad insists, "we may speak thus of the global coproduction of Enlightenment knowledge," the same can surely be said for the social sciences and intellectual history writ large.[60] Some might contend that this is a relativistic project—that there are indeed certain phenomena such as the Enlightenment or the French Revolution that should be understood principally by the normative claims, most often with European thinkers remaining at the heart of the conversation. Inspired by scholarship on the Haitian Revolution, this study takes a more multidirectional approach to authorship and influence.[61]

Regardless of how much Brazilians participated in the development of the French social sciences, they were rarely recognized for their efforts. One is hard-pressed, for example, to find references to Mário de Andrade in Lévi-Strauss's mature work. While the two were peers, friends, and colleagues in the historical past, one became internationally famous and the other less so. Even if Mário subsequently became translated and read worldwide, his story with Lévi-Strauss is not well known.[62] Part of this may be because Lévi-Strauss spent little time in Brazil, emphasizing his years in New York rather than in São Paulo as some of the most significant for his intellectual biography. His colleague Roger Bastide, on the other hand, remained in the country much longer and more explicitly situated himself within it—not only as his object of study, but as a source for methodology.

Gilberto Freyre called Bastide a "Brazilianized Frenchmen" late in his life, as Bastide had so fully adapted himself to his Brazilian intellectual milieu.[63] Bastide himself even claimed to have become "African" in Bahia.[64] In terms of his relationship with Mário, Bastide positioned himself on much more equal terms, citing him often and writing about him at length. Even so, Mário addressed Bastide formally as "professor." When Mário compared himself to Bastide, he saw himself "only as an amateur," and even refused to be part of a dissertation defense to avoid embarrassment.[65] Mário's deep sense of inequality, produced by "the cultural conditions with which we lived when I studied,"[66] meant that he always considered himself at the margins of the university and global intellectual life more broadly. The historiography, instead of complicating this narrative, has tended to reproduce it.

The unequal treatment given to Brazilian and non-Brazilian intellectuals in the social sciences and other areas of knowledge, however, is not only the blame of Europeans or North Americans. It is also part of what Lévi-Strauss saw as a "predilection of South America for France." In part, such a predilection could be "explained by a secret connivance based on the same inclination to be consumers, and to help others to be consumers, rather than producers."[67] The Brazilian elites who founded USP, for instance, could have trained students themselves so as to further consolidate regional or national thought. However, they chose not to. They preferred to subsidize the foreign, cosmopolitan cultural sphere instead of embarking on a kind of import substitution of ideas.

Gilda de Mello e Souza, a critic and sociologist of culture who knew Lévi-Strauss from her student days,[68] surely viewed Mário and Lévi-Strauss as equals. But when she wrote her interpretation of Mário's masterpiece *Macunaíma*, that definitional work of Brazilian modernism and forerunner of magical realism, she understood it in the theoretical framework of "bricoleur" advanced by none other than Lévi-Strauss himself.[69] Whereas Mário provided the raw material for her analysis, Lévi-Strauss provided the finished product—the "theory" to apply to the case study of *Macunaíma*. Much of Mello e Souza's analysis of Mário explained his ideas with constant reference to his life. Lévi-Strauss, on the other hand, floated above earthly determinants in her analysis, serving as a kind of contextless universal. In reality, Mário, like many others, helped Lévi-Strauss to achieve such a status. This is by no means to delegitimize Mello e Souza's work, which has been favorably reassessed by feminist scholars and surely valorizes Brazilian culture.[70] Instead, it is to demonstrate precisely how assumptions about the division of labor between Europe and Latin America were not only externally imposed but also constructed by dynamics internal to Latin American intellectual life.

EMPIRES AND KNOWLEDGE FORMATION:
BRAZIL, FRANCE, AND LATIN AMERICA

A number of empires traverse this story, some more material than others. Politically and economically speaking, I draw parallels between the French Empire and the Brazilian nation-state. The material conditions underlying these state formations predetermined how different parts of the empire in the French case and different regions of Brazil became imagined, understood, and controlled. In more metaphorical terms, I analyze what I have called "an empire of French cultural life" in Latin America and elsewhere.[71] And while this book is essentially about relations and exchange between Brazil and France, the United States inevitably emerges in both of these places throughout the twentieth century, affecting not only the economy and politics but also the formation of knowledge.

Although Brazil was no longer a self-described empire as of 1889, it, like France, continued to expand into new areas, displacing and exploiting different populations. Settlers of all races displaced indigenous peoples in pioneer regions (the likes of which Monbeig would come to see firsthand), and in cities and the countryside alike, political rights were rarely if ever extended to the entirety of the population. James Holston sees this as evidence of Brazil's difference vis-à-vis nations of the North Atlantic during much of the twentieth century, but if we consider France and other empires *as* empires, the regimes of differential citizenship have a great deal in common and were often connected.[72] Whereas those who study the Atlantic world have long been grappling with the question of the circulation of political forms and knowledge, this book advances such an approach for the modern period.[73] The two-way traffic of the Atlantic, after all, did not end with the steamship or the age of revolutions.

Historians of Brazil and Latin America have made the case that any serious attempt to explain differences in regional economic development would do well to consider racial politics and representation. Durval Muniz de Albuquerque Jr., for example, has shown how the discourses and images through which certain regions defined themselves as "advanced," "industrious," or "modern" have often served to justify regional difference along racial lines, counterposing the backward Brazilian Northeast to the progressive Center-South.[74] São Paulo, which had "whitened" itself in the late nineteenth and early twentieth centuries through massive European immigration, came to be seen as the "locomotive of Brazil," an engine for economic and cultural modernization.

Saying that Brazil was characterized by a kind of "Orientalism in One Country," as Barbara Weinstein suggests, is not the same as saying that the structuring discourses of otherness were produced entirely in a national framework.[75] Indeed, throughout Latin America, the views of elites about the relative progress of different communities or regions often coincided with those advanced by Europeans and North Americans. As Nancy Appelbaum has demonstrated, "writings by Colombians and foreigners coalesced to form a relatively cohesive discourse of Colombian regional variation."[76] Both Weinstein and Applebaum would recognize that the notion of "imperial eyes" advanced by Mary Louise Pratt extended well beyond a prototypical "network of literate Northern Europeans."[77] Latin Americans may be the victims of orientalism—or "australism," as José Moya prefers—but they also helped to produce it.[78]

It would be problematic if not entirely metaphorical to compare French imperialism with Brazilian "internal colonialism"—a neo-European project of development based upon expropriating land from indigenous peoples and controlling Afro-descendant populations.[79] As far as the social sciences are concerned, however, I argue that they in many ways coincided. Lévi-Strauss's anthropology came out of a tradition of colonial ethnography based at the Musée de l'Homme, and he explored Brazil's most remote corners; Monbeig's geography drew from work on settler colonialism in other parts of the globe, especially the US West and India, and sought to understand São Paulo's interior expansion; Bastide made comparisons between the Brazilian Northeast and French Africa, traveling between the state of Bahia and the Institut Français d'Afrique Noire in Senegal; and Braudel, too, constantly drew on his Algerian experience to understand Brazil, and vice versa. This is not to condemn their work, much of which critiques colonialism. It is, however, to understand the colonial conditions under which much of the French social sciences came into being—most often under the premise of reformist colonialism rather than on outright rejection of empire.[80] The French, trained in colonial forms of knowledge, also entered into a properly Brazilian colonial culture in São Paulo.

Across history different empires have sought to undermine each other through negative propaganda (the Black Legend of Spain in the New World perhaps being the best example) or to justify themselves through self-presentation as the most modern, civilized, and humanitarian.[81] Internally, the Brazilian state based in Rio de Janeiro and later Paulistas (from São Paulo state) sought to do the same.[82] By heroizing and mythologizing the Paulista *bandeirantes*, São Paulo's intellectuals explained and reified their state's distinct economic and racial development.[83] These *bandeirantes*, or trailblazers, a motley crew of seventeenth-century explorers, slavers, and fortune hunters, expanded Brazil's borders beyond those of the Treaty of Tordesillas. Those who studied the *bandeirantes* in the first third of the twentieth century, the "bandeirologists," lauded them for their bravery and their willingness to expand into the Brazilian interior while coastal inhabitants in places like Rio de Janeiro remained in indolence. They also contrasted the Portuguese-indigenous mixed stock of the *bandeirantes* to the African presence in other parts of Brazil. In literary and popular culture, such images pervaded the public sphere, especially in the *Revista do Brasil*, so poignantly analyzed by Tania Regina de Luca.[84]

Connected race thinking between Brazil and France had a long history, with Arthur de Gobineau using Brazil as a prominent example of the decadence caused by racial mixing.[85] By the end of the nineteenth century, such open white supremacy had been replaced by what we would now consider "scientific" racism. For example, the work of Raimundo Nina Rodrigues and his disciples, pioneers in the study of Afro-Brazilian religions, drew upon French criminology, much of it just as racialized as the work of Cesare Lombroso.[86] Anthropologist Arthur Ramos, a student of Rodrigues, relied heavily on the philosophy of Lucien Lévy-Bruhl, especially *Primitive Mentality*, to understand certain aspects of black culture in Brazil.[87] Even if Lévy-Bruhl insisted on abstraction and relationality, his division of the world into societies governed by rationality and those that were still "pre-logical" probably did more to consolidate racial categories than undo them.

Furthermore, Gilberto Freyre, an influential peer and colleague of the French social scientists and by most accounts Brazil's most important racial theorist of the twentieth century, became an apologist for Portugal's empire, especially in Africa.[88] Following World War II, his theories of racial mixing would be picked up by the French as they thought about their own empire in the midst of decolonization. Freyre's particular defense of empire, easy to condemn retrospectively, took aim at the US empire—both as a concrete instance of racial inequality and as an all-too-powerful force in shaping the categories by which people in other parts of the world thought about themselves.[89]

In this sense, despite their almost diametrically opposed politics, Freyre predated Pierre Bourdieu and Loïc Wacquant's critique of American scholars' "imperialist" racial categories.[90] This goes to show that, while the broader story I tell is of intellectual and social-scientific exchange between Brazil and France, the United States is never far away. After all, US social-scientific institutions, methodologies, and networks were present in both Brazil and France throughout the twentieth century.[91] As the century progressed, American influence began to dwarf the Francophile remnants of the Belle Epoque.

When asked about the decline of French influence in Brazil in 1935, Mário de Andrade wrote that in the domain of intellectual culture, "the French spirit dominated Brazil colonially in the second half of the nineteenth century."[92] Nonetheless, in recent times, there was no "diminishing of French influence, but instead an aggrandizement of Brazil."[93] In an added note to his own text, contained in his private archive, Mário lamented that the relative decline of

France corresponded to "the all-consuming cultural advance of the United States upon us."[94]

Mário admired aspects of (North) American culture, especially in music, engineering, and commerce. Nevertheless, he felt that "the North American spirit presents us with no normative ideal of equilibrium, restraint, and liberty that is useful to us."[95] With this in mind, he wrote the following:

> I want to freely affirm that the French influence was beneficial, and that it is still the best, that which most balances us, that which permits us the exercise of our true national psychology, that which requires of us the least of that we give up [being] ourselves.[96]

According to Mário—and many other Brazilian intellectuals in these pages—exchange with France came on more equal terms than with the United States. We do not lack examples of culturally dominated Brazilians who sought to reproduce metropolitan fashions, but there were those, like Mário, who found in France a model for intellectual life that did not require "that we give up [being] ourselves." André Dreyfus, the director of USP who had seen the continuous advance of US political, financial, and military influence in Brazil during the war, wrote the following about foreign cultural models in 1944: such influence "must at least be from a country whose civilization is close to ours, which is for us France, and not North America."[97]

The United States would become all the more important in Brazilian cultural life during and following the Second World War.[98] Still, prior to the 1960s, the French remained the crucial reference for many Brazilian social scientists, in part because Franco-Brazilian cooperation had laid the groundwork for studies on indigenous, Afro-descendant, and settler populations—works that brought fieldwork into contact with human geography, political economy, and other theoretical frameworks. This is the story of that cooperation as much as it is about the life and works of a number of prominent social scientists.

Finally, a couple of pages on "Latin America," which pervades the aforementioned analysis and continues through the text. The term has no stable or fixed meaning and was by no means unanimously accepted by either the French or the Brazilian scholars, past or present. When referring to Brazil and the broader region of which it was part, they often preferred "South America," a continental rather than ideological designation. Nonetheless, for both practical and analytic reasons, I continue to use the former term. Practically, it is a way of recognizing the US disciplinary framework in which this work sits. It also indicates that my analysis might speak to people interested in places like Mexico or the Caribbean that fall out of South America but are more easily included in Latin America.

Analytically, the term "Latin America" helps to unite some of the different threads on empire and the formation of knowledge. At once oppressive and liberating, it silences certain visions and makes others possible. While it might be allied with "indigenous" or "Afro-" America, it is neither of these, strictly speaking. "Latin America," by most accounts, is a French invention, designed to justify the occupation of Mexico. Nonetheless, as Michel Gobat explains, it also has a long history of being used as an anti-imperial concept, even preceding the French intervention.[99]

Regardless of who discursively "invented" Latin America, the societies that make up present-day Latin America share a great deal with Europe and North America in terms of their historical formation, ideas, and conceptions of the state—not the least of which is the liberal tradition. Rather than posit Latin America as "non-Western" or somehow fundamentally different from the United States, many scholars emphasize its common political, legal, and intellectual culture. As Greg Grandin argues, if anything, Latin America helped to "socialize" its northern neighbors.[100]

The interstitial positionality of many Latin American intellectuals as both cosmopolitan and local, privileged and excluded, tells a great deal.[101] For the most part, even in the colonial period they were neither the colonial mimic men analyzed by Homi Bhabha nor the interior thinkers analyzed by Partha Chatterjee.[102] To use the words of Mary Louise Pratt, they were part of a project of "planetary consciousness" that mapped the world and made it legible.[103] The difference is that they more often described their own countries rather than the world at large. In the international division of labor, their work, therefore, was either ignored or treated as raw material to be analyzed subsequently by metropolitan scholars, a fact lamented by Walter Mignolo, who even in 2000 felt the need to remind the field that Latin America is not only a source of "'cultures' to be studied by anthropologists and ethnohistorians but also [of] intellectuals who generate theories and reflect on their own culture and history."[104]

Language played a significant role, as it continues to today. When Arthur Ramos sent his work to Sigmund Freud, the latter simply responded that he didn't read Portuguese.[105] This is not, of course, to raise Ramos to the status of Freud, but instead to highlight the inequalities in exchange between those who inhabit the cultural and linguistic center of a given historical moment and those who are outside it. As a Brazilian author named Alice Leonardos da Silva Lima coyly put it to the anthropologist Paul Rivet: "I dare to write you even if I have a terrible fear that you will archive this letter in the Muséum as a contemporary ethnographic document of a Brazilian savage."[106]

Leonardos, Ramos, and the other Brazilians of this story were much closer to purported centers of global capitalism and cultural life than previously imagined. They had lifestyles very similar to—and in many cases, much more extravagant than—those of their European and North American counterparts. They knew them relatively well, corresponded with them, and even founded social-scientific institutions together. As I demonstrate in *Terms of Exchange*, they profoundly altered the thinking of their foreign peers. In other words, the so-called "Latin Americanization of central cultures," which Roberto Schwarz and others have sought to achieve since the 1960s, was already well underway in the 1930s.[107]

CHAPTER OUTLINE

By tracking this story of French-Brazilian cooperation from the founding of the University of São Paulo in 1934 into the 1960s, the book's six chapters show how Brazilian intellectuals went from depending almost exclusively on European social science to influencing French intellectuals. Narrative and chronology maintain the flow between the chapters, even though individual chapters are conceived thematically, often based on different types of sources and intervening in different historiographies.

Chapter 1 situates the founding of the University of São Paulo in the broader context of social-scientific, aesthetic, and political movements of the first third of the twentieth century. It analyzes the Paulistas' liberal vision leading up to and in the wake of the Constitutionalist Revolution of 1932, Francophile tendencies in the Brazilian social sciences, and the internal dynamics of Brazilian universities in the early years of the French missions.

Chapters 2 and 3 shift the focus to the cohort of younger scholars who would make Brazil part of their research agenda, including Bastide, Braudel, Lévi-Strauss, and Monbeig. Reframing previous historiographies on the politics of the French missions or individual scholars, these chapters examine intellectual dynamics within the University of São Paulo, notably the shift from a sociology based largely on the work of Émile Durkheim to more anthropological and geographical-based methodologies. While chapter 2 serves more as a sociology of how a set of scholars came together to transform the social sciences, chapter 3 looks closely at how Brazilian intellectuals such as Mário de Andrade and Arthur Ramos mediated the research of their French counterparts. The latter's early work on São Paulo's colonial expansion, indigenous anthropology, and Afro-Brazilian studies would not have been the same otherwise.

Chapter 4 analyzes the more mature work of the French scholars, highlighting their dialogues with Brazilian scholars such as Caio Prado Jr. and Gilberto Freyre. This work includes Monbeig's *Pionniers et planteurs de São Paulo*, Bastide's *Imagens do Nordeste místico em branco e preto*, Braudel's *The*

Mediterranean and the Mediterranean World in the Age of Philip II, and Lévi-Strauss's *The Elementary Structures of Kinship.* In addition to situating these works in the context of World War II and the emergence of France's collaborationist Vichy regime, this chapter argues for the importance of Brazil as a site of fieldwork and semiautonomous space for social-scientific development.

In chapters 5 and 6, the scholars return to France and the Brazilian social sciences come with them. In chapter 5, I argue that Brazil served as a central pillar for a cluster of non-European research based at the newly founded 6th section of the École Pratique des Hautes Études and published in *Annales.* Together, Monbeig, Bastide, Braudel, and a handful of others made *Tristes Tropiques* a success and made Lévi-Strauss's project of structural anthropology possible.

Finally, chapter 6 examines how French thinkers conceived of Brazilian race relations and imagined the French Empire in the midst of decolonization. By the 1950s, Brazil had ceased to be a kind of intellectual colony for the French, now contributing both social models and methodology. Certain students of the French, such as Florestan Fernandes, had since come of age, and Gilberto Freyre had finally been translated into French. In this postwar context, the intellectual partners that had previously been invisible emerged as important actors in the construction of the social sciences—in France and elsewhere.

This Brazilian presence and influence would by no means end French influence in the Brazilian social sciences, which remained prominent and still does to this day. However, these openly multidirectional exchanges in the postwar period would usher in a different kind of relationship between intellectuals in the two countries in question. Now, let us turn to the origins of the University of São Paulo, where this story begins.

CHAPTER ONE

São Paulo: The New Metropolis with a French University

The city of São Paulo is so curiously French in some of its aspects that not once during a whole week did I have the sensation of being in a foreign country.

GEORGES CLEMENCEAU, 1911

On January 25, 1934, the University of São Paulo (USP) was created with a new Faculty of Philosophy, Sciences, and Letters.[1] The first director of the new Faculty, the mathematician Teodoro Ramos, proceeded on behalf of the state of São Paulo to Europe, where "he had meetings with the French, Italian, and German governments so as to obtain, in the important university centers of Europe, professors of renown for the chairs of the new Faculty."[2] Germans and Italians were hired for mathematics and the hard sciences. Meanwhile, the French were given entire responsibility for the social sciences and an important stake in the university's conception.[3] Long-standing Francophilia among the liberal intelligentsia and the fact that France had yet to succumb to fascism decisively shaped these intellectual geopolitics at a time of internal political struggle in Brazil.

The Paulistas had just been defeated after rising up against the federal government in the prior two years (1932–34).[4] Dominant during the First, or Old, Republic (1889–1930), with six of its nine presidents coming out of the São Paulo law school, the Paulistas' role in national politics was significantly reduced under Getúlio Vargas.[5] As a consequence, they became increasingly frustrated with the centralized, anti-democratic, and corporatist governments of the 1930s. The newspaper with the largest national circulation, *O Estado de S. Paulo*, and the group surrounding it tied to the Partido Democrático (PD), decided to advocate for culture and education as a form of resistance.[6] Although supporting Vargas in 1930, the PD changed sides by 1932, advancing the cause of the middle classes who saw the new Vargas government as excessively populist and even fascist.

When armed resistance failed, the *O Estado* group adopted a new strategy: instead of engaging in politics as such, they invested in the idea of elite formation. Unable to control electoral politics at the national level, they could at least provide the new cadres and professionals that influence government and other related fields—or so they thought. As Irene Cardoso has argued, USP promised to advance liberalism and an anti-populist form of democracy through the training and reproduction of governing elites.[7] According to one of USP's founders, Armando de Salles Oliveira, an expansive "doctrine of equality" threatened to bring about "equality in servitude and misery." Opposing such doctrine, the Paulista elites sought instead a more abstract form of equality that would allow "any man to climb to the highest levels of social life and that permits the free extension of all creative forces."[8]

The journalist and public intellectual Júlio de Mesquita Filho, owner of *O Estado de S. Paulo*, and others had plans for a university at least since 1925. Nonetheless, the project only materialized after the conflict between São Paulo and the federal government.[9] Mesquita participated in the revolt, as did three other principal founders of USP: Salles Oliveira, brother-in-law of Mesquita and *interventor* of São Paulo from 1933–1935; educational reformer Fernando de Azevedo; and Paulo Duarte.[10] Duarte and Mesquita would return to Brazil under amnesty in 1934 after being exiled in Portugal.[11]

In 1933, in the midst of the conflict between São Paulo and the federal government, the industrialist Roberto Simonsen wrote:

> A considerable pleiad of intellectuals . . . grasped the urgent necessity to create schools of elite training that disseminated notions of politics, sociology, and economy, awaking and creating a national consciousness capable of orienting public administration. [This was] in accordance with the reality of our milieu and working, in this way, to stop the reigning incomprehension inside Brazil, of which São Paulo was and is the principal victim.[12]

For Simonsen, this meant the Escola Livre de Sociologia e Política (Free School of Sociology and Politics), a school he founded explicitly to train public administrators.[13] For others, it meant USP, which literary critic Sérgio Milliet remembered as bringing an end to anarchic civil wars and inaugurating "an intellectual and scientific revolution capable of changing Brazilians' social and economic conceptions."[14] All these men would have agreed with the American L. D. Coffman, then president of the University of Minnesota, who said that universities might teach politics, but "never advocate for, nor could advocate for, fascism, nor communism."[15]

This chapter examines how the social sciences in São Paulo came to be imagined in the years leading up to USP's founding. Whether for the modernists of the 1920s or the leaders of the Constitutionalist Revolution of 1932, French thinkers such as Émile Durkheim and Lucien Lévy-Bruhl proved an important point of reference. In what follows, I explore some of the personal, political, and ideological reasons for why this was the case and how it affected the institutionalization of university life and the social sciences in São Paulo, as well as in Brazil more broadly. I argue that Paulista elites drew upon the social sciences—and more particularly the French social sciences—as a means to nationalize aesthetic culture in the 1920s and as a way of creating cadres that could understand and overcome the political upheavals of the early 1930s.

The second section of the chapter considers some of the salient differences between the French scholars who went to USP and those who went to the University of the Federal District (UDF), in Rio de Janeiro, founded just two years later. Whereas UDF brought in senior French scholars as distinguished lecturers who disseminated French academic life *à la lettre*, the younger professors who began their university careers at USP were more inclined to incorporate Brazil into their research. This generational difference is crucial for understanding the dynamics within each faculty.

PAULISTA USES OF THE SOCIAL SCIENCES

São Paulo grew vertiginously in the first third of the twentieth century, both in population and height. In 1900, the city had 239,820 inhabitants; in 1920, it had grown to 579,033; and by 1940 it reached 1,318,539.[16] In forty years, the population had more than quintupled. São Paulo rapidly became Brazil's second-most-populous city (and third in Latin America), eventually overtaking the capital, Rio de Janeiro, in the 1950s.[17] For a country whose urban development had been almost entirely coastal, the major exception being Minas Gerais, São Paulo's emergence also had important geographical consequences, allowing Brazil to expand ever farther into the interior.[18]

Despite its Jesuit Seminary (Colégio) and the São Francisco Law School, the oldest in Brazil (est. 1827), São Paulo was largely a backwater town during the colonial period and the early nineteenth century. In the late nineteenth and early twentieth centuries, however, this changed rapidly. By the time USP was founded, São Paulo was not only Brazil's largest industrial economy but also, in many ways, its cultural avant-garde.

With the fertile land of the state of Rio de Janeiro largely exhausted by the end of the nineteenth century, Brazil's coffee production shifted west, and São Paulo's widely famed *terra roxa* (purple earth) allowed for the production of coffee at a scale never before seen in Brazil or in the world. As the state of São Paulo emerged as the principal producer of coffee in Brazil, exporting over eight hundred thousand tons annually as of 1935, its capital witnessed growth in just about every sector, industry included.[19] Paulista sociologist and literary scholar Antonio Candido still remembered São Paulo as a *malograda província* (unsuccessful province) prior to the 1920s, and really only qualitatively different after 1930.[20] But as Richard Morse has demonstrated, the transition "from community to metropolis" was already thoroughly underway by the early 1900s.[21] As just one indicator, by 1912 São Paulo had more circulating periodicals than any other state in the nation.[22]

The cultural sphere in São Paulo may have been incipient and not entirely "autonomous" during this period. As Sergio Miceli has argued, it depended heavily on the state and important patronage networks.[23] Nonetheless, few would deny the seismic changes that had taken place by the 1920s. The growth of the middle classes and the liberal professions brought about an emerging consumer base for print materials, and consequently, a demand for a new class of journalists, writers, and publishers. In the nineteenth century, Brazilian publishers printed their books in Europe, mostly in Portugal and France, and books were often sold in the same elite boutiques where one could find perfumes, clothing, and other imported goods.[24] Only in the early twentieth century did Brazilian publishers begin to actually print books—whether of national or international authorship—on Brazilian soil.[25]

São Paulo saw a proliferation of new bookstores, journals, and cultural movements. There was a veritable editorial "boom" in the 1930s, which in turn brought about an increasing specialization in production. The newspaper *O Estado de S. Paulo*, for example, expanded its number of editions and produced a separate review, the *Revista do Brasil*, creating "new forms of erudite production counterbalancing previously dominant literary and worldly materials."[26] This boom in production entailed professional diversification, and not just in cultural industries. It required everything from "the acquisition of press rotaries, the diversification of investments and editorial programs, the recruitment of specialists in different sectors of production and finishing, market-oriented innovations and sales strategies"[27] With such noteworthy diversification in the liberal professions, publishing being just one example, it is not surprising that new educational institutions emerged in order to train them.

São Paulo's expanding economy and its corresponding growth in the liberal professions and cultural sectors meant that it could support writers and intellectuals to an unprecedented extent. Rio de Janeiro, Brazil's capital since 1763, continued to claim a monopoly on the national institutions of intellectual recognition (Academia Brasileira de Letras, Escola Nacional de Belas Artes, and Instituto Histórico e Geográfico Brasileiro, to name just three), as well as Brazil's principal publishing market. Paulista intellectuals in the 1920s and 1930s nonetheless challenged Rio's centrality in the arts, literature, and, ultimately, the social sciences.

The Semana de Arte Moderna (Week of Modern Art), held in São Paulo in 1922, is by all accounts a watershed in Brazil's intellectual and cultural production.[28] Paulistas exhibited their paintings, performed prose, and distributed their writings in the Theatro Municipal and elsewhere. They proposed a new kind of art, supposedly free from Europe and its imitators in Rio de Janeiro. Convinced of their ability to revolutionize and Brazilianize the arts in Brazil, the modernists sought to transform the capital of Rio de Janeiro into a province and inaugurate São Paulo as the nation's new metropolis. Mário de Andrade, arguably the most emblematic of them all, wrote to his friend Manuel Bandeira: "My God, what vanity! These people of Rio will never forgive São Paulo for having rung the bell. I am not speaking of you. You are not from Rio. You are like me: from Brazil."[29]

Manuel Bandeira, originally from Recife, may not have been from São Paulo, but, according to Mário, he, too, was from Brazil. This distinguished him from intellectuals from Rio who had refused to recognize the seismic shift that he and his fellow modernists had inaugurated and who continued to look to Europe. According to Mário, intellectuals from Rio, unlike those from Brazil's interior and the Northeast, could make no claim to authentic Brazilianness.[30]

Mário, on the other hand, had never been to Europe. Traveling extensively in his own country instead, especially to the Northeast and the Amazon, he consciously sought to immerse himself in Brazilian culture, however far it may have seemed from bourgeois culture and "rationality."[31] He certainly read Lucien Lévy-Bruhl's *Primitive Mentality* with great interest, like so many of his generation who sought to relativize Eurocentric notions of progress.[32] However, unlike Lévy-Bruhl, he refused to reify indigenous culture as "pre-logical," whether as part of the poetic and artistic group known as *pau-brasil* (Brazilwood) or in his novel *Macunaíma*, in which the indigenous protagonist becomes a kind of ethnographer of modern, urban São Paulo.

As a metonym for the *pau-brasil* modernists, Oswald de Andrade's "Manifesto of Anthropophagy" (1928) explicitly critiqued Lévy-Bruhl's dichotomies between rational and irrational, primitive and modern, European and other that were so in vogue.[33] The idea of "antropofagia," to which Oswald, Mário, and Tarsila do Amaral all contributed, was literally to cannibalize European art forms, consuming them and using their energy to produce new forms of art more attuned to Brazilian realities; by desacralizing European art forms, Brazilians could escape the prison house of mimicry and create new kinds of art appropriate to their needs. As Barbara Weinstein has argued, "the celebration of hybridity and mixture," the use of folkloric elements, and a critique of the "turn-of-the-century fixation on whitening and Europeanization" are all part of the *pau-brasil* group's legacy.[34]

Beyond literature and the arts, São Paulo proved itself to be a leader in education and the social sciences.[35] Fernando de Azevedo had been a professor of Latin and literature at the Escola Normal (Normal School), a kind of teacher's college. He was also part of a broader Escola Nova (New School) movement in the 1920s that brought together reform-minded educators, administrators, and intellectuals. While the movement was very much national in scope, Azevedo's 1926 investigation into the state of education in São Paulo had "enormous repercussions" throughout the country, and surely contributed to his selection as the head of reform for public education in the federal district, Rio de Janeiro, between 1929 and 1932.[36] There, according to Maria Penna, he inaugurated "a veritable pedagogical revolution in the fields of primary and secondary education."[37] Furthermore, as the editor of the new book series Biblioteca Pedagógica Brasileira (Brazilian Pedagogical Library), Azevedo contributed to a growing collection of teaching material nationwide.

As a liberal reformist, Azevedo saw education principally as a means of integrating various social classes and professions into a rationalized, capitalist economic system. As opposed to the traditional divisions between faculties or schools (law, medicine, engineering), what Azevedo proposed were new disciplines that would allow for the "scientific" study of society.[38] According to Azevedo:

> Alongside the professional faculties already in existence, reorganized upon new bases, we must simultaneously or successively create, in every university branch, faculties of social and economic sciences; mathematical, physical, and natural sciences and philosophy and letters that, attending to the variety of mental types and of social necessity, should open up . . . an increasingly large field of scientific investigation.[39]

Azevedo was not alone in this quest for scientific approaches to social questions. Such ideas gained traction in São Paulo and throughout Brazil in the 1930s.

The state of São Paulo created the Departamento de Cultura e Recreação (Department of Culture and Recreation) in the municipality of São Paulo in 1935, a year after the founding of USP. Its goals were to "organize public education and recreational activities in the city, and to undertake social research as a basis for government action."[40] The *Revista do Arquivo Municipal*, published by the Departamento de Cultura e Recreação (henceforth Departamento de Cultura), also became an important publication for Brazilian and international research during this period.[41]

Historians and geographers, meanwhile, created a dynamic research group around the Instituto Histórico e Geográfico of São Paulo. The systematic archival research of historians such as Afonso d'E. Taunay, José de Alcântara Machado, and Washington Luís Pereira de Sousa—their Paulista-centered ideological biases notwithstanding—transformed the practice of history.[42] Their studies on the *bandeiras* and *bandeirantes* contributed to shifting Brazilian historiography toward the interior, a process that began in the 1920s and culminated in the 1950s with the works of Jaime Cortesão and Sérgio Buarque de Holanda. Rather than studying the imperial court or colonial cities, historians became increasingly interested in the mixed-race Portuguese and Indian trailblazers who defied the Treaty of Tordesillas and expanded Brazil's borders.

All these groups and movements—literary, artistic, and social scientific—point to an effervescence of cultural and intellectual life in São Paulo in the 1920s and 1930s. New scholarly institutions, journals, and innovative research distinguished the city's cultural landscape from its provincial origins and the heritage of the Old Republic that governed Brazil until 1930.

As James Woodard has shown, by the 1920s the republic came to be seen as incompetent, corrupt, and oligarchic.[43] The Partido Democrático, founded in 1925 on a reformist platform that advocated for the secret ballot and made gestures in favor of workers' rights, offered a significant challenge to the hegemony of the republican political regimes.[44] Gradual reform, however, would prove to be insufficient. The economic crash of 1929 and the political crisis of the following year sealed the Old Republic's fate. Brazil's economy was hit hard by the reduced demand of its trade partners, which drove down the price of coffee and other commodities precipitously.

In such a context, President Washington Luís's choice of the Paulista Júlio Prestes as his successor, both men coming from the Partido Republicano Paulista (PRP) and São Paulo, was a recipe for disaster.[45] The political economy of classical liberalism mixed with intervention on behalf of the coffee producers had become unsustainable with the rise of a national economy that was not only export based, but also more regionally integrated. In short, the producers of industrial and other goods demanded the same degree of protection as the coffee planters from São Paulo.

Prestes may have won the election, but Getúlio Vargas and the Liberal Alliance (Aliança Liberal) refused to accept defeat, ushering in a revolution that would bring down the government in 1930. At least initially, the São Paulo–based supporters of the Partido Democrático and the newspaper *O Estado de S. Paulo* supported Vargas. However, shortly after "the overwhelming majority of the Partido Democrático leadership in São Paulo decided to back the insurgent candidacy," they changed their minds to join the PRP, perceiving a "vendetta" against São Paulo and a loss of autonomy within the Brazilian federation.[46] By all accounts, the failed Constitutionalist Revolution, or civil war, in 1932 united Paulistas of all stripes (except a vocal minority on the left) and served as a pivotal moment in São Paulo's attempts at self-definition.[47]

The crisis of the 1930s also encouraged Paulista leaders such as Júlio de Mesquita Filho to more forcefully advocate for the social sciences as a way of understanding their political moment and of recuperating "reason" from mass politics. Their familiarity with French philosophers and sociologists encouraged them to look to France, especially to allies of Émile Durkheim who had made important inroads in Brazil in the previous decades, thanks in large part to the psychologist Georges Dumas. Both as a scholar and a diplomat, Dumas helped to shape French influence in South America throughout the first half of the twentieth century.[48]

As early as 1912, he lectured on Auguste Comte and Émile Durkheim in São Paulo, contributing to the diffusion of the *L'année sociologique* and its language surrounding "social facts."[49] By 1924, if not earlier, Dumas effectively served as the point person (*directeur adjoint*) for Brazil to Jean Marx, a former student of Marcel Mauss and collaborator of *L'année sociologique* who was now head of the Service for French Works Abroad.[50] This service, part of the French Ministry of Foreign Affairs, sought to promote French culture abroad, a strategy of winning over the hearts and minds of different nations in the turbulent interwar period.[51]

As part of such intellectual-cultural diplomacy, Sorbonne professor Paul Fauconnet spent several months in Brazil in 1927, giving a series of lectures on sociology, education, pedagogy, and other topics in São Paulo at the Escola Normal and the law school.[52] He subsequently contributed articles on a variety of topics to *O Estado de S. Paulo*.[53] Like that of Célestin Bouglé, Fauconnet's thought concerned "the philosophical thrust and the social implications of Durkheim's sociology," in this sense distinguishing him from Durkheimian "research scholars" such as Marcel Mauss.[54]

In 1932, from the front during the Constitutionalist Revolution, Mesquita wrote to his wife, Marina, "Bring me, tomorrow, the book by Bouglé entitled *Les idées égalitaires* [Egalitarian ideas], and ask Chiquinho for another by Durkheim on education. It was given to him by Fauconnet."[55] Azevedo's book *Princípios de sociologia* (1935), to which we will return in the next chapter, also drew heavily on the work of French sociologists, notably Fauconnet.[56]

Both Azevedo and Mesquita had studied at the São Paulo law school where Durkheim had almost certainly been taught.[57] Both were anti-communists and certainly to the right of Durkheim, who, although a radical, was close to Jean Jaurès. Nonetheless, one might speculate that it was more Durkheim's empirical knowledge of social relations in an increasingly industrialized world, rather than his political positions, that interested them. In particular, Azevedo and Mesquita must have read Durkheim's early works such as *The Division of Labor in Society* (1893) and "The Intellectual Elite and Democracy" (1904) as invaluable in their own quests to create a cultural elite.[58] Mesquita, who completed his secondary education in French-speaking Europe (Lausanne, Switzerland), and Azevedo may have also found resonance between their own educational project and that of France's Third Republic of maintaining social cohesion without radical changes to the social structure.[59]

Mesquita, who was exiled for his resistance to Vargas, must have identified with Dreyfusard intellectuals (of which Durkheim was one), and likely, as a fellow exile, with Émile Zola. Mesquita's father had covered the Dreyfus affair thoroughly, transcribing "articles by Zola, by Clemenceau, and Labory's defense" in *O Estado de S. Paulo*, and using it to differentiate himself politically from the PRP.[60]

French philosophy and social sciences, especially those of Durkheim and the Durkheimians, were central references for figures such as Mesquita and Azevedo, if not liberal Latin Americans more generally during this period.[61] With the Constitutionalist Revolution quashed and the project of conceiving a university before them, it is not surprising that these thinkers would play such a significant role in USP's conception. According to France's ambassador in Brazil, "The Paulista university would be of French essence, with the Anglo-Saxons and Germans bringing only . . . their practical spirit and technicity in teachings that do not touch at all on moral training."[62]

Ambassador Louis Hermite may have exaggerated USP's French essence, but the fact remains that the French controlled the entirety of the social sciences there. Louis Baudin, a law professor from the University of Paris, was not involved in USP's creation. A speech of his from 1935 at the Maison de l'Amérique Latine in Brussels, however, helps to explain the value of France in South American higher education:

> It used to be that the elites had the honor of speaking our language. It was a sign of distinction, but those elites have been challenged by the crisis, and they can no longer go soak up Europe. They have been often dispossessed by the power of the masses. Neither the economy nor politics are favorable for them, and both react against the intellectual. A certain Anglo-Saxon ideal threatens to install itself following the popular thrust.[63]

The political and economic crisis that Brazil faced in the 1930s brought into question the Old Republic's liberal tenets, and with them, the place of certain elites. The "masses" and Americanized mass culture, even in its embryonic forms, seemed to threaten their very ideas of civilization.[64]

USP was envisioned as a response to the populism of the 1930s that had unseated (or at least threatened to unseat) São Paulo's ruling classes. With its preference for philosophy, USP may have differed from its more empirical counterpart, the Escola Livre de Sociologia e Política. Both, however, shared a vision of a broader crisis of "civilization" in very abstract terms. Manoel Tosta Berlinck, an engineer and son of one of the Escola Livre's founders, remembers reading through a course catalog from the Sorbonne. Still shocked by the defeat of São Paulo's Constitutionalist Revolution at the hands of what he saw as irrational masses, he was "convinced that [Lévy-Bruhl] would explain why Brazil was that way."[65]

Roberto Simonsen wrote in 1933 that while "universal history" offered examples of great civilizations without a basis of popular education, "There is not a single example of a civilization that did not have a basis of intellectual elites, wise and strongly constituted."[66] In Simonsen's short book of reflections *Rumo à verdade* (The way to truth), largely dealing with the role of education and culture within a society threatened by new social forces, he cited French authors (Durkheim included) just as frequently as Americans. Even Simonsen, a trained engineer and industrialist concerned with practical sociology, argued that the crisis of the 1930s was one unsolvable solely by mechanization and rationalization: it demanded a new attention to the "spirit" of civilization, which the French represented so well.[67] Simonsen in many ways echoed the sentiments of Latin American liberals more generally, such as Uruguayan José Enrique Rodó, whose *Ariel* (1900) sought "a spiritual, peaceful, and learned Latin America" in opposition to "a materialist, bullying, and morally bankrupt North America."[68]

France, in the eyes of the Paulistas, offered a powerful example of liberal democracy and humanism, but it was by no means a model to be imitated directly. Somewhat ironically, France was used—or at least intended to be used—for the nationalization of Brazilian culture. Just as the modernists had largely appropriated French culture to inaugurate a new kind of Brazilian arts, or so they thought, the Paulista university would do the same.

Antônio de Almeida Prado, USP's first director, laid out this intention in his speech that opened the new Faculty of Philosophy, Sciences, and Letters:

> In truth, the diffusion of university education is what will fill the legitimate function of promoting the common instinct of Brazilianness and the universalization of national sentiment in every corner of the immense Brazilian territory. When numerous universities spread across it, taking in every direction the same level of culture, all Brazilians will identify with the same moral and intellectual background . . . And then, marked as one of the greatest of our history, the government that conceived of this idea, and put it into victorious

motion, will have accomplished the most decisive effort for the sake of the civic and cultural renaissance of the great Brazilian fatherland.[69]

The Paulista attempt to nationalize Brazilian culture by way of French appropriation would obviously take time—and indeed had been ongoing since the 1920s. It clearly took on new dimensions during USP's early years. But before we see how, let us turn to some of those French professors who made up the faculty, how they imagined their role, and what changed over time.

WHICH FRENCH PROFESSORS, WHICH FRANCE, AND WHAT SOCIAL SCIENCE?

When USP was founded, in 1934, it was not altogether clear who would make up its faculty. As we have seen, many Paulista intellectuals sympathized with the French, but at both the state and the national level, other alternatives made the choice anything but natural. Italians boasted a large demographic presence in São Paulo and Vargas's inner circle was much more interested in Italy and Germany than they were in France.[70] In this context, the continuous efforts of Brazilians such as Mesquita and the French psychologist Georges Dumas were invaluable in ensuring French control of the Faculty of Philosophy, Sciences, and Letters.[71]

Having successfully navigated the Brazilian politics of the Old Republic, Dumas took extra care to make sure that France would continue to play an important role in Brazil under Vargas. Before his previous trip to São Paulo, in 1931, he requested an audience with Vargas himself in the capital, Rio.[72] Among other questions to address at the national level, the subsidy for a newly founded chair of Brazilian literature at the Sorbonne was at stake.[73] Following this visit to Brazil, Dumas was decorated as an honorary member of the Society of Philosophy and Letters of São Paulo, a precursor to the Faculty of Philosophy, Sciences, and Letters.[74]

Dumas's long-standing knowledge of Brazilian elites encouraged him to see the 1930s as an opening for a new kind of partnership with France in the form of a Paulista university that would receive "French missions." It would be the culmination of his two decades of diplomatic work in building relationships between Latin America and French universities and *grandes écoles*.[75] When USP finally took shape, Dumas rushed to Rome to meet Teodoro Ramos, even though he knew that Ramos was subsequently coming to Paris.[76] He felt the need to ensure France's prominence among foreign professors recruited.[77]

In 1934 and, to a lesser extent, in 1935, Dumas's personal and professional network constituted the primary source for the recruitment of candidates as professors in Brazil. He sent a telegram to the geographer Pierre Deffontaines, for example, that reads: "Do you accept Brazil? See Garric."[78] Clearly, the selection process was informal, personal, and very last-minute. Furthermore, because of the relative lack of prestige associated with teaching in Brazil, Dumas initially had difficulty in recruiting professors to teach outside the capital and in keeping them in place. These dynamics ultimately paved the way for a cohort of younger scholars that would take the reins in subsequent years, less religious and politically to the left of their predecessors in São Paulo and contemporaries in Rio.[79]

Out of the six Frenchmen sent in 1934, only three were already teaching at the university level.[80] By July 1934, these six professors had arrived in São Paulo and had started to teach: Émile Coornaert, professor at the École Pratique des Hautes Études, was to teach the history of civilization; Robert Garric, professor at the University of Lille, French literature; Pierre Deffontaines, professor at the Institut Catholique de Paris, geography; Paul Arbousse-Bastide, sociology; Étienne Borne, philosophy and psychology; and Michel Berveiller, Greek and Latin literature.

After their first semester of teaching, all these professors sent reports to the Ministry of Foreign Affairs in France evaluating their courses and the success of the French mission in São Paulo. Coornaert's is by far the most direct.[81] While concerned about the declining readership of French books in Brazil and the negative consequences of growing nationalism, he nonetheless claimed to have "very cordial" relations with the academic authorities at USP. His students' academic preparation may have been almost "worthless," but they were "intelligent" and, "except for one or two, all worked very hard."[82] Coornaert quickly understood, however, that his role as a professor and unofficial diplomat was about much more than teaching.

From the beginning of the French missions, a public presence in the form of evening lectures connected to a broader public. It brought together, wrote Coornaert, "a small elite, rather proud of showing if not its culture, then at least its knowledge." He continued, "this elite, in large part very favorable to France," has, "at its head, with an admirable devotion, the leaders of the new Faculty." He insisted, too, that in the wake of growing fascism, "France is still the country least tinged" in public opinion.[83]

Clearly, the evening lectures mentioned by Coornaert were of critical importance to the French missions and the Paulista elite, at times more so than the professors' actual classes, which drew few students. However, in the case of Deffontaines, who inaugurated the Associação dos Geógrafos Brasileiros alongside Brazilians Luiz Flores de Moraes Rego, Rubens Borba de Moraes, and Caio Prado Jr., it meant a new research association closely linked to the university.[84] Deffontaines's wife, Geneviève, chronicled their daily existence in the form of a family diary. From this we know, for example, that upon arrival, the Deffontaines were taken to the Mesquitas' fazenda (plantation):

> July 12 and 13: Pierre and I went almost four hours by car to the Mesquitas to spend the evening and the following day at their "fazenda." Beautiful ride, deserted mountains, then . . . the first "fazendas." The Mesquita fazenda, one of the oldest, a pretty estate in the middle of plantations, great hall with ceramics, the patio.[85]

The Mesquita fazenda was a common reference for the French professors during this period, but Geneviève Deffontaines's conspicuous failure to mention other French professors in her journal entry suggests that the Catholic and relatively senior Deffontaines (Pierre was the second oldest in the group, after Coornaert) were the first to have been invited. Months later, Mesquita told Madame Deffontaines about her husband that "no professor has succeeded as he had in São Paulo."[86] Deffontaines would soon leave behind the budding Associação dos Geógrafos Brasileiros to join the newer, but in some ways more conservative, University of the Federal District (UDF) in Rio.

While both Deffontaines and the historian Henri Hauser presented cutting-edge research and teaching profiles during their tenure in Brazil, the larger part of French education in Rio was geared toward general knowledge (*culture générale*) and, to a certain extent, the diplomatic corps.[87] UDF's course listings from 1936 contrast sharply with those of USP. None of the field-defining "inaugural lessons" of the French missions dealt directly with Brazil or proposed a research program significantly different from that taught in metropolitan France.[88] This is not surprising, considering many of the disciplines in question—French literature, ancient history, classical languages, and art history, to name just a few.

The professors in Rio were also notably more Catholic than those who would stay at USP. Brazilian Catholic intellectuals were prominent in the foundation of UDF, causing problems for French professors associated with secularism—particularly the historian Henri Hauser.[89] The founders of UDF and USP disagreed less about whether France was to have a significant role in higher education and in the social sciences in particular, and more about *which* France would be privileged. The monarchist and Catholic France, the liberal and secular France, and the France of the left—most recently of the Popular Front—were all represented in Brazilian thought. If the elites of both Rio and São Paulo united in eschewing the Popular Front, Rio's intellectuals were,

generally speaking, markedly less liberal than those of São Paulo—if not necessarily more Catholic. The Deffontaines's private archive confirms this, even
if it is only partially representative of Rio's intellectual life. Deffontaines, like
Garric, left São Paulo in December of 1934 after only six months of teaching.

Pierre Deffontaines returned to France in January of 1935 after his first
semester of teaching at USP without knowing what he was going to do next.
He was received "warmly" by Dumas, and at the Ministry of Foreign Affairs he
was proposed "another mission in all of the republics of South America."[90] In
1936, however, he left São Paulo to help with the founding of UDF alongside
his longtime friend and colleague Robert Garric.

Paulo Duarte remembers Garric and Deffontaines as "quase padres à pai-
sana" (almost undercover priests), and Deffontaines specifically as "if not reac-
tionary, at least very conservative and full of prejudices."[91] The two Frenchmen
had long known each other as devoted Catholics and activists in the Équipes
Sociales, an organization that sought to quiet social unrest and "Bolshevism"
by spreading the gospel of fraternity in working-class neighborhoods.[92] Prior to
teaching at USP, Garric had spent 1933 teaching at a French secondary school
in São Paulo, where he also established a chapter of the Équipes Sociales at
the Centro Dom Vital. Nonetheless, his intellectual network was much more
Rio-based, at least in part due to his Catholicism.

When Deffontaines and Garric arrived in Brazil in 1934, they followed the
typical journey to arrive in São Paulo. They stopped first in Rio, then continued
on to the port of Santos, finally reaching São Paulo by train. Upon disembark-
ing in Rio, they were received by Garric's friends, the French general Baudouin
and his wife, as well as "Tristain d'Athaïde and a whole group of *équipiers*."[93]
Deffontaines's most important hosts in Rio were militant Catholics—a sharp
contrast with the São Paulo–based *O Estado* group. Furthermore, Garric, Deffontaines, and the Rio-based French professors in general had a privileged
relationship with the French military, foreign service, and even nobility.[94]

By 1936, when Deffontaines had returned to Brazil to teach at UDF, his
Catholic network in Rio appears to have been more significant than his professional network related to geography in São Paulo. His relationship with
the Monbeigs and his occasional trips to São Paulo for the Associação dos
Geógrafos Brasileiros kept him abreast of happenings at USP and in contact
with his Paulista hosts.[95] Still, Deffontaines's major affinities seemed to lie with
Catholics of the Centro Dom Vital. On the French side, these included writers
such as Georges Bernanos; on the Brazilian side, the "Schmidts".[96] Augusto
Frederico Schmidt, a Catholic modernist poet and editor, was heavily involved
in a political movement called *integralismo*, a Catholic and authoritarian movement with fascist overtones that had a strong following in Rio.[97]

At its beginnings, UDF was not imagined in very different terms than USP had been, except that the former was controlled by the federal district, the latter state controlled. The letters exchanged between Georges Dumas and Gustavo Capanema, for example, made no reference to Catholicism and are primarily concerned with the professionalization of intellectual life in Brazil.[98] Over time, however, as in many aspects of his tenure as minister of education and health, Capanema provided space to right-wing Catholics, intervening in the internal affairs of the university, which, although technically autonomous, resided in the federal capital. While Capanema is best remembered for his support of modernism, he was a practicing Catholic himself, and provided ample space to Catholics within his administration.[99]

In the tense political climate of Rio in the late 1930s, Capanema's intellectual openness gave way to practical considerations about preserving order and governmental stability. With both left-wing and, more importantly, extreme right-wing groups challenging the Vargas government, Capanema was forced to cede on certain appointments and policies. This meant, among other things, accepting the defeat of Anísio Teixeira's project of liberal education for UDF, a consequence of the backlash against the Aliança Nacional Libertadora and the recent Communist coup attempt of 1935.[100] It also meant appointing Alceu Amoroso Lima as dean and instituting a more rigorous ideological control of foreign professors in Rio.[101]

Henri Hauser, who taught at UDF from 1936 to 1939, and who was one of the more productive French scholars to have written during this period on Brazil, ultimately lost his job because of his left-wing tendencies. As the work of a pioneering social historian, his *Ouvriers du temps passé, XVᵉ–XVIᵉ siècles* (Workers from the past: Fifteenth–sixteenth centuries) is worth mentioning.[102] In a letter to the dean dated August 7, 1936, Hauser denounced the "exclusion of the old dean Afrânio Peixoto, considered too progressive"; and he decried the widespread public opinion that related "any manifestations of independent thinking" to Soviet Communism.[103] In 1939, after his three-year contract was up, Hauser was once again considered for teaching in Brazil by the French government. In his disfavor, the Ministry of Foreign Affairs remembered his all "too materialist conception of history."[104]

As of May 1939, Capanema was quite clear that all new professors "should have no hostile orientations toward right-wing tendencies."[105] By that point, the federally controlled University of Brazil, too, had replaced the extinguished UDF, a municipal university with some autonomy from the state. Despite having "identical conditions" in their contracts as those of the professors at USP, the professors in Rio worked in a very different ideological climate. While not all of them were on the right, Fortunat Strowski, for example, a member of the Académie Française and fierce critic of the Popular Front, was among the new recruits for 1939.[106]

In a speech from 1937, Strowski spoke on the subject of the "crisis of intelligence." He brought printed copies of his lecture to Brazil and dedicated one personally to Capanema, after an interview in which "an old professor found himself miraculously in agreement with a brilliant young minister."[107] France's intelligence, he argued, was threatened by the West's "comfort and industry" and the East's "politics of passion and instinct, mass politics practiced on a large part of the globe."[108] Strowski was by no means the first to define France's unique third way between capitalism and communism. Still, his solution for worker's alienation from rationalization is worth noting for its originality: "In the factory, what will be the veritable enemy [of the impersonal, mechanical, chain production]? Intelligence, individual intelligence, intelligence cultivated à la française."[109]

Strowski, like many conservative intellectuals of his generation, saw the 1920s and 1930s as a missed opportunity for France. In his memoirs of this period, largely colored by the initial losses of 1940, Strowski called the Popular Front "without brains"; it was a "fever" that should be called the "Crazy Front."[110] In this sense, Strowski, like most of the professors sent to Rio de Janeiro, was distinct from the younger professors sent to São Paulo, who were largely sympathetic to the Popular Front. But even more to the point, Strowski, at seventy, was at the end of his career—not as a researcher, but as a distinguished public lecturer.[111]

Regardless of their politics, the French professors in Rio were older (often at least twenty years older) and more established than the professors in São Paulo. From its beginnings, USP had to rely on young agrégés, such as Michel Berveiller and Étienne Borne. Although they had achieved the rank to be able to teach at the university, they did not yet have their doctoral degrees. By the second mission of 1935, not a single new arrival had a doctorate or a previous university position. Without the assurance that the French state would recognize them for having taught at the university level upon their return to France, they ventured to a land about which they—and just about everyone else they encountered in France—knew very little.

As we will see, the younger professors sent to São Paulo embraced a new role as researchers that differentiated them from the more traditional one of public lecturers. Coming of age in an era in which the French academy was increasingly geared toward empirical research and taking their first university jobs in São Paulo, they embraced the opportunity to complete doctoral-level work of which Brazil was an essential part. They continued the legacy of what philosopher João Cruz Costa called the *faculdadezinha*, or "little Faculty," that preceded them.[112] Nonetheless, they transformed it into something new—and with it, their own approach to the social sciences.

USP's long-term success relative to UDF and the University of Brazil (both of which were ultimately closed) has contributed to the mythification of the city of São Paulo and its intellectual life—a process initiated by the modernist movement in the 1920s. While both Rio and São Paulo had newly founded universities in the 1930s and notable French professors teaching at them, the differential recruitment of professors in each city and the conditions on the ground contributed to diverging trajectories. Whereas the older, more established professors in Rio altered their curriculum very little from what they taught in Europe, the younger, less-established professors in São Paulo sought to reconstruct their disciplines methodologically and empirically.

In what follows, I turn to these disciplines as they became conceived of and practiced at USP, focusing on the teaching and research of Lévi-Strauss, Braudel, Bastide, and Monbeig. These scholars, among others, departed from the traditional French model of erudite lecturer in Latin America and, to a lesser extent, in France. Their investments in recreating the social sciences in Brazil in the 1930s not only laid the intellectual basis for the social sciences in São Paulo and much of Brazil; they would ultimately affect the course of the social sciences in France, in quite profound ways.

CHAPTER TWO

Atlantic Crossings and Disciplinary Reformulation

When the second French mission arrived at the University of São Paulo (USP), in 1935, the group counted professors as young as twenty-six years old in its ranks. Their motivations for coming to Brazil may have differed, but a set of circumstances united them. Brazil gave them upward mobility and unprecedented academic authority. More often than not the only faculty member of their respective discipline at the newly founded university, young scholars were given considerable flexibility in defining their fields.

Furthermore, Brazil provided a stark contrast to the "Old World" that they left behind. Frequent references to Europe's decline after the First World War were common in intellectual circles, and not only in Germany, where Oswald Spengler's *The Decline of the West* was particularly influential. Since the fin de siècle, notions of reason and progress had been radically brought into question.[1] This became all the more true after the war that had exposed Europeans' own savagery.[2]

Within this broader context, the present chapter examines how these scholars used their new location, status, and academic authority to rework the social sciences. Through the lens of Pierre Monbeig, Claude Lévi-Strauss, Fernand Braudel, and Roger Bastide, among others, it considers the turn to empirical research and how group dynamics shaped interdisciplinary arrangements on the ground. As recent arrivals, these budding French social scientists had yet to become fully immersed in how Brazilians were dealing with similar questions. Even still, their contact with new populations, landscapes, and histories altered their vision of the world and the place of the social sciences within it. The next chapter will analyze the importance of Brazilian research groups such as the Associação dos Geógrafos Brasileiros and the Sociedade de Etnografia e Folclore for their work. First, we need to get a better sense of why these scholars came to Brazil in the first place and of their experience of geographical, social, and professional relocation.

For the French scholars who went to Brazil, the geographer Albert Demangeon's *Le déclin de l'Europe* (The decline of Europe) proved much more important than philosophies of decline, particularly for Braudel and Monbeig, who had had him as a professor. The economic crisis of the 1930s intensified the language around decline, particularly when many young intellectuals found themselves unemployed.[3] They faced not only a terrible job market but also the "guard dogs" of prestigious institutions—those careerist professors with little original thought of their own.[4] In any case, Brazil seemed like a good way out, at least if one were to consider Demangeon's portrait of Brazil as an emerging industrial economy, alongside the US and Japan.[5]

For Lucien Febvre, coeditor of *Annales*, South America offered nothing less than a "privileged field of study." As of 1928, he claimed, "Just about everywhere we are beginning to witness, relative to the questions that the history and geography of this immense continent bring to science today, some of the curiosity that was, for a long time, the prerogative of isolated ethnographers."[6] As opposed to the "indigenous and savage America," the emphasis of Febvre's article was on broader social and economic changes such as urbanization, electrification, and the development of export markets.[7]

Braudel would call Brazil a "new country," a term he associated with social mobility, economic dynamism, and an unprecedented mixture of peoples and ethnic groups.[8] In many ways, he was simply echoing the language of his Paulista contemporaries, such as Mário de Andrade, who called the city *récemnascida*, or newborn.[9] Sérgio Buarque de Holanda, in his now-classic *Raízes do Brasil* (Roots of Brazil), published soon afterward, would largely concur. For Buarque de Holanda, a student more of Weber than of the French, in Brazil:

> Few individuals knew how to dedicate their entire lives to a single vocation, without allowing themselves to be attracted by another apparently lucrative task. And even rarer are the cases in which the same profession stayed in the same family for more than a generation, as usually occurs in lands where social stratification reached a higher level of stability.[10]

Lévi-Strauss and, later, Monbeig would echo such comments in contrasting Brazil's dynamism and vastness to the Europe from which they came.[11] None went so far as to call Brazil "the land of the future," as the Austrian Stefan Zweig would soon thereafter,[12] but their initial contact left them with the impression of a land of opportunity. At least for them, it really was.

Brazil offered these four, much more than their first professorships, what Bastide would call, "an immense laboratory of experimental sociology."[13] Monbeig, Braudel, and Lévi-Strauss used similar language regarding their own fields—history, geography, and anthropology, respectively—and, more generally, the interdisciplinary social sciences that they helped to create. Whereas the links between these disciplines had been theoretical for the previous generation, they became eminently practical for the group in Brazil.[14]

In terms of strict chronology, Lévi-Strauss, Braudel, and Monbeig had more in common with one another than Roger Bastide had with any of them. Younger than Bastide by nearly a decade when they arrived in Brazil, they also taught in Brazil under significantly different conditions. Lévi-Strauss, Braudel, and Monbeig arrived in February of 1935, teaching alongside one another until 1938.[15] In São Paulo, they were given considerable leeway in defining their disciplines, and, with relatively few hours of courses and long vacations, they had time to get to know the interior of Brazil. Bastide only arrived in 1938, as a substitute for Lévi-Strauss, who had effectively given up his post at USP in order to conduct his ethnological missions. By that point, the social sciences at USP had been better institutionalized, and the negative experience of "absent" professors (notably Lévi-Strauss) as well as the stricter educational politics of the Estado Novo, meant that liberties afforded to the others would not be quite the same for Bastide. Although we will see much more of him subsequently, he therefore plays a minor role in this chapter.

These young professors of the French missions differed from many of their colleagues generationally, and Brazil would take on a much more significant role in their careers. As we saw in the previous chapter, French historians and geographers such as Émile Coornaert, Henri Hauser, and Pierre Deffontaines worked on Brazil during this period. In contrast to the younger cohort, however, they had participated in the First World War and had research careers prior to their time in Brazil.[16]

Of course, Bastide, Braudel, Lévi-Strauss, and Monbeig were not the only French scholars of their generation whose work would be inflected by their Brazilian experience. Some of these others even produced significant work on the country. For the most part, however, their short stays, subject material (particularly in the more strictly European subjects of philosophy, letters, and classical languages), and subsequent careers distanced them from Brazil. Some, such as the philosopher Jean Maugüé, left considerable marks in Brazil through their teaching, but their research agendas contrasted with those of Braudel, Lévi-Strauss, Monbeig, and Bastide, who transformed their time in Brazil into a sustained scholarly interest.[17]

PREVIOUS INTELLECTUAL TRAINING
AND THE PULL OF THE ATLANTIC

For Pierre Monbeig, Brazil offered a new terrain on which to conduct geographical research. Already advanced in his doctoral work on Spain, Monbeig had published on agrarian reform, among other questions.[18] The fact that he had published in both *Annales de géographie* and *Annales d'histoire économique et sociale* points to the historical dimension of his work, a continuation of the fruitful working relationships between geographers and historians from the previous generation.[19] The Spanish civil war ultimately interrupted the progress of his research and, with the rise of Franco, he vowed not to return to Spain.

In the midst of an academic crisis concerning how to complete his doctorate, he was doubly happy to receive a letter from Henri Hauser inviting him to Brazil: first, in a professional sense; second, for the sake of his doctoral studies.[20] Furthermore, he would have the opportunity to build upon the work on Brazil of French geographers such as Pierre Denis.[21] When Monbeig arrived in Brazil, he already had an advisor (Demangeon) and a set of questions from human geography. He was particularly interested in population movements, agrarian land use, and the relationship between lived experience and the broader political economy.

Lévi-Strauss, on the other hand, was not yet an anthropologist. Unlike most of the young anthropologists of his generation, he had not followed Marcel Mauss's seminar or participated directly in the network surrounding the Musée de l'Homme. When he left France, in fact, he was but an agregé in philosophy with no original teachings of his own. More to the point, he had little direct knowledge of the budding field of anthropology, largely depending on the familiarity of his wife, Dina, with physical anthropology and ethnography to frame his studies.[22]

Mauss, although continuing to identify as a sociologist, including at the Collège de France, where he had held a chair since 1931, had long insisted on the importance of ethnography for reviving comparative sociology.[23] As a founding member of the Institut d'Ethnologie in Paris, with Paul Rivet and Lucien Lévy-Bruhl, he encouraged students to conduct fieldwork. Rivet, a prolific fieldworker in his own right among Andean indigenous communities, was arguably even more important in this sense, especially for Jacques Soustelle, then in the field in Mexico.[24] Furthermore, as the president of the Société des Américanistes (Society of Americanists), Rivet served as a crucial mediator between Latin America and France—and not only in the study of indigenous cultures of the Americas.[25]

When given the opportunity to go to Brazil, the then philosophy teacher Lévi-Strauss immediately associated himself with Marcel Mauss and Paul Rivet. To Mauss, just before leaving, he wrote, "My wife ... and I will dedicate ourselves to fieldwork meant to provide us with material for a thesis"; to Rivet, "The orientation of our work in Brazil will depend, you know, essentially on the indications that you would be so kind as to give us."[26] Lévi-Strauss proposed meeting with both giants of ethnology prior to leaving, and he and Dina likely did. In that way they joined, at least in spirit, Mauss's students in their quest around the world to gain "total social facts" and Rivet in his linguistic and archaeological work on the Americas.

By the time Braudel arrived in Brazil, he had already undertaken a number of book reviews, published his first article on "The Spanish and North Africa," and was advancing rapidly on his thesis on Philip II of Spain and the Mediterranean.[27] As it had for his peers, Brazil offered a unique opportunity for his teaching and administrative career: his "first professional experience," in the words of his professor Henri Hauser, then teaching in Rio.[28] Even if Braudel would never dedicate himself exclusively to the country in his research, his contact with Brazil allowed him to extend the geographical and methodological scope of his work—a fact explored by previous scholarship and that this book addresses more thoroughly.[29]

Braudel claimed that he became intelligent in Brazil, but the intelligence he gained was as much social as intellectual in the more limited sense of the word. As we will see in the next chapter, Brazil opened Braudel's eyes to new landscapes, architecture, people, and histories, allowing him to see transatlantic trade, the colonial cities of Rio de Janeiro and Salvador, and, at least in his mind, the peasant of the Middle Ages so dear to Marc Bloch, Febvre, and *Annales*. Equally importantly, at an institutional level Braudel's tenure at USP permitted him to make history a central discipline within the social sciences, in part displacing the federative role played by sociology in the decades prior. As the "elder" of the young professors sent to São Paulo in 1935, Braudel had significant influence in shaping the curriculum at USP and in rearranging the power dynamics of the new Faculty of Philosophy, Sciences, and Letters. His seniority as measured by years of teaching and his accrued symbolic capital provided him with authority in the conflicts between Lévi-Strauss and Paul Arbousse-Bastide as well as with the Ministry of Foreign Affairs.[30] Braudel ultimately came to usurp Arbousse-Bastide's power as the head of the mission, putting his weight behind his junior colleagues to support their disciplinary objectives and negotiating the renewed contracts for the French professors with the Paulista administration as well.[31]

Whereas the other professors were searching for thesis topics, Braudel, the "preferred student of the historian Lucien Febvre," was already "quite advanced" on his thesis, if we choose to credit the memory of his colleague Jean Maugüé.[32] He brought cartons of European archival material and microfilm with him—so much that he needed to rent an extra room in São Paulo. But more important than the quantity of archives is Maugüé's memory that Braudel "never stopped consulting" his files.[33] As Lévi-Strauss would remember much later in life, in his speech inducting Braudel into the Académie Française:

> Very little our elder but much further along in your research, you already had a foot in higher education. A thesis underway put you, in any case, on the other side of the gap that separates new secondary-school teachers from a personage destined for great establishments [grandes établissements].[34]

Braudel, according to both Maugüé and Lévi-Strauss, was not only "ahead" of them, but in some ways in a category of his own. He had arrived at the other side of the chasm not so much because he had *in fact* arrived as because they perceived that he had. The "value" of Braudel's research program, personal and collective, was made possible by his colleagues' confidence in it; with little written, there was little to vouch for the importance of Braudel's research other than the belief that it was important.[35]

Brazil may not have been the same living laboratory for Braudel as it was for his colleagues, but it was important for his relationship with his future advisor Lucien Febvre, who had been building relationships with intellectuals in Argentina and Uruguay.[36] In his article "Un champ privilegié d'études: L'Amérique du Sud" (A privileged field of study: South America), Febvre had urged young scholars to look beyond Europe to a Latin America full of possibilities.[37] Braudel heeded this advice, and, after teaching for two years in Brazil, he finally met Febvre for the first time on a ship returning to Europe in 1937. The two continued to speak of Brazil into the war years and even after.[38]

Roger Bastide's engagement with Brazil would lag behind that of his younger colleagues, simply because he arrived three years later. His interests in the sociology of religion, mysticism, and religious syncretism would ultimately encounter fruitful terrain in Brazil in the later 1930s, as we will see. He may figure little in the events of this chapter, but his similarities with and connections to the other protagonists of the story merit foregrounding. Like Lévi-Strauss, Bastide was an agregé in philosophy looking for a thesis topic. During his years teaching at the secondary level before coming to Brazil, he explored a variety of subjects, ranging from politics to religion to poetry, and published his first sociological article, on the Armenian community in the French city of Valence.[39] He also published two books, Les problèmes de la vie mystique (1931) and Éléments de sociologie religieuse (1935).

Hailing from the south of France, Bastide was largely separated from Durkheim's followers and the Parisian sociological establishment. Coming to sociology as an outsider with little formal training, his interests were rather eclectic, and he knew he needed anchoring. His familiarity with *L'année sociologique* encouraged him to reach out to two of its more important researchers concerning a possible thesis: Marcel Mauss and the sociologist Maurice Halbwachs.[40] Halbwachs responded to a letter from Bastide in 1935, "Mr. Blondel informed me of your work that should become a thesis, and it appeared to both of us that the second subject . . . would be of interest. The social conditions of mysticism . . ."[41] After continued correspondence, Halbwachs wrote to Bastide from his summer vacation home in the Alps: "I above all wanted you to meet Mr. Mauss, so that you can bring him up to speed on what you want to do."[42]

A few months later, Bastide did exactly that. He wrote Mauss, sending along his *Les problèmes de la vie mystique* as well as a kind of prospectus for future work. Bastide expressed his "great admiration" for Mauss and sought out "the honor and pleasure of working with [his] help." This was notwithstanding his "philosophical opposition" to the "metaphysical undercurrents of Durkheimism."[43]

Bastide may have been surprised by Mauss's virulent criticism in response. Mauss chided Bastide for his appreciation of Max Weber and redeployed the Durkheimian arguments of "science" versus "philosophy" to disqualify Bastide's project as it stood. Bastide, who proposed to study mysticism sociologically, was imprecise in the sources that he intended to use in order to transcend the age-old question of the relationship between the subject and God. Mauss offered him two suggestions, the latter of which Bastide opted for in his move to Brazil. The first was to focus on "the social conditions of mysticism in Europe."[44] The second option would be to "leave history behind to arrive at generality"; citing India, China, and even Sufism, Mauss asked with considerable doubt, "Is the promised land of mysticism [really] the land of Christianity?"[45] Little did Bastide know that shortly thereafter he would receive an opportunity to study such questions in Brazil.

Ironically, Paul Arbousse-Bastide, the nemesis of Braudel, Lévi-Strauss, and, to a lesser extent, Monbeig, would be crucial in allowing Bastide to expand his studies outside Europe. Lévi-Strauss's insistence on teaching cultural anthropology and his frequent absences to conduct fieldwork cost him his job at USP—the very job that Bastide took up in 1938. In Brazil, Bastide met and grew to appreciate Lévi-Strauss, becoming a colleague, in a sense, by succeeding him.

Bastide and Arbousse-Bastide (no relation) had known each other for quite a long time prior to working together in Brazil. Their correspondence dates to

1922, and according to the memoirs of Arbousse-Bastide, they met in 1919.[46] In Brazil they would be referred to affectionately by their students as little and big Bastide—"Bastidinho" and "Bastidão."[47]

Weathering the storm that pitted Braudel, Monbeig, and Lévi-Strauss against him, Arbousse-Bastide wrote to Bastide, then in Valence: "I would very much like to have you as a colleague. You know, it is not impossible. A chair in sociology may be vacant one day or another and sociologists are rare at the University."[48] Arbousse-Bastide praised Bastide for his article in the *Revue internationale de sociologie* and let him know that he used it in his teaching.[49] After waxing nostalgic about Valence and the region of France that they affectionately shared, Arbousse-Bastide closed his letter: "The question of the chair for you in São Paulo is not platonic. Reflect on the idea. It would be for March 1938. Keep it to yourself because of the circumstances that I will explain."[50]

Bastide ultimately got the job, but, when he arrived in São Paulo in 1938, he had little more than a vague idea of working on African religions. He, like the others, would be transformed by his early years in Brazil, although at a different tempo. Arriving three years later to take up a post at a much more institutionalized university, he was unable to travel as extensively as his younger colleagues, nor depart as significantly from Durkheim. Nonetheless, the crossing of the Atlantic opened up his world—and by most accounts, even more so than it did for the others. For all the French scholars who went to Brazil, the three weeks it took to traverse the ocean by steamship served as an extended prelude— geographic, intellectual, and social—to their lives in São Paulo.

An unpublished letter by Monbeig to his wife, Juliette, provides a glimpse into the first-class ocean liners to Brazil. He describes an ambience of decadence and festivities, mixed together with a kind of colonial exoticism. On the *Campana* in the port of Dakar, Monbeig wrote: "Tired from the ball, the passengers are still asleep. There is not much noise in the smoking parlor, the only place that is cool enough to be able to write."[51] If Monbeig mostly wrote about his love for his wife and the health of his son (in his company for the voyage), he also alluded to the possible conflict between different "factions" of French on board and the tensions between these groups that the consul attempted to alleviate.

The "Franco-Argentines" wanted Monbeig and a French couple, the de Vogüés, to dress up for the equator party, much to his chagrin: "We refuse to dress up as Arabs for the equator dinner; can you imagine me dressed up in sheets and speaking Petit-Nègre? Charming!"[52] Monbeig insisted to his wife that he would be wearing a tuxedo to the "equator dinner," that he would not speak in Petit-Nègre, the pidgin colonial French developed for primitives in Africa, and that he was not particularly interested in attending in the first place.[53] And yet, all these things were in the realm of possibility for Monbeig and his immediate social circle of world travelers, international businessmen, and the slew of doctors, engineers, and administrators who circulated around the tropics. It was a world much different from the classical formality of the École Normale Supérieure where he was trained, but nonetheless a world within and against which he and his colleagues defined themselves as scholars.

Transatlantic travel had for some time contributed to a reformulation of French culture, especially in literature, music, and the performing arts. Ships were the kind of places where characters like Josephine Baker could meet Le Corbusier. And the Atlantic, whether "black," "white" or "red," provided inspiration to Parisian Brazil lovers including the authors Blaise Cendrars (who was actually Swiss), Jean Cocteau, and Paul Morand and the composer Darius Milhaud.[54] Entertainment, poetry, and even aesthetics, however, are considerably different fields than the social sciences.

Few of these earlier go-betweens with Brazil had the kind of institutional backing that the French missions examined in this book did, the major exception being the Claudel-Milhaud mission of 1917–18.[55] Paul Claudel, the French ambassador to Brazil, and Milhaud both officially represented the French state. Similarly, as low-ranking diplomats, the young French professors had their first-class travel paid for;[56] as professors, their salaries were covered in another country; and finally, as scientists, they would define themselves socially against the bohemians who had preceded them.

The journey to Brazil took them out of their libraries and classrooms and into the world of travelers. It also prepared them for positions of prestige and authority. The sudden upward mobility of first-class travel accustomed them to feeling more important and put them in direct contact with some of the ruling elites in and outside Brazil. Lévi-Strauss remembered the luxury of first-class accommodations on board the *Mendoza*, where he was "among the eight or ten passengers who, on a boat built to accommodate 100 or 150, had the deck, the cabins, the smoking room, and the dining-room all to themselves."[57]

Braudel's memories of grandeur are even clearer. Recounting his first trip to Brazil, in 1935, he said:

> The French government, desiring to complete the French mission, sent me on the transatlantic *Marsilia*, a ship that was so luxurious that, even before arriving in Brazil, I could establish contacts with all the men who dominated, from the outside, the economic life of Brazil. They were representatives of North American trusts, French insurance companies, etc. For a young professor of history, who mainly knew the world from books, it was an extraordinary first lesson.[58]

One of these men would become one of the architects of the 1964 military coup d'état as well, but that story will come later.

Atlantic travel provided a new geographic and social context for the French missions, all the while creating a space for its members to get to know one another.[59] Still on board the *Campana*, Pierre Monbeig wrote to his wife (then in France): "Last night, big discussion on the importance of history, ethnography, etc.—animated but without acrimony. Let's hope that it lasts! Mrs. Lévi-Strauss speaks of you often, she is a bit bored, I think, but did me a big favor in sewing a button on my jacket."[60]

The French professors were preparing themselves for the year to come. Monbeig put his finishing touches on his article on Febvre, and they certainly all had some reading to do. But whatever responsibilities they may have had, their light workload was interspersed with unending games of bridge ("our only distraction"), two-hour-long lunches, and "big discussions" of the social sciences that they were sent to teach. But before we look at the continuation of these big discussions at the university and in print, let us look more closely at these young scholars' first contacts with Brazil and the Paulista bourgeoisie.

ACQUIRING CAPITAL—SOCIAL AND CULTURAL

Crossing the Atlantic was the first of many steps in Braudel's, Monbeig's, Lévi-Strauss's, and Bastide's intellectual journeys in Brazil. In São Paulo, they were thrown into a rapidly developing urban landscape and a cultural universe in which they would have to define themselves. Taken under the wing of Júlio de Mesquita Filho and his newspaper *O Estado de S. Paulo*, they immediately became celebrities. For example, Braudel, Arbousse-Bastide, and the economist François Perroux's arrival in São Paulo on board the *Mendoza* was front-page news, and Lévi-Strauss's visit to the neighboring city of Campinas for the Week of the Child there merited a full-length article.[61]

A photo from 1936 of the Faculty of Philosophy, Sciences, and Letters exemplifies the ambience of formality and prestige that surrounded the French in Brazil. The ladies' furs and hats and the uprightness of the gentlemen suggest the seriousness of the whole endeavor. The French were to bring "culture" to the tropics, much as the mission of French artists did to the royal court over a century earlier.[62]

According to Lévi-Strauss, USP was "an ideological cover in the form of an urbane parliamentarianism," a project of "landowners who were gradually transferring their capital to partly foreign-owned industrial investments."[63] These "feudal landlords" invited the French to Brazil, partly as a "cultural front" and partly as "entertainment."[64] Lévi-Strauss's comments miss the particularly modern form of global capitalism that sustained these "feudal

FIG. 1 The University of São Paulo, 1936. Pierre Monbeig private archive. *First row, on right*: Juliette Monbieg. *Second row, from right to left*: Claude Lévi-Strauss (2), Pierre Monbeig (3), Fernando de Azevedo (6).

landlords"; however, his awareness of bringing at once "culture" and "entertainment" seems to fit the bill.

In São Paulo, the young scholars were given a platform on which to speak— and the financial assurance of their own importance. Pierre Hourcade, their colleague in literature from 1935 to 1937, wrote to the Ministry of Foreign Affairs of "exceptional material advantages" during his tenure in São Paulo.[65] Maügüe remembered Braudel's car and chauffer.[66] Whether downtown at the chic Hotel Terminus, where they stayed upon arrival, the Esplanada, where many of them moved to, or in the new bourgeois "garden" neighborhoods fanning off the Avenida Paulista, the French lived in some of the best real estate in the city.[67] Monbeig, who stayed at the hotel to save a little money before his wife and children came, boasted of the ability to live in such a garden neighborhood, Jardins: "The other colleagues, who are much better off than I thought, are leaving the Esplanada for their new homes. Let's do the same!"[68]

In addition to enjoying fine housing, the French scholars and their spouses benefited from domestic labor that allowed them to focus their energies on their work. Maügüe remembers Braudel's maid (*empregada*), and when Braudel returned to France in 1937, his replacement, Jean Gagé, wrote to Braudel's then assistant, Eurípides Simões de Paula, requesting that the domestic workers at his home speak Italian, a "language that we know, my wife and I, because we lived for three years in Rome."[69] Arbousse-Bastide wrote to his parents in 1938, "Our maid crisis appears to be finished. We will keep our little German maid and we have a cook."[70] Having a maid may have been a common practice in upper-middle-class families in France at the time; Emmanuelle Loyer noted the people that served Lévi-Strauss's extended family, and Monbeig in one of his letters to his wife spoke of a "panne de bonne" (lack of maid).[71] Braudel, coming from a colonial household in Algeria (his wife was a *pied-noir* from a wealthy family[72]), and Gagé, from Italy, were also clearly accustomed to having help. One thing, however, is for sure: these young professors were guaranteed a bourgeois lifestyle in São Paulo that was not accessible for their peers in France without accumulated family resources.

Finally, the French scholars had assistants at USP who helped to teach their courses and prepare their research.[73] Monbeig's assistant Maria Conceição Vicente de Carvalho, for example, was responsible for giving parallel lessons in Portuguese for those who did not understand Monbeig's French.[74] As for Braudel, his assistant Simões de Paula not only translated enormous amounts of course material into Portuguese for other students, but also conducted research. In a letter to the Portuguese historian (José?) Osório de Oliveira, Simões requested "information on and bibliography for the islands of the Atlantic (Azores, Madeira, Cape Verde, Canary Islands), Portuguese Africa, Brazilian wood, corn, and their respective transports" for Braudel's "course on the Atlantic in the seventeenth and eighteenth centuries."[75] In the most limited sense, we can see the work done by Brazilians for these young French scholars. But we might also consider the conversations that occurred in the classroom or in more informal settings—interactions that seldom show up in the archive.

João Cruz Costa, who would become USP's first philosophy professor of Brazilian nationality, served as de facto library for the humanities and social sciences during the university's early years.[76] Braudel remembered that it was in the library of "this humanist of extraordinary sophistication" that he "learned to see Brazil."[77] Unfortunately, the only letter from Braudel to Cruz Costa that remains, written off the coast of Brazil when Braudel was returning to France after his first year of teaching, is more touristic and sentimental than intellectual.[78] If his conversations with Cruz Costa cannot be reproduced, however, the general milieu can: a wealthy, highly literate bourgeoisie that was fluent enough in the French language and familiar with French academic culture to share ways of conceiving of the world, all while having an entirely different set of references that would enrich the French scholars' work.

Months prior to the younger French scholars' arrival in February of the following year, in November 1934, the Associação dos Geógrafos Brasileiros hosted an event at the Automóvel Club (Automobile Club) in homage to the professors Deffontaines, Arbousse-Bastide, and Coornaert. They had completed their first year of teaching, and for Deffontaines and Coornaert, it would be their last in São Paulo. The elaborate menu (in French) had as possibilities: "potage Malakoff, Robalo poché aux Sauternes Sauce Hollandaise, [and] Pintade à la mode d'Alcantara [with] petits pois à la française [and] marrons étuvés." The five-course meal came accompanied by a Graves Supérieur Moulin à Vent (1923).[79]

Prominent guests such as Antônio Carlos Couto de Barros and Geraldo Horácio de Paula Souza were present, as were students such as Caio Prado Jr.[80] Then enrolled in the course of history at geography at USP, Prado was already one of Brazil's most recognizable historians and geographers, having published two books: *Evolução política do Brasil* (1933) and *URSS: Um novo mundo* (1934). We will encounter him in the next chapter in São Paulo, and later in Paris, exiled due to his participation in the Aliança Nacional Libertadora.

The French professors' bourgeois lifestyle brought them into contact with high society that included not only artists and academics but governors and ambassadors, too. These are the people whom Lévi-Strauss encountered at the Automóvel Club and would later excoriate in *Tristes Tropiques*. But whereas Lévi-Strauss distanced himself from this world to the extent possible, most of the French professors embraced it as part of their larger responsibility. The Ministry of Foreign Affairs had recruited them and paid for their travel, after all.

A letter from Monbeig to his wife is particularly explicit about this aspect of his social life. After mentioning the lunches and meetings that he had with Couto de Barros and the governor, Adhemar de Barros, he elaborated on the range of people that expected his presence. These included the journalist, librarian, and researcher Rubens Borba de Moraes (who, like Couto de Barros, helped to organize the Week of Modern Art in 1922) and the secretary of the Association for French Abroad, Mr. Wernlé.

> Rubens proposed, and had accepted, the principle of a Franco-Brazilian dinner twice per month, at the Hotel Terminus, with gastronomy. As you can imagine, the Departamento de Cultura will supply the essential Brazilian element and the "mission" will complete . . . as Tuesday the Lévi-Strausses disembark at Santos, as Monday night, the French community is offering a dinner for Mr. Wernlé, secretary of the Association for French Abroad, on a mission in South America, you can see that my "vie mondaine" is quite busy. Positive indication for the mission, but I would pass it up easily. Particularly the Wernlé dinner that at $50 stupefies me terribly.[81]

FIG. 2 France-Amérique Committee, 1939. Pierre Monbeig private archive. Monbeig is at the center table (facing), fifth from right.

The biweekly dinners put together by the Departamento de Cultura were not necessarily as chic as the formal dinner for the secretary Mr. Wernlé, for which the photo of the France-Amérique Committee in 1939 might offer a plausible approximation. But they were nonetheless "gastronomic."[82]

Outside the Paulista metropolis, the French professors also took breaks from the urbane lifestyle. For Monbeig, this meant spending time in the interior of São Paulo state. Writing his wife about a family friend, Paul-Marie, who was likely looking for work in Brazil, he claimed: "If this sweet young man is not otherwise called upon, I think that he will find sugar plantations, the 'terrains' of Mesquita at Marília, and the orange cases of Couto de Barros [to be] all that he needs—and considering the customary hospitality here, without expenses."[83] It is unknown whether Paul-Marie made it to Brazil, but the letter attests to Monbeig's intimacy with São Paulo's social elite (the Mesquitas being the owners of *O Estado de S. Paulo*; Couto de Barros, one of the wealthier landowners in the state). Their hospitality gave him nice places to visit (countryside fazendas, or plantations) and an object of research (the geography of coffee production in São Paulo).

Not everyone was as close with the Mesquitas as Monbeig or Braudel, whom Júlio de Mesquita Filho would later call "um dos nossos" (one of ours).[84]

Lévi-Strauss, for example, claimed that his political quarrels with Mesquita may have ultimately led to his being fired from USP, in 1938.[85] It is possible that partisan politics came between them. What is more likely is that Mesquita, who had wanted European thinkers to Europeanize Brazil, took issue with the idea of encouraging research on oral or semiliterate cultures. Indeed, he had argued a decade before that many of Brazil's problems arose from the "African toxin" in Brazilian blood.[86]

Lévi-Strauss's retrospective account has been made more plausible by biography's treatment of his socialist activism prior to arriving in Brazil, even if the official historian of Mesquita (not surprisingly) claimed that there is no evidence to support such a claim.[87] My point is not to say, however, that everyone was friends—or, for that matter, that all the French professors shared equally in the elitist lifestyle that São Paulo offered. Rather, it is to situate the French professors socially and highlight the access they had to Paulista high society, economic and cultural. Lévi-Strauss, like Monbeig and Braudel, frequented the Automóvel Club and the Departamento de Cultura, notably less elitist but still with close ties to the Mesquitas and the *O Estado de S. Paulo* group.[88]

Geographically and socially, French professors were much closer to the elites of São Paulo and their luxurious *palacetes* (mansions, literally small palaces) than to the *povo* (the everyday people of the city).[89] They were also brought into the cultural sphere of the Brazilian modernists in their institutional phase, where impressionistic travels and the imaginative notions of cannibalizing European art forms were giving way to concrete studies about Brazilian culture.[90] The Paulistas not only invited the young French agregés to found their university in the first place, but also welcomed them to the best of their ability. They provided them with a place to speak, an audience to listen to them, and the "material conditions" to assure them that what they were doing was of importance. Monbeig, Lévi-Strauss, Braudel, and, to a lesser extent, Bastide rose to the occasion, taking on responsibilities that they never would have been offered back in France.

REDEFINING DISCIPLINES

Upon arriving in São Paulo, the young French professors were tasked with defining their respective disciplines. Over the course of their transatlantic journey, they went from secondary-school teachers, largely responsible in the French educational system for instilling *culture générale* (general knowledge), to professors who would single-handedly determine curricula. This is evidenced by their essays in USP's *Anuário*, or course directory, for the 1934–35 academic year and in their teachings more generally.[91] Except for in sociology, where Lévi-Strauss and then Bastide taught alongside the older Arbousse-Bastide, they had no direct supervision.

In this unprecedented position of curricular power, I argue, Lévi-Strauss, Monbeig, and Braudel sought to establish a federative social science, where the disciplines of geography, "cultural sociology" (or anthropology), and history could join forces to displace what they saw as the intellectual primacy of Durkheimian sociology. Elevating the place of geography in the social sciences, they proposed to understand cultural units rather than conduct general studies of humankind, the likes of which were all too common in France. Just a few years later Bastide would find the fertile terrain they had cultivated—where he, too, could affirm his distance vis-à-vis the dominant models of the social sciences as practiced in France.

Monbeig's essay in the *Anuário*, entitled "Didactic Orientation," is most closely addressed to the organization of teaching at USP.[92] While not necessarily any less methodologically oriented or ambitious in his own work than his colleagues, in this essay, Monbeig wanted the students to see geography as part of practical activity. Many students, he claimed, took "pleasure in grandiose frameworks, with questions that permit them to establish uselessly long debates . . . but that in the end lead to nothing." As opposed to such metaphysics, he wrote, "I would prefer that they knew geography, before discussing it . . . Geography is a science based on territory . . . It is not a branch of philosophy."[93] According to Monbeig, empirical research in geography was the precondition for any broader conversations about space, geopolitics, or economic development. Furthermore, geography as a science was of public utility.[94]

In "Didactic Orientation" Monbeig proposed to examine localized, regional geographies in his courses. Instead of taking the globe as his point of departure, he divided the world into smaller geographical units such as Monsoon Asia, Central Europe, North America, and, most importantly, South America. For the last unit, he wrote, "I would feel particularly satisfied if, next year, I could start this regional geography with a course on South America."[95]

By shifting his courses to South America, Monbeig not only effectuated the geographical transition of his own research from Spain to Brazil; he also set forth to develop a new dynamic between research and teaching (for him) and research and learning (for his students). For him, geography was about much more than "theory." It needed to be supplemented by "the study of the reality of the terrain."[96] This meant, above all, a departure from teaching ex cathedra, so common in the French system—and in Brazil, for that matter—and the development of new kinds of didactic materials such as maps, statistics, and iconographic documents.

Monbeig's own research would provide the material with which to teach about São Paulo, while students' questions and projects would lead them to understand phenomena such as "the cotton trade in São Paulo; the production and commerce of oranges in the world (considered from a Paulista point of view); a monograph on Cornélio Procópio, pioneer city; the demographic evolution of São Paulo; a map commenting on the textile industries in the city of São Paulo; the geographical conditions of development in São Paulo, and so on."[97] In this way, the geography program would be at the forefront of shifting courses on general knowledge (largely Eurocentric) to empirical questions dealing with São Paulo, as testimonies by Monbeig's students, such as Ruy Coelho, would later confirm.[98] Collectively, Monbeig and his students' efforts took hold in the Associação dos Geógrafos Brasileiros and in its journal *Geografia*.[99]

If the field of geography emerged in the French university system largely by way of Paul Vidal de La Blache and his followers, its growth seemed to taper off in subsequent generations. Monbeig, the advisee of the Vidalian Albert Demangeon, was part of a generation in which the highest percentage of *normaliens* (students of the École Normale Supérieure) in the history/geography track chose to specialize in geography. It subsequently declined.[100] The regional monograph, which had served as the model for the previous generation, had largely exhausted France's regions. As a consequence, the discipline was left intellectually unsure of the distinctiveness of its methodology, internally divided between more scientific geological impulses and more human elements, not to mention the emergence of applied geography dealing with urban settings and population management more generally.[101]

For Monbeig, having a precise object or methodology was less important than studying an area of the world where so much remained unknown. Geography, multidisciplinary by nature, would distinguish itself by its study of non-European spaces and of Brazil in particular. Precisely because of its wealth of poorly known phenomena such as "the formation of the South Atlantic, the atmospheric circulation above the American continent, [and] the conquest of the land by man," South America proved a region of great promise.[102] Studying these phenomena, both human and geological, would provide ample space for Brazilian geographers—and Paulistas in particular—to stand out at the International Geographic Union.[103] Of course, it would also allow Monbeig himself, a specialist of this part of the world, to stake out a place in the French social sciences. In the process, particularly in a discipline with relatively porous boundaries and characterized by significant interdisciplinarity, he would need to ally himself with his colleagues who were doing similar things. Thus, his reliance on Lévi-Strauss and Braudel.[104]

Lévi-Strauss's essay in the *Anuário*, "Cultural Sociology and Its Teaching," is at once radical and conservative.[105] It is, as Bourdieu wrote of Manet, the work of "a specific revolutionary"—of an insider who mastered the dominant codes of French intellectual life and who fought against those who dominated "the relatively autonomous universe" of culture from within that very universe.[106] In a sense, Lévi-Strauss effectuated a paradigm shift within the French social sciences, exploiting his temporarily peripheral position (vis-à-vis France) in Brazil and recruiting allies (notably Braudel and Monbeig) to defend him. In his essay, Lévi-Strauss put forth a methodological treatise on "cultural sociology," a phrase deliberately chosen to emphasize the fact that he was teaching in a sociology department and to define himself within the line of Durkheim's science.[107] He avoided the controversial term that he would later use to define himself against Durkheim and Paul Rivet—"anthropologie"—and in so doing sought to allay concerns about his teaching.[108]

Equally importantly, he cultivated a personal relationship with the director of the Faculty of Philosophy, Sciences, and Letters, Fernando de Azevedo, whose didactic book, *Princípios de sociologia*, he cited respectfully. When he thanked Azevedo for the book, he even "wondered why Brazil called upon us when there are scholars of your level here."[109]

In France, he wrote periodically to Paul Fauconnet, the Durkheimian professor at the Sorbonne, to let him know of his intellectual development and the progress of his studies.[110] And, to the best of his ability, he heeded Marcel Mauss's advice not to "burn our bridges with sociology."[111] Arbousse-Bastide, after considerable frustration in previous years, even wrote to his parents in 1937: "Levy S. [*sic*] admirably holds his courses on *pure sociology*."[112]

All that said, Lévi-Strauss's respectful approach to his predecessors and immediate colleagues masked the frontal attack that he was laying on the field of sociology. For Lévi-Strauss, the great majority of sociological works conceived the discipline as "a sort of universal method that allows for the elaboration of all problems where man is considered, to any degree, implicated."[113] This pretension to universality created "an insipid syncretic view of social studies," because each individual phenomenon would require "a respectable number of specialists."[114] Lévi-Strauss, of course, would attempt to define himself as such a specialist in his studies of Amerindian cultures. First, though, he needed to dismantle sociology, at once empirically and methodologically, only to later refashion it under very different terms.

If the debates of the previous generation pitted sociologists as "scientists" against speculative philosophers, Lévi-Strauss proceeded to use many of the same arguments to valorize "cultural sociology" (which was, remember, a coded term for ethnology) against Durkheimian sociology. First, he defined science not as an organizing principal, but rather as a set of empirical results. Then, he disqualified sociology as precisely the kind of speculative enterprise that it condemned in philosophy. And finally, he proposed archaeology and ethnology as the primary "results of scientific value that the study of human collectivities has provided until today."[115]

If in theory Lévi-Strauss preserved the role of sociology in studying human culture, in practice he reduced it to the level of speculation. Until archaeology and ethnology had provided sociology with sufficient empirical studies upon which to base larger claims, sociology itself needed to be sidelined. Once "fieldworkers" had applied themselves to all collectivities—"not only savages and disappeared peoples . . . but to modern society as well"—ethnology and sociology might fuse together again.[116]

Mauss, who was, after all, Durkheim's nephew and most loyal collaborator, had been working with his students precisely on the "savages" to which Lévi-Strauss referred. However, for Mauss, "culture" was never a term of particular importance and, on several occasions, he even discredited it.[117] Lévi-Strauss, then, was not proposing to be a Maussian in Brazil, but instead to practice a "cultural sociology" whose primary referents came from the field of anthropology in the United States. He wrote:

> As paradoxical as it may seem, we have reason to say that the object of sociology is not the social but the cultural. The social is comprised in the cultural, as one of its categories . . . That said, we are not contradicting Durkheim, quite the contrary. Durkheim perfectly understood the specificity of sociology; he had not yet conceived of its extension. When he affirms the specificity of social relations, it is relative to geographical, psychological factors, etc. . . . We add only this clarification to his commentary: the characteristic of specificity does not belong only to the social fact as such, but as it expresses one of its aspects, that it is one of the "complexes" whose ensemble constitutes the domain of culture.[118]

While Lévi-Strauss affirmed elsewhere in his *Anuário* essay that ethnology was by no means attempting to dominate sociology, in this passage he seems to be arguing for precisely that. Whereas the Durkheimians were interested in social facts (*faits sociaux*)—in particular the relationships that organized society into classes—Lévi-Strauss claimed that it was not understanding such facts in and of themselves that should be the object of sociology. Instead, it should be understanding how these facts are *expressed*.

For Lévi-Strauss, class, for example, might be useful in understanding certain cultural phenomena; however, rather than focus on class itself, sociologists should focus on distinct cultural forms. It is precisely for this reason that Lévi-Strauss cited Robert Lowie's *Culture and Ethnology* (1917) and, later in the essay, Alfred Kroeber as inspiration. These American anthropologists, both students of Franz Boas, were primarily interested in cultural expression and language rather than in social organization as such.

The kind of cultural relativism that Lévi-Strauss gained from such readings was shared by the Brazilian Gilberto Freyre, who had studied with Boas at Columbia University.[119] Freyre's *Casa-grande e senzala: Introdução à história da sociedade patriarcal no Brasil* (1933; *The Masters and the Slaves: A Study in the Development of Brazilian Civilization*, 1946) had revolutionized the Brazilian intellectual field and is seen today as the precursor to the history of everyday life, the history of slavery, and even of *Annales*.[120] Freyre insisted on the essentially African nature of Brazil and praised racial mixing, frontally challenging the eugenicists of the period. Braudel, Monbeig, Arbousse-Bastide, and Bastide all had their own relationships with Freyre to which we will return later, but not Lévi-Strauss, even if it is likely that he read works by him.

Coming back to the essay itself, Lévi-Strauss, despite his rhetorical insistence on preserving Durkheim, largely cited him in selective ways to justify his own departure from French sociology. In closing his essay, he anticipated his critics:

> It is not less thorny to believe that the adversaries of cultural sociology, with their Marxist grievances, consider it an American invention. Without a doubt, the cultural point of view has illustrious defenders in the United States; but it also finds there its fiercest adversaries. And the list of European theorists of culture is no less imposing: Rivers, Elliot Smith in England, Ratzel, Graebner.[121]

Lévi-Strauss not only had intellectual stakes in his position vis-à-vis Marxism (and, for that matter, socialist sociologists in France who insisted on class analysis); he also had to justify his field geopolitically. Lévi-Strauss's citations alone demonstrate that he had little interest in promoting the "French essence" of the university, which ultimately put him at odds with faculty members such as Arbousse-Bastide who sought to ensure the diffusion of sympathy toward France and her cultural life. (Remember, they were partially paid by the Ministry of Foreign Affairs.)

But if Lévi-Strauss departed from the generation of French social scientists that preceded him, he drew closer to his immediate colleagues Monbeig and Braudel. "Cultural sociology," he argued, was much closer to newer empirical sciences than it was to philosophy, the cornerstone of French academic life. In a concluding remark, Lévi-Strauss insisted on the role of geography. He deplored the "almost complete absence of the links between sociology and geography, on one hand, and sociology and ethnography, on the other," insisting that, with respect to the optional course for sociology students on human geography (taught by Monbeig), "physical geography is no less indispensable."[122] The student Caio Prado Jr. took such teachings to heart as he prepared his masterpiece *Formação do Brasil contemporâneo*.[123] Lévi-Strauss shared this interest in geography with his colleagues Braudel and Monbeig, participating in the meetings of the Associação dos Geógrafos Brasileiros. All three of them found the German ethno-geographer Friedrich Ratzel useful for their work, and their affinities with *Annales* opened them up to scholars working on social, psychological, and anthropologically oriented understandings of collective belief and behavior.

While Monbeig and Lévi-Strauss sought to define their respective disciplines, Braudel's age and seniority allowed him to make more general statements about the social sciences, establishing the relationships between different disciplines in both theory and practice. His contribution to the *Anuário*, "The Teaching of History and Its Guidelines," like Monbeig's "Didactic Orientation," is a task-oriented essay intended to define the discipline of history for the university authorities, the general public, and, above all, his students in São Paulo. And yet, at the same time that Braudel considered practical issues regarding his courses, he broadly redefined the field of history and its relationships to newer disciplines such as geography and ethnology. For Braudel, like for Monbeig, Brazil was a "laboratory"; its students benefited from direct observation in "economic and modern history that the European student will not possess as precisely or completely."[124]

Braudel claimed to have considered limiting the essay "strictly to its useful and technical conclusions," but ultimately chose a much more extensive approach. This, he said, was "because here, in a young country, where the future expands without pause and regularly surpasses the promises of the present, our actions take on a gravity, an intensity, that come from their importance."[125] Braudel's notion of a young country determined not only his paternalistic tone, but also his course of action.[126] His Brazilian audience, he thought, deserved much more than his practical conclusions; they needed, in fact, to be elevated to his cultural level.

> The title of this chair—the History of Civilization—is in and of itself an educational program . . . The title gave its chair a dominion without limits, and the entire annals of Humanity, in time and in space, were entrusted to his study. This attitude was perhaps a tacit recommendation for us to elevate ourselves as much as possible, above that which is related exclusively to erudition.[127]

Braudel's essay offered a kind of philosophy of history, shedding light on the increasing spatial and temporal dimensions of his own work. His chair in São Paulo had a "dominion without limits," encompassing, indeed, "the entire annals of Humanity."

Braudel made it clear in this essay, moreover, that his role as historian in Brazil was much more than a scientific one. The historian, "this master of time travel," had a distinct interpretive role and an imagination that distinguished him from the scientist.[128] In fact, history for Braudel, at least in this early stage of his career, appeared to fall halfway between literature and science. "Much like a novelist," Braudel wrote, "the historian creates life."[129] Evoking Michelet and his ability to resurrect the past, Braudel served as a poignant example of what several authors have noted already: that history, and the social sciences in France more generally, have "long been dominated by the literary field."[130] In the case of São Paulo, Braudel's analysis demonstrates the limits of empirical research, the maintenance of the importance of philosophy in the French curriculum, and the insistence on generality that distanced the French professors from their American and European contemporaries at the Escola Livre de Sociologia e Política.[131]

Braudel used the metaphor of the past as a mirror shattered into a thousand pieces. While claiming that "the intact mirror exists"—indeed, that there is an objective thing that is the past—Braudel admitted that it is "much beyond our ability to see."[132] Only by bringing together the fragments of the broken mirror, studied in isolation by political economists, statisticians, geographers, jurists, sociologists, and ethnologists, could the historian begin to see the mirror as a whole. For Braudel, since historians lacked their own specific scientific vocabulary, they must necessarily synthesize those fragments to arrive at something higher.

The conflict between historians and sociologists over who could lay claim to all-important synthetic analyses depended on the raw materials—"the broken fragments" of the mirror. If, in São Paulo, this took the form of disciplinary infighting, it came from a long struggle between practitioners of history and sociology over which would become "the" social science.[133] While the Durkheimians frequently sought to make use of history as a science auxiliary to sociology, supplementing their larger ambitions, historians challenged the validity of universal social theory, even if they embraced the "social" as a fundamental aspect of their research.[134] For Braudel, Monbeig's geography and Lévi-Strauss's ethnology would be particularly important in this regard. As the elder of the group, he could claim an important role as a federator, all the while supporting his younger colleagues—most notably Lévi-Strauss.

Braudel distinguished history from the newly emerging social sciences. History, he insisted, did not have the same need to be defined and positioned "in the general field of intellectual life" as did the newer social sciences. Unlike those disciplines, "born yesterday or that will be born tomorrow," for Braudel, "history has existed, in fact, since intelligent reflection began, since the first legends that man told."[135] And yet, Braudel insisted that history, too, was a social science—indeed, the oldest of all of them.

For Braudel, it was nothing less than "the *totality of social life* that the historian looks for and recomposes."[136] For over a decade, the editors of *Annales*, Marc Bloch and Lucien Febvre, had been attempting to practice such a history in their writings and as editors. Their work on *mentalités*, particularly Bloch's *Les rois thaumaturges* (1924; *The Royal Touch*), laid the basis for the kind of "total" understanding of a historical era to which Braudel referred. While the term *mentalités* was not always explicitly employed by the journal's founders (other terms such as *outillage mental* appeared early on), this "spirit of the Annales" pervaded the journal from its beginning.[137]

Braudel took his predecessors' total methods to another level, as his experience in São Paulo permitted a new kind of interdisciplinarity. The founders of *Annales* had been particularly receptive to the geography of Paul Vidal de La Blache, using the spatial and temporal understandings of the discipline to overcome the limitations of political histories that defined much of French historiography. Braudel, too, drew from this geographical understanding.[138] His vision was even more comprehensive, making reference to the emerging field of ethnography and the social sciences more broadly. According to Braudel, "The social sciences form a block, a coalition." Furthermore, "Ethnography, sociology, political economy" and "the link with geography that was very well thought out" merit close attention by students of history.[139]

Braudel's references to ethnography and geography referred specifically to these disciplines as practiced at USP.[140] Whereas Monbeig's *Anuário* essay addressed some of the practical consequences of the relationship between history and geography, in terms of coursework and professional outlets for students, Braudel took a more encompassing approach, expounding on the role of the historian within an interdisciplinary context. Braudel, the elder, seized the opportunity to clarify his view of history's unifying role within the social sciences, not only advancing its institutional position at USP but also foregrounding its intellectual centrality vis-à-vis sociology.

Monbeig, Lévi-Strauss, and Braudel—each with his own disciplinary objectives—had enough in common generationally, institutionally, and intellectually to join together in Brazil. They sought to create a new social-scientific paradigm, one where fieldwork, archives, and new kinds of data would displace abstract notions and universal histories, particularly when they dealt with places outside Europe. This meant distancing themselves from the classical humanities centered around erudition and from Durkheimian social philosophy. In the university setting, this aspect of Durkheim's legacy had increasingly displaced his emphasis on empirical study, much to the frustration of a younger generation inspired by Karl Marx, whether or not they considered themselves Marxists.[141] Paul Arbousse-Bastide, it seems, was their primary victim.

Arbousse-Bastide, after all, was the official head of the French mission. He had no specified powers, but as the elder of the group (nearly ten years separated him from Lévi-Strauss and Monbeig, three from Braudel), someone who had been in São Paulo since the foundation of USP, in 1934, and loyal to Georges Dumas and Durkheim, he was less likely to take risks that might jeopardize French "influence" in Brazil. He also seemed to be from a different generation, whose values surrounding order and respectability clashed with those of the younger professors.

This conflict between Arbousse-Bastide and the others primarily revolved around the second chair of sociology, whose creation he helped to negotiate and that Lévi-Strauss occupied. When the younger professors arrived in Brazil, he wrote optimistically about his colleagues, if with little precision concerning their names: "Levy Strauss and his wife, Hourcade, Maugué (Protestant), Lévy Strauss friendly; the new team younger and less homogenous."[142] But his sympathy would turn sour with the frontal attacks that they launched on his understanding of his discipline of sociology and on his authority more generally.

Lévi-Strauss's "Cultural Sociology and Its Teaching" demonstrated his departure from French sociology toward North American ethnology. He later remembered how his position in "rebellion" against Durkheim created serious difficulties for him:

> Georges Dumas placed at the university, from the first year, a young relative of his who was a sociologist. When I arrived as the second sociologist, if I may say, he intended to put me in a subordinate position. It was not to my taste, and since I resisted, he tried to fire me in the name of the Comtian tradition of which he was a specialist—and that my teaching betrayed. The bosses of the university, who were also those of the newspaper *O Estado de S. Paulo*, offered him a complacent ear. I needed to depend on the solidarity of some colleagues who passed away: Pierre Monbeig and Fernand Braudel, who supported me with the authority that he [Braudel] already had.[143]

Lévi-Strauss's above-quoted interview, from 1988, has all too often been taken as gospel, but, like all testimonies, it is incomplete. The characters are present in his narrative (Dumas, Braudel, Monbeig, and the unnamed Arbousse-Bastide), but the reasons for the conflict have been intellectualized (Comtian or positivist tradition versus Anglo-American ethnology) instead of specified.

Arbousse-Bastide's testimony from the era, while equally partial, nonetheless helps us to understand the conflict in more practical terms. The archives of the Ministry of Foreign Affairs, to which Arbousse-Bastide wrote frequently, reveal some of the internal power dynamics of the mission, including Braudel's refusal to recognize Arbousse-Bastide as "chef" and the wider conflict over Lévi-Strauss teaching ethnology. However, a private letter from

Arbousse-Bastide is most explicit about the personal aspects of his conflict with Lévi-Strauss.

Arbousse-Bastide, writing to his parents in Paris, informed them that he had written not only publicly to Jean Marx, head of the Service for French Works Abroad, about his problems with the younger professors, but also privately to Dumas. If Marx refrained from bringing Lévi-Strauss back into line, he wrote, "I will not hide [from Dumas] that the Brazilians will conclude that France does everything to create disorder."[144] The "disorder" was much more than a methodological question concerning the social sciences; it was at once political, generational, and organizational. For Arbousse-Bastide, the mission suffered from "le vague et officieux" (the vague and quasi-official). "This deplorable politics," he said, "is surely due to the atmosphere in France, which continues in uncertainty and the terror of responsibility." He was referring to the Popular Front, which was formed in 1936. Its participatory organization and anti-hierarchical utopias traversed not only the political class but also higher education.[145] This fact alone separated him from at least Monbeig and Lévi-Strauss, who were active supporters of the new government—the latter also part of the Musée de l'Homme network.[146]

Lévi-Strauss put a kink in USP's liberal politics, and, as Arbousse-Bastide wrote, in its schedules as well:

> We received a telegram this morning from the Ministry. It seems that Maugué [*sic*] and Monbeig will be back March 3. For the rest it seems complicated. Levi requested to undertake an expedition in the middle of the year. São Paulo does not seem to be working out. I find it a daring and childish demand in the present circumstances that a professor leave in the middle of the year. Perhaps we will have new professors, but São Paulo is no longer disposed to be taken for a ride by Paris.[147]

If Monbeig and Maugüé were dependable in showing up to their courses on time, the rest of the younger professors negotiated their professorial duties while attending to other projects. In the same year that Braudel terminated his contract early (1937), Lévi-Strauss's constant negotiations about time for fieldwork put Arbousse-Bastide in a difficult position.[148] The contracts from 1938 clarified that during the semester, professors were no longer free to leave the state capital, "except for practical work in the company of students, upon the authorization of the Directory [university administration]."[149]

Arbousse-Bastide was primarily interested in maintaining order and reputation, assuring the Paulistas not only that the French were abiding by their contracts but also that they were respectable in a gentlemanly sense of the word. From an academic standpoint, he preserved Durkheim as the central reference for both French sociology specifically and sociology in general, writing the introduction for the Portuguese translation of *The Rules of Sociological Method* that would be used as a textbook in Brazil.[150] He was, however, no dogmatist. In his own essay for the USP *Anuário*, Arbousse-Bastide proved open to many of the empirical criticisms that his young colleagues made of the discipline.[151]

What becomes clear is that Lévi-Strauss, Braudel, and, to a lesser extent, Monbeig's challenge to Arbousse-Bastide was not simply academic. It also involved lifestyles choices and personal values. A large part of this probably had to do with Arbousse-Bastide's background in World War I and ideas around order and discipline, not to mention patriotism. Arbousse-Bastide expected an esprit de corps moved by the desire to spread French influence in Brazil, and he found a group of individuals—a "new team younger and less homogenous"—looking out for their own advancement.

Over time, the lectures of broader public interest that had figured so prominently in the first mission to USP gave way to more specialized groups such as the Associação dos Geógrafos Brasileiros and the Sociedade de Etnografia e Folclore, where Dina Lévi-Strauss was, in both cases, particularly active. The younger scholars invested their energies in research, helping one another to build new research institutions. Monbeig, for example, presented on "the cartographic representation of human phenomena" at the Sociedade de Etnografia e Folclore, in turn contributing to a larger project of mapping folkloric traditions in Brazil.[152] Lévi-Strauss, meanwhile, helped to develop his colleague Monbeig's journal *Geografia*, where he published his initial fieldwork on the Bororo; Dina Lévi-Strauss did the same on the Indians of Bolivia.[153]

With the same agregé degree in philosophy that her husband and Arbousse-Bastide had, Dina Lévi-Strauss came to Brazil on the false promise that there was work for her at USP too. With USP unable (or unwilling) to hire her, she became particularly active with the Departamento de Cultura, ultimately giving courses in anthropology and conducting her own fieldwork.[154] Recent scholarship has shed light on Dina's teachings, especially in physical anthropology, and on her role as a founding member of the Sociedade de Etnografia e Folclore.[155] The sources themselves make it difficult to know to what extent she directly influenced the ideas of those around her, but her close relationships with intellectuals such as Mário de Andrade and commitment to collaborative, hands-on research clearly made a mark on the practice of knowledge formation in São Paulo in this period.[156]

Outside the classroom, the Lévi-Strausses and Monbeig worked alongside students, organizing geographical and ethnological fieldtrips in the city of São Paulo and its surroundings.[157] This was not only pedagogically different than anything that Arbousse-Bastide had seen; it was socially different as well—a place where men and women mixed and where the relationship between ranks was less clear. Monbeig, on an excursion with the Lévi-Strausses in Londrina, wrote to his wife, Juliette, an active member of the Associação dos Geógrafos Brasileiros, back in São Paulo, "Arbousse is stupid with his thoughts concerning the participation of women on excursions. I am really sorry that you aren't here."[158]

Lévi-Strauss's criticism of Durkheim and his unorthodox courses in which he brought students to the ethnic neighborhoods of São Paulo already made him a difficult underling. His relatively egalitarian relationship with Dina was yet another point of divergence from the generation of scholars who preceded him in São Paulo.[159] Whereas for Arbousse-Bastide, coed rustic traveling was taboo (even among husband and wife!), the others had a different perspective. The Monbeigs, not surprisingly, got along quite well with "Madame Lévy-Strauss" during their travels.[160]

Ultimately, Lévi-Strauss sacrificed his job at USP for the task of fieldwork. In the words of Arbousse-Bastide: "Lévi-Strauss is quitting to dedicate himself to ethnography and will be replaced by . . . Roger Bastide." With this shift in personnel, Arbousse-Bastide continued, "the mission will change entirely if there are no new dramas." Regretting the departure of Pierre Hourcade, a literary scholar and loyal friend, Arbousse-Bastide reserved the following for Lévi-Strauss: "May he go be with the savages but leave us in peace."[161] Lévi-Strauss did just that.

Bastide, then a professor at the Lycée Hoche, in Versailles, missed out on the early years of the French mission to USP. When he arrived in Brazil, gone were the glory years when disciplines were poorly defined, when the French professors had significant control over their own time and were paid for additional hours worked,[162] and when USP had significant curricular autonomy from the federal government. All this would change with the Estado Novo, in 1937. By the time Bastide arrived, in 1938, being a French intellectual in Brazil inland from the coast was not cause for immediate celebrity, either.

Generationally distinct from the younger scholars who preceded him and linked by friendship to Arbousse-Bastide, Bastide may seem at odds with the trio of Monbeig, Lévi-Strauss, and Braudel. His devout, if flexible, Protestantism contrasted with their agnosticism. And yet, he would experience Brazil in similar ways. It would be a place for him to escape from "Durkheimian dogmatism" and a sociocultural entity that would offer him new possibilities to think through (and teach) the sociology that he was attempting to construct.[163]

Ironically, Arbousse-Bastide's choice replacement, Bastide, quickly became friends with Lévi-Strauss. From São Paulo, Bastide wrote Paul Rivet at the Musée de l'Homme in 1939, "I have only had indirect news from Lévy-Strauss since his departure from Brazil. If you see him, please send to him and Madame Lévy-Strauss my words of friendship."[164] In their absence, Bastide did his best to continue the work of the Sociedade de Etnografia e Folclore, presenting on "Afro-Brazilian methodology" in 1939.[165]

 Despite their differences, Bastide, Braudel, Lévi-Strauss, and Monbeig shared a desire to move the social sciences away from Durkheim and to experiment with new kinds of interdisciplinary arrangements in which philosophy would play a less significant role. In São Paulo, they were given considerable authority in defining their disciplines, and, as I have shown, they used this authority to advance questions of geography and culture, at times at the expense of "social facts." Braudel, Monbeig, and Lévi-Strauss's quarrel with Arbousse-Bastide exemplifies how these questions were at once intellectual and generational—a means by which they defined themselves against what came before them.[166]

Methodological reformulation, however, was only part of the reason that Brazil was a "laboratory" for the French social sciences. As a country considerably different from what the French social scientists had read about and seen in Europe and its empires, they needed to adapt their methodologies to it. The next chapter explores their early fieldwork in Brazil's interior and elsewhere and their exchanges with Brazilian intellectuals that made their immersion in Brazil so productive.

CHAPTER THREE

Getting to Know Brazil: The New Country behind the Methodology

For most foreigners who visit Brazil for the first time, the country is nothing short of exotic. When the French scholars first arrived in Brazil in the 1930s, it surely felt even more so. Except for what they may have seen at the Musée du Trocadéro (precursor of the Musée de l'Homme), or at the *bals nègres* in Paris (this was still before the time of Carmen Miranda's international stardom), Brazil's lush forests, tropical mountains, and its indigenous and Afro-descended peoples left them with feelings of awe and fascination. For this reason, some of the French scholars' early writings indeed differ little from travel writing. Over time, however, they started to get to know their host country. Socially, this meant entering into Paulista high society. But it also meant looking beyond the rapidly industrializing city of São Paulo, whose population more than doubled between 1920 and 1940, to Brazil's historic capitals and its interior.

This juxtaposition of the urban and the rural proved particularly important for the young French scholars. Even when their research took them far afield, they had unusual resources at their disposal for the kinds of "primitive" subjects they sought to know. Brazilian researchers had laid the groundwork for them, albeit in nonuniversity contexts. This meant that, prior to conducting fieldwork, the French social scientists had a unique opportunity to read and converse about the country before them. Different from in colonial contexts where researchers were either a direct or indirect representative of state power, in Brazil French social scientists worked alongside highly educated mediators who were themselves in the process of discovering Brazil.

Despite the fact that French explorers and travelers had a long history of writing about Brazil, little scholarship of importance had appeared in France in the first decades of the twentieth century, with the exception of the geographer Pierre Denis's *Le Brésil au XXᵉ siècle* (1909).[1] Lévi-Strauss, for example, remembered reading the accounts of the admiral Villegaignon and the missionary Jean de Léry's *History of a Voyage to the Land of Brazil*, both from the sixteenth century, as if they were still relevant to Brazil in 1934.[2] What is clear is that, prior to their arrival, the French scholars were almost entirely unfamiliar with Brazil and Brazilian authors, even if some of the greats, such as Machado de Assis, had been published in French.

In an age in which the disciplines of geography, anthropology, and, to a lesser extent, history were linked with European empires, Brazil—and Latin America more generally—fell between the cracks as neither metropolitan nor colonial.[3] As public figures, the professors who made up French missions to Brazil represented the French state and more often than not the interwar policy of *mise en valeur*, by which colonies would be made "valuable."[4] As researchers, however, they did not serve the French state, whether in its archaeological pursuits in the Near East, mostly in French protectorates, or in its ethnographic missions in Africa, to name just two. Brazil as a noncolonial space had yet to be completely "controlled" in the Foucauldian sense, at least as far as the French gaze was concerned.[5] This certainly limited preexisting scholarship, but it also gave the young French social scientists an unprecedented opportunity to define their research on non-European peoples among their Brazilian counterparts. This chapter examines some of their most important exchanges, whether in dealing with applied studies on pioneer zones and indigenous anthropology or in more abstract ideas about temporality and the interpretation of culture.

In the 1930s, Monbeig traveled all over Brazil, from the coffee plantations of São Paulo to the cacao plantations in southern Bahia and the new city of Goiânia, on Brazil's central plateau. Accompanying Monbeig on some of these expeditions, Lévi-Strauss also went farther afield, in search of indigenous populations in their most unaltered form. Braudel traveled to Salvador, Brazil's first capital. Bastide, who only arrived in São Paulo in 1938, would have to wait until later to get to know Brazil's other regions. Nonetheless, his immersion in Brazilian literature familiarized him with new landscapes and cultures, as did his meanderings within the city of São Paulo. These travels were crucial for each individual scholar's research, as well as for their solidarity with one another.[6]

Brazil was an exotic place not just for foreigners but for Brazilians themselves, especially elites. Mário de Andrade joked to his compatriots: "You know the French word for monkey but you don't know what a guariba is."[7] Mário's quip served as a stinging criticism of Brazilian Eurocentrism, an alienation from the American continent that the *pau-brasil* group had attempted to move beyond. It also helps to illustrate the juxtaposition of worlds within Brazil: the urban and the rural, the human made and the natural, the European and the indigenous, to name just a few.

The French were astonished by these juxtapositions, especially the presence of standards of living in many ways comparable to those of Western Europe alongside populations who seemed like they were from another era. Writing to Marcel Mauss, Lévi-Strauss claimed that "ten kilometers from the skyscrapers of São Paulo, we can already find completely medieval lifestyles."[8] In Caio Prado Jr.'s terminology, "colonial" would be a more appropriate word than "medieval," whether during the colonial period as such, during which Portugal represented a new mercantile system, or in his present, characterized by a particularly modern export-commodity economy in São Paulo and elsewhere.[9] Nevertheless, the dialectic between the urban world of São Paulo and Brazil's interior—between colonial remnants and modernizing areas— distinguished the work of Monbeig, Lévi-Strauss, Braudel, and Bastide from that of many of their era who worked on places outside Europe.

The French scholars gave their courses almost entirely in French, but they were not working on a blank slate. Their students, colleagues, and friends guided them in their understanding of Brazil in everything from giving them access to their own private libraries to hospitality at their fazendas. The French may have never become Paulistas, but they were not lone explorers, either. Their thoughts, their travels, and their research, autonomous from the colonial state, were filtered through a Brazilian bourgeoisie whose literary and artistic production had been particularly fervent in the decades preceding their arrival.

MONBEIG AND PAULISTA EXPANSION

For Monbeig, the meetings of the Associação dos Geógrafos Brasileiros and his excursions with students allowed him to get to know the geographical highlights of his immediate surroundings: the peak of Jaraguá, the Paraíba Valley, and the various rivers upon which the city of São Paulo was built.[10] On rare occasions, he went further afield, particularly in the company of colleagues and friends such as Lévi-Strauss, René Courtin, and Jean Maugüé. Braudel, assiduously working on his archival material, stayed in São Paulo for these excursions.

FIG. 3 Photograph of Braudel, Maügüé, Dina Lévi-Strauss, and others. Claude Lévi-Strauss, Claude Lévi-Strauss Archive, Bibliothèque nationale de France.

Maügüé remembered these travels fondly, not only the challenges of long car rides along dirt roads but also the collective experience of contact with the Carajá peoples.[11] During a trip to the state of Goiás, he marveled at how Lévi-Strauss deciphered "gestures that for Courtin and me were merely picturesque."[12] Recounting this trip some years later, Lévi-Strauss wrote in the third person:

> After five days spent extracting their automobile from varyingly perilous situations, they enjoyed the exquisite spectacle of a colonial-style city whose houses were painted with tender colors. This perpetuates the image that they offered, already in the eighteenth century, to its first inhabitants.[13]

At first glance, these travels appear more like tourism than the birth of the social sciences, something that Lévi-Strauss admitted to Mauss.[14] Some of them, however, were in fact quite rigorous, such as those made in the company of the geographer Emmanuel de Martonne.

When de Martonne arrived in São Paulo, in 1937, the geography faculty doubled, from one to two professors. Monbeig would thenceforth teach human geography, whereas de Martonne would teach physical geography—much more associated with the geological features of land, such as rock formations and waterways, and with climate science.[15] At the age of sixty-three, de Martonne was a genuine elder to the French mission and had taught physical geography of tropical regions at the Institut National Agronomique.[16] René Courtin wrote to his parents about the trip taken in September 1937: "Last week, I was once again able to take part in a nice trip with two colleagues, four students, and the illustrious geographer de Martonne, the son-in-law of Vidal-Lablache [*sic*] who, as I probably already wrote to you, is at the University for three months."[17]

This excursion was to Itatiaia in the Serra da Mantiqueira (around three hundred kilometers northeast of São Paulo). After a grueling 2,800-meter trip up the mountain by car and the rest by horse and by foot, de Martonne made a memorable impression on Lévi-Strauss:

> Martonne improvised a lecture that, for me with a literary training, seemed like an admirable explication de texte. I understood that a landscape, looked at and analyzed by a master, can be a passionate reading, as capable of training the mind as a play by Racine.[18]

Lévi-Strauss's time spent alongside de Martonne may have helped to consolidate the geological perspectives of ethnography that had interested him since his student days. For Monbeig, de Martonne's mastery of the natural and geological aspects allowed him to make broader claims about the purely scientific nature of geography (theretofore very much a social science). Still, de Martonne's geological excursions were not the only ones important for the young scholars. Even the more touristic expeditions had their benefits in terms of building friendships, acquiring new research materials, and coming into contact with Brazilian intellectuals from other regions.

In his first year of teaching, in 1935, Monbeig had begun his fieldwork on frontier zones, depending heavily on the previous work of the journal *Geografia* as his point of departure. Caio Prado Jr., for example, had already published on the distribution of landed property in the state of São Paulo and even on the different ethnic groups who had come to settle Paraná, the state directly south and west of São Paulo, where the pioneer city Londrina was founded in 1934 (the same year as USP).[19] Monbeig's research on the North Paraná Land Company complemented such research and resulted in his article for *Geografia* in which he analyzed "settlement with a new kind of financing of a large enterprise of the capitalist type."[20] A previously unpublished photograph of Dina and Claude Lévi-Strauss on horseback helps to elucidate other more personal aspects of Monbeig's travels.[21]

Monbeig's friendship with the Lévi-Strausses was forged through their shared experiences of travel.[22] If their properly intellectual relationships con-

FIG. 4 Dina and Claude Lévi-Strauss in North Paraná. Pierre Monbeig, Bibliothèque nationale de France, Collections de la Société de géographie. Géographes Français, Fonds Pierre Monbeig.

cerning the disciplines of geography and ethnology laid the foundations for a fruitful collegial relationship, more personal day-to-day experiences consolidated and reinforced their solidarity with one another. Even when they traveled separately, they were present for each other, materially and sentimentally. When Monbeig traveled to Uberaba and Uberlândia, in Minas Gerais, he brought with him a sweater given to him by Lévi-Strauss that "fit him quite well."[23] As we shall see, when the Lévi-Strausses undertook their Serra do Norte expedition in 1938, Claude wrote frequently to Monbeig, having him serve as his intermediary with Mário de Andrade.[24] Quickly, their friendship evolved around the shared circumstances of having a family in Brazil: for the Monbeigs, their children; for the Lévi-Strausses, Claude's parents, Raymond and Emma.[25]

If the young French scholars learned a lot through their travels into the interior, they also benefited from the "laboratory" of São Paulo. The city's rapidly expanding economy demanded labor, both national and international; the internal migration of people provided the French with a vision of other regions of Brazil prior to their own travels. In his first published essay on Brazil for *Annales de géographie*, "La population de l'état de São Paulo" (The population of the state of São Paulo), Monbeig wrote of "immigration" from other regions of Brazil, whether through the port of Santos or by foot from Minas Gerais or Espírito Santo.[26]

While Monbeig distanced himself from the objections of Paulistas to this new population, he nonetheless considered the newcomers to São Paulo as different and even possibly responsible for the recent rise in cases of malaria.[27] Monbeig would later become a fierce critic of the exploitation of the laboring classes in Brazil, but at this early stage he seemed little inclined to openly critique his Paulista hosts. If São Paulo had become relatively familiar in his first year after arriving, the rest of Brazil remained an irremediable other.

Indeed, Monbeig's writings about his travels suggest a kind of Paulista-centrism, according to which the dynamic agricultural and industrial center of Brazil contrasted with the stagnant coastal regions. In 1938, Monbeig had the privilege of circling the new city of Goiânia by air before landing to spend a couple of days there. His description of Goiânia, founded in 1933, reflected the ideology of the newspaper *O Estado de S. Paulo*, including a widespread belief that São Paulo held the keys to Brazil's future. Just four years after São Paulo's crushing defeat by the federal government, Monbeig affirmed São Paulo's place in settling Brazil's interior: "I wanted . . . that the first message sent from Goiânia to the federal government be written: 'Bandeirismo is not dead.'"[28]

In the decades prior to his arrival, the Instituto Histórico e Geográfico of São Paulo and intellectuals in its orbit offered Paulistas a way of conceiving of São Paulo's distinct economic and racial development.[29] Alongside the socio-historical accounts that explored the life of the bandeirantes, most notably José de Alcântara Machado's *Vida e morte do bandeirante* (1929), the figure of the *bandeirante* came to justify São Paulo's supremacy within the nation. Rather than as the Indian slavers that they were, the *bandeirantes* came to be known as humble trailblazers who beat the odds to expand Brazil's borders. Monbeig took this language of Paulista exceptionalism to another level, encouraging state-led commercial expansion into neighboring states before the federal government could do so. He argued that this would not only bring value to the *sertão* (dry backlands); it would also ensure that Paulista entrepreneurs would reap the benefits.[30] In this sense, Monbeig's language around the valorization of the *sertão* is strikingly similar to the French colonial *mise en valeur*.

New to air travel, Monbeig also insisted on its role in making the backlands a more accessible and hospitable place: "Nowadays, settlers want to be in contact with the rest of the world and to feel secure—and airplanes can be a good instrument in this sense."[31] From an entirely technical point of view, aerial perspectives provided him with new approaches to human geography, heretofore limited primarily to military reconnaissance missions. From above, he could witness "the perfect zoning," the "forest belt," and the "desolate land-scapes" (all his words) farther out, all at the costs of *O Estado de S. Paulo*, for which he was writing.[32]

In addition to Goiânia, Monbeig went to Bahia. In South Bahia, the land of cacao, he also insisted on *mise en valeur*, criticizing the moral dimensions of both the rich and the poor that prevented Brazil's development.[33] Instead of saving while prices were high, the rich spent their money on cars and trips to Europe.[34] As for the poor, he lamented their moral misery and "the low salaries that prevent the constitution of families." This ambience led to theft and murder, which he read about in Jorge Amado's novel *Cacau* (1933).[35]

The brevity of Monbeig's visit to Bahia rendered his analysis particularly superficial and moralizing, but it nonetheless revealed to him a world that looked very much colonial, where inequalities had strikingly clear racial connotations.

> The coexistence of two completely different economies, two societies that ignore each other's existence: on one hand, the big towns, a minority where the white element predominates, living in the rhythm of European or North American modern life; on the other hand, in the small towns and above all in the immense regions of the interior, a majority where the element of color predominates, more or less pure Indian or African, cut off from the rest of the world, possessing little money, selling and buying almost nothing from the outside world, remaining at the stage of a closed economy and of artisan-ship, where certain archaic techniques subsist until today. This disequilibrium between the two elements of the population is particularly perceptible in the states of the north of Brazil, much less so in the states of the south.[36]

Monbeig's reification of the North versus the South was surely a product of his Paulista ideology—just as was his insistence on the quasi-autarky of the interior of Brazil. Monbeig, however, was not interested in exploring the dimensions of this perceived autarky. He preferred instead the case study of São Paulo, an internal colonization of tropical space that followed in the path of his mentor Albert Demangeon's studies of colonial India.[37] In many ways, São Paulo, as a settler colony, was closer to French North Africa than other parts of its empire.[38]

If Monbeig traveled to Goiânia by air and Bahia by ship, the majority of his travels took place within the closer "pioneer zones" of the state of São Paulo. There he sought to understand "how rural colonization takes place and how a human landscape is born."[39] Monbeig's first major article on Brazil, published in *Annales* in 1937, laid the groundwork for his doctoral thesis. In addition to providing a precious description of the settlement of the state of São Paulo, it also reproduced the ideology around Paulista exceptionalism. This is perhaps not all that surprising given that Rubens Borba de Moraes, Júlio de Mesquita Filho, and another of the Mesquita clan, Raul Ferraz de Mesquita, are quite explicitly thanked.

Monbeig appropriated the word "dynamism"—"dear to the Paulistas," he notes—to describe the phenomenon of expansion into the interior.[40] Compared to the people of "the littoral, which was the great center of population in the colonial era, but which has since gone to sleep," the Paulistas, he claimed, were the principal actors who were taking possession of the land.[41] But if Monbeig insisted that "the state of São Paulo in its entirety" is a pioneer state, he found that the "moving frontier" was the best place to observe the forms of human geography created along the regions of deforestation. The term "moving frontier" appears in English in Monbeig's writings, indicating his appropriation of US sources about the settlement of the West. Building off the work of Frederick Jackson Turner, historians and geographers used the notion of frontier to define the American nation based on its moving western edge.[42] Monbeig did the same for Brazil based on São Paulo's push into the interior.

For Monbeig, "the pioneer zone of São Paulo is a melting pot of races."[43] All elements thrown into the pot may not have been equally valuable or assimilable, with the "physically depressed" Bahians and the Japanese immigrants arousing controversy. For Monbeig, however, "even though the Japanese question is serious, there is no doubt concerning the assimilation of other Brazilians, Europeans, and also Syrians."[44] Just two years later, in a book review, he was even more optimistic: "The 'Brazilianization' of immigrant children is well known in the countryside of meridional Brazil, where it is not hard to find Germans [and] Japanese living the same lifestyle as the 'caboclo,' having adopted the same agricultural techniques, style of house, diet, and mentality."[45]

For Monbeig, the pioneer zone of São Paulo served as a laboratory for a number of questions, of which demographics were just one. New landscapes and agrarian economies were in the process of being constructed, forcing new articulations between rural communities and the nation. He continued:

> Mr. Lucien Febvre pointed out how such a description of the forest starting in the very city of Rio de Janeiro was likely to enlighten us about the cities of antiquity, Massilia, for example [Roman Marseille]. The description of the modern pioneer zone can have the same historical interest.[46]

Monbeig's travels brought him into contact not only with pioneer zones that to him resembled the settler colony par excellence, the United States; they also provided an empirical case of urban-rural development that could interest historians and classicists focused on the origins of urban life. Monbeig's comparisons between Brazilian cities and those of Europe in antiquity or between São Paulo and the American West may today seem a bit of a stretch. They nonetheless gestured to two communities on which the discipline of geography depended at the time of its consolidation: historically minded academics, on one hand, and present-minded planners and business people, on the other.

LÉVI-STRAUSS AND THE SEARCH FOR
UNTOUCHED AMERINDIANS

While Monbeig researched the evolving frontier zones—the "new" Brazil, as it were—Lévi-Strauss imagined himself to be in the era of contact between Europeans and Native American communities. At the very least, his pretention to become an ethnologist depended on him finding and writing about the most "primitive" communities possible, untouched by European civilization. His story is the most well known of any in these pages, but it is worth the effort to continue to deconstruct the Malinowski-like image of a lone man among the savages, a process begun by the Brazilian anthropologist Luiz de Castro Faria some time ago.[47] Not only did Lévi-Strauss benefit from the guidance of his elders in Paris; he also encountered a fruitful community in which to conduct his research in São Paulo as well as some of the funding to undertake such research.

In his second semester of teaching at USP, in November 1935, Lévi-Strauss was preparing his first set of expeditions, in which he would encounter the Bororo, among other peoples. He wrote Mauss:

> You certainly were right in telling us that the state of São Paulo is above all archaeologically interesting . . . Some Indian groups, obviously very deculturalized, still offer, in the state's interior, a real interest. . . . There is still an enormous amount of work to do here; of course, we would prefer to work on the Andean plateaus. But if ethnographic studies were seriously conducted here, we would have an enormous amount of documentation that could be organized instead of being lost in the collections of amateurs and antiques dealers . . . There is an immense peasant mass disseminated about the forest, living in conditions reminiscent of several centuries ago.[48]

Mauss warned Lévi-Strauss of looking too much to the Andes, encouraging him to focus instead on "the small rivers of the Amazon." The archaeological findings of highly developed terra-cotta techniques in the Amazonian basin had led Mauss to believe that Lévi-Strauss might find there "the existence of a great civilization."[49]

Lévi-Strauss's correspondence with Mauss, the director of the Institut d'Ethnologie in Paris and an active participant at the Musée de l'Homme, demonstrated his concern for approval not only in what to look for but also in where to look for it. São Paulo, with its "deculturalized" Indians in the interior, may still have offered ethnographic material, but the state's rapid expansion and settlement pushed them farther and farther north and west. Lévi-Strauss expressed interest in the "immense peasant mass disseminated about the forest," but, as an anthropologist, he was principally concerned with finding an object worthy of study: an intact people.

During their first summer vacation, in the months between November 1935 and March 1936, the Lévi-Strausses traversed some 1,500 kilometers up the Paraná River and into Mato Grosso.[50] Along the way, they encountered the Kadiweu (often spelled "Caduveo" in Lévi-Strauss) and Bororo.[51] Writing about the Kadiweu village Nalike from the field to Mário de Andrade, Lévi-Strauss expressed both the aesthetic and folkloric aspects that interested the former. The women painted their faces with "a prodigious refinement." Lévi-Strauss promised to bring back numerous examples of pottery as well as the "interesting testimonies of legends and social organization of the past" that exist until this day.[52]

Upon returning to São Paulo, Lévi-Strauss communicated to Mauss that he and Dina had been able to "collect about four hundred designs executed directly by indigenous women that attest to a refinement and an absolutely prodigious decorative inventiveness."[53] These "first-class ceramic arts" certainly suggested "an ancient and great civilization," but, according to Lévi-Strauss, the Kadiweu were now in "complete decomposition," to the point that "ten years from now, they will have completely disappeared." In comparison, the Bororo of the Rio Vermelho gave the Lévi-Strausses "an idea of urgency" and elicited enough interest in them to undertake "an exhaustive study." According to Lévi-Strauss, those Bororo who had not yet been brought into contact with the Salesian missionaries presented a "just about intact" social organization.[54] Mauss's earlier insistence on looking for that "great civilization" in the Amazon basin, rather than along the Andes, may have been a determining factor in keeping Lévi-Strauss on track.[55]

According to Lévi-Strauss, Bororo social organization was defined by "reciprocal exchanges and obligations from clan to clan, of the type that led you to expand the area of potlatch"; "the subdivision of clans in matrimonial classes" and "the coexistence of an economic hierarchy with the hierarchy of clans."[56] Because of Mauss, Lévi-Strauss was already thinking well beyond the specificity of his own fieldwork, which he admitted was "ridiculously short."[57] Thanks to his engagement with Mauss's The Gift and with the author himself, Lévi-Strauss began to observe the social building blocks around reciprocal gifts and kinship that would later orient his dissertation, *The Elementary Structures of Kinship*.[58]

In the months following their return to São Paulo, the Lévi-Strausses presented the pottery and indigenous artifacts that they had collected at the Departamento de Cultura, which had helped to finance their expedition and would do so for others.[59] They also gave a talk at what *O Estado de S. Paulo* called the "Clube dos Geógrafos Brasileiros," surely the Associação dos Geógrafos Brasileiros. According to the newspaper write-up, Lévi-Strauss "found the forest-dwellers [*selvícolas*] of the region in the same state in which Von den Stein [*sic*] found them, stating that one could currently apply what that illustrious traveler said, in its entirety, with respect to the Bororo civilization."[60] In other words, nothing had changed since the nineteenth century, when the German ethnologist Karl von den Steinen had conducted fieldwork among the Bororo.

Lévi-Strauss's ethnography, "Contributions sur l'organisation sociale des Indiens Bororo" (Contributions on the social organization of the Bororo Indians), began the transformation of the philosophy agrégé into a respected international anthropologist. Covering village structure, economic organization, and, perhaps most importantly, the codes that governed clan, lineage, and marriage within the Bororo communities, Lévi-Strauss's article represented a significant departure from the philosophical speculations of his earlier lectures in São Paulo.[61] It certainly didn't hurt Lévi-Strauss to have had a rather artistic childhood alongside his portraitist father, as he reproduced the Bororo hunting bows, arrows, and penis shafts by hand.

Lévi-Strauss's period of fieldwork among the Bororo may have lasted but a few weeks, but it proved incredibly fruitful. Curt Nimuendajú, the German-born ethnologist and unsung hero of Brazilian anthropology, claimed that his article, "in few pages, brings very valuable material."[62] He also expressed his surprise to another German-born ethnologist, Herbert Baldus, that "this man, who only recently began in ethnology, managed in so little time to become acquainted in such a profound way, that he understood with so much precision the sociological conditions of the Bororo, who are indeed not simple."[63] Clearly, Lévi-Strauss's initial fieldwork experience was a crucial component of his turn toward ethnology. Through such experience, he accumulated recognition, materials to publish and display, and, even, indigenous philosophies that came to influence his later work.

If Lévi-Strauss later claimed to be "rebelling" against Durkheim, as we saw in the previous chapter, the reception of his work among the Durkheimians and their allies was quite friendly indeed. Paul Fauconnet, to whom Lévi-Strauss sent his article, replied to "mon cher ami": "I read your Bororo with interest and pleasure."[64] As for Lucien Lévy-Bruhl, author of *Primitive Men-*

tality and professor at the Institut d'Ethnologie, he even expressed jealousy: "Your letter thoroughly interested me, and I must admit that it makes me fight the sin of envy. What I wouldn't have done, in my time, for the privilege of spending a few months with the Bororo!"[65] Lévi-Strauss's firsthand knowledge, according to Lévy-Bruhl, gave his work a "precious advantage."

Beyond France, Lévi-Strauss's article also brought him international recognition, particularly in the United States, where anthropology was a much more established field. Upon receiving Lévi-Strauss's study, Alfred Métraux, then ethnologist at the Bernice Pauahi Bishop Museum, in Hawaii, wrote: "I must congratulate you on this monograph that is without a doubt one of the most important on a South American tribe over the course of the last ten years."[66]

After writing his doctoral theses on Brazil, based upon entirely secondhand material, Métraux moved to Argentina to become the founding director of the Institute for Ethnology at the Universidad Nacional de Tucumán.[67] In Paris, he had worked under the supervision of Paul Rivet and Mauss. It is not surprising, therefore, that he was excited about Lévi-Strauss's work on Brazilian Indians. Métraux's enthusiasm also brought Lévi-Strauss into contact with the anthropologist Robert Lowie, whom Lévi-Strauss so admired. Métraux, who was in the process of becoming a prolific fieldworker himself, sent Lowie a copy of the article with the introduction: "This article is a good example of what is to be found in South America when somebody with broad interests attempts to study a tribe seriously." Lowie in turn, wrote Métraux specifically to request more personal information on Lévi-Strauss.[68]

While Lévi-Strauss was giving lectures on subjects such as "the social life of monkeys," he was also preparing to exhibit his findings in Paris.[69] The objects collected during his and Dina's fieldwork in 1935–36 would be put on display at Georges Wildenstein's gallery in Paris with an exhibition on "the Indians of Mato Grosso."[70] Under the patronage of Jean Zay, then the French minister of education, and the Brazilian ambassador Luis Martins de Souza Dantas, the exhibit was a formal event that wowed visitors and spiked scientific curiosity.

Just a month later, Rivet, director of the Musée de l'Homme, wrote to Paulo Duarte requesting information about his personal collection; Rivet was particularly embarrassed by the "poverty of our collections relating to northern Brazil" and thought that Duarte might have items of interest for the Musée.[71] Knowing how much the Musée de l'Homme was interested in such material, the Lévi-Strausses changed their tactics. The Serra do Norte expedition that they were preparing and that would last from March through December 1938 would not only provide the fieldwork necessary for Claude's doctoral thesis.[72] Henceforth, it would take on museological dimensions as well.

Since Brazil was not a French colony, however, Lévi-Strauss's expedition into the interior required authorization from the Brazilian government and financial support from Brazilian agencies. He could not count on the Minister of the Colonies as the Dakar-Djibouti mission that had traversed Africa had before him.[73] Instead, he was subject to the Brazilian government's decree 22698, which regulated circulation within the country as well as "natural, artistic, historic, and ethnographic material goods."[74] In Brazil, the last official mission to the Serra do Norte was conducted by Marshal Rondon, about which the ethnographer Edgard Roquette-Pinto had provided a memorable account in *Rondônia* (1917). However, that was a state-sponsored expedition by Brazilian authorities to extend the telegraphic line into the interior, a project of national unification that explicitly sought to minimize foreign influence.[75] Naturally, it benefited from a freedom of circulation impossible for Lévi-Strauss.

Emmanuelle Loyer explains with acuity the challenges that Lévi-Strauss faced in negotiating the supervision by Luiz de Castro Faria during the grueling expedition. Accordingly, Lévi-Strauss provided "intellectual and financial leadership"; Castro Faria, "strategic leadership," with the power to end the mission, if necessary, and alter its itinerary.[76] However, Castro Faria's constant supervision of the mission, particularly in regard to contact with indigenous populations that the Serviço de Proteção aos Índios ostensibly protected, was not Lévi-Strauss's only obstacle.[77]

To make matters worse (for Lévi-Strauss and the French), the aforementioned decree stipulated that all collected materials would be divided equally between Brazil and the foreign mission, complicating an expedition intended to bring back ethnological objects to France.[78] This only further complicated the unfortunate situation that Lévi-Strauss ultimately faced at the customs house at the port of Santos, in which his bags, "despite being appropriately declared," were temporarily seized under the misunderstanding that they contained merchandise.[79] Fortunately, a set of contacts in Rio and in São Paulo allowed Lévi-Strauss to overcome many, if certainly not all, of the bureaucratic hurdles for his expedition.

The considerable impression that Rivet had made upon his Brazilian hosts in the 1920s, including the anthropologist Heloisa Alberto Torres, paved the way for his student Métraux.[80] The Lévi-Strausses, too, benefited from Torres's generous hospitality—now, as the deputy director of the Museu Nacional.[81] Without her, the Serra do Norte expedition likely would have never materialized. In a letter to Rivet, Lévi-Strauss wrote that the Supervisory Commission of Scientific Missions (stipulated by decree 22698) "gave Mademoiselle Torres carte blanche, and I wanted to tell you all of the kindness she demonstrated in arriving at this result."[82] Torres's latent anti-Semitism and concerns over the Museu Nacional's prestige (vis-à-vis São Paulo) may have colored her reception of the Lévi-Strausses.[83] Nonetheless, the charismatic Torres, by

FIG. 5 Anthropologists at the Jardim das Princesas (Museu Nacional). SEMEAR—Seção de Memória e Arquivo do Museu Nacional; BR MN JF.O.MN, DR. 107/10. *From left to right*: Claude Lévi-Strauss, Ruth Landes, Charles Walter Wagley, Heloisa Alberto Torres, Luiz de Castro Faria, Raimundo Lopes da Cunha, and Edison Carneiro.

far the "most charming of friends" for the Lévi-Strausses, was an invaluable resource.[84]

If Torres helped to get the Lévi-Strausses' project through the federal government, it was Mário de Andrade in São Paulo who in part made it economically and logistically feasible. According to Lévi-Strauss in his correspondence with the French minister of foreign affairs, the Departamento de Cultura subsidized the mission to the tune of ninety contos.[85] This, of course, was in addition to the three hundred thousand reais that the couple had received for their previous films, which include footage of the Bororo and Kadiweu, popular festivals (e.g., Mozambique, Cavalhada, Congado in Mogi das Cruzes) in the greater São Paulo area, and *forró* and cattle farming in Mato Grosso.[86] The Lévi-Strausses' exhibition of pottery at the Departamento de Cultura the previous year—and Dina's friendship with Mário—had paid off.[87] The mission, therefore, was "Franco-Brazilian," not only because the federal government required Brazilian supervision but also because the funding of the mission was partially Brazilian.

Additionally, the participation of the Departamento de Cultura brought important recognition to the mission, thenceforth under the protection of the powerful Adhemar de Barros. Barros, writing to the then *interventor*, or federally appointed governor, of São Paulo, José Cardoso de Melo Neto, requested that he communicate their arrival and research to his peer in Mato Grosso.[88] (Barros himself would be the next *interventor* of São Paulo.)

The quixotic aspects of the Serra do Norte expedition are well captured by Lévi-Strauss's biographers. Patrick Wilcken, for example, portrays the bulkiness of this "team of twenty men, fifteen mules, thirty oxen, a few horses, tons of equipment and a truck."[89] In this sense, the Serra do Norte expedition was certainly much closer to nineteenth-century exploration than the majority experience of early twentieth-century lone ethnologists. During an unexpected stay in the Brazilian backlands, Lévi-Strauss even wrote Mário that they had the occasion "to hunt, and to taste what will henceforth be the best of our day-to-day: parrot soup, armadillo *cozido*, roasted deer and hog, all sprinkled with *buriti* wine, is that not a menu for an explorers' club?"[90]

Although doing his best to immerse himself among the natives, Lévi-Strauss never forgot his French friends back in São Paulo. He communicated to Monbeig that he took his daily bath in "the sacred river that flows through crystalline waters . . . among fish and young naked indigenous women." He continued, "Courtin would be very happy here."[91] Monbeig, abreast of Lévi-Strauss's travels, was among the first to review his recent ethnological work—one of the many transformations by which his fieldwork would be recognized as having scientific value.[92] This goes to show that, however far away from "civilization" Lévi-Strauss may have gone, he was always thinking back to his colleagues in São Paulo, his stepping-stone back to France. We will see more of this in the next chapter, but first, let us turn to Braudel, who saw a very different Brazil.

BRAUDEL, BAHIA, AND *MENTALITÉS*

Braudel, a bit older and more consumed by his work on European archives, was less drawn to the thrill of travel in Brazil than some of his peers. His ambitious thesis, in any case, did not allow for it. While the others were set on seeing the "new country" before them, Braudel returned to Europe during all of his summer breaks (European winter) to spend time in the archives. If Lévi-Strauss imagined himself as having arrived in Latin America in the age of discovery, Braudel was mentally and physically on the other side of the world. In the archives of Dubrovnik, Croatia, that held the Ragusa mercantile registers, he remembered seeing in 1936, "for the first time, . . . the Mediterranean of the sixteenth century."[93]

Braudel's essay on the teaching of history, discussed in the previous chapter, attested to the advantage that Brazilian students had in seeing historical phenomena happen before their very eyes. Despite his limited travels in Brazil, Braudel, too, benefited from such a perspective. As Caio Prado Jr. wrote, referring to either Braudel or Pierre Deffontaines: "A trip through Brazil is often . . . an incursion into the history of a century or more into the past. One time a foreign professor told me that he was envious of Brazilian historians who could personally witness the most vivid scenes of their past."[94] This idea of time travel to "backward" areas of Brazil, I would like to suggest, allowed Braudel to play with different temporalities—not in the archives, but in real life. Braudel would later use a story of the appearance of fireflies in Bahia as representative of a historical "event," but his testimony from the era is what concerns us for now.[95]

Braudel's "vivid, unorganized impressions" about Bahia were due to "the brevity of his trip and the randomness of his travels."[96] Like most tourists, Braudel was impressed by Salvador's churches and convents, even if "made a bit uncomfortable by the exaggeration of baroque."[97] His larger discovery, however, was not the city of Salvador itself, but the dimension that it gave him of the larger state, "almost half the size of France."[98] From the state's capital city, he found himself imagining "Indian hunters, adventurers, seekers of emerald, gold, and precious stones, cowboys on horseback, dressed in leather . . . how many men were necessary for the conquest of this space for the benefit of a new city and a new civilization!"[99] Here, Braudel echoed the distinction between the civilized Brazil of the coast and the primitive backlands so well exemplified by Euclides da Cunha in *Os sertões* (1902), a book that he would later review.[100]

If Bahia represented a "new civilization" for Braudel, it was nonetheless much older than São Paulo—even if the colony of São Vicente, in what became São Paulo (1532), actually preceded Salvador's founding (1549) by seventeen years. Whereas São Paulo resembled Chicago or New York, according to Braudel, Salvador "smelled like Europe."[101] Braudel's olfactory allusion remains cryptic, but less so is his intepretation of social organization. Bahian society, "for me who is a bit Paulista, gives me the impression of an old society, that is to say a coherence."[102] Bahia seemed to him more established when compared to São Paulo, which "stupefies" with its "social fluidity" and its "lack of resistance in the fact of economic imperatives."[103] It was, consequently, less apt to change.

Having lived in French Algeria, where social relations proved extremely rigid, at least insofar as the separation between colonizer and colonized was concerned, Braudel found São Paulo to be a refreshing change of scene.[104] His fascination with São Paulo's rapid urban development, relatively fluid social classes, and history of interior settlement exemplified by the *bandeirantes* also had a great deal to do with his Paulista hosts. Identifying himself as "a bit Paulista," he was convinced by many of the tropes of São Paulo's identity tied to modernity, social progress, and entrepreneurial ethic. He wrote:

> We perceive, above all, a coherent society, capable of collective movements, that knows its classes and their demands; that has its nouveaux riches, as all societies do, but who knows how to recognize them; that has its social problems. In São Paulo, people commonly say, "We don't have social problems." I responded to a friend that made this remark: "It's because you do not have society." By "society" I obviously mean rigid society, in the European sense of the word . . . There is in the north [of Brazil] some of this European rigidity that creates social problems.[105]

For Braudel, São Paulo was so new that it did not yet have time for social stratification. Opened toward the frontier, São Paulo had an escape valve the likes of which American historians had used to understand why the class conflicts of Europe in 1848 did not have the same repercussions in the United States. The north of Brazil, in contrast, suffered from "European rigidity."

Braudel admitted that social problems exist in "all societies, whatever their configuration," but of course, São Paulo was not yet a "society."[106] Its social hierarchies, according to him, were not yet imprinted upon the consciousness of the masses.[107] This contrasted starkly with French Algeria, which he saw as "a failed Brazil."[108] The dynamic, quickly changing city of São Paulo in the 1930s also provided a striking contrast to the more slowly moving Mediterranean of the sixteenth century that occupied his thinking nearly every day—thinking that built upon the work of the *Annales'* editors on long periods of historical time that privileged continuity over change.[109]

Braudel's description of Bahia, while recognizing certain aspects of change—new roads into the interior and urban construction and, perhaps most importantly, the use of the steamship—nonetheless focused on the unchanging. As Caio Prado Jr. claimed, traveling to Brazil's interior was "an incursion into the history of a century or more into the past." Braudel wrote, "A walk along Bahia's shores allows one to see the sailboats, generally without draft, that arrive in the city full of merchandise—these same sailboats that Von Martius, more than a century ago, had the chance to use."[110]

The historical object of *mentalités* that we can find in Bloch and Febvre's work (whether or not they always called it such) had largely dealt with peoples tied to the land. Braudel attempted to apply their methods to the Mediterranean and its world of navigation, commerce, and port cities. The Bay of All Saints (*Bahia* literally means "bay") and the surrounding Recôncavo region were, for Braudel, "the Bahian Mediterranean."[111] Carole Reynaud-Paligot has demonstrated how the *Annales'* use of *mentalités* for non-European populations resembled their treatment of peasants, often falling into the realm of a kind of ethnic psychology that changed very little over long historical periods.[112] This is surely in part due to the influence of Lévy-Bruhl upon them.[113] Braudel's description of a timeless and eternal Bahia reflects this, even if indirectly.

Salvador made Braudel think of other cities of antiquity as "masters of their own destiny, resolving their day-to-day affairs on their own, penetrated by rural life that envelops them and gives them life." "Did not Bahia," he asked, "live in this way for a long time—this antique way of life, producing its sugar, planting its fruit trees, using fish oil from its fisheries for lighting?"[114] Bahian everyday life, he claimed, exemplified its history: "the simplicity of a refined politeness, the art of original cuisine, and, above all, the taste for moderation."[115]

For Braudel, Bahia was a laboratory, a source of imagination much closer to his research as a historian than São Paulo. Bahians long mourned the move of the capital from Salvador to Rio de Janeiro, and it is no surprise that Braudel sensed a certain *saudade*, or longing, for the Portuguese past. His reflections, however superficial, nonetheless point to his shift toward geography and its relatively immobile time—something he had more trouble seeing in Paris, São Paulo, or the modern port cities of the Mediterranean than in Salvador.

Braudel, like Lévi-Strauss and Monbeig, used Brazil as a place not only to reflect on the world and his discipline but also to establish himself within a transatlantic network of scholars. The next chapters take a closer look at those Paulista historians such as Caio Prado Jr., Eurípides Simões de Paula, and Alice Piffer Canabrava with whom Braudel continued to collaborate well beyond his Brazilian years. This section closes with a more serendipitous encounter.

Upon Braudel's definitive return to France, he finally met his future advisor, Lucien Febvre. According to Braudel:

> In October 1937, in Santos, as I was definitively leaving Brazil . . . I came upon Lucien Febvre, who was coming back from a series of lectures in Buenos Aires. Those twenty days crossing the ocean were for Lucien Febvre, my wife and me, twenty days of conversations and laughs.[116]

It is difficult to imagine that Braudel and Febvre, who had never met each other personally, would have become such good friends and close colleagues had it not been for the shared Atlantic crossing. In Paris, neither of them would have had much time to spend with each other. Aboard the transatlantic steamer, however, they had three weeks of lunches and dinners.

By the time Braudel had left São Paulo, the French mission had changed considerably. USP had seen two graduating classes of bachelor's degrees, and, as students continued their studies and research, the very necessity of foreign professors seemed to be brought into question. The Faculty in São Paulo embarked on a project of "nationalization" that sought to "replace as soon as possible the foreign professors with national elements and in particular the current assistants of these foreign professors."[117] Furthermore, the liberal and leftist professors faced a new political situation in Brazil that looked upon them quite unfavorably. Roger Bastide, to whom we will now turn, navigated this new context quite successfully, making better use of his Brazilian interlocutors than any of his peers had. In so doing, he compensated his limited travels with extensive readings.

BASTIDE, LITERATURE, AND SOCIOLOGY

Recruited by Paul Arbousse-Bastide, Roger Bastide filled Lévi-Strauss's position in the midst of a crisis as much concerned with practical questions (who would teach sociology, what would students learn) as political ones (the Popular Front). But if Bastide was not part of the trio of Braudel, Monbeig, and Lévi-Strauss in the period 1935–37, he nonetheless embraced the new academic context that they had done so much to create when he arrived in 1938. Less amenable to travel, Bastide began his initiation to Brazil primarily in São Paulo. He did so in ethnic neighborhoods, in his readings, and in his correspondence with Brazilians outside the state, including with Mário, henceforth based in Rio de Janeiro.[118]

Afro-Brazilian religions fascinated Bastide immediately, not only because of his previous interests in mysticism and Christianity but also because of the wealth of the field of research into which he entered. By the 1930s, Afro-Brazilian studies were already transnational in nature and an exciting subfield of anthropology where fieldwork played a particularly significant role.[119] Then in his second year in Brazil, Bastide wrote Marcel Mauss: "I can now go farther. Move to direct research—'fieldwork,' as the Americans say."[120] This was only after having read, commented on, and assimilated the works of Brazilian authors such as Machado de Assis, Sérgio Buarque de Holanda, Gilberto Freyre, and likely Caio Prado Jr.

When Bastide first arrived in Brazil, slavery and its aftermath immediately consumed his attention. His first public lecture at USP was on the sociology of slavery as part of the fifty-year anniversary of abolition in Brazil.[121] Although the original text no longer exists, the newspaper article covering his lecture provides us with its general thrust.[122]

In his lecture, Bastide posed the question of how slavery evolved in two contradictory tendencies: "On the one hand, the history of forced labor, with its three stages—slavery, servitude, paid labor—is the history of the gradual emancipation of the human condition; on the other, modern colonial slavery appears as a singular aggravation of ancient slavery."[123] There was nothing particularly new about Bastide's claim that ancient slavery was more humane than colonial slavery. What is interesting, however, is that one of Bastide's very first observations in São Paulo was how much worse colonial slavery was than its equivalents in Europe.

Bastide associated slavery with the patriarchal family, specifically referencing Egypt and China, but probably referring also to Gilberto Freyre's *Casa-grande e senzala*. Why this patriarchal family persisted in the contemporary period remained one of the fundamental paradoxes for Bastide; in Europe, he argued, the dominant model was the "conjugal family," but in places like Virginia, and by extension, Brazil, slavery and the patriarchal family took root.[124]

As a philosophy agregé, Bastide made generalizations that spanned time and space. The longer he stayed in Brazil, however, the more Bastide shifted his focus from the abstract and general to the empirical realities of Brazil. His life experience and research there made him question the differences in social treatment between whites and blacks, as well as the repercussions of the "contact between two cultures."[125]

At this early stage in his research, these questions were much more day-to-day than they were part of a broader project. Take, for example, Bastide's contribution to the Rio-based journal *Dom Casmurro* of his "Brazilian meditations on a São Paulo market":

> I love to wander among the crowd of buyers and merchants, on this square where the sun and the clouds alternatively throw spots of shade and of fire. High-pitched [squeaking] Japanese, mulattos that swing smoothly on their hips, Portuguese, talkative Italians, busy Brazilians who suddenly feel invaded by some kind of marvellous dream that keeps them immobile for a minute, serious in a concentrated lyricism. Distressed chickens, attached by their feet; stands of butter and of greens: bananas, pineapples, savory riches of the earth. And these juicy oranges that a black child bites. All of this fills the spirit and the heart.[126]

Bastide's meditations on the Brazilian marketplace demonstrate his interest in the racial politics of everyday life of São Paulo. Observing "this melting pot of so many races in such a small space of a few square meters," Bastide wondered, "Is not the drama of Brazil in the mixture of opposed races, in the silent struggle that continues in every person from here, between all of the contradictory heredities"?[127]

Bastide's language of "opposed races" and "silent struggle" between "contradictory heredities" contrasted with his description of the end of slavery in his first lecture—or at least, with the *O Estado de S. Paulo* journalist's inter-pretation of it. According to the newspaper write-up, Brazil's abolition meant "assimilating to the Latin people what is best of the black spirit, permitting the free cooperation between all citizens in the common effort, in a collectiv-ity that makes the strength and grandeur of today's Brazil."[128] Between his lecture in May 1938, when Bastide was applauded for his ideas about the "free cooperation" of "all citizens," and July 1938, when he published in *Dom Cas-murro*, he became much more aware of the violence of Brazilian society. Like Freyre, he was convinced that "the mixing of races" in Brazil was "a drama" full of violence, but one that nonetheless promised the creation of a new kind of multiracial society.[129]

In his article on the São Paulo market, for example, Bastide cited the Arabic, Germanic, and Italian influences on the population of the south of France in a positive light. The wars of the Middle Ages, for Bastide, resulted in a mixture of peoples who would have otherwise remained separate. With this example in mind, it was not for the "Latin people" to see blacks as antithetical, but rather, to assimilate "the best of the black spirit."[130] Bastide, like the other French scholars, was not particularly profound—nor particularly correct—in his analysis of blacks in São Paulo; and yet, these early articles demonstrate a real sociological interest that distinguished his thought from the questions of mysticism that had motivated him in France.

Bastide's journey to Brazil brought him "out of the study and into the field," transforming his broad philosophical statements into concrete sociological testimony.[131] In different ways, this very process of coming down from the universal to examine particular empirical phenomena characterized Braudel, Lévi-Strauss, and Monbeig as well. As far as Brazilian writers were concerned, however, Bastide attempted to do something much different: to elevate them to the level of the universal—and in so doing, to create the conditions of possibility for a cross-fertilization of ideas. Machado de Assis, the mixed-race author of the novel *Dom Casmurro* (for which the journal was named), was one of those authors who belonged to "the intellectual patrimony of human-kind as a whole."[132] According to Bastide, Machado's "glory went beyond his country, extending itself around the world. It is because he is Brazilian that he is universal."[133]

Machado de Assis, of course, was not a risky choice for a writer to elevate to the level of universal. In *The Posthumous Memoirs of Brás Cubas* (1881) alone, Machado proved his familiarity with what was in his time called uni-versal history, citing authors such as Molière, Voltaire, and Shakespeare and historical figures including Cromwell, Cavour, Bismarck, Lucrezia Borgia, and Napoleon. His writings were even sometimes critiqued as insufficiently "national," much more concerned as they were with the interior lives of bourgeois residents of Belle Epoque Rio de Janeiro than the country as a whole. But more importantly, Machado was one of Brazil's most established writers—and founder of the Academia Brasileira de Letras, which propagated his memory.[134]

Bastide's homage to Machado, however, went well beyond celebrating an established *lieu de mémoire*. Machado was, alongside Dostoyevsky, one of the most important writers in exploring "subterranean man," thereby contributing to the "renewal of contemporary psychology." In an homage to Machado published in *Dom Casmurro*, Bastide thanked the International Institute of Intellectual Cooperation for its Iberian-American collection and translation of *Dom Casmurro*, even if he clarified that it was *The Posthumous Memoirs of Brás Cubas* that made him "the original precursor" of a Proust or a Pirandello.[135]

Bastide, however, was not only interested in acclaimed writers of the stature of Machado or in positivists such as Euclides da Cunha. He also paid attention to lesser-known movements in poetry, and in particular to the relationships between aesthetics and sociology that he found in Brazil. "Only Brazil . . . a land of poetry . . . could permit the doctrine of Comte to be fulfilled lyrically, and finished in music."[136] Since the late nineteenth century, positivism had taken root in Brazil, to the point where Rio de Janeiro inaugurated its Positivist Church in 1897, also known as the Temple of Humanity. The historian Sérgio Buarque de Holanda sought to explain positivism's hold on Brazilian elites as due to their "lack of intellectual maturity" and "confused thought," reported Bastide.[137] But rather than designate political ideologies in Brazil as false copies from "more socially advanced nations" or symptoms of "political and social adolescence,"[138] Bastide saw Brazilian positivists as creating a new kind of art.

Bastide questioned how a French "intellectual" construction (positivism) could pass to the "sentimental or even mystical" realm. This transformation, he thought, "must be sought out in . . . Brazilian *bondade* [goodness], in this grand desire of love that characterizes a whole people and that found its philosophical systematization precisely in the cult of Humanity."[139] Bastide's attribution of sentimentality to Brazilians—as well as inherent goodness—is an essentialization as equally invalid as Buarque de Holanda's "lack of intellectual maturity." But whereas for Buarque de Holanda, Brazil was lacking in certain attributes (notably rationality and organization), Bastide insisted on the creative value of irrationality and disorganization.

Brazilians such as the positivist Martins Fontes proved the possibility of hybridity—the fusion of a highly determined world (Comte) with a much more personal interpretation (the lyrical). In postrevolutionary France, Comte sought to move beyond religion's irrationality as well as the excesses of philosophy, providing a conservative post-Catholic view of the social order. For Bastide, Comte's thought as it was understood in Europe—a rigid and systematic set of principles—prevented innovation in the aesthetic domain.

Martins Fontes, on the other hand, who followed neither "pantheism," nor "socialism," nor "franciscanism" directly, could more easily embrace the "aesthetic possibilities of positivism."[140] His eclecticism, "scientific poetry," contrasted with the rigidity of the French positivists. According to Bastide, Martins Fontes "was attracted above all by the most new and mysterious forms of speculation, like the theory of matter and of metaphysics."[141]

Bastide saw Brazil as an "immense laboratory of experimental sociology," both because of its contact of cultures and because of the new methodologies that were being developed to examine such phenomena. According to Bastide, the state of the field of Afro-Brazilian studies did not yet permit "a complete systematic description."[142] Brazilians nonetheless developed their own methodologies. These included the ethnological method of Raimundo Nina Rodrigues, the sociology of Gilberto Freyre, the psychoanalysis of Arthur Ramos, and new linguistic studies, according to Bastide's lecture at the Sociedade de Etnografia e Folclore, in São Paulo.[143] Bastide read Brazilian authors not only to get at Brazil's underlying empirical reality but also to import their methodological contributions into the field of sociology more generally.

During his first years in Brazil, Bastide began to develop a network of contacts, often outside São Paulo, that would help him to focus his research.[144] One such contact was Arthur Ramos, about whom he likely first learned through Marcel Mauss's review in L'année sociologique.[145] Bastide wrote Ramos, professor at the Universidade do Brasil, in Rio de Janeiro, and author of As culturas negras no Novo Mundo (Black cultures in the New World), requesting bibliographic citations and guidance: "In this world of Afro-Brazilian things, a guide is necessary, and if it does not bother you too much to sometimes be an informed and perspicacious guide for me, it would be a great honor and I would be very grateful to you."[146] Bastide sought "intellectual cooperation" between France and Brazil, particularly in regards to studies of black populations. He wrote of a future French mission to the Antilles, under the direction of Rivet, and looked forward to serving as an intermediary with the Institut Français d'Afrique Noire, in Dakar.[147]

Sometime in the first half of 1939, Bastide invited Ramos to participate in the International Congress of Sociology in Bucharest (Romania) and informed him that he had sent some of his work to colleagues at the Musée de l'Homme, in Paris.[148] Because of heightened international tensions, however, the Congress never happened.[149] Later in 1939, Bastide intended to visit what Ramos had called his "Afro-Brazilian Museum," in Rio de Janeiro, and attend a candomblé in Niterói, where he was invited by Josué de Castro, a sociologist from Pernambuco who was then teaching at the Universidade do Brasil.[150] Regrettably, he had to cancel his visit to Rio for family reasons and due to fear that war could break out at any time.[151]

Much as he did with Ramos, Bastide also informed Gilberto Freyre of his "Afro-Brazilian project," inviting him to participate in the conference in Bucharest.[152] Freyre, then in the US, declined the request to give a paper at the conference.[153] He nonetheless thanked Bastide for the "amicable references made by you and other French professors at the University of São Paulo to my work."[154] As we will see in the next chapter, their relationship only continued to grow into the 1940s, when Bastide visited Freyre in Pernambuco as part of his travels in the Northeast.

Bastide may not have met the major figures of Afro-Brazilian research, nor witnessed the communities most relevant for their work. São Paulo had a significant Afro-descendant population but not yet one nearly as large as Rio, Minas Gerais, or the Northeast. Even so, during his first two years in Brazil, Bastide traveled extensively through his readings, encountering a diversity of regions at different "historical stages."[155] Citing a work by the historian Pedro Calmon, he wrote for the benefit of his French colleagues: "The traveler, by going into the interior of the country, goes successively from contemporary civilization to the colonial society of the eighteenth century."[156] In June 1939, Bastide finally started to prepare his travels to the "part of Brazil where the Negro influence is the strongest": the Northeast made famous by novelists, folklorists, and anthropologists alike.[157]

Albeit still a novice in Afro-Brazilian culture, Bastide had already proved himself capable of assimilating Brazilian authors. Even before he had traveled widely in or written extensively about Brazil, Bastide was recognized by the young Senegalese Léopold Sédar Senghor as an ally and an expert on "the Renaissance of African culture in Brazil."[158] Senghor, who had already done so much for the negritude movement, even preferred Bastide's writings on the subject to those of Freyre, but this may have principally been because of Bastide's mastery of French.[159]

THE END OF A GOLDEN AGE?

By the time Bastide began his tenure in Brazil, Braudel had returned to France and been elected to the École Pratique des Hautes Études. There he would be responsible for covering "the Iberian Peninsula from the Middle Ages through the eighteenth century, with by extension a part of the entire western Mediterranean, and Iberian expansion in America."[160] Largely occupied with his return to Paris and his teaching there, Braudel nonetheless corresponded with his former assistant Eurípides Simões de Paula and maintained contact with USP through another student in Paris, Branca da Cunha Caldeira.[161] In a letter written at his father-in-law's country home in Tiaret, Algeria, he announced to Simões, "Branca's work is finished. It is solid, surely the best historical work that we have on contemporary Argentina."[162] He also maintained an interest in Eduardo d'Oliveira França, despite the quality of his work paling in comparison to that of his female colleague. He hoped d'Oliveira França would find a post at "our Faculty."[163]

Upon his return to France, Braudel continued to cultivate his interest in Brazil and in Latin American history, as evidenced by his numerous review essays.[164] However, Braudel's research interests migrated back to the Mediterranean and to Algeria in particular, where his wife Paule came from and his father-in-law lived. In *Annales*, he questioned the future of the "indigenous mass, otherwise poorly rooted and now held entirely, as in a net, in the mesh of European culture."[165]

Lévi-Strauss continued to visit São Paulo throughout 1938 and into 1939, despite no longer having a formal position at USP. He and Dina were highly respected, particularly by their students, who offered them a farewell tea at the Automóvel Club prior to their departure for Mato Grosso. One of their students, Décio de Almeida Prado, praised Dina for being a woman scientist—and still remaining a woman (*mulher*)![166] Their "tea" was publicized in the society section of the newspaper, advertising guests such as the USP founder and former São Paulo governor Armando de Salles Oliveira. Contrary to certain claims, this proves that the Lévi-Strausses were not marginalized within USP, but, instead, that they knowingly ended their contract in order to conduct research.[167]

O Estado de S. Paulo closely followed their research in Mato Grosso, and the Lévi-Strausses' return to São Paulo.[168] In January 1939, the Sociedade de Etnografia e Folclore organized an event for them in homage to all that they had done and what they would do for Brazil in France. One speaker at the event, unidentified in newspaper coverage, hoped that the results of Lévi-Strausses' mission would bring recognition to the Sociedade in the "Old World": "not because of the indigenous material that you are transporting, but because of our accentuated interest in ethnography and folklore, sciences that awake enthusiasm in intellectuals of the most advanced countries of the globe."[169]

As late as February 1939, Claude Lévi-Strauss was still in Brazil, presenting his last lecture at the Sociedade de Etnografia e Folclore, on "the sentimental life of the Nambicuara."[170] By March, he had returned to Paris. Relieved of his teaching obligations until the fall of 1939, when he was supposed to take up a post at an all-girls secondary school in Versailles, Lévi-Strauss had a few months to "unpack, catalog, and label all of the six hundred objects brought back from the second expedition." Absorbed by this laborious task, he prepared to integrate his collection into "the Latin American collections of the Musée [de l'Homme], next to those of his professor and thesis advisor [*directeur*] Paul Rivet."[171]

Monbeig stayed on with Bastide to teach at USP under much different terms. The glory days of the French presence in São Paulo seemed to have come to an end. As Fernando de Azevedo, then director of the Faculty, wrote to Gilberto Freyre: "The University and culture, in S. Paulo, are crossing a critical phase, of the most serious that it has gone through. Already, the work of destruction has begun."[172] In the reigning political climate in Brazil, of nationalism and even *integralismo*, neither Monbeig nor Bastide was sure how long he would be able to keep his job. They therefore dedicated themselves to their teaching and to planning for their return to France.[173]

In the months after World War II broke out, in 1939, the French Ministry of Foreign Affairs decided to leave the two men in place. Braudel and Lévi-Strauss, back in France, were mobilized. The war would take them in different directions, but the Brazilian years offered these scholars an important starting point for their research and their wartime trajectories. Whether they stayed in Brazil or found themselves elsewhere, Brazilian authors would follow them as their work matured and the world turned upside down.

Four Approaches to Global and Social-Scientific Crisis

World War II would profoundly disrupt the French social sciences, and those scholars who make up this story were by no means exempt from the tribulations of France's debacle, occupation, and Vichy. Beyond their patriotic roles as soldiers and resistants, however, Bastide, Braudel, Lévi-Strauss, and Monbeig all pursued their scholarly work. This chapter examines some of their wartime exchanges with Brazilian intellectuals such as Gilberto Freyre, Caio Prado Jr., and Arthur Ramos that proved so crucial for their ideas about settler colonialism, religious syncretism, transatlantic trade, and kinship structures.

Braudel spent much of the war in officers' prison camps in Mainz and Lübeck, Germany, surrounded by Gaullists;[1] Lévi-Strauss was in New York, at the New School for Social Research's Latin America Center and the École Libre des Hautes Études, a "university in exile" for French-speaking academics in New York during the war;[2] and Monbeig and Bastide stayed in Brazil throughout the entirety of the war, teaching at the University of São Paulo. These French social scientists, like so many scholars during the war, were cut off from their families, academic resources, and/or basic material comforts. Nevertheless, compared to their peers and superiors, their situation was enviable, even in Braudel's case. All four of them continued with their work. Furthermore, their confidence in Free France led them to believe that they were continuing to construct "French" science from abroad, despite the challenges of wartime life.[3]

While the great majority of Frenchmen were being mobilized in early 1940,

Monbeig wrote Lucien Febvre to report on the important geographical work that he had been undertaking. After a "long voyage to Mato Grosso" that "had given [him] a good harvest for [his] thesis," Monbeig wondered if he could help to publicize *Annales* or the *Encyclopédie française*, if they were available, or be useful to France in any other possible way.[4] As for Lévi-Strauss, when he reported to the Rockefeller Foundation in 1945 at the end of the war, he claimed:

> We were able to benefit from the physical and mental security that those who stayed in Europe were deprived of. And, what's more, these last four years, instead of being lost in the all-consuming task of simply surviving or fleeing, were made beneficial and fruitful and were enriched by our contacts with American professors, with American university life, and with American libraries.[5]

Whether in Brazil or the US, then, these two scholars were insulated from the war and able to advance in their research.[6] Unlike the Germans—"permanent exiles," according to Martin Jay's formulation—the French were only temporarily displaced.[7]

Despite the territorial, disciplinary, and methodological distance that separated them, the intellectuals at the heart of this book shared an understanding of France's demise as caused not only by politics but also by a failure of the social sciences. Monbeig's published lecture from 1942 on the crisis of the social sciences, *La crise des sciences de l'homme*, best exemplifies such a concern.[8] In it, Monbeig rejected the racist pseudoscience of the likes of eugenicist Alexis Carrel. He also criticized hyperspecialization and excessive empiricism that prevented students and researchers from asking larger questions about society and humankind's relationship to nature. In their own ways, Bastide, Braudel, and Lévi-Strauss sought to overcome such compartmentalization as they, too, advanced on their respective projects.

The idea was not to deny the merits of empirical social science altogether. After all, Lévi-Strauss, Monbeig, and Bastide built upon a mixture of Brazilian fieldwork and methodological engagement with North American scholarship. Instead, they sought to construct a style of work that was at once empirically rigorous—that is to say, based on local knowledge—and broader in scope. This required a synthesis of previous French social-scientific models and the new circumstances in which this younger generation found itself.

The universalizing projects of the Durkheimians and *Annales*, Marcel Mauss's understandings of "total social facts," and those of the French school of geography of human societies in their physical world: all of these had to be repurposed in light of the new international circumstances. As Christophe

Charle has shown, in the period prior to the war, French social scientists maintained a significant international presence through numerous "ambassadors" abroad.[9] In the postwar period, French social scientists would make up for their comparative disadvantages in applied research by offering reinterpretation and synthesis. At a privileged crossroads between Europe and the Americas, North and South, empirical research and French epistemology, the intellectuals of this story anticipated this sea change.

Monbeig's and Bastide's debts to Brazil, intellectual and professional, ran deepest, especially since the men stayed there during the entire course of the war. Monbeig continued his work in the states of São Paulo and Paraná for what would become his dissertation, *Pionniers et planteurs de São Paulo*, and his secondary dissertation, on the city of São Paulo.[10] These years were crucial for Monbeig's study of tropical settlement and commodity agriculture. Meanwhile, Bastide traveled for the first time to the Brazilian Northeast, to take part in Brazilian "African" religions, especially candomblé, and popular celebrations that would lay the basis for his future work. Like Monbeig, he depended intimately on Brazilian interlocutors and mediators, whether they were students, professors, intellectuals, or people that made up the communities he studied. Bastide's published books between 1940 and 1945 include *Imagens do Nordeste místico em branco e preto* (Images of the mystical Northeast in black and white), *Poetas do Brasil*, and a number of articles that laid the groundwork for his dissertations.[11] Brazil offered Bastide a unique intellectual culture, as well as ethnic and religious synthesis that piqued his interest in the sociological and literary realms.

For Braudel, Brazil served to open the Mediterranean, as he considered transatlantic trade and economic conjunctures more generally. His dialogue with the historian Caio Prado Jr. and the sociologist Gilberto Freyre were particularly important in this regard. Braudel's review of Freyre's work from 1943 best illustrates this engagement with the Brazilian social sciences during the war, but a closer reading of his dissertation, *The Mediterranean and the Mediterranean World in the Age of Philip II*, also reveals other connections, as we will soon see.

Lévi-Strauss, who lived in New York during the war, had a different experience. In addition to dialoguing with Brazilian intellectuals, he used his previous fieldwork on what he saw as the most "elementary of populations" (among them, the Bororo and Nambicuara) as a basis for his structuralist method. To be sure, his intellectual engagement with Brazilian scholars during the war years did not compare to that of his colleagues, but his ability to navigate between South and North American ethnology contributed to universalizing his thought and constructing *The Elementary Structures of Kinship*. When he brought back his "great book" to liberated France, he wrote Paul Rivet, it would allow "young anthropologists and sociologists" to be placed on "equal footing with their foreign colleagues."[12]

During the war and after, Brazil remained present in the thoughts and social lives of these four scholars. Monbeig and Bastide, living in Brazil and largely cut off from cultural and scientific information coming from France, had little choice but to further engage their host country. For Braudel and Lévi-Strauss, engagement with Brazil was a much more deliberate choice. Distanced from the country geographically, they nonetheless found Brazil a useful place to think with, or, as Lévi-Strauss would later say, "bon à penser."[13] At times, it served as little more than an abstraction; at others, a utopia of a mixed-race society. Nonetheless, the country continued to penetrate their thinking, whether through the materiality of a book or the idea of the most elementary structures of kinship.

Neither Bastide nor Monbeig produced anything as widely heralded as Braudel's *The Mediterranean* or Lévi-Strauss's *The Elementary Structures of Kinship*, but I explore their work here at equal length. These lesser-known giants enriched and transformed their respective fields, whether in understanding the role of capitalism, commodity markets, and the human geography of colonization, or in proposing new approaches to the anthropology of "complex" societies, characterized by religious and cultural syncretism. Their contributions are in many ways as universal as those of Braudel on the world economy or those of Lévi-Strauss on kinship.[14] However, their looser ties to France served as an obstacle to their reception in their home country, and by extension to the international publication market based in Paris.

This chapter, the most properly intellectual-historical of the book, examines the individual, private moments that scholars inhabit as they research, think, and write. Like chapter 3, it is divided into four parts, each having to do with the genesis of a particular scholar's oeuvre. That Monbeig, Bastide, Braudel, and Lévi-Strauss all engaged with Brazil as an empirical and methodological space for reconceiving the social sciences attests to the power of their earlier collective experience. In the next chapter, we will see how such experience, network, and knowledge would be invaluable for the reconstruction of the postwar social sciences. For now, however, let us turn to their work itself.

MONBEIG AND THE GEOGRAPHY OF COMMODITY EXPANSION IN THE TROPICS

During the war years, Monbeig traveled extensively throughout Brazil, not only in the state of São Paulo but also in Mato Grosso, Paraná, Santa Catarina, and even up to Ceará, in the Northeast. This allowed him to see certain patterns and to more clearly focus his object of study: the process of Paulista expansion. Since the end of the Constitutionalist Revolution, in 1934, Vargas tolerated and managed to co-opt significant sectors of the Paulista elite. The "March to the West," which began as official state policy in 1937, brought new migrant populations to the Brazilian plateau and the Amazon. These areas, intimately connected to international markets and the intensification of commoditization, offered Monbeig a fruitful site of fieldwork for observing human geography in its making, complementing his work in São Paulo.

Two of Monbeig's sites for fieldwork in São Paulo were particularly important: Barão de Antonina, in the Southwest, and Marília, in the Northwest. Both of these pioneer towns exemplified the processes of urban-rural codevelopment on which Monbeig based his models for understanding geographical expansion and colonization in the tropics. When considered alongside his extended bibliographical and geographical analysis of cities, Monbeig's writings about this early fieldwork evince their role as the basis for *Pionniers et planteurs* and his secondary dissertation, *La croissance de la ville de São Paulo*, which will be discussed subsequently. Here, I argue that his fruitful comings and goings between fieldwork and libraries in São Paulo allowed him to establish his research empirically and to consider the field more broadly, as evidenced in his published lecture *La crise des sciences de l'homme*.

Monbeig had traveled to Barão de Antonina, a *colônia*, or settlement, in 1938. At the time, the town, which was founded in 1930, had only 316 families and was eighty-eight kilometers from the closest railroad station.[15] For Monbeig, "Barão de Antonina afford[ed] a good example of the modern ways of life in the state of São Paulo" in addition to "a concrete expression of the Brazilian policy of colonization."[16] In contrast to coastal settlements, Barão de Antonina's position in the interior of the state made it a prominent example of the changing human geography of São Paulo and Brazil as a whole.

Because of his training under Albert Demangeon, Monbeig was inclined to focus more on human geography than on natural landscapes.[17] But whatever preconceived ideas he brought to Barão de Antonina, what struck him most was the influence of humans upon nature, not vice versa. According to Monbeig, "Man has been active enough so that one can hardly speak of a natural landscape."[18] Deforestation, agricultural burnings, and other human-made modifications had made the initial fieldwork of Vidalian geography (i.e., sketching a landscape) utterly meaningless.

Barão de Antonina's population and economy differed from other land occupations in the state, particularly the "ragged clearings of the caboclos" and the "grandiose monotony of the classical landscape of the coffee fazendas."[19] For Monbeig, Barão de Antonina's landscape was "characteristic of the state of São Paulo and of Northern Paraná, where small farmers are installed in the forest."[20] These small farmers were largely of recent European descent, when compared to the mixed-race caboclos, on the one hand, and families of Portuguese and Spanish descent that had immigrated earlier, on the other.[21]

Monbeig's experience at USP alongside Lévi-Strauss clearly influenced the ethnographic lens with which he approached Barão de Antonina and his subsequent research.[22] One can see this in his attention to different kinds of (im)migrants, their houses, and their customs, both in his analysis and in his photography. His article on Barão de Antonina, for example, examines the Polish and German rancho house of wattle and daub, with roof of thatch; the Brazilian's house, with brick walls and primitive thatched roof; the Lithuanian's, with clay walls and roof of corrugated iron and tiles; as well as those of Ukrainian, Swiss, and Romanian settlers.[23]

However distinct these groups appeared one from another, they did not exist in clusters. In fact, the way that the land was divided and sold (*loteado*) precluded such a possibility. According to Monbeig's research, the results were "indisputable": "The foreign families that I visited, although they do not deny their attachment to their native lands, are proud to call themselves and their children Brazilians—or, rather, Paulistas."[24] Furthermore, state projects like that of Barão de Antonina and others in Rio de Janeiro state were succeeding in creating "citizens" rather than ethnic communities or "cysts," to use the nativist language of the time.[25] The different groups may have preferred to work with their own and celebrate certain traditions as a community, but they ultimately socialized with one another, particularly in the settlement headquarters (*sede do nucleo*).[26]

Monbeig himself at times reproduced a broader cultural imaginary that privileged white immigrants over Brazilian migrants.[27] Nevertheless, his willingness to engage immigrant communities on their own terms allowed him to document Paulista psychology and ideology at an everyday level. European immigrants living in Barão de Antonina proudly called themselves Paulistas, and less so Brazilians. This very fact points to a state or regional discourse around superiority that was at once economic, political, and racial.[28]

State intervention, Monbeig argued, created the conditions for true assimilation, preventing the mushrooming of the rural proletariat (*proletariats ruraux*). In Barão de Antonina, Monbeig claimed, "assimilation takes place at Brazilian school, where children of all colors and all nationalities are brought together."[29] To be clear, not all children attended school, and even those who did would not necessarily mix as adults. Nonetheless, Monbeig saw Barão de Antonina as a "new step in the settlement of the country," which should calm Brazilian concerns about foreign groups, particularly in the face of growing nationalism and war.[30] Barão de Antonina provided an important example of an agricultural community and a test for Brazil's ability to integrate different kinds of (im)migrants. In contrast, Marília, in the more rapidly growing Northwest of São Paulo, provided an example of a new regional hub—an invaluable position from which to see the articulations between the urban, suburban, and rural in the expanding commodity economy.

Marília was a "pioneer city," considered by many poorer migrants from other states as an El Dorado.[31] Intimately tied up with the advance of the state and its coffee economy westward, it was over two hundred kilometers from the capital of São Paulo. The state's Comissão Geográfica e Geológica had been drawn to the region in the 1910s for its fertile soils, and the subsequent opening of rudimentary roads led to settlement and farming there.[32] As for Marília itself, it was based on the *espigão* (crest of a narrow plateau or relatively broad ridge), an ideal position for rainwater, soil, and a number of other factors.[33] Embryonic in the first decades of the twentieth century, Marília's development really took off in 1928, with the arrival of the first trains. According to those who were there for those early years, it had the feel of the "Far West": "Everyday, one could witness the arrival of new pioneers who camped in the middle of tree trunks, rapidly building mud shacks [*cabanas de terra*] before constructing a better house on their own lot."[34]

For Monbeig, Marília served the classic role of *boca de sertão*, a term familiar to most Brazilians. The term *sertão* is nearly impossible to define, as it was and remains a constant source of debate.[35] For Monbeig, *sertão* was most nearly rendered in French as *bled* or *brousse* (English: backwater or sticks), and *boca de sertão*, as door to the backwater.[36] Pierre Deffontaines previously defined it as "the mouth upon open lands," clearly neglecting to mention indigenous inhabitants.[37] Writing of Marília in the same article, he claimed: "Marília was an absolutely empty and unknown *sertão* in 1925, and is today a capital of 20,000 inhabitants, more important than many old towns of the littoral."[38]

Marília, first for Deffontaines and then for Monbeig, served as the prototypical pioneer town. "Born with the railroad," it was for some years the last stop on the Paulista railway.[39] But what exactly was its function? For Monbeig, Marília, like other *bocas de sertão*, was at once a marketplace for the buying and selling of goods, a storage place for diverse items (*armazém*), an administrative center, and an embryonic industrial hub intimately tied to agricultural finished goods. Marília in particular had multiple cottonseed-oil factories.[40]

Coffee may have laid the foundation for Marília's wealth, but over time the city's development was less tied to the commodity itself and more to the process of outward expansion. Cotton production, largely by Japanese and Japanese-descended migrants, allowed for the diversification of the agricultural economy on less fertile soils.[41] But much more importantly, Marília's influence on those areas beyond the reach of the railway contributed to a diversification of sectors, ranging from infrastructure (clearing forests and making roads) to banking and storage (especially agricultural). In turn, this contributed to the growth of the real estate industry, with the buying and selling of lots ever farther away from the town itself. This entire process ultimately brought about the *mise en valeur*, or development, of the Alto Paulista region.[42] Because of the coffee economy and agricultural expansion, Marília and places like it had the "essential factors for the movements of population in the state of São Paulo."[43] As such, they were the state's biggest demographic beneficiary.

Barão de Antonina and Marília provided the principal field sites for Monbeig. Research into other towns and cities, as well as private archival sources from the coffee-producing elite, allowed him to better understand the economy behind Paulista expansion. Based on his contacts and social position, he was able to visit numerous fazendas in the state of São Paulo, to check their account books, and obtain otherwise inaccessible documents about the transportation of goods by railroad.[44] Often bringing along students whose "inquiries" informed his work, he also had statistical information drawn up by São Paulo's Department of Lands, Colonization, and Immigration.[45]

Meanwhile, the city of São Paulo provided the resources, namely access to new books in his field, for Monbeig to think more methodologically about his endeavor. In São Paulo's libraries Monbeig brought himself up to speed with geographical works coming out of France, England, the US, and Germany. This dialectic between fieldwork and bibliography, of raw material and finished goods, allowed Monbeig to continuously evolve in his thinking over a long period of time. It also paralleled his understanding of pioneer cities, which initially served agricultural functions and progressively specialized, only to once again contribute to settlement and agricultural exploitation further out still.

The first systematization of such thinking can be seen in Monbeig's article "O estudo geográfico das cidades" (The geographical study of cities), published in 1941.[46] In it Monbeig gave particular attention to his own training in France, but also incorporated other, Brazilian and North American influences.[47] While Monbeig analyzed the work of his French colleagues in Rio, Deffontaines and Philippe Arbos, he also incorporated the work of American geographers who examined networks of towns in Ohio, Michigan, and New York. Finally, Monbeig explicitly highlighted the Chicago school of sociology, which proposed ethnographies of different ethnic "communities." In particular, he likely benefited from exchanges with Emilio Willems and Donald Pierson at the Escola Livre de Sociologia e Política.[48]

This is not to mention Monbeig's continuous dialogue with his Brazilian students and peers, especially Eurípides Simões de Paula, Gilberto Freyre, Raul de Andrada, Olga Pantaleão, Maria Conceição Vicente de Carvalho, and Caio Prado Jr., to name just several. A number of these scholars, including

Gilberto Freyre, presented with Monbeig on the theme of urban geography at the ninth Brazilian Congress of Geography, in 1940, in Florianópolis, Santa Catarina state.[49] Although not in attendance, Prado, upon request by Monbeig, offered his "Nova contribuição para o estudo geográfico da cidade de São Paulo" (New contribution to the geographical study of the city of São Paulo) to be read out.[50]

All of these different conceptions helped Monbeig to rethink the future of human geography, by encouraging intensified interdisciplinary collaboration. Furthermore, in new urban spaces where humans and nature were in the process of mutual construction, the relatively autonomous natural regions so dear to the French school of geography proved increasingly difficult to locate. In urban contexts where topography is disguised, Monbeig wrote:

> The geographer finds himself, then—more than in any other terrain of his research—led to work with the help of historians, sociologists, and economists, and even more, to consult urbanists, the technicians of the city. In this way, the eminently synthetic character of human geography finds itself accentuated in the inquiries of urban geography.[51]

The geographer, instead of being a pure scientist tied to geology, could become the "coordinator, but not the dictator" of collective social-scientific inquiries.[52] The first step in this process was to leave behind the geographically determinist perspectives. In this article and in his subsequent work, Monbeig emphasized human agency and, above all, history.

The physical and natural environment would continue to play a role in Monbeig's work, but the shift toward urban geography made other questions more immediate. These included land occupation and the spatial organization of "factories, offices, stations, men, and capital."[53] With the appropriate documentation and research, such a shift could allow for measuring the "influence of the city on rural milieus, on small urban groupings, and on its dependency relative to more powerful concentrations."[54] In other words, Monbeig outlined a regional approach, defined not by topography but by human activity. In it, larger cities remained central, but were constantly in dialogue with smaller urban centers in the countryside.

However tenuous, Monbeig's method for urban geography laid the basis not only for his secondary dissertation, *La croissance de la ville de São Paulo* (The growth of the city of São Paulo), but also for much of his work on pioneer zones. This urban geography required the superimposition of successive maps to see spatial development historically;[55] close study of demographic patterns, with particular attention to changing densities in different spaces, whether it be a neighborhood in a city or an agrarian setting;[56] and functional analysis of types of neighborhoods, intimately linked to communication, infrastructure, and transportation of people and goods.[57] If this tripartite method were followed, Monbeig argued, geographers could write a series of monographs, each on a different aspects of cities and their surroundings, progressively building on each other's work. "Great science is not made in a single stroke, but is elaborated slowly by the accumulation of elementary data," Monbeig wrote.[58]

All while attempting to make urban geography into a science, Monbeig insisted on preserving its human aspects—those elements that make up the "soul of the city." In "O estudo geográfico das cidades," Monbeig cited Freyre's notion of the "symphonic quality" of landscapes, warning against "exaggerated scientificity" that precluded "comprehensive interpretation."[59] For Monbeig, the excessive emphasis on scientific aspects risked dehumanizing cities and people: "No one believes," he claimed, "to have shown man [to be] . . . a herd of cattle."[60]

The very human nature of the social sciences was one of Monbeig's concerns that transcended his field-based research, as evidenced in his sixty-two-page pamphlet *La crise des sciences de l'homme*.[61] *La crise* reflected Monbeig's outrage with Nazism, Vichy, and collaborationist scientists. But, interestingly enough, Monbeig also emphasized his frustration with American empiricism and hyperspecialization—an exaggerated science for science's sake that prevented a more general and systematic approach to studying humanity. Arthur Ramos would echo such considerations a year later in a similar lecture, on "the social sciences and postwar problems," subsequently brought out by the very same publisher.[62]

Monbeig specifically targeted two types of human science: ideologically inspired human science, especially in Germany, and utilitarian human science, especially in the United States. As for the former, he mentioned German pseudoscientific racism and geographers working explicitly to advance geopolitical goals.[63] He also singled out Frenchmen such as biologists Charles Nicolle and Alexis Carrel, the latter of whom affirmed, according to Monbeig, that "those who today are proletarians owe their situation to hereditary flaws of their body and their mind."[64] As for utilitarian human science, Monbeig lamented the increasing demands on the human sciences to reproduce the logics of natural sciences and to justify themselves in economic terms.

As Monbeig claimed, "To express myself in business terms, exact sciences 'pay,' and for that reason they are excused a great deal. But to study the folklore of the blacks of Bahia or the savages of the Andaman Islands, it does not 'pay.'"[65] It is easy to see that Monbeig was justifying his colleague Roger Bastide's research—the likes of which the market would not bear. (As we will see later, with Monbeig as the director of the social-sciences department at the Centre

National de la Recherche Scientifique, the state could be used to fund such research.) In the most general terms, Monbeig sought to rectify the fact that,

> for more than a quarter century, white humanity has lost confidence in itself and confidence in its future. It became frightened by the mechanization that it had created and it fears the material progress that it unleashed. What is too certain, alas, is that the peoples of European civilization, of all social classes and on every continent, no longer distinguish what path they are engaged in and allow themselves to be dominated by fear. [66]

The fact that Monbeig divided humanity into racial categories and located the crisis of human science entirely in white humanity's fears and doubts demarcates what he saw as the boundaries of science. But Monbeig was also in the process of undoing and reconstructing his own mental categories. Western Europe and capitalist science were responsible for the destruction of arable land, "one of the most tragic episodes of the conquest of the planet by the white race."[67] He exhorted his audience, both those present at the conference in Rio and his readers more generally, to look beyond the exploitation of nature and capitalist development. "It is not nature that we need to dominate," he wrote; "it is social and economic man that we need to transform: that is the domain of the human sciences."[68]

Part of the problem of the present moment, Monbeig argued, was that the sciences obeyed "abusive segregation," "hyperspecialization," "excessive splitting up," and too often were divided into "scientific clans."[69] The North Americans, Monbeig claimed, were largely responsible for this culture. Some of them, he claimed, insisted so much on technical and empirical work that they warned their students against "ideas, number one enemy of social science."[70] True, Monbeig welcomed certain aspects of the American social sciences. In geography, for example, his American colleagues had led the way in renovating cartography.[71] However, like those of his colleagues, Monbeig's project for the human sciences largely sought to transcend the American model, notably the one promoted by the Rockefeller Foundation.[72]

Instead of being "barricaded in his specialty" and "entrenched behind technique," Monbeig was open to the more general perspectives offered by Freyre and Mauss. The human sciences in their footsteps could help to arrive at the "total man" (a repurposing of Mauss's "total social facts") and, more specifically, at "the psychology of the total man."[73] This was not only a methodological imperative. It also required the reorganization of research on humankind and society.

Monbeig saw collective and interdisciplinary research as the precondition for arriving at "total man." For him, *Annales* was the epitome of such research in journal form, known for advocating the study of "total history," even if the crystallization came later.[74] But so were practical studies that brought natural and human scientists together on projects, such as in the United States or in French and British colonies in Africa.[75] While he remained vague about what these projects should be, he nonetheless encouraged bridging the gap between "our own ivory towers and the real world." "This will require," he argued, "the radical transformation of our habits of thinking and our university organizations."[76]

During the war years, Monbeig's published fieldwork in São Paulo and Paraná had given him the empirical credentials necessary for a geographer. Throughout these years, he worked closely with students of his such as Antonieta de Paula Souza and Maria Conceição Vicente de Carvalho, with both of whom he organized the publication of *Geografia de hoje* (Geography of today).[77] Monbeig also had the unique possibility of coming in and out of fieldwork, spending time in the capital city to consult secondary literature and keeping up with advances in the international geographical field and in the human sciences more generally. All of this would serve him when he returned to France as a key reorganizer of the human sciences, a task that he had been addressing at least as early as 1943.

BASTIDE, BETWEEN SOCIOLOGICAL THEORY, LITERARY CRITICISM, AND AFRO-BRAZILIAN STUDIES

During the war years, Roger Bastide and his colleagues were largely cut off from new material being published in France, and equally importantly, from their French intellectual milieu. Arguably more than any other professor in Brazil, Bastide embraced this distance as an opportunity to integrate himself into Brazilian culture. He did this through his readings in Brazilian literature, poetry, sociology, and folklore, but also through his intellectual network and a set of questions that would thoroughly root his research in Brazil. These were: How might one go about studying the "profound psychology" of Afro-Brazilians? And how, as a sociologist, could he understand Brazilian lyricism and mysticism?

In the early years of the war Bastide's interrogations of these questions remained at the level of secondary and literary sources. However, as he sharpened his questions through analytical essays, as well as through literary criticism, he increasingly began to approach Brazilian culture not from the outside but from within a set of references common to Brazilians themselves. Informed by the Chicago school and Durkheimian approaches to psychology, Bastide's fieldwork on the macumbas of São Paulo and African religions in the Northeast beginning in 1943 encouraged him to propose a participation-based epistemology in light of his own initiation into candomblé.[78]

First in *Imagens do Nordeste místico em branco e preto* and then in his monographic study of candomblé, Bastide fully embraced the study of "Afro"-Brazil. Henceforth, the question of syncretism would remain central for his work, notably in his essay "Contribution à l'étude du syncrétisme catholico-fétichiste" (Contribution to the study of Catholic-fetishist syncretism), in his dissertation, and beyond.[79] However, Bastide never abandoned his work as a literary columnist and theorist, interweaving questions of aesthetics, lyricism, and mysticism into a comprehensive approach toward Brazilian culture.[80]

Prior to his travels to Brazil's Northeast, Bastide's fieldwork had been limited to short visits to religious ceremonies in São Paulo and Rio de Janeiro. A letter he wrote to Arthur Ramos in September 1940 gives a sense of this: "I passed through Rio this year. But at a sad moment: my father-in-law dying, my wife who wanted to leave for France had just embarked in Rio, the news of Italy's entry into the war forced me to hold her back... and in those moments, I did not have the courage to come see you."[81] Nonetheless, even when Bastide's movement was restricted, it did not prevent him from traveling through his readings.

Two essays in particular demonstrate quite clearly Bastide's penchant for experience through the lens of other observers: "Psicanálise do cafuné" (Psychoanalysis of cafuné), from 1940, and "Introdução ao estudo de alguns complexos afro-brasileiros" (Introduction to the study of some Afro-Brazilian complexes), from 1942.[82] In them, Bastide blended a variety of travel literature, fiction (including poetry), and social-scientific sources. Both essays are clearly products of their time, with ethnocentricities regarding gender, sexuality, and race. They nonetheless suggest themes that would permeate Bastide's later work and methodology, specifically his understandings of the transmission of culture—where possible from the bottom-up—of racial prejudice in industrial society, and of the possible cross-fertilization between sociology and psychoanalysis.[83]

Bastide's "Psicanálise do cafuné" opens with the following image, found in a nineteenth-century travel account by the Frenchman Charles Expilly:

In the hour of intense heat . . . the ladies, retired inside their residences, lay down in the lap of their favorite *mucama* [servant], delivering their head to her. The *mucama* passes her indolent fingers again and again through the thick head of hair in its luxuriant skein of silk. She delicately scratches the roots of the hair, pinching the skin with skill.[84]

Bastide was fascinated by this image that had so horrified Expilly. The *cafuné*, precisely this habit of having one's head massaged and scratched, seemed to him a distinct sociological and psychoanalytic phenomenon.

There is and was, of course, nothing specifically Brazilian about having one's head scratched. But the way that it took place, Bastide argued, was not only regionally located in the sugarcane-producing Northeast but also socially located in its class and sexual structure—that of the plantation dependent on slave labor. Rimbaud had explored how the removal of head lice had given him "another pleasure beyond the simple pleasure of cleanliness, a voluptuousness, of the sexual order."[85] Bringing the psychological to bear on the social, Bastide inquired into what the particular form of head scratching by black servants and maids on the heads of generally whiter ladies could tell about the Northeast, where African slavery had been such a prominent determinant of social structure. It might also help to explain why, according to Bastide, the Paulistas were resistant to the *cafuné*.[86]

As a sociologist, Bastide proposed to explain the transformations of the use of the gesture in different periods in Brazilian history. At first, the "African habit" was adopted for utilitarian purposes (i.e., for the removal of lice). Over time, however, it became transformed into a symbolic gesture, associated with sexual desire, as well as comfort and relaxation.[87] The collective history of Angolan slaves giving head massages to their white masters likely laid the basis for the term's penetration into the Portuguese language. To this day, Brazilians of all colors and genders give one another *cafunés*, and Bastide's analysis of bottom-up cultural transmission from historical sources provides a fascinating archaeology of the term, clearly distinct from the increasingly technical sociology practiced in the United States, at the Escola Livre in São Paulo, and even in France.

So, too, does Bastide's early analysis of "Afro-Brazilian complexes." As in "Psicanálise do cafuné," Bastide drew heavily on psychoanalysis, attempting to understand Afro-Brazilians not as objects for jurists, doctors, or anthropologists, but instead as subjects of their own reality. This approach laid the groundwork for his mature work on the question, culminating in the coauthored study with his student Florestan Fernandes, *Relações raciais entre negros e brancos em São Paulo*, to which I will return in chapter 6.

Unlike Arthur Ramos, who had studied surviving elements of Africa in the New World, Bastide emphasized the *Brazilian* aspect of Afro-Brazilian culture.[88] In this sense, his approach was much more historical than that of his predecessors, who tended to see Afro-Brazilian religions—and culture more generally—as either some kind of remnant of "primitive mentality" traceable back to Africa or form of social maladjustment, particularly in Brazilian cities. In "Introdução ao estudo de alguns complexos afro-brasileiros,"

Bastide furthered the second approach. However, instead of treating urban Afro-Brazilians as some kind of amorphous mass that emerged out of slavery (and that was therefore structurally determined by the aftermath of slavery, as Fernandes would later argue), Bastide attempted to understand individual psychology and choices. At times essentializing his subjects, Bastide's psychoanalytic approach nonetheless represented an important shift toward addressing the question of post-abolition subjectivity.

Bastide had not yet conducted the interviews or surveys of Afro-Brazilians that would come to define his later work. His argument concerning "Afro-Brazilian complexes" largely depended on secondary and literary sources. They ranged from "pathological" sources about mental illness according to race (including firsthand accounts from the states of Rio, Pernambuco, or São Paulo) to secondhand interpretations of pathologies found in writings about legal medicine and spiritism, and finally to more literary sources from post-emancipation societies.[89] Bastide drew heavily on Afro-Brazilian and African-American writers, including Luiz Gama, João da Cruz e Sousa, and Claude McKay, as privileged sources.[90] Such primary material provided insight into questions about belonging and prejudice that Bastide would reflect upon in his conversations with students, as well as with a broader public.

All of these sources provided Bastide with an argument parallel to that of Chicago-trained Donald Pierson: that post-abolition North America tended toward a regime of castes, while South America tended toward a regime of classes.[91] In Brazil, according to Bastide, "The differentiation between blacks and whites subsists . . . but does not impede social ascension."[92] Recognizing that there was a color line, but a much more fluid one than in the United States, Bastide then proceeded to ask how such a color line influenced individual psychology.

Bastide's essay argues for what would become his hallmark: that sociology and psychoanalysis can be used to mutually enrich each other. For Bastide, the individual id is produced not only by one's family experience but by social formations in which the family operates.[93] To put it simply, the basis for psychoanalysis in bourgeois Vienna could provide a methodology, but not an essential prototype, for mental categories in different places. Bastide wrote:

> The color line has an influence on the formation of complexes, even infantile ones—but this color line acts differently in different total situations of age, sex, education, and social milieu, economic or geographic, that should not, therefore, be neglected in our analysis.[94]

Nowadays, Bastide's emphasis on the multiplicity of black experience might come across as banal. However, in contrasting Brazil with the United States,

Bastide highlighted internal variation. This was not only a pluralist intervention: it was, indeed, a recognition that history—and the history of slavery and
abolition—unfolded very differently throughout the Americas.

Before we continue to travel with Bastide through his own imaginations of
Afro-Brazilian psychology, it is worth explaining that these essays, however
imperfect, were grounded in Brazilian intellectual life in a way that no other
French intellectual had attempted. Bastide relied heavily on the work of others, particularly since he had not yet conducted fieldwork. Arthur Ramos,
for example, whom Bastide addressed most specifically in the beginning of
"Introdução ao estudo de alguns complexos afro-brasileiros," had sent Bastide
his "inaugural lesson" as well as other materials on racial and cultural contact.[95]
The famed folklorist Luís da Câmara Cascudo, whom Bastide cited in the same
essay, responded to his "illustrious brother" about the different characteristics
of Brazilian folklore and their ethnic connotations.[96]

Gilberto Freyre allowed Bastide to experience the Northeast, even without
ever having been. In Freyre's article "Aspectos de um século de transição do
Nordeste" (Aspects of a century of transition in the Northeast) Bastide found
"odors of Brazil in olden times with its Negros, its mills, its traditional festivals,
its *moleques* [boys], and its street processions."[97] Freyre's *Casa-grande e senzala*
and *Sobrados e mucambos* (translated as *The Mansions and the Shanties*) were
among his most frequent citations. But it was Freyre's *Região e tradição* (Region
and tradition), which he had dedicated to Bastide, Monbeig, and Arbousse-
Bastide, that Bastide found to be at once so promising and dangerous.

For Bastide, *Região e tradição* was promising in that it allowed for "the
preservation of Brazilian values against certain dangers of European or North
American standardization"; it was dangerous in that it risked hardening,
sclerifying, and museifying Brazilian culture. Bastide wrote to Freyre:

> I, who was born in Provence, near Carmague, where the bulls and the horses
> play an analogous role to those of the "Other Northeast," where there are pas-
> toral people like in your country, where the gypsies are sacred each year—their
> mysterious Queen in the fortified church of Saintes Maries de la Mer—I feel
> very close to you. I measure the danger against which you and your friends
> must have fought . . . Do not content yourselves with winning the battle, as
> Mistral won that of our Provence. It is always necessary to keep watch so that
> others, who may seem to be your disciples—but who might not be but clumsy
> profiteers—do not come to ruin what you have achieved.[98]

Bastide had always been interested in the singularity of Southern France, distinct from any hegemonic French project centered in Paris. In São Paulo he

was remembered as a Provençal as much as a Frenchman.[99] What is interesting in his correspondence with Freyre about the Northeast is that he did not see it as some kind of unknowable other (as many in São Paulo did), but instead as a place capable of inspiring a sense of belonging analogous to his own for Southern France. The magical Northeast was like Provence, with vivid colors, odors, and feelings that, in a way, escaped the rationality of places like São Paulo.

The central problem for Bastide with Freyre's work, however, was that it risked depriving "tradition" of any kind of dynamism. This was at once a problem that limited aesthetic evolution and an urgent political one. Frédéric Mistral, to whom Bastide referred, was the first French Nobel Prize winner for literature who did not publish in French, but instead in Provençal. A number of right-wing writers, including Charles Maurras and others associated with the group Action Française, would take up Mistral's regionalism and traditionalism in the service of Pétain's traditionalist revolution.[100] Despite Bastide's concerns about the more conservative aspects of Freyre's thought, Freyre nonetheless made him want to visit the Northeast more than any other region. "It is true that I am nostalgic for the Northeast," he wrote Freyre. "I would like to see everything, to study it," regretting that "the war has prevented me."[101]

Just a few months later, Freyre sent Bastide two of his books, *Guia prático, histórico e sentimental da cidade do Recife* and his "collection of studies on the English." Bastide thanked Freyre, contrasting these "packets of poetry" from the Northeast with "our São Paulo, industrious and industrial." In them, Bastide could feel "the living land, flowering with all sorts of flavorful fruits from the tropics," and see "blots of color, Negro songs, dreams of Recife along its clear waters." All of this was, for Bastide, a "carnal delight."[102]

Freyre, in turn, was very happy to receive Bastide's letter, "so full of sensibility, penetration, and generosity." He did not know when he might come to São Paulo to commemorate his books alongside the "good friends" that he had there, but he did insist "as a friend that [Bastide] visit Pernambuco and come to this house in Santo Antonio de Apipucos."[103] Freyre and Bastide continued to correspond about a variety of subjects—including whether or not there were restrictions on people of color entering into religious societies—until Bastide finally visited in 1944.[104] In the meantime, Bastide continued to travel through literature, as he always had.

Bastide's innovative literary criticism alternates between using texts as documents (of social reality) and using them as a lens through which to explore how form thematizes more abstract aesthetic and identitarian problems. Marxism aside, it is reminiscent of some of Theodor Adorno's work.[105] Two texts saliently evidence this: "Incorporação da poesia africana à poesia brasileira" (Incorporation of African poetry into Brazilian poetry), a synthesis of Bastide's work on Afro-Brazilian poets such as João da Cruz e Sousa and Antônio Gonçalves Dias, and "Machado de Assis, paisagista" (Machado de Assis: Landscape painter).[106]

Bastide's "Incorporação da poesia africana à poesia brasileira" provides a panorama of "African" poetry in Brazil from the colonial period through the nineteenth century and into the 1940s. Capacious in his approach, Bastide included white Brazilian writers who had incorporated African or Afro-Brazilian characters in their poetry, Afro-Brazilian poets themselves, and African rhythms, tones, or pronunciations that entered into poetry—in sum, anything in Brazilian poetry referencing or having to do with Africa. Bastide traced four distinct periods in the history of this "African" incorporation into Brazilian poetry. The first was of exoticism, in which exceptional and mythical Africans, especially warriors, became part of the pantheon of Brazilian independence. This genre flourished in the early nineteenth century, giving way to a period in which Africans were romanticized for their "docility, resignation, and suffering."[107] In the third period, beginning in the late nineteenth century, sentimentalism was cast aside, allowing Afro-Brazilian poetry to finally become social, best captured by Castro Alves.[108] This poetry was "Hugoano" (referring to Victor Hugo), in that it demanded social change, particularly abolition. In the final stage, Bastide argued, the social was transformed through symbolism, free verse, and the "the discovery of unprecedented lyricism."[109] Such poetry, according to Bastide, incorporated the more profound elements of African culture, especially its rhythm and aesthetics.

For Bastide, the history of "African" poetry in Brazil was at once internal and external. Its flourishing was certainly not possible under slavery and still not during the First Republic, where Africanness was seen as an obstacle to the Brazilian nation.[110] Nor was it possible in an era in which Parnassian poetry and naturalism dominated. For as long as the external "real" predominated over the internal and metaphysical real, according to Bastide, African poetry could not penetrate fully. Indeed, symbolism needed "to first break Parnassian norms" for "the poetry of Africa [to] flourish in Brazil."[111]

This poetry of Africa, however, had Brazilian specificities. At least since Pablo Picasso's African Period and the Harlem Renaissance, black figures and artists had emerged in a global context, influencing artists in Brazil. But with "Europe chanting the pure Negro" and "America chanting the Westernized Negro," Brazil preferred to chant "the flavorful moment of syncretism and of metamorphosis."[112] Bastide considered that "the Afro-Brazilian is first jerked away from the outside, by way of his folklore and ethnography"; over time, however, "The poet allows himself to elevate himself in his song, the Negro's own song."[113] Accordingly, "The work of transfusion has concluded; the blood of the man of color already flows in the veins of Brazilian poetry."[114] For Bastide, the final stage of Brazilian poetry had been reached: the triumph of African incorporation had ended the dialectic.

Bastide gave critical attention to Afro-Brazilian poets such as Cruz e Sousa. But while he increasingly sought to understand Afro-Brazilian poets on their own terms, he also sought to consider them within a broader pantheon of Brazilian writers. Bastide's Afro-Brazilian literary criticism was part and parcel of his criticism of more widely recognized writers such as Manuel Bandeira, Oswald de Andrade, Mário de Andrade, and Carlos Drummond de Andrade. With the last two, he was in epistolary, if not always face-to-face, contact.[115]

Bastide's intimacy with Brazilian literary culture can be seen in his essay on Machado de Assis as a "landscape painter," in which he deconstructed the arguments of Machado's posthumous critics. Since Sílvio Romero's polemic against Machado at the end of the nineteenth century, many critics considered Machado "anti-Brazilian."[116] Another of Machado's detractors, Aurélio Buarque de Holanda, claimed that "he lacked . . . a feeling . . . for the land, his landscape, and his people"; Cassiano Ricardo called him a "great Brazilian writer of an anti-Brazilian spirit."[117] For Bastide, Machado's use of landscape permeated his work, despite its surface-level absence. Machado "did not permit descriptions for entertainment, truly artificial adornments in books"— that is to say, description that did not somehow develop his characters or move the story forward.[118] Instead, he preferred to represent nature as a character with a specific role.

In Machado, Bastide wrote, "landscape must have its own signification and finality that serve to facilitate the comprehension of men." It must not be "a mere rigid painting."[119] In this sense, nature or landscape would never be the center of any given segment of prose. Bastide considered nature in Machado's writings to be a device that allowed for the suppression of the "interval that separated characters"; it "mixed in with them . . . integrating itself in the dough with which he constructs the heroines of his novels."[120]

Bastide refused to seriously consider the criticisms of Machado as "anti-Brazilian" insofar as they were based on landscape. Such nationalist criticisms tended to reify Brazil as an essentially timeless, tropical place, and risked subjecting human agency and psychology to environmental and ethnic determinism. Machado's exploration of the interior life of Brazilians incorporates landscape, but it does so subtly, leaving space for more universal themes. For this reason, the late Antonio Candido hailed Bastide's "Machado de Assis, paisagista"; Bastide had effectively demonstrated that Brazil was much more than its environment, even if it played a significant role in the country's development.[121]

Bastide's literary criticism during the war and after allowed him to continue his immersion in different parts of the country, even when he was unable to travel outside São Paulo. What is clear in his correspondence is the extent to which Brazilian authors appreciated his readings. As one example, a lesser-known poet from Pernambuco, Ascenso Ferreira, wrote Bastide to thank him for his "interpretation of the human meaning of my poetics"—that no Brazilian critic had yet to perceive.[122] According to Ferreira, Bastide "represent[ed] the French spirit crystalized in the chairs of the Sorbonne, which will always be the most important cultural center of the world!"[123] Ferreira was clearly charmed by the fact that a French university professor had written about his poetry in the first place, independent of Bastide's interpretation. Consciously or not, Bastide benefited from his Frenchness in his role as a literary critic. Still, his warm reception by Brazilian writers and intellectuals demonstrates that their relationships were most often reciprocal.

Since 1938, when he arrived in Brazil, Bastide looked forward to traveling to the Brazilian Northeast, especially the two colonial cities of Salvador and Recife. But time and time again, for professional, familial, or geopolitical reasons, he was prevented from doing so. This led him, as I have demonstrated, to approach African cultures through a variety of lenses, the most important of which were literature and sociological and anthropological writings by Brazilian intellectuals. Finally, in 1943–44, he made an extended trip over USP's summer vacation. It was the precondition for him to get in "personal contact with African religions"—and most especially the candomblés of Bahia and Xango of Recife.[124]

Roberto Motta has demonstrated how such fieldwork brought about "a thematic, theoretical, and methodological revolution" in Bastide's work.[125] The results of his initial fieldwork can be seen in several articles, many of them adapted for publication in *Imagens do Nordeste místico em branco e preto* and other studies closer to home, on the macumba of São Paulo.[126] They are also present in Bastide's first scholarly work on candomblé, including "O Cerimonial da polidez" (The politeness ceremonial) and "O Lundum do Padre" (roughly, "the priest lundu"), as well as in his *Estudos Afro-brasileiros* (1973), recently re-published and made more widely available in *Poètes et dieux*.[127]

Bastide, the first to recognize the superficial nature of his fieldwork, wrote Arthur Ramos that he would need "to live there [in Bahia] longer [and] penetrate more deeply."[128] In any case, he had found a religious community that would continually inspire him from that moment on. "Candomblé philosophy," he wrote, "is not a barbarian philosophy, but a subtle thought system, that we have not entirely deciphered."[129]

Bastide was certainly not the first anthropologist or sociologist to sympathize with and humanize his subjects, in turn valorizing their cosmologies. By the time he wrote the above words, for example, he had read Marcel Griaule's work on the Dogon civilization. Nonetheless, Bastide's intervention in seeing candomblé as "normal" rather than as a pathological phenomenon was quite significant for its time. "One must judge this religion, not by way of the concepts of White Men," he wrote, "but by trying to penetrate into the souls of the faithful, looking to think as they think."[130]

Surely Bastide's Christianity was part of the reason that he so embraced candomblé. The *orixás*, sort of demigods, all have associations with Christian saints—a fact that Bastide would come to understand as evidence not of the Christianization of candomblé but of a "a system of functional equivalents" shared between the two religions.[131] For example, in Rio de Janeiro the *orixá* Oxóssi has a functional equivalent in Saint Sebastian. Because of his own religious background, Bastide was better inclined to understand faith and abandonment of rationality than previous researchers, who had approached candomblé from a clinical perspective. In mysticism, however, Bastide found African and Christian practices to be diametrically opposed:

> Whereas the latter moves toward the fusion of the soul into God—by way of a slow ascent through the darkness of the senses and of the spirit—the other consists in a descent of the gods that come to possess the soul. As a consequence, it [African mysticism] consists in passing from the supernatural to the natural.[132]

Bastide's very description of candomblé possession seemed to contradict the idea that there was anything particularly mystical about it. But it also served to make possession, often considered by outsiders as a pathology, equivalent to Christian mysticism, which Bastide valued highly. Bastide believed that once he had moved beyond superficial descriptions of the "fetishist religion of Bahia," he could begin to enter candomblé spirituality on its own terms. This would require a monograph on "all of the *terreiros*, at least the most traditional ones."[133]

What sparked Bastide's interest most in his travels in Bahia was the representation that Bahians made of Africa. Candomblé signified the presence of Africa in Brazilian culture par excellence.[134] For Bastide, however, Africa's presence was much more ubiquitous. Contrasting black Bahians to North Americans, he claimed, "Africa, here, is a pride and a fidelity; no inferiority complex, but the intuition to conserve a heritage of beauty and goodness, the will to not let oneself be lost in Brazilian civilization, but to integrate into this civilization so as to enrich it."[135]

After visiting Bahia, Bastide continued to Recife, "the Venice of Brazil."[136] There Bastide visited Freyre at his house in Apipucos, a once-rural area that is now a *bairro* (neighborhood) of Recife. But if Bastide was grateful for Freyre's invitation and for their conversations, Recife did not win him over in the same way that Salvador had. It was simply not the "mystical" place that Bastide had hoped it might be. In *Imagens do Nordeste místico*, Bastide wrote that in Recife the "Negro . . . is proletarized, caught in the grind of hours, machines, and industries."[137] Surely, Freyre's description from *Sobrados e mucambos* must have seemed dated, if not inaccurate from the beginning. In any case, the "proletarized" black worker to whom Bastide referred hardly echoed Freyre's description of the attenuated "antagonisms of class and race" that "formed an average, a middle, a mixed Brazilian contemporanization of lifestyles [and] of cultural standards."[138]

Although Bastide very much enjoyed seeing Afro-Brazilian religious communities and taking part in *carnaval*, for him the city lacked the *joie d'esprit* that candomblé requires.[139] Nonetheless, Recife and Salvador were part of a broader phenomenon that Bastide admired in a very Freyrian way: the "harmony" of races. The "typical civilization" of the Northeast, according to Bastide in 1944, was one in which "all social classes and all colors [join in] the same cadence, musically cementing the communion of Brazilian hearts."[140]

In the Northeast, Bastide had finally made it to a region that would sustain his interest for the years to come. Upon his return to São Paulo, Bastide started to practically envision his dissertation on candomblé, publishing his first ethnographic article on the subject.[141] He also reinforced his contacts with the religious communities he had visited, who would provide him with information from a distance until his next visit. Henceforth people such as Askhelão de Abreu, president of the Sastria Lordes *terreiro* in Salvador, would occupy as much of his time and correspondence as the writers and intellectuals with whom he had exchanged previously.[142]

Much to Bastide's chagrin, however, the different worlds in which he circulated were not entirely mutually intelligible. During the previous years, he had published on sociological theory, literary criticism, and Afro-Brazilian themes, shifting between his roles as public intellectual and university professor. By 1944, times had changed. USP was becoming more specialized, and he had embarked on a doctorate.

When Bastide asked Mário de Andrade to be part of an examining committee at USP, Mário graciously refused, admitting, "It would be intolerable for me, considering my moral conception of culture, to see myself in an examining committee at the University."[143] Mário, who was then suffering from severe depression in Rio de Janeiro, feared he was too much of an amateur. He wrote: "If I had the levity to sit down in the examination bench of the University, in disciplines in which I recognize myself amateur, afterward I would not have any more courage to look at myself in the mirror. These oppressive mirrors that I invoked in my verses, just as Cruz e Sousa invoked, and that will possibly denounce miscegenation as much as blood."[144] Mário's feelings of guilt for not having further specialized in ethnology, as well as his recognition of his own problems with being a mulatto, surely affected Bastide, especially after Mário's death just months later. Seeing a friend feel so "denounced" for his mixed race may have been the beginning of the undoing of Bastide's notions of racial harmony. Some years later, he would become more explicit, writing, "Miscegenation is not, contrary to what is [often] claimed, the index of the absence of prejudice, but can perfectly coexist with it."[145]

During the war, Bastide continued to cultivate his signature hybrid approach, applying it to a wide range of subjects. Mixing social-historical and ethnographic research, literary criticism with the interrogation of non-traditional "intellectual" sources (the black press, Afro-Brazilian religions, and folklore), Bastide sought to arrive at the most total of Brazilian experiences: ethnic and religious syncretism. In the next two chapters, we will see how this continued to develop in *Le candomblé de Bahia* (The candomble of Bahia) and *Les religions africaines au Brésil* (The African religions of Brazil). For now, however, it is worth pausing to look at the properly Atlantic aspects of Braudel's work and Brazil's place within it.

BRAUDEL, THE *LONGUE DURÉE*, AND THE OPENING OF THE MEDITERRANEAN

In your place, I would be very preoccupied with not neglecting the continent discovered by Alvarez Cabral. We need to not lose contact (I emphasize this) . . . You would become at once Mediterranean and Brazilian. We need both.

Febvre to Braudel, 1942[146]

Fernand Braudel, as an officer imprisoned by the Nazis, spent much of the war thinking, writing, and testing out his ideas while many of his fellow compatriots struggled with day-to-day existence. Surely distraught at the collapse of France, Braudel was also separated from his family and his belongings, including his notes and books. However, compared to most of his colleagues— except, of course, the Vichy collaborators—he had greater ability to continue his work, in his case on what would become his 1,600-page magnum opus, *The Mediterranean and the Mediterranean World in the Age of Philip II*.

There is something heroic and even mythical about Braudel having written parts of his dissertation in captivity.[147] While by no means attempting to take away from Braudel's merits, this section considers his intellectual production during the war in its broader social ecology. For indeed, if it is amazing that Braudel produced his first great work in prison, he was neither the first to do so (consider, for example, Antonio Gramsci, with *Prison Notebooks*; Graciliano Ramos, with *Memórias do cárcere*; or, perhaps Braudel's favorite, Miguel Cervantes), nor was he alone in his endeavor.

Throughout his time in prison, Braudel corresponded regularly with his advisor Lucien Febvre about different drafts.[148] He also gave courses to fellow French prisoners, as French officers in German prisons had the autonomy to establish educational institutions and even to provide degrees. As far as war-torn Western Europe was concerned, the prisons in which Braudel lived were not such unfavorable places to continue intellectual work, particularly for someone who refused collaboration with the Nazis.[149] Furthermore, Braudel had access to German libraries at Lübeck and Mainz and permission to receive outside material, including several books that Febvre sent him.[150]

Braudel claimed that if it had not been for his captivity, he "would have written an entirely different book."[151] It is clear that he made up for the challenges of research with a renewed intellectual and spiritual purpose that insulated him from the outside world. During this period, if we take him at his word, Braudel's view of history took on "its definitive form."[152] Rejecting the traditional history of events, Braudel focused on longer periods of historical time, what he called "conjunctures" and the *longue durée*, or long duration. "In part," he claimed, this was, "the only existential response to the tragic times that I was going through. All of the events that bombarded us from the radio and in the newspapers . . . It was necessary to go beyond them, to reject them, to deny them . . . to believe that history, destiny, were written at a much deeper level, to choose the observatory of long periods of time."[153] In this sense, Braudel was not simply taking refuge in the past, but in a specific view of the past in which the role of events, good and bad, faded in comparison to geography and broader structural processes. This was tantamount to recognizing that the moment he was living through—the tides of war, Nazi Germany, and Vichy—was merely temporary.

Braudel's *Mediterranean*, which laid the cornerstone for his later work, proved highly influential in the historical profession for at least two reasons: it established a framework for examining multiple temporalities and contributed to rethinking history's relationship to the other social sciences. Braudel divided *Mediterranean* into three parts, dealing with the *longue durée*, the conjuncture, and the event, respectively, continuing *Annales*' shift away from political history and its focus on events. If Braudel's most recognizable contribution, then and now, was his conceptualization of long duration, in what follows I consider the dynamic nature of the conjuncture, departing from the timeless, geographical Mediterranean. I argue that Brazil, and Latin America more generally, encouraged Braudel to rethink the Mediterranean's place in the sixteenth- and seventeenth-century world in the context of an expanding global economy.

Latin America's place in Braudel's understanding of the conjuncture is most evident in the second part of *Mediterranean*, "Collective Destinies and General Trends," and in fragments of its first drafts, published as "L'histoire, mesure du monde" (History, measure of the world).[154] The importance of Latin America for his masterpiece becomes even clearer upon a close analysis of Braudel's review of Gilberto Freyre's work and his correspondence with Caio Prado Jr.[155] Building off of these sources and drawing them back to Braudel's intellectual experience in the 1930s, this section posits Latin America as a continuing source of inspiration for Braudel throughout World War II.

However far away Brazil may have been, it continued to serve as an experiential and intellectual reference for Braudel's work—namely, in thinking about the importance of transatlantic trade in opening up the Mediterranean Sea or in recalling everyday life at the peripheries of capitalism. Braudel's Brazilian years, in this sense, represented not only an intellectual opening that allowed him to better understand historical conjunctures but also an experience of seeing the past before his own eyes. When Braudel visited Salvador along "the Bahian Mediterranean" in 1937, he claimed to better see the inner workings of port cities such as Genoa and Venice in the sixteenth and seventeenth centuries.[156] These cities were integrated into both international capital markets and their adjacent countrysides, which supplied them with food, goods, and consumers.

Unlike some of his colleagues who went to Brazil, like Monbeig and Bastide, Braudel never fully shifted the center of his scholarly attention to Latin America. The mass of European documentation that he brought with him to Brazil occupied his research during the years he spent there. (Remember, he had to rent out an additional hotel room in São Paulo for his archival material.) It is no surprise, therefore, that the primary sources for Braudel's dissertation were overwhelmingly European—and most specifically, Spanish, French, and Italian. But if Braudel's *Mediterranean* was always primarily a European history, it would become a foundational text for Atlantic and World History because of its embrace of spatial expansiveness.[157] In what follows, I aim to shed new light on how Braudel's firsthand experience in and knowledge of Brazil allowed him to make broader claims about structural phenomena, including international trade, prices, and the world economy.

In his *Mediterranean*, Braudel held steadfastly to the very importance of the Mediterranean Sea and its wider commercial-geographical region, against the claims of a variety of economists, sociologists, and historians who argued for its decline in the sixteenth century. American historian Earl Hamilton had argued two decades prior that the discovery of the Americas and the arrival of the mineral riches that they offered Europe "precipitated one of the greatest price revolutions occurring on a specie basis in modern times, if not in all of history."[158] According to Hamilton, this price revolution helped Europe to turn the corner after a century of declining prices that "handicapped business enterprise."[159] Rejecting such claims, Braudel supported the idea that "the European conjuncture determined everything from afar"; after all, he claimed, "in the heart of European countries, the price revolution started before Christopher Columbus."[160]

Furthermore, Braudel argued that the primacy of the Mediterranean persisted much longer than commonly thought. Its defeat had not yet been "consummated" at the beginning of the seventeenth century, "one hundred years after the date that the majority of general histories officially give as that of the death of the old queen, dethroned by the new king of the world: the Ocean."[161] To historians who overemphasized the emergence of England as an oceanic power (whose defeat of the Spanish Armada would have signaled the decline of the Mediterranean), Braudel responded that "it is not on the new routes of the world's Seven Seas, but instead in the Mediterranean, that English supremacy was constructed, at its start."[162]

Nonetheless, one of Braudel's most important contributions in part 2 of *The Mediterranean* was to demonstrate how gold and silver coming from the Americas entered into the Mediterranean economy and how it affected prices.[163] Braudel, in many ways, continued the work of Earl Hamilton, cited above.[164] Braudel, his advisor Febvre, and the group surrounding *Annales* were especially attentive to Hamilton's work, reviewing some of the articles that would make up his 1934 classic *American Treasure and the Price Revolution in Spain, 1501–1650*. Febvre analyzed the state of the field of price-history research, emphasizing the role of sociologist François Simiand in France and Earl Hamilton for studies of Spain;[165] he promised to keep *Annales'* readers abreast of research into price history and wrote a short introduction to Henri Hauser's article on the International Scientific Committee on Price History, which was financed by the Rockefeller Foundation and led by Sir William Beveridge of the London School of Economics;[166] and most importantly, he reviewed Hamilton's article "American Treasure and Andalusian Prices, 1503–1660," in 1931.[167]

Braudel, who had met Hamilton at the Spanish archives in Simancas, in 1928, followed suit, reviewing the latter's article on monetary inflation in Castille just months later.[168] He called it first-class, "de tout premier ordre."[169] However, according to Braudel, Hamilton tended to see Spain as a monolithic entity. In this sense, Spain would have been both the principal beneficiary of the imports from its empire and the most negatively affected by its own excesses. Braudel, eschewing a national perspective, instead emphasized the role of Genoese bankers as early capitalists.[170] They negotiated the terms by which precious metals imported into Spain were prospected, shipped, distributed, and used as a basis for larger commercial transactions.

The Iberian Peninsula may have been the center of the Spanish Empire, the greatest world power in the sixteenth century and the first empire where the sun never set. However, it was never really the center of capitalist development. Spain's failure to industrialize was not, as some might argue, because of Spain's lack of a Protestant ethic or an inherent indisposition toward capitalism.[171] For Braudel it was instead because of how Spain's finances, money, and debt were managed. Seville, the symbol of Spanish wealth from the Americas, had to deal directly with Genoa, which served as its bank and therefore commercial intermediary with the New World.[172] He clarified: "The Peninsula, insufficiently urbanized, disposes only of foreign intermediaries, whose real interests lie with their own countries, for the hard work of commerce. However, they play a necessary role, as in this or that South American country today, or rather, of yesterday (1939)."[173] Braudel repeatedly criticized Philip II of Spain for not having established a national bank, which could have helped to keep Spanish profits in the Iberian Peninsula. In the passage just quoted, however, Braudel argued for a more demographic understanding of dependency: the insufficient urbanization (and one could say workforce specialization) of export economies meant that they often had to rely on foreigners to conduct their business: "Philip II seems to me to have often been in the position of a South American government of the nineteenth century, rich in products, its mines, or its plantations, but disarmed just as much vis-à-vis international finance. Such a government was free to get angry, even to strike back, but then it would have to submit, delivering its resources, its command posts, and be 'understanding.'"[174]

Beyond this demographic factor was a geographical and commercial one. Italy lay at the crossroads between the Mediterranean and Germany, as well as much of Northern Europe. For this reason, it ensured Spanish payments to the North, especially to the Spanish Netherlands and its financial center, Antwerp. (France, the most direct route to Northern Europe, was frequently at odds and even at war with Spain during the sixteenth century, whereas the allied Habsburgs in the Germanic states offered a more reliable path.) Furthermore, Italian towns and cities benefited directly as middlemen, extracting the surplus value of American silver, which became increasingly valuable as it made its way East, first to the Levant, then to Persia, and all the way to China. In the period 1557–1627, Braudel wrote, "In every direction, Genoese capitalism quickly established its primacy." It was indeed "the Genoese century."[175]

Spain as a whole was the richest country in the Mediterranean during the reign of Philip II, but it remained overwhelmingly agrarian. Two urban centers of the Mediterranean in particular—first Venice, then Genoa—served as the veritable banks and commercial entrepôts for polities that were territorially richer and much more powerful than they were.[176] Venice and Genoa, alongside Milan and Florence, formed "a tight urban quadrilateral" that served as the Mediterranean's economic center. They benefited from "the imperatives of large-scale, long-distance commerce," building upon the forces unleashed by the accumulation of capital to expand and revolutionize their textile industries.[177] Meanwhile other places, such as Sicily, this "sort of Canada or Argentina of the sixteenth century,"[178] furnished wheat and other agricultural goods such as wine and olives for the urbanized centers. Capitalist cities and their surroundings, then and now, rarely produced either sufficient food or raw materials to sustain themselves.

When compared to Italy, Portugal and the Atlantic are far from central to *The Mediterranean*. Braudel's anecdotal use of explorers and chroniclers such as Jean de Léry demonstrates this clearly.[179] But if Braudel decided not to follow closely Febvre's advice to be both "Mediterranean and Brazilian," he nonetheless considered the South Atlantic as an important closure to his argument about the long sixteenth century.

Unlike Hamilton, who saw Spanish minerals as radically altering European economic development, Braudel gestured toward the seventeenth century and the arrival of Brazilian gold via Portugal as one of the primary factors in the Mediterranean's decline. This is not to say that Portugal or Brazil became the center of capitalist development, but rather, that they served as part and parcel of the shift from the Mediterranean to the Atlantic. The Atlantic, according to Braudel, had already become "the center of the Earth" in the time of Philip II.[180] That said, it would have to wait until the following century to entirely dethrone the Mediterranean.

In this sense, the defeat of the Genoese represented not "the bankruptcy of finance or paper . . . but the expansion of another kind of capitalism favored by a geographical revolution, signaled by the discovery of America and that would take more than a century to be accomplished."[181] To put it in the words of Caio Prado Jr., who published his principal work, *Formação do Brasil contemporâneo*, during Braudel's internment, this new world economic order served to "dislocate the commercial primacy of the central territories of the continent, through which the old route passed, to those that form the oceanic façade: Holland, England, Normandy, Brittany, and the Iberian Peninsula."[182]

"The first boom of Brazilian gold," Braudel claimed, citing Brazilian industrialist and economist Roberto Simonsen, marked the end of a "conjuncture of silver" centered in Spain and Genoa.[183] With the arrival of Brazilian gold in Lisbon, England, and other places in Europe in the late seventeenth century, the Mediterranean would no longer find itself at the "center of this gold inflation, as it had for so long been at the center of silver inflation."[184] At least part of this process of decentering Spain's Mediterranean, according to Braudel, was the flourishing of "Jewish" capitalists, many of whom had converted to Christianity after having been deported from Spain during the Inquisition—and who found in Portugal and its empire a more welcoming home.[185]

Braudel, who we must remember had lived at length in Algeria, manifested his antipathy throughout *The Mediterranean* for the Arabs and Moriscos (Iberian Muslims converted to Christianity) who had been deported from Spain.[186] He saw them as "inassimilable" and therefore antithetical to Western civilization.[187] Nonetheless, World War II and the excesses of European eugenics left him fascinated with Gilberto Freyre and his ideas of racial mixing. Braudel cited Freyre about Portugal serving as a kind of bi-continent, bridging the Mediterranean and North Africa[188] and enriching Spanish culture, arts, and cuisine.[189]

The extent to which Braudel had read Freyre in Brazil remains a mystery, but by World War II his engagement became clear. Febvre, who had insisted on Braudel being both "Mediterranean and Brazilian," was surely responsible for sending several of Freyre's books to Braudel in prison. These served Braudel for his extended review of Freyre's work, published in *Mélanges d'histoire sociale*, Febvre's continuation of *Annales* under a new name during the war.[190] If not through Braudel himself, Febvre had become aware of Freyre's importance through his colleagues. Monbeig, for example, wrote him in 1940: "There is a sociologist in Brazil with the name Gilberto Freyre, who writes good things on the Northeast. Would *Annales* possibly accept several articles by him?"[191]

Braudel's review "À travers un continent d'histoire: Le Brésil et l'oeuvre de Gilberto Freyre" (Across a continent of history: Brazil and the oeuvre of Gilberto Freyre) suggests Freyre's importance for Braudel's thinking about a number of questions. The first is the historical Atlantic or Atlantic World, particularly its role in the decentering of the Mediterranean with the rise of transoceanic trade. The second is Freyre's methodological framework for doing social history, analyzed at length by Peter Burke.[192] And finally, Freyre's work seems to have offered Braudel a kind of New World utopia in contrast to his experiences of social and racial discrimination in Algeria and now Nazi-occupied Europe.

Two groups that appear throughout Freyre's works are the Dutch, who controlled his part of Brazil (Pernambuco) from 1630 to 1654, and New Christians, or marranos (Christianized Jews of medieval Spain), many of whom had their origins in Spain or Portugal. Through reading Freyre, Braudel saw how the Brazilian Northeast—this "civilization of sugar"—contributed to "the putting into place of European capitalism, that of Flanders and Holland."[193] For Braudel, this was the legacy of the New Christians—those converted Jews, "mostly Sephardic, who came from the Iberian world directly or by way of

Holland, England, or Hamburg."[194] Although Braudel criticized Freyre for not focusing enough on New Christians, it was Freyre who had brought them to Braudel's attention in the first place.

Freyre had argued that however white a Brazilian was, he or she could not deny the influence of his or her black heritage.[195] Braudel, horrified by the anti-Semitic, xenophobic, and white-nationalist sentiment in Europe, was particularly sensitive to this kind of argumentation about racial mixing. He embraced Freyre's emphasis, for example, on understanding the role of blacks in the "difficult construction of Brazil, where they did much more than the [Amer-]Indian, and even as much as the Portuguese," as well as mixed bloods of the empire—"lawyers, doctors, politicians, and sometimes writers of talent."[196] Furthermore, Braudel found little problem with Freyre's dismissal of indigenous culture, perhaps because of his own belief that the *indigènes* impeded progress in Algeria.[197]

One of Freyre's central (and now most infamous) claims was that Brazilian slavery was gentler and more humane than that of other countries, particularly the United States. According to Freyre, even if there remained a social and racial difference between masters and slaves, the considerable presence of miscegenation in Brazil meant that the color line proved less rigid, particularly for the manumitted and their descendants. In 1943, Braudel "wanted very much to believe that . . . this sexual promiscuity, this polygamy . . . will have contributed, as Gilberto Freyre claims, to soften the inevitable conflict between the *senzala* [slave's quarters] and the *Casa Grande* [Master's house], to 'democratize' morals and create—this time without possible refutation—a mixed race of which future generations should largely bear fruit."[198] Whether or not Braudel considered Freyre's model of race relations to be desirable or even possible outside Brazil, he nonetheless found it compelling in the heyday of a war, racial and religious discrimination, and ultimately ethnic cleansing in Europe. Such an optimistic discourse about Latin America will return in the next two chapters, especially with regard to African decolonization.

For now, it is worth reiterating that, however much Braudel dedicated himself during the war years to the Mediterranean Sea, he nonetheless found in Latin America a useful complement to his intellectual project. By helping Braudel to conceive of the Mediterranean in its Atlantic dimensions, South America also brought closure to Braudel's *Mediterranean*. Spain and Portugal's American empires served to clarify Braudel's periodizations, his understandings of the world economy, and, at certain key moments, his conceptions of historical time more generally. For Braudel, the empires also represented the emergence of new models of social and ethnic relations that were more harmonious than those in Spain during the sixteenth century or in Europe in the middle of the twentieth.

LÉVI-STRAUSS, CULTURAL ANTHROPOLOGY, AND
THE MODELING OF KINSHIP STRUCTURES

Claude Lévi-Strauss's public wartime activities, whether as part of the Latin America Center at the New School or Free France, serve as important reminders of the persistence of Brazil in his trajectory. However, as compared to Monbeig, Bastide, and Braudel, who continued to engage with the Brazilian social sciences, Lévi-Strauss's dissertation provides us with a kind of puzzle: why were Brazil and Brazilian Indians so notably absent from *The Elementary Structures of Kinship*? In this section, I argue that however far Brazilian thinkers may have been from Lévi-Strauss's models of "structure," the Brazilian Indians among whom he had spent time in the 1930s were invaluable for the term's conceptualization.

The Elementary Structures of Kinship now stands as a classic in the field of anthropology.[199] In the decades following its initial publication, in 1949, its influence extended well beyond anthropology, making waves in philosophy, literature, and the social sciences in general. Simone de Beauvoir called it a resounding awakening ("un éclatant réveil") and insisted that its audience was not principally made up of specialists; instead, she continued, *The Elementary Structures* dealt with "the mystery of society in its entirety, the mystery of man."[200] Lévi-Strauss's fame only grew with the later publication of the two volumes of *Structural Anthropology*—collections of essays that offered a new method: structuralism.[201] Convinced of the value of *The Elementary Structures* while he was writing it in New York, Lévi-Strauss promised his advisors Paul Rivet and Marcel Mauss that he was preparing a social-scientific monument to bring back to postwar France.

In what follows, I dissect this massive, specialized work, examining the conditions of possibility for its realization. This should complement scholarship that considers Lévi-Strauss's contributions to kinship studies, all while further contextualizing his oeuvre during the wartime exile that followed his Brazilian years.[202] Lévi-Strauss's specific arguments about "culture"—and, of course, the "structures" upon which it is based—evidence his appropriation of the language, concepts, and themes of social science outside France. This scientific and cultural capital would serve an important purpose in the construction of *The Elementary Structures*.

Brazil and Brazilian indigenous peoples had allowed Lévi-Strauss to consolidate his reputation as an anthropologist, a precondition for his recruitment in the US. Just months after his arrival there in 1941, Alfred Métraux wrote to Julian Steward at the Smithsonian Institution about Lévi-Strauss. (Steward was then organizing what would become the seven-volume *Handbook of South American Indians*.) Métraux was clear: "We shouldn't lose the opportunity of using the services of a man who is the only one in the world who knows the Indians of western Brazil."[203] Although Lévi-Strauss's contribution to the *Handbook* would only see publication in 1948, during the war years he published articles on "The Social Use of Kinship Terms among Brazilian Indians," "On Dual Organization in South America," and "Guerre et commerce chez les Indiens de l'Amérique du Sud" (War and commerce among Indians of South America), among other topics.[204] Only once Lévi-Strauss had earned recognition as an anthropologist of South American Indians could he stray from the particular and return to the universal, making broad statements about kinship, nature, and culture that largely transcended his fieldwork.

Lévi-Strauss's wartime experience not only removed him from French ethnography in its "infancy" but also led him into the heart of American anthropology.[205] He frequently saw Franz Boas at Columbia University and also Métraux, who passed through New York City regularly.[206] His participation in the *Handbook of South American Indians* formalized his entry into a network of anthropologists that included Alfred Kroeber and Robert Lowie, in addition to Ralph Linton, Ruth Benedict, and Margaret Mead—by then prominent public figures.[207] Unlike anthropologists and sociologists in France, in New York Lévi-Strauss had extended access to libraries during his formative years.

Whereas so many of his generation were fleeing, hiding, or fighting, Lévi-Strauss spent his days at the New York Public Library, reading and taking notes on anthropological literature with which his contemporaries in France were almost entirely unfamiliar. This literature transformed his thinking. He wrote to Rivet, then in Mexico, to inform him of how and why his dissertation, originally about "the sociology of Mato Grosso," had become something much more ambitious. It all began when he set out to write a book on incest. This "little book," he explained,

> transformed into a work of considerable dimensions that seems to me more appropriate as a dissertation, also for the intellectual needs of France the day after victory. During this past year, I have committed myself to putting together everything that had been written on family organization in England and the United States (in Australia, too) during the last ten years. I present these results in a systematic publication that is not a compilation, because I insist on surpassing the current positions and in defining what could be—if I am not too ambitious [to say]—the position of the French school of tomorrow.[208]

Instead of continuing in the vein of a specialized monograph on Brazilian Indians, Lévi-Strauss decided to do something much more "systematic." By synthesizing and "surpassing the current positions" of ten years of publications in the English-speaking scientific community, he could define or at least help to define "the French school of tomorrow." Lévi-Strauss sought to present "a system of the forms of kinship." In this way, it was not to be a "sociology according to old formulas" (specifically those of Edward Westermarck or Durkheim), but instead a "treatise of logic applied to certain primitive institutions."[209]

To explain his treatise of logic, Lévi-Strauss assured Rivet that he was building upon the new science of linguistics rather than philosophy. Inspired by how phonology had given linguistics a new universal language, he sought to do the same in anthropology with structures. It is in this sense that his famed friendship with Roman Jakobson, a Russian exile associated with the Prague school of linguistics, was so important. But even prior to Lévi-Strauss's theoretical maturity and collaboration with Jakobson's journal *Word*, the two wrote each other specifically about Lévi-Strauss's work on indigenous languages and Karl von den Steinen's *Durch Central-Brasilien* (Through Central Brazil).[210]

Rivet's response to Lévi-Strauss must have been skeptical, because Lévi-Strauss's subsequent letter to him was highly defensive.[211] (We should remember that Rivet emphasized fieldwork and physical anthropology in his own work and teaching.) Lévi-Strauss regretted that it "it is difficult to explain to you, even in a long letter, the exact nature of my undertaking."[212] He nonetheless tried his best, reiterating his claims of the importance of bringing a synthetic work back to France, as well as emphasizing the empirical basis for it: 1,500 books and articles that he had scrutinized and analyzed during his time in New York.

> I have the feeling ... that I am constructing a "great book." If I can bring it back to liberated France, young anthropologists and sociologists will find in it a basis that will place them on equal footing with their foreign colleagues. They will not only know everything that has been done during these past years in other countries, but perhaps more. Because I hope, in certain domains at least, to have accomplished for primitive sociology several decisive steps forward. And if I can contribute, in my specialty, to make it so that there is, at war's end, a young, bold, and innovative French science—that will have assimilated all recent contributions, and at times, surpassed them—I think that I will have well used my years in exile.[213]

Lévi-Strauss insisted with Rivet that his work was "positive," rather than philosophical. He envisioned positive research based upon facts, however, not as the kind of case study common to American anthropology, but instead as a much more general synthesis.

A monograph on a given people, such as the Nambicuara, would not give him such an opportunity. *The Elementary Structures* would, much like Durkheim's *The Elementary Forms of Religious Life* that preceded it. But if *The Elementary Structures* was largely written in the US and based on American secondary literature, it would have to wait until Lévi-Strauss's return to France to be published as a finished product. This may have been because of what Lévi-Strauss perceived as a "growing disinterest" of Americans for "theoretical works" during the war—even his still "small book on incest."[214] For a French audience, however, his creation of a broad philosophical system indebted to Comte, Durkheim, Lévy-Bruhl, and Maurice Granet would be much more appealing.[215]

Lévi-Strauss's object of analysis, elementary structures of kinship, were "those systems which prescribe marriage with a certain type of relative or, alternatively, those which, while defining members of the society as relatives, divide them into two categories, viz., possible spouses and prohibited spouses."[216] Much of his analysis dealt with nomenclatures surrounding specific marriage prescriptions and prohibitions in "primitive society," such as the preference for parallel cousins versus cross-cousins.[217] However, Lévi-Strauss imagined his work as "an introduction to a general theory of kinship systems."[218]

In his own words, the purpose of *The Elementary Structures* was "to show that marriage rules, nomenclature, and system of rights and prohibitions are indissociable aspects of the one and same reality."[219] But instead of focusing on a given tribe or people, as most anthropologists did, Lévi-Strauss followed in the footsteps of the American Lewis Henry Morgan, whose classic book *Systems of Consanguinity and Affinity of the Human Family* depended on hundreds of surveys from all around the world.[220] The book, published in 1871, had in a sense "invented" kinship as a field of study.[221]

Lévi-Strauss's penchant for systems rather than case studies can been seen in his 1944 article on chieftainship among the Nambicuara. Instead of simply recounting his fieldwork experience or the empirical minutiae from his research notes, Lévi-Strauss defended his "very ponderous introduction" and subsequent forays into political philosophy. "I do not believe," he wrote, "that the data which I am going to present, if considered only as data on a chieftainship among a hitherto little-known group, would honestly deserve one hour of attention." He continued, "similar facts have been recorded many times."[222]

The Nambicuara, both in this article and in *The Elementary Structures*, served as the abstractly conceived most primitive form of humanity, which allowed Lévi-Strauss to theorize on the relationship between nature and culture. Little interested in understanding the long history of the Nambicuara, Lévi-Strauss instead preferred to focus on the present and treat it as timeless: "The Nambicuara society functions, in the present, as one of the simplest forms of human society to be conceived."[223] Simple forms or structures were the focus of Lévi-Strauss's dissertation, which excluded both "Africa and our own contemporary society."[224] These two, among others, were characterized by "complex" systems of marriage and kinship, whereby the transfer of wealth and free choice, among other factors, complicated marriage prescriptions.[225]

Lévi-Strauss initially intended to publish his dissertation in three volumes: "The Elementary Structures," "The Complex Structures," and "Family Attitudes."[226] However, his entire enterprise depended on simplified models that made only the first possible. His system of structures, homologous to binaries in mathematics or phonemes in linguistics, sought to strip relationships down to their essential and most discrete characteristics. In this sense, once relationships were categorized in a system of binaries (say, for example, maternal versus paternal cousin), they could be abstracted into an interchangeable set or system that no longer had to do with a given group.

Lévi-Strauss used his binary approach most extensively to think through the common marriages between cross-cousins. In many societies, the children of a brother and sister could marry, because they were "crossed" (whereas the children of a brother and a brother or sister and a sister could not). Instead of focusing on the marriage choices of a single family, Lévi-Strauss expanded the binary outward, incorporating a broader array of possibilities—or, to use the language of mathematics, permutations. Surely, Lévi-Strauss's conceptualization of such relationships in abstract terms was influenced by mathematician André Weil, who contributed an appendix to *The Elementary Structures* entitled "On the Algebraic Study of Certain Types of Marriage Laws (Murngin System)."[227] (Weil taught at USP for some years starting in 1944, in large part thanks to Lévi-Strauss.)[228]

In Lévi-Strauss's system of elementary structures, which was indeed based on models created by other field-workers, we can visualize how prescriptions and prohibitions work within a limited set of relations, whether between paternal and maternal cousins or in certain moieties that complement each other in totemic relationships.[229] But it is not clear how "complex" structures would work using such abstract models. The logical abstractions that Lévi-Strauss universalized for "primitive society" were not as convincing—even to him— once a society became historical and complex.

This did not prevent him, however, from emphasizing generality over specificity. He reproached American anthropologists, in this sense, for missing the forest for the trees. They failed to recognize that ostensibly different forms often represented "a difference of degree, not of kind; of generality, and not of type." Instead of privileging some region of the world (Egypt, Mexico, and Peru being prominent examples) or a certain period of the history of civilization, one would therefore do better to direct inquiry to "certain fundamental structures of the human mind."[230]

By moving away from local empirical instances, Lévi-Strauss could scale the globe in his formulations of elementary kinship structures: from Eastern Siberia in the north to Assam (India) in the south, and from India in the west to New Caledonia in the east.[231] By and large, this geography extended the one Mauss had established in *The Gift*, which centers on the edges of the Pacific, especially Polynesia, Melanesia, and the Pacific Northwest, the noteworthy home of the institution of potlach. Analyzing "primitive" institutions that laid the foundations for forms of law and economics, Mauss claimed: "Naturally we know that they have another extension, and it is only provisorily that the research stops here."[232]

In extending Mauss's geographical and civilizational approach, Lévi-Strauss's understandings of universal logics of kinship, or "structures," largely excluded the "primitives" that he knew so well from South America. Like in Mauss's *Gift*, too, the formalization of such categories was necessarily incompatible with attention to local specificities, leaving little room for Lévi-Strauss's fieldwork in *The Elementary Structures*. As Lévi-Strauss would later claim in his introduction to the work of Mauss, *The Gift* provided, for "the first time in the history of ethnological thought, an effort made at transcending empirical observation and attaining deeper realities."[233]

The two essential arguments in *The Elementary Structures* are as follows: first, that the prohibition of incest is the "threshold" between nature and culture and, second, that the exchange of women is the fundamental basis by which kinship systems are constructed. The first argument represented a philosophical reckoning with a long list of precedents—ethnologists such as Lewis Henry Morgan and Edward Burnett Tylor, sociologists such as Herbert Spencer and Durkheim, and also Sigmund Freud.[234] The second provided the system, or "structure," that would prove it.

For Lévi-Strauss, the existence of the incest prohibition could not be explained using precedent methodologies, as it was neither natural (based on human biology), nor social (based on conscious human choices and imposed rules), nor psychological (based on the timeless human psyche). Instead, it was the precipice between nature and nature's own overcoming, most commonly known as human society. In his words, "the incest prohibition is at once on the threshold of culture, in culture, and in one sense, culture itself."[235] Culture, in this sense, was no longer natural but not yet social, instead serving as the transition between the two.

According to Lévi-Strauss, man was cultural before he was "social." Prior to the development of complex social structures such as class, humans nonetheless had the aptitude to "think of biological relationships as system of oppositions." Those oppositions were essentially between "the men who own and the women who are owned," whether they be spouses, sisters and daughters, or women acquired from other groups.[236] Accordingly, humans—but really, men—"renounce their close relatives and . . . look beyond this circle for the partners with whom they will unite sexually and socially."[237]

Lévi-Strauss's male-centered argument that associated culture and kinship systems with exchange of women has since been thoroughly critiqued by feminist critics and empirical studies on more matriarchal societies.[238] His own disciple, Françoise Héritier, preserved his logic, but insisted that men, too, could be exchanged, and, as Maurice Godelier has demonstrated, research among various matriarchal societies has largely invalidated Lévi-Strauss's interpretation.[239] For our purposes, the question is not about the validity of such distinctions, which belongs to the domain of kinship studies. It is instead to consider the production of *The Elementary Structures* within the context of exile in New York and Brazil in Lévi-Strauss's recent past.

Lévi-Strauss's exile has been analyzed at length as an aesthetic, artistic, and social experience—encouraged by his own text "New York post- et préfiguratif" (New York post- and prefigurative).[240] But it was the social-scientific and not the artistic language that Lévi-Strauss would later bring back with him to France. As Laurent Jeanpierre has so poignantly analyzed, Lévi-Strauss's role as an intermediary between an international social-scientific space based in the United States and a more national one in France structured his return to Europe, especially after a year as French *conseiller culturel* (cultural counsel) in New York.[241] Since his years in Brazil in the 1930s familiarized him with the Ministry of Foreign Affairs, we could say that this habitus was somewhat of a continuation.[242]

When Lévi-Strauss was in Brazil, he navigated between professional obligation to spread the legacy of Durkheim and his intellectual interests in American anthropology. As we saw in chapter 2, he called his enterprise "cultural sociology." But his full immersion into American anthropology in wartime New York, as well as the disruption of French social-scientific institutions, encouraged him to make a cleaner break with both French vocabulary around the study of man and its methods. His correspondence with Rivet sheds light on this. When Lévi-Strauss wrote Rivet asking him to join the École Libre des Hautes Études, he outlined the disciplines that were taught there, including, of course, anthropology. Rivet rallied to the École Libre but questioned Lévi-Strauss's use of the word "anthropologie."

Why in hell do you think the word "Anthropology" will be better understood in America than the word "Ethnology," considering that the greatest American scientific institution that occupies itself with our science took, in 1879, the title The Bureau of Ethnology? Is it because the North Americans do not yet understand the goals and field of action of this glorious organization? All of this seems unclear to me. I insist therefore that the designation "Ethnology" be maintained.[243]

Rivet, far from nitpicking with Lévi-Strauss over nomenclature, was thoroughly vexed by his protégé's use of the word "anthropologie." This word in particular had a long history in France, and Lévi-Strauss's argument of convenience (that Americans would more easily understand anthropology than ethnology) failed to convince Rivet.

In France, "anthropologie" had its own scientific institution, the Société d'Anthropologie, synonymous with Henri Vallois. Not only did the Société d'Anthropologie have a much more physical approach (largely based on body and skull measurements), but it had long competed with Rivet and his network around the Musée de l'Homme. Although Vallois himself, Rivet's successor at the Musée de l'Homme, remained within the pale of good science, French fascism served to transform the competition between ethnologists and "anthropologistes" into outright antagonism. Best represented by the Swiss George Montandon, naturalized French by Vichy, "Anthropologie" during the war years became increasingly associated with the fascist and anti-Semitic project.[244]

Lévi-Strauss, however, decided to leave such French antagonisms aside. As he would later formulate, he saw the study of man as progressing from ethnography (essentially fieldwork), moving to ethnology (the extension of ethnography, often at a broader regional level, synthesizing a number of firsthand ethnographies), and finally arriving at anthropology—a kind of meta-analysis of various ethnologies.[245] Lévi-Strauss had proven himself as an ethnologist with his studies on the Bororo and Nambicuara. According to his definition, however, he would only become an anthropologist with a broader, synthetic study. Rivet may not have been aware of Lévi-Strauss's intent in this respect. Nevertheless, his call to order for Lévi-Strauss to maintain his project as "ethnology" was highly suggestive of both word choice and what he considered proper research.

Beyond parsing words, Lévi-Strauss and Rivet's subsequent correspondence concerning the former's dissertation (analyzed above) points to a heightened tension in regard to abstract, universal arguments and concrete manifestations of a given group or people. In doing anthropology rather than ethnography, Lévi-Strauss was, in a sense, distancing himself not only from his own fieldwork but also from fieldwork in general. Others had conducted it before him, and with their ethnologies he felt that he could arrive at something higher, much as Mauss had in *The Gift* without ever having been to the non-European societies that lay at its basis. As Edmund Leach has argued, in this sense, Lévi-Strauss still retained "the grander more macrocosmic viewpoint of the nineteenth century."[246]

Mauss served as a transitional figure between armchair anthropology and the field. Lévi-Strauss, in returning to Mauss in the 1940s, embraced comparative ethnology in a time of increasing specialization. He obviously had Mauss in mind as a mentor and ally when he wrote to him about his expectations for returning to France after the war—and indeed as someone who would allow him to continue working in universal terms. This was in sharp contrast to Rivet, who seemed to think that Lévi-Strauss could benefit from more fieldwork. Lévi-Strauss wrote Mauss in 1944:

> My sincerest desire is to return immediately to France to a post (Musée de l'Homme, Institut d'Ethnologie, Hautes Études?) that would allow me to consecrate myself entirely to scientific work. Dr. Rivet is OK with this, but would like that I stop for a time in Mexico so as to get the Institut Français Ibéro-Américain up and running that he proposed that I head.[247]

Lévi-Strauss had already completed his work on the family and social life of the Nambicuara, but his contribution to the "renaissance of scientific thought in Europe" was of much larger dimensions and ambition.[248] It was, he continued in his letter to Mauss, "the extension of your thought," although in a different domain: "the typology of systems of kinship and a systematization of the rules of marriage."[249]

In wartime New York, with France occupied and then liberated, Lévi-Strauss sought to synthesize his experience among the "primitives" in the field with over a thousand other accounts to arrive at something new: a universal theory or system that he had previously reproached the Durkheimians for attempting to build. Only it was "cultural" rather than "social" facts that he sought to explain—an appropriation of American terminology to bring back to postwar France. By then, except for Georges Davy, who noted the lack of class analysis in Lévi-Strauss's dissertation, and Georges Gurvitch, little remained of the Durkheimian school against which Lévi-Strauss defined his project.[250]

When the war came to an end, Lévi-Strauss accepted the job as *conseiller culturel* for the French foreign service in New York. There he not only continued to work on *The Elementary Structures*, which would be published in 1948, but also further established the conditions for dialogue between French and American intellectuals and social scientists. This mediation would provide him with the tools and the habitus for negotiating between his two future roles: as a French intellectual in the United States and as an American-trained social scientist in France.

CONCLUDING REMARKS

During the war years, Monbeig, Bastide, Braudel, and Lévi-Strauss all drew upon Brazil as an object of study, intellectual network, and sustaining framework for their thinking as they developed their mature work. While Monbeig and Bastide engaged most directly and explicitly with Brazilian social science during their years spent in Brazil, Braudel, too, found Brazil important, for his understandings of the Mediterranean. For all three, exchange with Brazilian social scientists helped them not only to think about their respective projects but also to offer alternatives to what they saw as the crisis in the social sciences. Distinct in their methodological approaches and the forms through which Brazil entered into their writings (for Braudel it was a distant reality, filtered through books; for the others, it was much more direct), they all built upon their early research from the 1930s.

Lévi-Strauss differed from the other three men in that his thinking gradually moved toward US-based social science and to formalizing models that moved beyond both his own fieldwork among Brazilian Indians and fieldwork in general. This disciplined effort to bring back an important synthesis of ethnology and methods to liberated France was designed to allow French social scientists to compete with their American counterparts. For Lévi-Strauss, Brazil would come roaring back in the postwar, with and alongside publications by his colleagues from the 1930s. Then, they were no longer young, inexperienced scholars questioning the foundations of the social sciences at USP, but back in the heart of French academic life, trying to construct new institutions together.

In the final two chapters, the threads of each individual's work will be drawn back together. Monbeig's understandings of human geography, Bastide's meditations on cultural synthesis and syncretism, Braudel's temporal frameworks tied to geography and international trade, and Lévi-Strauss's structuralism all contributed to renovating the French social sciences in the postwar period. However different their respective projects may have been, their work built upon Brazilianist research, helped to further institutionalize it in Parisian intellectual life, and brought questions related to the world economy, social structure, race, and indigeneity to the fore.

CHAPTER FIVE

Brazil and the Reconstruction of the French Social Sciences

L'unité du tout est encore plus réelle que chacune
des parties.

MARCEL MAUSS

If the war years saw French social scientists scattered around the globe, in the postwar period, most of them came back to France. Unlike the German refugee scholars who were "permanent exiles," the French scholars residing abroad were more often than not temporary visitors. Except for Bastide, who stayed longer to teach in Brazil and preserve French influence there, by 1946, the other three French scholars at the core of this story were back in France teaching and planning their next moves. As I argue in this chapter, by the early 1960s, often with the help of one another, they came to occupy—and indeed to create—central positions in the social sciences.

The role of Brazil and Brazilians in the development of these scholars' individual projects should now be clear. This chapter examines how their shared network and set of references informed their work in the postwar, at both intellectual and institutional levels. Culminating with a discussion of Braudel's geohistorical *longue durée* and Lévi-Strauss's structuralism, I demonstrate how some of the most seemingly divergent research agendas came together at a critical inflection point for the social sciences.[1]

By the mid-1940s, USP had trained its first PhDs. Of these, it is only natural that Braudel would be more invested in Brazilian historians; Monbeig, in geographers; and Bastide, in sociologists and anthropologists. As for Lévi-Strauss, he left no Brazilian heirs. Beyond the professor-student relationships, however, a much wider web brought together French and Brazilian scholars as peers and collaborators.

In the period following World War II, Brazilian universities hired newly minted Brazilian doctors instead of French professors, becoming increasingly autonomous from France.[2] Nevertheless, the exchanges between the two countries in many ways intensified. Travel became easier and quicker with airplanes, even if most people still continued to make the trip by ship, and with it came a more global circulation of books and ideas. With this changing context in mind, the next chapter analyzes the centrality of a number of Brazilian intellectuals, some of them physically present abroad.

Here, however, the question is of a different nature, emphasizing instead exchanges between the professors who made up the missions to the University of São Paulo in the 1930s upon their return to France. Braudel alone exchanged some sixty letters each with Lévi-Strauss, Bastide, and Monbeig; and Lévi-Strauss and Bastide, too, exchanged roughly the same number.[3] Indeed, in Braudel's, Bastide's, and Lévi-Strauss's archives, few correspondents—French, Brazilian, or otherwise—were more important than those professors whom they knew from Brazil. This chapter asks, therefore, how did these social scientists draw upon Brazil as an experience, a network, and a resource as they navigated French academic life?

The very experience of having taught and researched in Brazil helped to solidify a cluster of French scholars not only interested in Latin America but also supportive of one another's projects institutionally. As Braudel, Lévi-Strauss, Monbeig, and Bastide navigated France's "long reconstruction," they collectively engaged in their own professional reinsertion, drawing upon international experience outside the French university to ultimately create and occupy new positions within it.[4] Other scholars would do the same, although with a much more North American emphasis. These include sociologists such as Raymond Aron, Georges Friedmann, and even the economist François Perroux, who, in addition to having taught in São Paulo, benefited from early contacts with the Rockefeller Foundation and American economists.[5]

Although Bastide and Monbeig would later be elected to the Sorbonne, in 1958 and 1961 respectively, this cluster's force mostly took root outside the traditional French university system and the *grandes écoles*—at the Collège de France, at the newly founded 6th section of the École Pratique des Hautes Études (the precursor to today's École des Hautes Études en Sciences Sociales), and at the Musée de l'Homme. These scholars published together in *Annales* and made Brazil more visible in their respective disciplines. They also contributed collectively to the production of Lévi-Strauss's *Tristes Tropiques*, both as a text and as an event in the public sphere. Building on these publications, they debated the possibilities for interdisciplinarity and "structure"—emerging together in the process as central figures in the French social-scientific landscape.

With the liberation of France, Braudel was freed from his German POW camp and allowed to resume his position at the 5th section of the École Pratique des Hautes Études, in Paris. He continued to teach there while he finished *The Mediterranean*, which he defended in 1947. Lévi-Strauss, although returning briefly to Paris upon liberation, lived in New York through 1947, serving as the first *conseiller culturel* (cultural counsel) in the US for the French foreign service. In 1948, just months after returning to France, he defended his dissertation, *The Elementary Structures of Kinship*. Except for brief visits to France, for work related to the newly founded Centre National de la Recherche Scientifique (CNRS), Monbeig remained in Brazil until December 1946. At that time, he moved his family to Strasbourg, where he became professor of colonial geography at the very university where Febvre and Bloch had worked together in the 1920s.

As for Bastide, he continued teaching at the University of São Paulo and conducting fieldwork on candomblé, oftentimes alongside Pierre Verger, with whom he would ultimately travel to Africa.[6] By 1951, he taught only a semester per year in Brazil, leaving definitively in 1954. As he explained to Braudel, "My wife, above all, for two or three years now, cannot bear the extreme temperatures in S. Paulo, and we desire to return to France to come back to the regular rhythm of the four seasons."[7]

For these French scholars, as for almost all Frenchmen, the postwar moment signified readjustment. After over four years of occupation, their country was in tatters, and the long process of reconstruction and purging (*épuration*) would provide both new challenges and opportunities for them.[8] Specifically, they needed to convert their extensive international experience into something of interest to French academia, a process that was neither easy nor linear. After so many years surrounded by other references, scholars, and institutions foreign to France, they needed to resituate themselves and make up for lost time.

Whether under the auspices of the foreign service or by other means, all four of these scholars maintained close relationships with Latin America and Latin Americanists in France. The Service des Oeuvres Françaises à l'Étranger had maintained Bastide and Monbeig in place through the war and its aftermath, and the service served as one of the spaces in which such relationships became consolidated. In February 1945, Henri Laugier, first president of the CNRS and cofounder of the École Libre des Hautes Études, in New York, presided over a meeting at the foreign service in Paris that included professors Coornaert, Deffontaines, Lévi-Strauss, Maugüé, and Émile Bréhier—all of whom had taught in Brazil—in addition to the likes of Paul Rivet and Jacques Soustelle.[9]

Furthermore, Rivet, Paulo Duarte, and others inaugurated a new Brazil center within the Musée de l'Homme called the Institut Français des Hautes Études Brésiliennes (French Institute for Advanced Brazilian Studies). At its inaugural session, Rivet, Georges Dumas (the architect of the Franco-Brazilian exchanges), Laugier, Henri Bonnet (then serving as ambassador in Washington), and Lévi-Strauss gave speeches.[10] They emphasized the need to move beyond diplomacy and high society, which had characterized organizations such as the France-Amérique committee in the interwar years. They also proposed endowing the Musée de l'Homme with a library for Brazilian studies as well as resources for teaching, citing as a precedent the Institut d'Ethnologie that Mauss, Rivet, and Lévy-Bruhl had created in the 1930s.

These initiatives, however fragile some of them ultimately proved, point to a renewed and expanded interest in Latin America and Brazil among social scientists. The question remained of how such interest might become institutionalized in programs with specialist professors and budgets for new research. This question would initially be resolved, at least in part, by the founding of the 6th Section of the École Pratique des Hautes Études, in 1947, dedicated to "sciences économiques et sociales." The newly founded institution, created by Febvre, Braudel, and Charles Morazé, grew alongside its unofficial journal, *Annales*. Little by little, it would gain the recognition and financial autonomy to act upon Febvre's manifesto from 1928, "Un champ privilegié d'études: L'Amérique du Sud" (A privileged field of study: South America).[11] Febvre's project would become the pulsing heart for new Latin American research—as well as one of the more innovative sites for social research in general.

Of course, Febvre, Braudel, and the group around the 6th section of the École Pratique des Hautes Études by no means had a monopoly on Latin American research in France. Nonetheless, they served as its nuclear core, putting scholars in communication with one another, strengthening partnerships between France and Brazil, and providing an important point of departure for Bastide, Lévi-Strauss, and Monbeig as they reentered French academic life and its epicenter in Paris. For this, *Annales* was crucial.

ANNALES AND LATIN AMERICA AFTER WORLD WAR II

Braudel had been writing about Latin America for *Annales* since the 1930s, in reviews of works on the Spanish and Portuguese Empires, and he continued to cover the region during the war, in his review of Gilberto Freyre's oeuvre for *Mélanges d'histoire sociale*.[12] In the immediate postwar, Braudel's interest in Latin America only expanded. Notably, he reviewed Caio Prado Jr.'s work, published his first article from his dissertation, "Monnaies et civilisations: De l'or du Soudan à l'argent d'Amérique" (Currencies and civilizations: From the gold of Sudan to the silver of America), and coedited a special issue of *Annales* in 1948 that dealt exclusively with Latin America.[13]

If nothing else, these sources and others demonstrate a heightened interest in Latin America among postwar French social scientists. For many, the continent provided a lens through which to view broader ethnic, historical, and developmental processes in a moment of global restructuring. The success of Lévi-Strauss's nostalgic *Tristes Tropiques*, which harked back to a time before imperialism and economic development, provides a window onto this interest in Latin America. But, as I will show, *Tristes Tropiques* was but the tip of the iceberg. An increasingly institutionalized Latin Americanist research base in Paris, especially at the École Pratique and its journal *Annales*, lay beneath the surface.

Almost immediately upon returning to a more or less "normal" professorial lifestyle in the fall of 1945, Braudel took back up correspondence with Caio Prado Jr., whom he had last wrote in 1940, before the war broke out. That January, likely from the front, he had responded to Prado's end-of-the-year greetings, where his immediate horizon was Germany. He wrote Prado, "I think about our conversations from yesterday. I hope that there will be more tomorrow."[14]

In November 1945, Braudel wrote Prado again for the first time since before the war, after seeing his friend Jean Maugüé in Paris.[15] In a long conversation about "Brazil and all of our Brazilian friends," Maugüé, who had just returned from Brazil, informed Braudel of a "marvelous" new book by Prado. Braudel requested a copy for review in *Annales*. He also announced himself as the new coeditor, alongside Lucien Febvre, of the journal, soon to appear under a new name. For the journal, he hoped to establish "as close relations as possible abroad, with your country especially, about whose history we know too little here."[16]

Prado naturally sent Braudel his books, for which the latter thanked him. Along with his reply, Braudel sent Prado a press release for *Annales*, hoping that he could spread word about the journal to Brazilians who desired "contact with a history that is not exclusively and sadly historicizing."[17] Furthermore, Braudel requested that Prado put him in touch with the "elusive" Freyre. Prado did both of these things. Indeed, he had already served as an intermediary between Freyre and the French mission to USP in previous years.[18] This time, he informed Braudel of Freyre's address at the constituent assembly in Rio, as Freyre had entered national politics and left his native Recife.

Braudel's exchanges with Prado were motivated by very specific goals for *Annales*, notably further collaboration with Latin American historians and with Freyre in particular. They also suggest how French social scientists imagined Brazil and Latin American more generally as a utopia in the postwar period. Braudel himself very much appreciated Freyre's emphasis on racial mixing, as well as the hierarchical but supposedly nondiscriminatory relationships between different groups in Brazil. It was not only Brazil's racial mixing, however, that served as a contrast to Vichy France. In a time of neo-Malthusian thinking, it was also its geographical immensity.

> If you knew, my dear friend, how much every dictatorship is detestable, odious, wherever it may come from. How much liberty is indispensable, in this place with little elbow room, at the edge of Europe where we are located! In Brazil, I imagine that space, the enormity of space, balances everything, making ridiculous in advance—and disarming—any attempt at coercion. But it is likely that you see that with another eye than me, that you think differently.[19]

Sitting at the edge of Europe with "little elbow room," France's geography appears, in this light, as part of the explanation for Vichy. Brazil, on the other hand, regardless of its political regimes, had space to "balance everything" and "disarm all attempts at coercion." Prado certainly saw this question with a different eye than Braudel, considering Brazil's recent history of authoritarianism and his recent prison sentence. Incidentally, he would be arrested again just months after Braudel sent this letter.

Braudel imagined Brazil as a space of liberty and of new possibilities. Even if his own research was into the sixteenth and seventeenth centuries, Braudel wrote Prado once more to clarify: "The Brazil of today interests us as much if not more than that of Villegaignon or P. Anchieta."[20] Braudel had already learned a great deal about colonial Brazil through Prado, both from their previous contact and from his recent readings of *Formação do Brasil contemporâneo* and *História econômica do Brasil*.[21] These readings would prove important for Braudel's first article from his dissertation, "Monnaies et civilisations" (1946), as well as his broader understanding of economic conjunctures, evidenced in his 1948 review in *Annales*.

Beyond this textual influence for Braudel, Braudel's contact with Brazilians such as Prado merits further consideration. Why, in a moment of French reconstruction, when Braudel was investing his energies alongside Lucien Febvre to create the 6th section of the École Pratique, were partners such as Prado and Freyre so essential? Braudel repeatedly invited the two to contribute to *Annales* and to become members of its patronage committee, aimed at establishing relationships between France and the rest of the world.[22] He saw Latin America as a crucial ally for the French; it embodied a kind of "Latin" humanism, continued to provide new opportunities for fieldwork in various disciplines, and served as a strong institutional connection for advancing both French social science as a product as well as various scholars' individual careers.

As of 1946, the subtitle for the new *Annales* was "Économies, Sociétés, Civilisations," and in it Monbeig published the first article having to do with South America. "South America," he wrote, "is decidedly in style."[23] "Our young people," wrote Monbeig, "are taking back up the old myth of El Dorado—and let's not forget the Europeans who believe to have found in the South American republics a hiding place as secure as it is profitable for their capital in distress."[24] While distancing himself from superficial travelers and investors, Monbeig nonetheless sought to build on this broader public interest.

In his article, Monbeig emphasized the tensions between industrialists and agriculturalists in terms of the national and broader world economy.[25] Of course, Prado had explored this at length in his own work, highlighting the opposition between industrialists who preferred an agricultural market aimed at feeding workers and the export-based sectors tied to cash crops. Despite its "agricultural" vocation, Monbeig reminded his readers, "Brazil lacks wheat."[26] Anticipating dependency theorists, he wrote, "The serious question is to know up to what point Brazil can advance in this way," considering its unequal position vis-à-vis North America, "the great financial and military power of the Western hemisphere."[27]

Monbeig's article, the first of the Latin American articles in the new *Annales*, was soon followed by Braudel's extended review of Prado. Then, in 1948, South America's presence really took off, in an issue dedicated entirely to the continent, introduced by articles from two members of the old guard who had encouraged Latin American research during the interwar years, Lucien Febvre and Paul Rivet (see chap. 1). With contributions from Bastide, Monbeig, Roger Caillois, Pierre Chaunu, Frédéric Mauro, the Portuguese Vitorino Magalhães Godinho, the Brazilian João Cruz Costa, and Braudel himself, among others, the issue contained over two hundred pages of recent work and reviews.[28]

In his introductory essay, "L'Amérique du Sud devant l'histoire" (South America in the face of history), Febvre largely repeated the themes and optimistic tone of his 1928 quasi-manifesto.[29] *Annales* was interested in these countries from the South, he claimed, because over all they were not yet "sedentary," "stabilized," or "bourgeois"; for this reason, "these countries appear to institute, for us, under our eyes, perpetual human experiences, political and social."[30]

Rivet in many ways echoed Febvre, although paying more attention to racial mixing. In his essay, "Sur l'Amérique latine: Propos d'un ami" (About Latin America: Words of a friend), Rivet emphasized the geographical, ethnic, and linguistic diversity of Latin America, harshly criticizing European travel writers and diplomats for their ignorance and essentialisms.[31] Nonetheless, despite this diversity, Rivet claimed that language and the Catholic religion "constitute in Latin America a common substratum for all peoples that make it up—and a solid substratum."[32] Brazil, he recognized, was an exception to the common language of Spanish, but, of course, Portuguese is a Romance language too.

According to Rivet, the primary distinction between North and South America was racial mixture rather than religion or language. Optimistic about modern technologies and infrastructure, Rivet saw them as tending to reduce the centripetal tendencies of Latin American regionalism and contribute to realizing "national, cultural, and physical unity." This "singularly enthralling spectacle of a world constituting itself" seemed to be a harbinger for a future that would be relatively free from racial prejudice. "While in the United States, this unity is retarded or even hampered by a racial prejudice," Rivet claimed; "it does not encounter, for this reason, any obstacle in Latin America, or at least no absolute obstacle." Elites in Ecuador and Peru harbored racial prejudice, he continued, but as for Mexico and Brazil, "Racial prejudice does not exist."[33] (Clearly, Rivet had bought into José Vasconcelos's idea of the "cosmic race.")[34]

Rivet seemed to have preferred whiter or whitening Latin American countries for models, especially Argentina and Brazil. For example, he lauded the fact that over the past century and a half Rio essentially went from a "black" to a "white" capital.[35] But his remarks were far from categorical, and his interest in human prehistory made him believe that, in the long term, mixing was more often good than bad. The three "types of humans" presently mixing in the New World, he claimed, were analogous to those from the upper Quaternary period, in which "the Cro-Magnon race, which was certainly white," mixed with "the mongoloid Chancelade race, that is to say, probably yellow," and the Grimaldi race, related to "the current black races of Africa and Oceania." Since these three races and their subsequent mixture with future invaders of Europe gave birth to the population of France and Western Europe, Rivet coyly claimed, "We can say that this brewing of such diverse elements did not give too bad results, neither from a physical, nor a cultural, point of view."[36]

Still traumatized by the war, Vichy, and the racist pseudoscience that took over the Musée de l'Homme after the Nazis executed some of his students, Rivet saw hope in Latin America. "I am convinced," he said, "that if, by misfortune, old Europe falls into darkness, her cultural heritage, humanism, free critique, and free creation will find depositaries in Latin America worthy of preserving and making her flourish again."[37] Europe might fall into darkness, but it would always have its "depositaries" in Latin America, the new sprouts of European civilization.

Whereas Rivet provided a general panorama of racial mixing in Latin America, Bastide focused on the survival and transformation of "civilizations of color."[38] "Dans les Amériques noires: Afrique ou Europe?" (In the Black Americas: Africa or Europe?) was his first essay published in France dealing with his research conducted during the war. If Rivet had seen racial mixing in

FIG. 6 Bastide in Ifanhin/Briki (Benin). Pierre Verger © Fundação Pierre Verger.

an overwhelmingly positive light, Bastide was more ambivalent. For Bastide, "the original African civilizations" had been disturbed by the "destructive action of white civilization"; in some cases those African civilizations had "mixed with their white rivals to create the most lovely and unexpected cultural mosaics," but many were destroyed outright.[39]

Febvre wrote a brief introduction to Bastide's essay, emphasizing the original, and indeed "revolutionary," truth that recent research on African culture in the Americas told; in it, he insisted on Bastide's role in the "great renewal of anthropological and sociological studies throughout the entirety of his country of adoption."[40] Bastide's affinities with African culture were inflected through his conflicted French identity. As a Protestant from the south of France, Bastide had his own difficulties with the hegemonic and homogenizing project of the French nation-state. In the same way that he celebrated the Cathars, who had resisted the Inquisition, or writers from the Midi who put forth an alternative to Parisian literary culture, he celebrated the African civilizations in the Antilles and in Brazil that had overcome separation from their homeland, slavery, and subjugation. In this, they differed from their counterparts in the United States, where "the Negro has become just about completely assimilated to Anglo-Saxon culture."[41]

Bastide spent a considerable amount of ink reviewing the work of Chicago-based sociologist E. Franklin Frazier, who had argued that while African familial structure had disappeared in Bahia, its religious support in candomblé had remained intact.[42] For Bastide, institutions such as the "purchase" of a wife following religious initiation were far more than vestiges or empty representations. The "purchase" of a wife was the "survival of the old African religion" in symbolic terms, even if no longer as rigid as in Africa. Nonetheless, Bastide confirmed that the custom still structured social relations, referencing his fieldwork and *Imagens do Nordeste místico em branco e preto*.[43]

The concept of reinterpretation had allowed Melville Herskovits to advance the idea that "Africanisms have not completely disappeared, even where they do not show on the surface."[44] For Bastide, however, Herskovits sometimes went too far in attributing African causes or roots to contemporary institutions among black peoples in the Americas such as obligatory collective labor (*mutirão* and *trocar dia*) and the relationships between Catholic and African divinities. As a way of understanding the former institution, Bastide preferred the notion of convergence between phenomena of different origins; for the latter, "mystic correspondence."[45] For Bastide, the coincidences between Catholic saints and *orixás* had more to do with self-preservation than confusion; Afro-Brazilians created analogies between Catholicism and their religion so as to appear to be good Catholics, rather than because they sincerely "reinterpreted" their religion according to Catholic cosmology.

Complementing the articles from Bastide, Rivet, and others, much of the rest of the issue of *Annales* consisted of shorter reviews and essays, of which Braudel single-handedly wrote twelve. His reviews spanned nearly the entirety of Latin America, from the Southern Cone of Chile, Argentina, and Brazil to Venezuela, Cuba, and the Antilles. Explicitly building upon a different article by Bastide, he called for a survey of the intelligentsia of South America. Writers such as the Argentine Ezéquiel Martínez Estrada and Freyre, "our brothers in spirit," could offer *Annales* "their passions and their ideas, admirable or detestable." They could do this "by way of their experience as men, [and by this] I mean to say by way of their countries themselves."[46] According to Braudel (who, unlike Bastide, did not have a subtle understanding of African culture), Freyre and the Brazilian Northeast that he described might offer an alternative to the Antilles, with its "influx of savage, frustrated blacks, brought too quickly and numerously from Africa."[47]

Much like other articles in the *Annales* special issue on Latin America, Braudel's essays emphasized the difference between "Anglo-Saxon" and "Iberian" America.[48] He distinguished them not only analytically but also prescriptively, as if the young Latin American countries should not forget their essayist past, avoiding fragmentation and the specialization of the American academy. Whereas Émile Coornaert praised the Brazilian historian João Fernando de Almeida Prado for his "solid book," holding it up as an excellent example of erudition and "total history," Braudel added a supplement to Coornaert's review claiming much the opposite.[49]

Almeida Prado's studies, Braudel wrote, did not always present "their riches in the best way."[50] "Erudition is only a means, a start," Braudel reminded Almeida Prado; "Sooner or later, you will need to give us great frescoes."[51] While Braudel himself was heavily invested in professionalizing history, he nonetheless discouraged Latin American historians from becoming overly erudite. To do so would miss the forest for the trees. History should grow out of literary, philosophical, and essayist culture rather than attempting to supplant it entirely.

Throughout his essays in the special issue, Braudel advanced the idea that "American history is linked to that of the Atlantic (and vice versa, by the way). In fact, it is one and the same history."[52] Bringing attention to the work of his Brazilian student, Alice Piffer Canabrava, Braudel encouraged an expansive scale of research that we would now consider the history of the Atlantic World. He also gave space to his students Pierre Chaunu and Frédéric Mauro, whose first scientific articles were published in this issue of *Annales*.[53]

Prior to World War II, French researchers who worked on Latin America had few specialized places to publish beyond the *Journal de la Société des américanistes*. *Annales* would be one of the first and most important journals to emerge in the postwar period to fill this void, publishing articles and reviews on Brazil and Latin America throughout the 1940s, 1950s, and beyond. Unlike earlier attempts to federate Latin American research, however, *Annales* had serious institutional backing. No longer dependent in the same way on underfunded learned societies, it had its base at the École Pratique des Hautes Études, to which we will now turn.

BRAZIL IN THE FRENCH SOCIAL SCIENCES, FRENCH SOCIAL SCIENCES IN BRAZIL

From the 1930s onward, Brazil had served as a relatively autonomous space in which the French could develop social-scientific methods and institutions. Their Brazilian collaborators left their mark in a variety of ways, even if they never had the kind of power wielded by American philanthropic organizations such as the Rockefeller and Ford Foundations in determining research agendas and curricula. The story of the role of American foundations in shaping the postwar French social sciences and in Braudel's role at the École Pratique des Hautes Études in particular has been told.[54] I would like to suggest that Brazil remained an alternative source of support and a space for influence throughout this period.

Brazil was not incidental to, but rather crucial for, the nucleus around the 6th section of the École Pratique. As Argentine scholar Fernando Devoto has argued, the group around *Annales* sought to overcome their "real and presumed marginality with a powerful strategy of internationalization that would compensate for, with its external relations, its domestic political and institutional obstacles."[55] For Braudel, Latin America and Brazil especially supported an important patron-client network, and through it he could provide publishing outlets, lecture tours, and even sabbatical semesters to his colleagues and peers. These included not only scholars interested in Brazil, such as Febvre, but also some who perceived Brazilian universities as a break from their Parisian responsibilities and an opportunity to spread their influence abroad. This was especially the case for Georges Gurvitch, editor of *Cahiers internationaux de sociologie*, and by most accounts the most central figure in postwar French sociology.[56]

In March 1947, immediately after defending his dissertation, Braudel returned to São Paulo for the first time since 1937. There he inaugurated a visiting-scholar program that would last well into the 1950s. With his former student Eurípides Simões de Paula now the director of the Faculty of Philosophy, Sciences, and Letters, Braudel decided to renew the French missions to USP, although in a different form. In the postwar, Brazilians were most often the full faculty (*catedráticos*); the French, visiting scholars. By reconnecting with his interwar friends in São Paulo, Braudel helped to secure jobs for his Brazilian allies at USP and to guarantee a sphere of influence for the French social sciences in Brazil, where USP still remained the premiere university. He personally helped to organize the stays of Coornaert, Febvre, Morazé, and Gurvitch, among others.

By the middle of 1949, Coornaert and Febvre, both historians at the Collège de France, had spent time in São Paulo. For Coornaert, USP's first historian, it was a return after a fifteen-year absence. According to Simões, Coornaert was "well received by the university and by his former students."[57] Because of his stature and the fact that it was his first time in São Paulo, Febvre received an even warmer welcome. Not only were his lectures well attended, but he was also given the "key to the city, a reception at city hall, a school parade, banquets, speeches, the Marseillaise sung by those present"; naturally, he was incredibly moved—*comovidíssimo*.[58] In the same letter, Simões informed Braudel of the launch of what would become the *Revista de história*, USP's history journal, in 1950. Braudel's, Febvre's, and Coornaert's lectures from previous years would be among its first publications.

For Braudel and Coornaert, who had taught at USP in the 1930s and had loyal former students, it is not entirely surprising that they would return to São Paulo. For Febvre, however, at the age of seventy, the trip to Brazil in 1949 demands further explanation. Of course, reading the work of Brazilians such as Freyre and hearing so much about Brazil through his students and peers had piqued Febvre's curiosity. Beyond a simple curiosity about Brazil, however, Febvre had concrete plans for furthering relationships between France and Brazil and locating them within the 6th section of the École Pratique, of which he was president and cofounder.

Febvre, who spent several months in Brazil traveling the country, was hosted in variety of venues, including in Recife. In the nation's capital, Rio, he gave lectures at the Escola Superior de Guerra, Itamaraty (Ministry of Foreign Affairs), the Ministry of Education, and the Universidade do Brasil. However, in Rio he spent more time with literary figures such as Augusto Frederico Schmidt—and even Albert Camus, with whom he spent at least an afternoon—than with academics.[59]

It was from Rio that Febvre addressed his programmatic article "Vers une autre histoire" (Toward another history) to France's principal philosophy journal, the *Revue de métaphysique et de morale*.[60] In his article, Febvre promoted the legacy of *Annales*, his work alongside Bloch, and Braudel's *Mediterranean*. He also sought to enlighten philosophers and the general learned public (philosophy still held a dominant position in France) about the "pioneer zones" of history, clearly referencing Monbeig's work.[61]

Febvre's shift from historical research to the memorialization and institutionalization of *Annales* corresponded temporally with his trip to Brazil. While at the same time bringing *Annales to Brazil*, he also sought to prove that *Annales* was global in scope, methodologically and geographically. By signing his article for *Revue de métaphysique et de morale* from Rio de Janeiro, Febvre demonstrated a level of familiarity with Brazil and Latin America and staked a claim for a social science that transcended European and colonial borders.

Bastide and others, both Frenchmen and their students and colleagues, organized Febvre's visit so as to maximize its efficacy. As Bastide wrote Braudel prior to Febvre's visit: "All of us in São Paulo are particularly happy about Monsieur L. Febvre's visit."[62] The Paulistas, concerned about being able to take advantage of the presence of Febvre, wanted more than a stopover. Organizing lectures, class visits, meetings, and dinners for Febvre, they hosted him for a total of three weeks in September 1949.[63] There, he wrote Freyre, he gave a "record" twelve lectures in fifteen days, in the "decidedly devouring city" that is São Paulo.[64]

Febvre lectured on a variety of subjects at both USP and the Escola Livre de Sociologia e Política. Alice Piffer Canabrava, Sérgio Buarque de Holanda, and João Cruz Costa, all three of whom would publish in *Annales*, showed him around. So, too, did Eduardo d'Oliveira França, Braudel's student who would soon be appointed to USP's history department.[65] Ultimately, Febvre's lecture "O homem do século XVI" (Man in the sixteenth century) would be the first article published in the flagship journal of USP's history department, the *Revista de história*.[66] Thus spoke Febvre:

> Who doesn't know of São Paulo and its University in our Parisian milieu? Who is not familiar with, among French historians and geographers, this Faculty of Philosophy where so many of us came—in a spirit of complete confidence and of total friendship—to collaborate in this great work, work of union between your great country and ours? The marriage of someone very young, Brazil, with an old man, France (and I ask you to forgive me for inverting the sexes) that, however apparently disproportionate, had quite a happy outcome.[67]

Febvre's comment about the extensive familiarity of Parisian historians and geographers—if not intellectuals more broadly—with São Paulo may have been overstated, a kind of flattery. It nonetheless suggests a different kind of relationship between Paris and São Paulo than in the interwar years, when philosopher Célestin Bouglé was convinced that the latter's outskirts were full of Indians.[68]

Nevertheless, the unequal relationship between the two remained. Beyond the "spirit of complete confidence and total friendship" between France and Brazil, the differences between them were both of seniority and of quality. France, the old man, had married Brazil, the very young woman (this despite the fact that in Romance languages France is feminine and Brazil, masculine). And yet, their marriage had "quite a happy outcome"—particularly for France, which not only had a vibrant and curious protégé but also one that was rather well off. As much as the bride herself, the dowry may have been worth the marriage.

For Febvre, Braudel, and Charles Morazé, the third cofounder of the 6th section of the École Pratique, the nuptials (and excuse my excessive use of Febvre's metaphor) demanded immediate attention after the separation caused by the war. Morazé went twice to Brazil, first in 1949 alongside Febvre in Rio and then in 1950–51, when he served as visiting professor of politics at USP. Over the course of these stays, he participated fully in high society and collected ideas for what would become his book *Les trois âges du Brésil*.[69]

The attention that these historians gave to Brazil in this postwar moment of intellectual and institutional effervescence was second only to the United States, whose foundations actively participated in the 6th section of the École Pratique, and perhaps to Germany, which remained an important reference for French social science and *Annales* in particular. It is only natural that in addition to reasserting French influence in Brazil, these historians sought to make Brazil more visible within the École Pratique.

Bastide provided them with constant support on the ground in Brazil through 1954 and brought Brazilian themes into French intellectual life. Thanks to Febvre and Braudel, Bastide was elected to the École Pratique in 1950, before ultimately entering the Sorbonne in 1958, upon the completion of his doctorate and publication of his monograph *Le candomblé de Bahia*. Even if Bastide kept his post at USP until 1954, he had already fully begun his transition back to France in 1950. In that year, during break between semesters, he gave a series of lectures on black religious syncretism, messianism, and the African legacy in Brazil, as well as more general ones on Brazilian thought, art, and literature.[70] These lectures made his work visible at the Musée de l'Homme, the Sorbonne, and, most importantly, the École Pratique, where he would soon be hired. Just prior to his election, Bastide wrote Braudel to request his "precious support." "It would be a great joy," he wrote, "to be able to enter the École des Hautes Études to work on questions that are very dear to my heart."[71] (Bastide's wording here suggests that the 6th section was commonly known as the École des Hautes Études well before its official name change in 1975).

Febvre, the president of the 6th section of the École Pratique, wrote Bastide to inform him of his election, emphasizing that he would supervise research instead of teaching in the "dogmatic ex-cathedra" style.[72] Bastide knew that his position was highly coveted. Without the firm support of Braudel and Febvre himself, who fought against "so many contrary winds and hostile tides," as well as his "long and rich Brazilian experience," Bastide certainly could not have obtained such a positive result.[73]

At an institutional level, Bastide served to preserve the relationships between the École Pratique and USP. Braudel wrote: "It seems to me quite logical that you would not abandon your chair in São Paulo, and I would not see any downside should you, during the first two or three years of your teaching . . . in Paris, *faire un tour* in São Paulo." Braudel reminded Bastide that he himself had "known and appreciated" splitting his time between Paris and São Paulo in such a way earlier in his life.[74]

Shortly before Febvre wrote Bastide that he would have no worries from "this boss" and complete liberty in determining his curriculum,[75] Braudel informed him of the extreme flexibility of teaching schedules. With Bastide still in Brazil, he wrote, "Take your time to come back to Paris. Your courses

will begin when it will be possible for you to teach them and you can inter-
rupt them when it will be time to go back to Brazil."[76] Bastide's continued
presence in Brazil was clearly of significant value to the École Pratique. Once
Bastide was back in France, at the École Pratique, Braudel had him give lectures about Brazil elsewhere, for example at the École des Sciences Politiques
(Sciences Po).[77] Latin America and Brazil in particular were in style, and Bastide's lectures would generate further attention for the group of specialists at
the École Pratique.

Lévi-Strauss, much like Bastide, depended on his intimate relations with
Braudel and his Brazilian experience for his hiring at the École Pratique. Upon
learning of his selection, albeit on a nonpermanent basis, he thanked Braudel
"for the considerable part" that he had played in making this happen.[78] Emmanuelle Loyer considers Lévi-Strauss's "half-success," or incomplete belonging
to the dynamic and innovative 6th section of the École Pratique, as a kind of
setback, but we must not overstate it.[79]

In 1948–49, Lévi-Strauss taught on "the social structure of primitive populations in Central Brazil" at the 6th section, and the following year, on "the
place and future of so-called primitive populations in the world."[80] Even after
being elected to the chair held by Marcel Mauss at the 5th section of the École
Pratique (previously called of "religions of non-civilized peoples"), he had his
courses on social structure cross-listed at the 6th section of the École Pratique
as "social anthropology," a term that he emphasized had been in common use
outside France for the past twenty years or so.[81] As for Febvre, he clearly valued
Lévi-Strauss's work on Brazil, and seems to have been influential in both the
publishing of the article "Histoire et ethnologie" in *Revue de métaphysique
et de morale* (to which we will return shortly) and his hiring at UNESCO.[82]

The recruitment of Bastide, Lévi-Strauss, and others to the École Pratique
allowed it to become a hotbed for Brazilian research, but the connections
between the École Pratique and Brazil went far beyond empirical research.
Brazilian universities had become an important, now-institutionalized audience for French social scientists who never conducted research in Brazil. By
providing coveted visiting-teaching positions to scholars such as Georges
Gurvitch and Georges Dumézil, Braudel furthered an important patron-client
network out of which the 6th section of the École Pratique emerged. This, in
turn, further strengthened the École Pratique's position in alliance with certain scholars at the Collège de France and Sorbonne, both in Latin American
research and in other fields.

Braudel and the sociologist Georges Gurvitch had been corresponding
since 1949, when Gurvitch called Braudel "the sorcerer of the Mediterranean."[83]
A couple of years later, Braudel arranged for Gurvitch to teach at USP. He

wrote his old friend João Cruz Costa: "Gurvitch is at the present moment very fatigued, alas, of this Parisian life and the fights with such and such a colleague. Brazil would be for him a kind of paradise ... Do what you can for him ... even the impossible!"[84] To his former student and director of the Faculty Eurípides Simões de Paula, he wrote, "I entrust it to you in asking you to make it work." Gurvitch needed a "break from his crushing work at the Sorbonne" and time to work on his book, *Déterminismes sociaux et liberté humaine.*[85] He was recruited to teach at USP later that very year.[86] One can only imagine that such a favor furthered the relationships between Braudel and Gurvitch—and by extension the École Pratique and the Sorbonne—that would lead to Gurvitch's article "Continuité et discontinuité en histoire et en sociologie" (Continuity and discontinuity in history and sociology) for *Annales.*[87]

While to a lesser degree than for Gurvitch, Braudel used his influence for the benefit of other French scholars passing through South America. For Dumézil, then in Peru, Braudel asked that Simões "request two or three lectures, and perhaps more," as well as to contribute to his expenses.[88] Loyal Simões did not disappoint.[89]

What becomes clear through these examples—and through this section in general—is that Braudel's institution building at what would become the École des Hautes Études en Sciences Sociales depended heavily on Brazil as an intellectual network. Beyond the budget at his and Febvre's disposal were also opportunities for visiting professorships and lecture tours in South America—resources which only consolidated the international prestige of the "École des Hautes Études" as well as of the scholars who made it up. In postwar Brazil, France's intellectual prestige seemed to be recuperating from the setbacks of Vichy, in no small part due to the reactivation of ties from earlier. Bastide received his honorary doctorate from USP in 1951, Braudel in 1954. In France, Brazil's place in the French imaginary grew as well. Beyond institutional and symbolic reasons, it is time to consider more properly intellectual ones.

THE FUNCTIONING OF A CLUSTER: THE "EVENT" OF LÉVI-STRAUSS

If the immediate postwar period saw a heightened interest in France for Brazil and Latin America, by the 1950s that interest generated demand for new books in the social sciences and for a broader reading public. Monbeig published *Pionniers et planteurs de São Paulo* in 1952, after having worked on the topic for nearly two decades. He also published his secondary dissertation, *La croissance de la ville de São Paulo* (The growth of the city of São Paulo), reviewed by Febvre, as well as a book for the general public on Brazil for the collection Que sais-je?[90]

Beyond these studies, Jacques Lambert published *Le Brésil: Structure sociale et institutions politiques* and Morazé, his *Les trois âges du Brésil*, both of which Bastide favorably reviewed.[91] Brazilians themselves, such as the sociologist Antônio Carneiro Leão, also gave lectures at the Sorbonne and other venues, some of which were published in French.[92] Furthermore, in both the social-scientific and literary worlds, which so often intersected, translations of Brazilian authors began to appear, not the least of which was Jorge Amado's *Capitaines des sables* (*Captains of the Sands*) and Bastide's translation of Freyre's *Casa-grande e senzala*.[93]

In this broad context of Brazilian publications, Lévi-Strauss's *Tristes Tropiques* (1955) is particularly emblematic, crystallizing French intellectuals' interest in Brazil. My goal here is not to recapitulate arguments made by others about the literary, philosophical, or properly anthropological value of Lévi-Strauss's most well-known work,[94] but instead to understand its reverberations within a specific social-scientific community whose locus was at the École Pratique. If *Tristes Tropiques* served as a leitmotif for the growing interest in Brazil, it also represents an important moment for understanding how the French-Brazilian collaboration from the 1930s came back to France.

Lévi-Strauss's ruminations on his youth, civilizations past, and the crisis of Western civilization echoed those of Febvre and his colleagues Bastide, Braudel, and Monbeig. He hit a nerve for a kind of *saudade*, or longing, for a France prior to the industrialization and mass culture of what we call now the *trente glorieuses* (1945–75).[95] As an antidote to this France, *Tristes Tropiques* invited reflection on questions as wide-ranging as ecology, human diversity, and even happiness.

As I argue here, *Tristes Tropiques* was far from a solitary work of genius. Lévi-Strauss's colleagues from his Brazilian years helped to produce this work at the level of content and broader relevance. The "event" of *Tristes Tropiques*, a watershed of Brazilianist research and reflection, served to reunite the professors from 1930s São Paulo in the public sphere. If their "rebellion" against Durkheim had brought them together previously, by the end of the 1950s, they had come full circle. Now in positions to construct the social sciences anew, they reclaimed Durkheim's goal of establishing a comprehensive science of humankind. Lévi-Strauss, who had fought so hard to distinguish anthropology from Durkheim's project, would ultimately dedicate *Structural Anthropology* to him.[96]

The São Paulo that Lévi-Strauss remembered in *Tristes Tropiques* had little to do with what his colleagues had seen in the postwar era. Between 1940 and 1952, São Paulo's population had exploded from roughly 1.3 to 2.3 million, and the city had rapidly industrialized with the war effort, the correlative import substitution, and expanding consumer demand.[97] Braudel saw this transformation with his own eyes in 1949, but it was an aerial photograph a few years later that shocked him most. He wrote Cruz Costa, "I received your last postcard with São Paulo's hallucinating forest of houses. Where is our youth, in the hollow of the Esplanade!"[98]

Brazil, which the scholars had considered a "young country," also represented their own youth. When he dedicated his book to "Dona Julieta" and Pierre Monbeig, he wrote, "In memory of the youth that they have known to preserve so well."[99] Lévi-Strauss remembered Brazil in *Tristes Tropiques* as a land of opportunity, both professionally and experientially. The country provided him—like it had Bastide, Braudel, and Monbeig—his first university job and access to new social and geographic realities. As an anthropologist, he had also been given the "supreme reward" of "being the first white man to visit a particular native community."[100] Lévi-Strauss's reflections in *Tristes Tropiques* about growing old suggest not only a certain kind of disillusionment but a closing of possibilities with time at both a personal and a global level.

Lévi-Strauss's colleagues Bastide and Braudel largely focused on civilizations past, whether the legacy of African culture or the Mediterranean in the early modern era. They concurred with Lévi-Strauss's thoughts concerning the unfolding crisis of Western civilization.

> Our Western civilization, which has created the marvels we now enjoy, has only succeeded in producing them at the cost of corresponding ills. The order and harmony of the Western world, its most famous achievement, and a laboratory in which structures of complexity as yet unknown are being fashioned, demand the elimination of a prodigious mass of noxious by-products which now contaminate the globe. The first thing we see as we travel round the world is our own filth, thrown into the face of mankind.[101]

This filth consisted of concrete runways in the Polynesian islands ("the whole of Asia is beginning to look like a dingy suburb"), shantytowns across Africa, and, of course, the actual pollution of the environment. Echoing his critiques of the homogenizing influence of the West on the rest of the world from *Race et histoire* (1952; *Race and History*)—a work to which we will return in chapter 6—Lévi-Strauss regretted that "Mankind has opted for monoculture."[102] Here, as elsewhere, he echoed Monbeig's indignation at the environmental impact of certain kinds of agricultural expansion. Specifically, Monbeig's description of Western settlement in *Pionniers et planteurs* must have sparked Lévi-Strauss's interest, surely laying the basis for *Tristes Tropiques*'s section on the frontier.[103]

Compared to the pioneer front, the relatively untouched Amerindians of Brazil's far interior provided Lévi-Strauss with possibilities for seeing earlier manifestations of the world prior to the "monstrous and incomprehensible catalysm" of European civilization.[104] Lévi-Strauss had no illusions about the decline from the sixteenth century onward of the Kadiweu, Bororo, Nambicuara, and Tupi-Kawahib populations he had studied. But he did feel that he got as close as possible to the very peoples studied by chroniclers such as Jean de Léry and André Thevet, chroniclers about whom he had been reminded by Florestan Fernandes's recently published book on Tupinambá society.[105] These chroniclers also allowed him to reflect on the presence of those very populations—the "savages"—in French Enlightenment thought more generally, especially in Montaigne, Voltaire, Diderot, and Rousseau, his favorite.

In his review of *Tristes Tropiques* for *Annales*, Jean Cazeneuve contended that Lévi-Strauss was renewing an earlier tradition of *voyage philosophique* in French thought.[106] Indeed, Lévi-Strauss's analysis of the Nambicuara chieftancy served as a broader reflection on Rousseau and his analysis of concepts such consent, contract, and reciprocity between individuals and the state.[107] Among the Nambicuara, Bororo, and Tupi-Kawahib, Lévi-Strauss had looked for "a society reduced to its simplest expression."[108] Lévi-Strauss never claimed to reach the state of nature, but instead the transition between nature and culture represented by the neolithic era—precisely the "threshold" between the two analyzed in *The Elementary Structures of Kinship*.

Lévi-Strauss's *voyage philosophique*, however, went well beyond political philosophy. In it, he examined the quest for knowledge, difference, and adventure in contemporary society: those very forms that informed his opening: "I hate travellers and explorers."[109] Lévi-Strauss, in his travels to some of the remotest inhabited places on the Earth, discovered just how futile travel could be. On the one hand, he manifested his elitist yearning for the good old days before travel became a mass phenomenon—not only to the tropics but also to the French Riviera.[110] On the other, he expressed a much deeper malaise of the unfreedom of the modern self. The world had become what Theodor Adorno had called "an open-air prison."[111]

Even after taking the professional risk of teaching in Brazil, then sacrificing that very job to go far into Brazil's interior under very challenging conditions, Lévi-Strauss could not escape from himself. He found himself reproducing what felt like repetitive, even bureaucratic activities: "setting up camp, slinging hammocks and mosquito nets, putting the baggage and packsaddles out of reach of termites and tending animals."[112] In his own words, "my attempted escapism had turned into bureaucratic routine."[113] Beyond recording its author's personal dissatisfaction, Lévi-Strauss's *Tristes Tropiques* also proved pessimistic about overpopulation, environmental degradation, and the destruction of traditional cultures.

Compared to other, more striking forms of alterity, or more satisfying ways to pass the time, his travels appeared futile, and he therefore discouraged others from completing similar journeys. Anticipating Foucault's *Madness and Civilization*, he opened *Tristes Tropiques* with the idea that the afternoon he had spent at the Parisian psychiatric hospital Sainte-Anne provided him with an experience that "no contact with savage Indian tribes" could.[114] And instead of encouraging new research on those very tribes, he ended his book with a "fond farewell to savages and explorations."[115]

The central paradox of *Tristes Tropiques* is that without his extensive travels in Brazil—and, to a lesser extent, in Asia—Lévi-Strauss could not have written the book that he wrote. In any case, he certainly would not have been able to publish it in the collection Terre Humaine, edited by the explorer, anthropologist, and geographer Jean Malaurie. If Malaurie had made it to the North Pole, and Lévi-Strauss, the innermost regions of South America, for everyone else authentic travel was dead; the search for untouched populations, in vain. Even if such populations did exist, the inability to communicate with them would make the entire voyage meaningless.

Lévi-Strauss echoed *Annales'* description of Latin America by criticizing the immensity of superficial literature on the countries in question. At a personal level, Lévi-Strauss was coming to terms with his own age and disinterest in conducting similar expeditions. In terms of social critique, he suggested a specific role for social scientists as experts of travel, both serving to dispel the misconceptions about other cultures and preventing the spread of a new kind of travel to the tropics that was rapidly transforming traditional cultures, often for the worse.

Ironically, Lévi-Strauss's book, with its photos of exotic peoples, contributed to exactly the opposite. As a best seller, it ignited interest in Brazil and the Amazon among the general public, rather than quelling it. For the cluster of researchers working on Latin America, it helped to reactivate the bonds created in 1930s São Paulo—bonds that would help to propel Lévi-Strauss from a self-described outsider into a professor at the Collège de France. Bastide, Braudel, Monbeig, and Febvre were all important allies in this process.

Monbeig had long supported Lévi-Strauss's work, and when he reviewed his *Vie familiale et sociale des indiens Nambikwara* in 1951, he surely gave his friend a morale boost about the interdisciplinary value of his work.[116] Lévi-Strauss's ethnographic manuscript, published in the *Journal de la Société des américanistes* three years prior, served as the central part of *Tristes Tropiques*. Indeed, much of the actual text about the Nambicuara in *Tristes Tropiques* is reproduced from Lévi-Strauss's earlier study. For Monbeig, Lévi-Strauss's work brought "an invaluable enrichment to our understanding of Brazil's interior and the Indian populations of South America."[117] Furthermore, it did so by escaping from the pure fascination with primitive sociology.

In addition to his review, Monbeig's own publications seem to have awoken Lévi-Strauss's Brazilian side. In so doing, they allowed him to examine his own object of study with a broader lens. Monbeig's *Pionniers et planteurs* (1952) emphasized the role not only of climate and topography but also of human activity in shaping the tropics. It did so through the exploration of the psychology of expansion and the *bandeirante* mentality upon which it was based.[118] Lévi-Strauss drew upon the work of Monbeig and also of Buarque de Holanda, who had preceeded him in advancing research into "the psychological determinants of the movement of Portuguese colonial expansion in the lands of our America."[119] In 1948, Lévi-Strauss had, along with Rivet and Febvre, helped to organize Buarque de Holanda's visit to Paris, where he gave several conferences, one of which would be published in *Annales*.[120]

The people and landscapes found in the work of Monbeig and Buarque de Holanda largely made up Lévi-Strauss's chapters "São Paulo," "Towns and Countrysides," and "Pioneer Zone." They also likely encouraged him to describe the various people whom he observed and depended on in his earlier voyages, such as Emydio, whose hand was blown off by his own rifle and whom Lévi-Strauss sent from the Serra do Norte expedition by plane back to Cuiabá.[121] Whereas ordinary people such as Emydio had no place in a traditional ethnography, in which direct contact between the observer and the natives was privileged, they did in *Tristes Tropiques*.

Like Monbeig had done for Lévi-Strauss's ethnography, Bastide emphasized that the value of *Tristes Tropiques* extended far beyond Latin America. In his review for *Présence africaine*, Bastide claimed that it was "the very situation of the ethnologist in the modern world that is brought into play."[122] He then argued for *Tristes Tropiques*'s importance for Africans and Africanists who were in the thick of important debates about tradition and modernity as well as their relationship with Europe. (Guinea would be the first French African colony to declare independence, in 1958; the rest of French West Africa would follow shortly thereafter.) Beyond its ethnological relevance for describing a rapidly changing world, *Tristes Tropiques*, Bastide highlighted, possessed literary value.

He wrote, "I had . . . the same kind of pleasure reading Lévi-Strauss as in reading Proust."[123] What differed were the kinds of images that the respective authors used to reflect upon *temps perdu*, as well as the kinds of subjectivity they sought to describe. While Proust evoked gustative images of foods that "melt, that dissolve in the mouth, that become juices and flavors," Lévi-Strauss evoked mineral ones of "sand, hard rocks, geological strata."[124] And whereas the Proustian novel sought lost time at an individual level, "Proustian ethnography looks for human lost time, [with] human meaning collective."[125]

Bastide's review resonated with Lévi-Strauss, who thanked him for the formulation of a "minerological Proust." Lévi-Strauss "had very consciously used it as inspiration."[126] As for *Annales*, was not reconstituting past societies in their totality precisely their objective? The attention that Febvre, Braudel, and *Annales* gave Lévi-Strauss upon the publication of *Tristes Tropiques* suggests that they, too, appreciated the Proustian contemplation of societies past and present. This was despite significant methodological and disciplinary differences, particularly in what concerns temporality.

Febvre wrote Lévi-Strauss, telling him that he read the book of his "Brazilian experiences" in a single sitting (*d'un trait*). For Febvre, it was an exceptionally rich book with a surprising point of view: "It not only allows one to reflect on exotic questions and destinies, but allows one to discover, behind the already well-known ethnographer of great stature, a man who voluntarily uncovers and even unmasks himself." Febvre concluded, "What richness and thought in your work, what quality and meditation, what aristocracy of style"![127]

Having intended to review *Tristes Tropiques* for *Annales*, Febvre passed away before he could do so, in 1957.[128] Because of the delay, when Jean Cazeneuve's review was ready, it was published in the very same issue of *Annales* as Braudel's much-acclaimed article "History and the Social Sciences: The *Longue Durée*."[129] Braudel had received a copy of *Tristes Tropiques* from Lévi-Strauss upon its publication, in 1955, for which he thanked and congratulated him.[130] Since then, however, Lévi-Strauss had published his programmatic *Structural Anthropology*, to which Braudel felt he needed to respond.

Braudel and Lévi-Strauss were in the midst of debating notions of structure and temporality—alongside and at times against the uses of neighboring disciplines. Bastide had organized a conference on the word "structure" in January 1958, at the École Pratique des Hautes Études.[131] There, Lévi-Strauss discussed the uses of the concept alongside the mathematician Georges-Théodule Guilbaud, linguist Émile Benveniste, psychologist Daniel Lagache, sociologist Georges Gurvitch, economists André Marchal and Edmond Malinvaud, and philosopher Maurice Merleau-Ponty. Braudel presided over the session.[132]

Lévi-Strauss's presentation must have left Braudel with the impression that the structures that he had elucidated in *The Mediterranean* had little to do with those that Lévi-Strauss presented as a research program.[133] While Braudel advanced both the geohistorical *longue durée* and the economic conjuncture, Lévi-Strauss argued for a synchronic—and essentially timeless—structuralism. Epistemologically speaking, these programs were very different and even antagonistic. As I showed in chapter 4, Lévi-Strauss constructed rather abstract models of human culture, based upon internal mental structures. Braudel, on the other hand, built history out of structures largely external to humans (namely, geography, climate, and economic materialism). He and Lévi-Strauss not only asked different questions based upon their respective disciplines but arrived at them through conflicting approaches—the internal and external being just one prominent example.

Nonetheless, the relations between Lévi-Strauss and Braudel proved largely symbiotic. Their debates ultimately served to advance both of their interests, bringing them into the limelight as theorists of the social sciences and not simply researchers with published monographs. In hindsight, they helped to strengthen, rather than weaken, their respective disciplines across the social sciences and in the public view. Precisely because they were from different fields, the debate between them helped to carve out their positions, both intellectually and institutionally. Braudel could claim the 6th section of the École Pratique as a kind of antithesis to structuralism, all while supporting Lévi-Strauss in his quest for admission to the Collège de France.

The year after the 1958 conference on structure, Lévi-Strauss published *Structural Anthropology*. The opening chapter, "History and Anthropology," had originally appeared as "Histoire et ethnologie," alongside Febvre's paradigmatic "Vers une autre histoire."[134] In it, Lévi-Strauss distanced himself from historical schools of anthropology and sociology, whether evolutionist or diffusionist in their thinking. Not only were such approaches "conjectural and ideological," but "they do not teach us anything about the conscious and unconscious processes," either for individuals or for collectivities.[135]

The historian, he argued, depended on the study of documents from "amateur ethnographers" from the past. For this reason, were historians not "as far removed from the culture they described as is the modern investigator from the Polynesians or Pygmies"?[136] The major difference between history and anthropology, according to Lévi-Strauss, was that "history organizes its data in relation to conscious expressions of social life, while anthropology proceeds by examining its unconscious foundations."[137]

These unconscious foundations, according to Lévi-Strauss, became clearest through the analysis of synchronic structures, the likes of which Roman Jakobson had argued for in linguistics (phonemes) and as Lévi-Strauss himself had in anthropology (elementary structures). Synchronic elements would allow the anthropologist to arrive at "a single structural scheme existing and operating in different spatial and temporal contexts."[138] In such a way, the anthropologist could analyze a particular institution or set of relations that spanned space and time without having to prove how they came to exist in different places or at different times. Instead, one could attempt to understand the fundamental logics behind them, logics that had more to do with mathematical permutations of mental processes than they did with concrete realities.

Despite his emphasis on synchronic versus diachronic structures, Lévi-Strauss did not wish to delegitimize history, quite the contrary.[139] "Any good history book," he claimed, "is saturated with anthropology."[140] As a poignant example, he referred to Febvre's *The Problem of Unbelief in the Sixteenth Century*,[141] closing with the following: "If anthropology and history once begin to collaborate in the study of contemporary societies, it will become apparent that here, as elsewhere, the one science can achieve nothing without the help of the other."[142] Nonetheless, as Lilia Schwarcz has suggested, Lévi-Strauss's olive branch to history offered a particular reading of history, one that was much closer to the event-based (*événementielle*) history that Braudel and *Annales* defined themselves against.[143]

Braudel's "History and the Social Sciences: The *Longue Durée*" drew upon what he saw as the most useful aspects of Lévi-Strauss's structuralism, all the while neutralizing its ahistorical dimensions. With considerable irony, Braudel asked, "Do the human sciences emerge from a supplementary effort of definition or from additional bad moods?" He called new tendencies in the social sciences "illusory," preoccupied with "false problems," and criticized Lévi-Strauss for his use of "unconscious history" and dependence on the "juvenile imperialism of 'qualitative' mathematics."[144]

We must not overemphasize these differences, however. Braudel himself wrote, "Let us not be unjust; there is an interest in these quarrels and these refutations. The desire to affirm oneself against others is necessarily at the origin of new curiosities: to deny the other is already to recognize him."[145] Throughout his article, Braudel cited Lévi-Strauss's work extensively—everything from *The Elementary Structures of Kinship* to his famous debate with Roger Caillois and even his efforts at UNESCO to advance mathematical models in the social sciences.[146] Even if Braudel disagreed with some of the conclusions of UNESCO's findings, he insisted that UNESCO's work (and Lévi-Strauss's in particular) was of "great interest."[147] Furthermore, Braudel made it clear that he considered anthropology and history to be of "the same adventure of the mind."[148] Lévi-Strauss's work may have been ahistorical, but Braudel found it to be "the most intelligent, the clearest, [and] the best rooted in the social experience from which all must depart."[149] Perhaps most importantly, it established new dialogues between formal mathematical modeling and the social sciences.

At the surface level, the debate between Lévi-Strauss and Braudel—between structuralism and the *longue durée*—appears necessarily antagonistic. Nonetheless, their public disagreements, while significant, covered up a much more supportive relationship in the private sphere, based upon a strong sense of solidarity, if not friendship. Braudel, who had already been elected to the

Collège de France, in 1949, was well aware of Lévi-Strauss's multiple setbacks there. This time, in 1959, he was in a position to help.

Braudel must have sent a copy of "History and the Social Sciences" to Lévi-Strauss, as evidenced by the archive of the Laboratoire d'Anthropologie Sociale.[150] In October 1958, Lévi-Strauss wrote Braudel to inform him of his candidacy, looking forward to the chance to "visit you, and to receive your opinion and your advice."[151] By February 1959, the month before the Collège de France would decide, Lévi-Strauss wrote to thank Braudel for his "tenacity," without which his election would have never become reality.[152] Braudel kept him on edge about the end result, likely more out of formality than anything else: "I still hesitate, but believe I will vote for you on March 15"; he nonetheless said that he would "take great pleasure" in speaking with Lévi-Strauss afterward.[153]

Lévi-Strauss was, of course, elected to the Collège, with the chair of social anthropology. This position would serve him as he constructed the Laboratoire d'Anthropologie Sociale, thenceforth France's premier anthropological research center. That is in itself another story. What concerns us here is that Lévi-Strauss arrived at the Collège not only through his knowledge of Brazilian Indians but because of his friends and allies from his days teaching in Brazil. Brazil had come back to France as both an object and a collective subject, centered around those that made up the French missions to USP in the 1930s. In his inaugural lecture at the Collège, Lévi-Strauss claimed to have accumulated an epistemological debt from the Brazilian Indians with whom he had spent time.[154] As I have shown, he also contracted a symbolic debt with his peers who had helped him to become more than a collector of curiosities.

At Christmas 1959, Bastide wrote Paulo Duarte after having spoken with Lévi-Strauss at the Musée de l'Homme. They had spoken of Duarte at length and of Lévi-Strauss's preparation for his inaugural lecture. Quite serendipitously indeed, "This conversation took place in front of the showcase where several magnificent feather headdresses of Tupi Indians from Brazil were displayed!"[155]

On January 5, 1960, Lévi-Strauss gave his inaugural lecture. In it he claimed that anthropology had come into maturity. This occurred the day that

> Western Man began to understand that he would never understand himself, as long as on the Earth's surface, a single race or a single people would be taken for him as an object. Only then, anthropology could affirm itself for what it is: an enterprise, renewing and atoning for [the sins of] the Renaissance, of extending humanism to the dimensions of humanity.[156]

Lévi-Strauss had taken South America's promise as a research field to its most extreme extent, relativizing the very centrality of the West.

Bastide had already been doing this for some time, by engaging extensively with Brazilian intellectuals and members of the communities he studied. He would nonetheless take such a critique even farther in *The African Religions of Brazil*, claiming to have indeed become "African," if a syncretic New-World African.[157]

> In fact it is possible in Brazil to be a Negro without being African, and contrariwise, to be both white and African. I can therefore say at the threshold of this book: Africanus sum, inasmuch as I have been accepted by one of those religious sects, which regards me as a brother in faith, having the same obligations and the same privileges as the other members of the same degree. The experience to be recounted here is lived experience.[158]

Neither Monbeig nor Braudel would offer such a radical critique of Eurocentrism, but they in their own ways had helped to shift Europe away from the center of conversation. It is easy now to attribute this change to the broader postwar context of decolonization and a new international system of which the UN was part. This forgets, however, just how important intellectuals themselves were in producing this shifting discursive landscape.

If anything, the rise of South America within postwar French social science was more than a simple reflection of a broader zeitgeist. *Annales* and the 6th section of the École Pratique des Hautes Études served as centers to federate knowledge about South America across disciplines and to concretize the ambitions of the generation of Rivet and Febvre from the interwar period. Through such collective efforts, Braudel, Bastide, Lévi-Strauss, and Monbeig worked closely together in everything from publishing to achieving research positions.

In the 1960s, the characters of this story gradually drifted in separate directions as their own oeuvre became increasingly autonomous. Bastide continued to publish on Afro-American culture and a variety of other topics; Monbeig led research groups at the CNRS, some of which dealt with Brazil; Lévi-Strauss transitioned from social structure and into studies of myth, a journey that began with *The Savage Mind* (newly translated as *Wild Thought*) and continued through *Mythologiques*.[159] And Braudel undertook his second major work, a trilogy on capitalism and material life.

One principal question remains, however, and that is to know why Brazil proved so interesting for French social scientists in an era of decolonization. In the next and final chapter, Brazil will appear not only as an object of study or as a network for these French scholars' intellectual projects. It will take the form of two Brazilian social scientists, Gilberto Freyre and Florestan Fernandes, debating over whether Brazil was a haven for racial equality.

CHAPTER SIX

Racial Democracy, *Métissage*, and Decolonization between Brazil and France

In the 1950s, Brazilian sociologist Gilberto Freyre became an important figure in French social-scientific and intellectual life as his books on colonial Brazil, plantation society, and slavery started to be translated from Portuguese into French.[1] Fernand Braudel considered Freyre's work to be "singularly innovative," as well as an important introduction to a country whose "original values matter . . . for all of humanity."[2] Apropos Freyre's most famous work, *Casa-grande e senzala*, translated into French as *Maîtres et esclaves*, Roland Barthes emphasized: "The conjunction of a racial history still entirely fresh and of a great intelligence nourished by the most advanced disciplines has given Brazil this prestigious book."[3] Lucien Febvre and Georges Gurvitch, editor of France's premier sociological journal, *Cahiers internationaux de sociologie*, visited Freyre at his home in Pernambuco. They invited him to France, where he presented his work at the Sorbonne, the École Pratique des Hautes Études, and a several-day workshop at the Château de Cerisy-la-Salle, in Normandy.

What did these French intellectuals see in Freyre? And why did they continue to value his work, even after it began to be challenged in Brazil, the US, and at UNESCO, in the heart of Paris? This chapter argues that in a period in which decolonization was already underway, Freyre piqued the interest of French social scientists looking to overcome the growing antagonism between colonizer and colonized. Coming out of the worst ethnic genocide in history, in which the French government actively took part, a number of French intellectuals embraced racial mixing, or *métissage*, in part to denounce racism and the proponents of ethnic purity and in part to blunt independence movements emerging in the colonies.[4]

The Portuguese, with the help of their Brazilian friends such as Freyre, constructed a tempting model of a people adapted to the tropics by nature and prone to mixing with subject populations.[5] This "luso-tropical" ideal of harmony and miscegenation contrasted with both the one-drop rule and the French civilizing mission.[6] Beyond his style, Freyre's luso-tropicalism was what most interested the French. Indeed, Roger Bastide framed the 1956 conference for Freyre in Cerisy-la-Salle with the question: "What should we think of the 'luso-tropical' solution to the racial question of which Gilberto Freyre has become the defender?"[7]

Freyre, as early as the 1930s, defended Portugal's role in the colonization of Brazil, favoring renewed ties with Portugal so as to forestall new forms of political, economic, and cultural colonialism. Specifically, he was wary of the United States, England, and the capitalist world system that they largely controlled. If unchecked, he argued, these countries would seek to impose their way of life on places like Brazil and parts of the Portuguese Empire— "the luso-tropics." Freyre insisted on the particularly "human" character of Portuguese colonization (in contrast with that of the Anglo-Saxons), based on racial mixing (*mestiçagem*):[8]

> This human character of Portuguese colonization, if in Brazil it had its broadest and happiest expression, is nonetheless common to Portugal's colonial efforts in general. Everywhere that this type of colonization predominated, racial prejudice appears insignificant, and *mestiçagem* is psychologically, socially, and might we even say, ethically active and creative.[9]

Freyre lived in Jim Crow America during his undergraduate studies at Baylor University. In Waco, Texas, infamous for the lynching of Jesse Washington, in 1916, just a year after the release of *The Birth of a Nation*, Freyre witnessed the poverty of black neighborhoods and heard firsthand of lynchings, even claiming to smell them.[10] Regardless of the necessarily constructive elements of Freyre's memoirs, these years were an experiential "coming to consciousness" for the young Freyre—a series of events that produced his own subjectivity as non-American.[11] This experience encouraged him to look for models other than the United States, and ultimately to insist on Brazil as an antithesis to countries such as South Africa in which formal, legal racial segregation predominated. By the 1950s, however, at the height of the Cold War, Freyre's idea that Brazil was a "racial democracy" took on a more specific meaning: as a third way between the US and the Soviet Union, not only economically but also racially.[12] This was particularly the case in what he saw as the most authentically Brazilian region: the Northeast.[13]

In the US, Freyre thought, the politics of difference prevented "new combinations"; in the Soviet Union, while racially tolerant, "red orthodoxy," he argued, prevented free expression. In comparison to the superpowers, Brazil was both racially and economically welcome to mixing. In the 1950s Freyre became increasingly associated with the Portuguese colonial mission—touring the Portuguese Empire, lecturing on the Portuguese openness to racial mixing and downplaying the role of the exploitation of black labor by whites.

Freyre's personal ties with French social scientists such as Braudel, Febvre, Gurvitch, and Bastide were crucial for his generous reception in France. But, as I argue, what made Freyre's luso-tropicalism stick was the ways in which it paralleled French Republican ideology and Latin humanism in a moment when France's African colonies, especially Algeria, more vociferously and violently demanded independence.[14] Freyre's accounts of "racial and humoral mixture," to use Barthes's words, offered a tempting alternative in the form of racial mixing to the rise of ethnic nationalism and anticolonial struggle.[15]

While it is doubtful that such ideas profoundly affected race relations or population control in the colonies,[16] French social scientists' fascination with miscegenation in the postwar period provides fertile ground for a kind of archaeology of French attitudes toward race. In what follows, I consider Freyre's place within this stratum, the critiques leveled against him by UNESCO, and the counter social-scientific models offered by the likes of Florestan Fernandes, Lévi-Strauss, and even Bastide, who saw in Freyre's project a possibility for emancipation, however limited its present validity may have been.

FREYRE'S FAVORABLE FRENCH RECEPTION

As we have seen, since the 1930s, Freyre maintained cordial and even friendly relationships with Paulista intellectuals and the French professors who had helped to found the University of São Paulo.[17] Paul Arbousse-Bastide wrote a long preface to Freyre's *Um engenheiro francês no Brasil* (A French engineer in Brazil), published in 1940, expressing great honor for having been invited to do so and offering his most "amiable homage" to Freyre.[18] Recently, Braudel had reviewed his work and requested his participation in *Annales*.[19] Freyre's most important French ally, however, was Febvre; the latter's visit to Brazil helped to consolidate Freyre's position at the height of French academic life.

Febvre's itinerary in Brazil in 1949 and in Latin America more generally was by no means centered on a visit to Recife, Freyre's hometown.[20] Freyre, however, made a point of ensuring Febvre's presence in Recife, in addition to the traditional bastions of French university influence—São Paulo and Rio de Janeiro. Upon Febvre's arrival, Freyre penned an article titled "O professor Febvre no Brasil" (Professor Febvre in Brazil), outlining the credentials and intellectual background of this eminent visitor. A myriad of such articles appeared in Freyre's column in the Rio-based newspaper *O Cruzeiro*, but the fact that he sent this one to Febvre suggests he was using it as a way of introduction.[21] Febvre, writing from São Paulo, thanked Freyre for the "charming article" that "touched him."[22]

Unfortunately, Febvre's archive contains no letters from Freyre, but Febvre's letters to Freyre, as well as his notebooks from his trip, allow for a partial reconstruction of his visit to Recife. It was his last stop on a whirlwind trip that took him to several places in Chile and Porto Alegre, São Paulo, Belo Horizonte, and Rio in Brazil.[23] After his trip, upon his return to Paris, Febvre wrote to his "cher ami":

> I am once again Parisian. And above all, descended from heaven, my mind still filled with the beauties of America. I write to thank you. Because you guided the entire end of my voyage, in the most touching and effective ways. I saw Recife, her wide landscape of whitewater and clouds, her charming bridges as old as those of Europe . . . her narrow roads with the talkative people of humble stock. I saw Olinda, her old churches, her remarkable convent of Saint Francis . . . I saw, one morning, Gilberto Freyre's home, and all around it his so typically Pernambucan garden, with its old trees and young flowers . . . I saw one of your young relatives who entertained by himself an old talkative, mannerful [*gesticuleux*] Negro, with lively eyes.[24]

Febvre's vision, little more than picturesque, was based upon one of Freyre's books that he had given him: *Guia prático, histórico e sentimental da cidade do Recife* (Practical, historical, and sentimental guide to the city of Recife). Of course, for Febvre the "talkative, mannerful Negro" was very much part of that landscape—not as a historical subject, per se, but as decoration like the trees and flowers. This, too, is not entirely different from Freyre himself, who, despite valorizing African civilizations in some abstract sense, never really considered Africans or Afro-Brazilians as agents in historical processes.

Freyre not only showed Febvre around Recife. From Febvre's letter, it appears as though Freyre accompanied him to places as far away as Goiana and Igarassu in Pernambuco.[25] Freyre introduced Febvre to popular folkloric traditions such as *cavalo-marinho* and *bumba-meu-boi*, "dazzling" him with

FIG. 7 Postcard of *bumba-meu-boi*. Archives de l'École des hautes études en sciences sociales, Archives de Lucien Febvre.

all that "he did not know" about Brazil.[26] For Febvre, Brazil, considering its regional diversity, was nothing short of a "miracle": "what a subject for meditation!"[27]

Febvre's curiosity about Brazil—and his enthusiasm for Freyre as a person—may have been the primary reason for the French translation of *Casa-grande e senzala*. When Febvre informed Roger Bastide of the latter's likely hiring at the 6th section of the École Pratique des Hautes Études, he requested that Bastide "suggest one or two texts" for translation.[28] *Casa-grande e senzala*, which Bastide ultimately translated as *Maîtres et esclaves*, was evidently one of them. Febvre wrote the preface.

In his preface, Febvre praised Freyre, highlighting his *Annales*-like methodology of doing social history and his approach to racial mixing.[29] Febvre's reserves and criticisms about *Casa-grande e senzala* were largely tempered, if not removed entirely. Gurvitch wrote to Freyre in June 1952, "Mr. Lucien Febvre has already written a preface for your beautiful book, but he is in the process of rewriting it, because he was more severe than he would like. I will take care of it. Braudel too."[30]

Drafting up criticism and toning it down is part of the dialectic of much academic writing, leaving no smoking gun of censorship in Febvre's final preface. That said, Gurvitch's "I will take care of it. Braudel too" suggests that

Febvre's criticism was discouraged by his peers. In the absence of Febvre's original drafts, we cannot say whether Febvre's reservations about *Maîtres et esclaves* were more methodological or political. We do know, however, that Gurvitch and Braudel saw to it that they were toned down or eliminated in the final version of his text.

In his preface, "Brésil, terre d'histoire" (Brazil, Land of History), Febvre leaned toward the picturesque, describing the "fusion of races" and the "new society that was elaborated between the equator and the [Tropic of] Capricorn." This society, he continued, offered "a palette of graded tones, from leather-red to rosy white."[31] Febvre, however, was far from blind to the violence and brutality of slavery. Febvre, more so than Freyre, emphasized the annihilation and exploitation of non-European peoples that laid the foundation for Brazilian society. He wrote:

> It is easy to accumulate testimonies, narratives of so many horrendous acts: blacks tied, living, by the mouth to a cannon and receiving the projectile through their body or *mulatresses* loved by their master, whose jealous white wife, for once and for all, ordered that they rip out her beautiful eyes—and that they serve them at dessert, entirely bloody, to the unfaithful husband. It is no longer worth our while to bemoan paternalism when we need to scream out man's suffering. But, alongside such scenes, there are others, many others, more consoling for humanity. And, I will say, as a historian, with greater consequences for the future.[32]

Febvre's criticism of Brazilian slavery, so abrupt after his light-hearted and colorful description of Brazil, overpowers and even contradicts the rest of his preface. Indeed, it is likely this section that he was working through when Gurvitch said, "I will take care of it." For Febvre, however, it appears less that he was convinced by Freyre's historical treatment of the Portuguese colonizer as inherently benign, and more by the promise of racial mixing in the future. In a Europe recently destroyed by war and ethnic cleansing, and in a French Empire that seemed increasingly divided into two camps, colonizer and colonized, Febvre looked to South America as a source of inspiration. Europeans, "haunted by what the world is becoming," he claimed, "are turning their eyes in an anguished search, toward these immense South American lands—so rich in promise."[33] South America, Febvre insisted, brought to light "the largest problems that are facing, in 1952, the carriers of the old European civilization."[34]

Among these problems, probably the most important was the right of "peoples of color" to be free from the "yoke" of "the civilized white man."[35] Febvre defended this right, but worried about increasing divisions between societies and their visions of progress—something that he personally experienced vis-à-vis "Science," with its increasing capacity to "annihilate Humanity."[36] (He was probably referring to the atomic bomb.) The world, instead of addressing its most pressing questions, Febvre claimed, "entered into revolution."[37] And it is here, and precisely here, that Febvre saw Freyre as providing "a grand lesson in Brazilian history": "a privileged experiment in the fusion of races, the exchange of civilizations. This Brazil, a melting pot [*un creuset*]."[38]

Prior to writing his introduction to *Maîtres et esclaves*, Febvre had his own ideas for understanding French history as one of racial mixture. In his manuscript, written in 1950 and only published posthumously, entitled *Nous sommes des sang-mêlés* (We are mixed bloods), Febvre insisted that France had always been a "mixed" civilization.[39] Even if Febvre was primarily concerned with the different European origins of France (ranging from the primordial synthesis of Gauls and the Franks to late nineteenth- and early twentieth-century immigrants), there is no question that his positive treatment of racial mixing led him to valorize Freyre's work. But Febvre was far from alone in embracing Freyre in France. The promotion of *Maîtres et esclaves* was particularly well planned, both inside and outside the academy.

In addition to Febvre's support in placing his book within the academic mainstream, Freyre counted on Gurvitch's support for its dissemination. Freyre and Gurvitch likely met in Paris in 1948 at UNESCO and corresponded as early as 1952.[40] Gurvitch served as Freyre's intermediary with Roger Caillois at Gallimard about the forthcoming publication of *Maîtres et esclaves*, discussed various possibilities for going to Brazil, and expressed interest in his forthcoming book on Asia and Africa, "which we look forward to."[41] Ultimately, Gurvitch received an invitation from the University of Pernambuco and the Casa Rui Barbosa in Rio, where he lectured in the fall of 1952. Freyre, in return, could count on Gurvitch's support in France.

Upon Gurvitch's return to Paris from Brazil, just months after the publication of *Maîtres et esclaves*, he wrote Freyre to keep him abreast of its reception: "I can assure you that your book has been *very successful in France*. It was discussed at length in *Combat*. We speak of it often, and it was even cited in discussion during a recent session at the Faculty of Letters. They say that it sells well." In addition, Gurvitch insisted, "Our friend Braudel and I are actively working to prepare some good surprises for you upon your arrival in Paris this spring. The École Pratique des Hautes Études and the Centre d'Études Sociologiques are looking forward to your lectures."[42]

Gurvitch's reference to *Combat* was not the only indication of a broader reception in France. Roland Barthes reviewed *Maîtres et esclaves* in *Lettres nouvelles*, and Jean Pouillon did the same in *Les temps modernes*.[43] In Gurvitch's own *Cahiers internationaux de sociologie*, the Africanist Georges Balandier reviewed it, too.[44] The French, according to Bastide, understood the book's "human significance alongside its scientific value."[45] Beyond the reviews that Bastide knew were in the works in *Annales* (Braudel) and *Cahiers internationaux de sociologie*, he highlighted a review in *Christianisme social*, a Protestant journal that he had contributed to throughout his life.[46] Bastide had not always agreed with Freyre's conclusions, but that did not prevent him from translating *Casa-grande e senzala*, just as Febvre's reservations about Freyre's possible minimization of the cruelty of slavery did not prevent him from writing a generally favorable preface.

In France Freyre was on the rise both inside and outside academia. Heralded for his affinities with *Annales*, he became one of two non-French and the only non-European on the director's committee of the Fondation Marc-Bloch.[47] His personal connections with Braudel and Gurvitch ensured the dissemination of his work among historians and sociologists. And literary figures inside and outside the Sorbonne embraced his particular brand of Latin humanism. Freyre's unquestionable emergence in 1950s France, however, is only part of the story. For at precisely the same time, his work was coming under attack in Brazil and in Paris—but not in French universities.

THE UNESCO PROJECT ON RACE RELATIONS AND THE CRITIQUE OF RACIAL DEMOCRACY

In the years 1951 and 1952, the United Nations Educational, Social, and Cultural Organization (UNESCO) organized and funded research into race relations in Brazil.[48] This field research followed UNESCO's statements on race by social scientists, including Lévi-Strauss, and biologists and geneticists from the previous years.[49] A large part of Brazil's selection as a case study for race relations had to do with the fact that UNESCO's first director of the Department of Social Sciences, Arthur Ramos, was Brazilian.[50] (Freyre was offered the job after his participation at the UNESCO conference on "tensions affecting international understanding," but turned it down.)[51] Swiss-born Alfred Métraux headed up the newly created section on race relations in that very department.[52]

In September 1952, with research underway, the *UNESCO Courier* published a special issue on "A Report on Race Relations in Brazil." Métraux's introduction, "An Inquiry into Race Relations in Brazil," laid out the justification for such a study.[53] He sought to answer the fundamental question: "Is the [racial] harmony real or apparent?" The underlying question was whether Brazil was a model for replication. Did Brazil's racial model provide an example to the rest of the world, or was its claim to be a land free from racial prejudice a construction by intellectuals such as Freyre and by foreigners such as Febvre, immediately impressed by Brazil's "palette of graded tones"?

Métraux had long been interested in Brazilian racial relations. His enthusiasm for Freyre's work as early as 1940 is evident in their correspondence, and even in his article "Brazil: A Land of Harmony for All Races?," from 1950, he had no problem with characterizing the Portuguese as relatively humane.[54] According to Métraux himself, they "never attached much importance to race" and "inter-married freely with all native peoples they conquered and colonized."[55] Freyre claimed that in Bahia Métraux had recognized "that in Brazil there is almost no racial problem. That color prejudice does not create drama, crises, or agitations here as it does in other countries. That this is due to a historical formation different from that of North America or South Africa."[56]

After Métraux traveled throughout Brazil, meeting with his research teams in Salvador, Rio, Recife, and São Paulo, and receiving their initial results, however, his inquiry matured. In the name of science, he sought to critically test the gains of the "racial democracy" so frequently "remarked on by travelers and sociologists."[57] While Métraux still held out hope for positive examples of race relations in Brazil, he forthrightly questioned the validity of preexisting scholarship—and implicitly that of Freyre. Nonetheless, Métraux recognized Freyre's international clout and advanced as diplomatically as possible. He therefore sought to keep Freyre affiliated with the project, but at a sufficient distance to prevent Freyre's vision from overriding the findings of those who had actually conducted sociological research.

Freyre was one of the first people Métraux visited in Brazil on behalf of UNESCO. After their meeting in the fall of 1950, Métraux wrote in his diary, Freyre "accepts in principle to write about the theme of the ascent of mulattos and blacks and to use . . . unpublished documents."[58] The following summer, still in the initial phases of UNESCO's research, Métraux confirmed a contract with Freyre concerning an introduction that Freyre would write for the final publication of the various regional studies underway in Salvador, Rio de Janeiro, Recife, and São Paulo.[59] In the meantime, Freyre had added a chapter to his *Sobrados e mucambos*, on the "system of miscegenation in patriarchal and semipatriarchal Brazil," in which he doubled down on his claims about the *reciprocity* between cultures, rather than domination, implied by racial mixing.[60] Through an examination of subsequent correspondence, we can understand the conflicts that ultimately led Freyre to back out of the project altogether— much to the chagrin of Métraux, who wrote to Freyre in March 1952:

> René Ribeiro tells me that before writing your introduction you were waiting for the manuscripts prepared by the different research teams. Here, I think that

there is a misunderstanding. If you remember our conversation correctly, you will recall that I asked for an introduction of historical character, that is to say a panorama of the history of blacks in Brazil from the sixteenth century until today. Your introduction should help to give a temporal depth to a study of contemporary sociology. In other words, I would ask you to summarize, for the European public, the masterpieces that made you famous . . . It is therefore not necessary for you to have read the different sociological contributions for you to write your introduction.[61]

Métraux, still fond of Freyre's interpretation of Brazil and convinced of the value that it would bring to UNESCO's report, insisted on the specificity of Freyre's preface as being "historical" in a compilation of studies of "contemporary sociology." In effect, Métraux sought to have it both ways: on the one hand, he wanted to have Freyre, a talented writer and public figure, as a symbolic part of the UNESCO inquiry, and on the other, he hoped to effectively silence Freyre's criticism of the respective regional studies. The latter's "historical" knowledge may have been interesting, but in no way did it make him an adequate judge of the scientific investigation that followed.

Métraux faced "huge disappointment" with Freyre when the latter's requests for a change in the nature of his contribution became nothing less than "impossible."[62] Freyre never wrote the introduction, and in retrospect, we can more fully understand why. It would have been a humiliating experience for the veteran intellectual, so well-known for his interpretation of race relations in Brazil, to be relegated to "history" while younger scholars, including several non-Brazilians, would take his place as the sociologists of the next generation.

Furthermore, in a period of decolonization, in which his luso-tropicalist discourse began to take on much more concrete meaning vis-à-vis Portugal's empire in Mozambique and Angola, Freyre could not let the more critical studies of Brazilian race relations offered by UNESCO have the last word. In 1951 and 1952, Freyre toured the Portuguese Empire, in Africa and Asia, serving as a state representative of Salazar's regime.[63] He advanced his ideas of the Portuguese peoples' affinities with the tropics and relatively benign treatment of subject populations in the colonies.

Several months had passed since Métraux and Freyre's "disappointing" correspondence when it became clear that neither would have his way. While Freyre did not write an extended historical essay, he did publish a two-page-long piece on "The Negro's Role in Brazilian History," directly following Métraux's introduction discussed above.[64] It would be the last of Freyre's contributions to UNESCO's studies, well before the final publication of its results. In his essay, Freyre reemphasized his claim about Brazil's relatively humane slavery. He also claimed that, in contrast to the situation of "workmen in the new factories of Europe during the early nineteenth century . . . it was better to be a slave in a typically patriarchal sugar or coffee plantation in Brazil."[65]

Bastide and his team of Brazilian colleagues (many of whom were former students) mounted one of the more direct challenges to Freyre. Since the 1920s, Freyre and his regionalist movement had defined Recife and the Northeast as distinct from São Paulo. It was not this fact, but instead the "artisanal" nature of his sociology that was challenged by a more professional generation of sociologists at USP.[66] Beyond generational and interpersonal rivalries, those who worked on UNESCO's study on race relations shifted a historical perspective on race relations to a contemporary one—in a highly industrialized city of over two million people with an increasingly specialized workforce.

Bastide's essay in the *UNESCO Courier*, on the pages immediately following Freyre's essay, outlined the stakes involved in such a shift. In "São Paulo: The Octopus Town," Bastide firmly situated his study within a "democratic" Brazil in the midst of "industrialization." That industrial Brazil, he argued, was "helping to improve the position of the coloured people as a whole[, meaning that] the classic master-and-man relations are no longer applicable to the relations between whites and blacks at work."[67] Unlike the period immediately following abolition, in which freed slaves could achieve certain social positions based on paternalist relationships with their former masters (benefitting from certain kinds of education or sources of employment in urban centers), a new, more democratic period had arrived, Bastide argued, one in which all people, by law, could achieve and compete as equals in the workforce.

At the same time as Bastide praised democratic and industrial advances in Brazil, insofar as they created opportunities for more equitable relationships between blacks and whites, he also recognized that progress toward achieving racial equality was neither linear nor inevitable. Pointing to "stereotypes and ideologies," Bastide analyzed how traditional slave-owning families attempted to keep blacks in their place and how newer European and Middle Eastern immigrant families sought to distinguish themselves from blacks in an increasingly competitive workplace.[68] While Bastide remained generally optimistic about how an integrated workforce would contribute to the overcoming of stereotypes and prejudices, his initial analysis suggested that there was such a thing as prejudice based on skin color, if not race, in Brazil. To a certain degree, this corresponded to Freyre's own criticisms of industrialized São Paulo, where he saw "Americanized" race relations—that is to say, where white immigrants were given more opportunities than darker Brazilians who had been natives for hundreds of years.[69]

All that said, Bastide, like Freyre, maintained a rather harmonious view of

Brazilian race relations. It was his student, course assistant, and, later, fellow professor Florestan Fernandes who more directly attacked Freyre's theses. Bastide's and Fernandes's respective views, as we will see, came out more clearly in their respective parts of their joint study, *Relações raciais entre negros e brancos em São Paulo* (Race relations between blacks and whites in São Paulo).[70]

Of the participants in UNESCO's studies on race relations in Brazil, Fernandes was among those most critical of Freyre. In Bahia, for example, American anthropologist Charles Wagley and his team criticized the "prejudice of skin color" so apparent in that state, but ultimately confirmed earlier studies that found racial discrimination as such to be nonexistent.[71] Fernandes, on the other hand, saw the "terrible system of slavery" and the "maladjusted" black labor force that it created upon abolition as the indirect causes for discrimination.[72]

The first part of Bastide and Fernandes's study, penned by Fernandes and entitled "Do escravo ao cidadão" (From slave to citizen), offers a historical analysis of slavery and its aftermath. In it Fernandes decried the institution of slavery for its role in the deformation of the black working classes, demonstrating how the transition to free labor little changed the conditions of black workers. Abolition, he argued, was an important means for landowners and capitalists to "secure" a labor force, rather than to free it.[73]

Furthermore, Fernandes argued, "slavery degraded its human source of labor to such a degree that it made economic recuperation extremely arduous, difficult, and slow."[74] Blacks, once free, were "reabsorbed" slowly into the labor system, occupying the least desired and worst-paid jobs. This created "flagrant inequality that separates blacks from whites in the professional structure of São Paulo"; he continued, "people of color neither participate, as a rule, in the guarantees offered by well-remunerated services or social representation, nor in the benefits drawn from free initiative in the urban economy."[75]

Fernandes always prioritized class over race as an analytic category.[76] In this article, for example, he appeared to have agreed with Freyre that the economic system during the beginnings of slavery was more important than race, per se.[77] However, later in Fernandes's analysis, his position became clearer. Whatever economic preconditions may have shaped the systems of inequality, "it was color that began to indicate more than a physical difference or a social inequality"; and it was based upon color that a permanent system of exploitation was created, founded on "the supremacy of the white races, the inferiority of the black races, and the natural right of the former to violate their own ethical code, to exploit other human beings."[78]

Whereas Freyre considered racial inequality as an epiphenomenon of the structural relationship between master and slave, Fernandes's analysis of white supremacy revealed that slavery was much more than an economic system.

It was a set of cultural norms that reified and reinforced the social division of labor. In response to Freyre's insistence on miscegenation as the foundational proof of Brazil's racial harmony, Fernandes argued that color prejudice

> did not look to avoid nor even to restrict miscegenation, but, on the contrary, to make sure that miscegenation occurred without substantially affecting the reciprocal positions of the two racial groups of the social system . . . Despite all of the contact, intercommunication, and intimacy that has always existed between blacks and whites, the two racial layers constituted two separate cultural and social worlds, mutually antagonistic and irreducible.[79]

For Fernandes, Freyre's idyllic world shared by masters and slaves was not an exaggeration or a selective interpretation; it was a lie. These two "mutually antagonistic" cultural and social worlds were what characterized the plantation system. Furthermore, according to Fernandes, "The tendency to define it [miscegenation] as an indicator of the absence of prejudice, on the part of Portuguese colonizers and their descendants considered white, does not find analytically consistent proof."[80]

In industrialized São Paulo, sixty years after abolition, an unconscious racialization served to keep people in their place. Fernandes clarified that he was not insinuating that whites "deliberately and obstinately" attempted to prevent blacks and *mestiços* from equal treatment. Instead, he emphasized an "essential fact": that "equality before the law does not guarantee blacks and *mestiços* an integral participation in all social rights," particularly for those rights that are "assured to whites beyond the legal system, by way of the economic situation and social position."[81]

Fernandes's structural and even categorical treatment of racial inequality in São Paulo left Bastide, long a sympathizer of Freyre's work, in an ambiguous position. On the one hand, he respected Fernandes's findings and those of his other students who contributed to the study; on the other, he insisted on limiting the generalizations of those findings. In such a way, Bastide could leave open the possibility that São Paulo's industrialization and the highly competitive urban workplace that it created may have been the causes of new kinds of racism rather than a characteristic of Brazilian race relations in general. Bastide's sections of *Relações raciais entre negros e brancos em São Paulo*, as well as his correspondence with Fernandes over the final version of the study, indicate precisely this tension.[82]

Bastide's conclusion in many ways reflected that of one of his interviewees, a white man who claimed, "We Brazilians . . . have the prejudice of not having prejudice."[83] Much less categorical than Fernandes, Bastide attempted to understand the contradictions in discourse and representations. Why was it that so many blacks and whites alike in São Paulo insisted that there was no racism there? While condemning racism in general, Bastide would not do the same for São Paulo, where, he insisted, "attitudes vary from one individual to another, creating a spectrum that goes from the maximum of prejudice to its total absence."[84] Bastide, versed in psychology and inspired by Gabriel Tarde, had never abandoned the individual as a category of analysis for sociology. But here, it was not only the individual in some abstract sense that Bastide was attempting to preserve; it was the very possibility of the generality of Freyre's visions of racial democracy.

The correspondence between Bastide, in Paris, and Fernandes, in São Paulo, highlights certain tensions between them. On multiple occasions, Bastide expressed concern about their study having "a harmonious unity, without repetition, nor possible (?) contradictions."[85] Bastide's request of photos from Fernandes, "showing blacks and whites in their celebrations, in communion, or on the contrary!" is suggestive, too.[86] Whereas Bastide emphasized relative racial harmony, while allowing for, as in any society, racist attitudes in certain segments of the population, Fernandes constantly drew Bastide back to seeing racial (and above all, class) discrimination. If it were not for Fernandes, whose structural arguments dealt with inequality and "color prejudice" (a term Bastide himself argued that they should use, instead of "racial prejudice"), *Relações raciais entre negros e brancos em São Paulo* likely would have come to different conclusions.[87]

Even if Bastide agreed with Fernandes's analysis for the cases that they studied—the interviews that they conducted largely did show the presence of color prejudice—he insisted that they be "prudent" in generalizing their results. "To what extent are the cases here valid for the ensemble of people of color? We need to be prudent with the conclusions and to verify each time, confronting our results with general statistics."[88] Surely Bastide's insistence here was one of a responsible sociologist, making sure to limit his claims and not overstep his bounds. Furthermore, the largely qualitative research conducted by Bastide and his team had to be contextualized within broader phenomena. It was exactly this that Bastide attempted to do in his own part of the study, even if Fernandes's structural-historical interpretation remained the dominant thread of the study as a whole.

Whereas Fernandes wrote three chapters for *Relações raciais*, Bastide wrote two and the introduction. In one of his chapters, "Manifestações do preconceito de cor" (Manifestations of color prejudice), Bastide separately analyzed four different groups: traditional slave-owning families, largely of Portuguese descent, and recent Syrian, Italian, and Portuguese immigrants. He ultimately concluded that "the stereotype of color is, at the bottom of it, a class prejudice."[89] According to Bastide, overt racial discrimination became stronger as one went up the social ladder. Among the middle and upper classes "discrimination emerges in the form of more or less severe restrictions on social or even professional activity."[90] Here Bastide cited, for example, two law professors who were prevented from being promoted at a university and a dentist whose competition used his race as a way of dissuading clients. Bastide also mentioned the most infamous cases of segregation at sporting clubs and dancing venues, and even the case of the hotel where African-American dancer and actress Katherine Dunham was barred entry.[91]

Despite how Bastide's introduction to *Relações raciais* emphasized the multiplicity of experiences in prejudice on both the producing and receiving ends, by the conclusion of "Manifestações do preconceito de cor" he seemed to have convinced himself of the prevalence of racial discrimination. However, he did not mean to indict Brazilian society as a whole. Just like Freyre and Donald Pierson, who considered the Northeast of Brazil to be a positive example of racial harmony, Bastide insisted on the "absence of color prejudice as that which prevails in the United States"; in industrialized São Paulo, however, where blacks ascended "no longer as isolated individuals, but as a social group," color prejudice was more prevalent.[92]

The black community in São Paulo had had its own political organizations and newspapers since the last decade of the nineteenth century.[93] By the 1950s, with Teatro Experimental do Negro and other groups, black intellectuals began to more openly advocate for themselves collectively.[94] Compared to in the United States, however, these race-based organizations were relatively few. The US black community's separate organization led Freyre and other Brazilian intellectuals (including black ones) to fear that Brazilian blacks were becoming increasingly Americanized, importing the categories of racial discrimination to justify separation.[95] While recognizing many of the beneficial aspects of independent African-American organization that sought to overcome the difficulties of institutional segregation (credit unions, universities, professional schools, etc.), Bastide nonetheless preferred the "Brazilian solution," of racial mixing, to that of the United States:

> the United States, prohibiting in certain cases weddings between blacks and whites, rejecting them everywhere, leaves a subsisting state of tension between the colors that Brazil, thanks to intense miscegenation, is unfamiliar with. The incessant mixture of blood progressively makes the oppositions of color disappear, forging them together in a "*morena* race," and tending to abolish the racial problem in the best way possible, simply erasing the races.[96]

Bastide's hope—that a new *morena* race would overcome divisions between blacks and whites—went against what he himself had witnessed in São

Paulo. He nonetheless continued to be wary about race-based organization, which brought into question the French Republican ideals of guaranteed equality of all citizens before the law and their treatment as individuals vis-à-vis the state; in his mind, such organization also challenged Brazilian racial democracy. One option was to recognize that French and Brazilian ideologies were highly racialized and needed to be discarded for the sake of reducing inequality.

Another option, which Bastide and many others preferred, was to put faith in the full realization of these ideologies and state formations as anti-racist and egalitarian. Despite his own empirical research that had proved just the opposite, Bastide maintained hope in formal models of social equality in Brazil and in France. Like many in the Musée de l'Homme network, he held on to a republican anti-racism that encouraged reformist projects for the colonies based on the principle of "association" rather than decolonization. And while at times critical of Freyre, Bastide translated *Casa-grande e senzala* into French, finding in it an important source for helping Europeans to understand Brazil as a model for a multiracial society with new possibilities. Things looked quite different to Fernandes, the son of a Portuguese-descended domestic worker who had shined shoes prior to becoming an academic. There was no mirror or model to hold up other than the social reality out of which he had pulled himself, and which he saw as such a tremendous obstacle to people of color in Brazil.

Despite their differences, together Bastide and Fernandes offered a powerful sociological critique of Freyre. By insisting on the prevalence of "color prejudice" and even discrimination in São Paulo, they rejected Brazil's self-representation as a racial democracy. They, like other researchers who participated in UNESCO's project on race relations, responded to Métraux's question, "Is the harmony real or apparent?" by demystifying Brazil's self-image as a racial democracy. For Fernandes, the path to real progress lay through trade unionism and the incorporation of blacks into a working class;[97] for Bastide, at least in 1953, it was further racial mixing, a Freyrian solution indeed. Both of them, however, much more than a weapon to take down Freyre, sought a way to bring prestige to USP's sociology department. Dethroning Freyre, nationally speaking, was as much about claiming São Paulo's preeminence as it was about differences in interpretation of racial phenomena.

In Brazil, Freyre, known as *the* Brazilian sociologist for much of the 1930s and 1940s, increasingly became a figure of the past—an essayist or even a literary figure. His ultimate refusal to contribute to UNESCO's study on race relations can be understood within this context. Delegitimized as a sociologist by being asked to limit his preface to historical background, he was also refused the possibility of commenting on the work of the newcomers such as Fernandes. Whereas Freyre counted on his training under Franz Boas in the United States in the 1920s to ensure his continued preeminence, by the 1950s his discipline had matured with advances in empirical research that made Freyre increasingly appear to be a dilettante.[98]

Bastide and Fernandes's findings, as well as UNESCO's in general, brought into question both Freyre's ideas of racial democracy and his status as a sociologist.[99] But if an international organization headed by Métraux had helped to bring him down, Freyre would nonetheless have an afterlife in France among not only historians and philosophers but sociologists as well.

FREYRE'S CONTESTED PLACE IN FRANCE DURING DECOLONIZATION

In 1956, after the appearance that year of the French translation of Freyre's *Nordeste* and three years after the publication of Bastide and Fernandes's *Relações raciais*, Gurvitch and Sorbonne philosopher Henri Gouhier organized a several-day conference for Freyre at the château in Cerisy-la-Salle.[100] This conference, entitled "Gilberto Freyre, un maître de la sociologie brésilienne," continued to valorize Freyre, despite severe criticisms of his work by Brazilians, Americans, and, to a lesser extent, by Bastide himself. Although the aging Febvre did not attend, Braudel, Arbousse-Bastide, Caillois, and others did.

While Freyre's method and way of doing history may have predated *Annales*, earning him the sympathy of Braudel and Febvre in particular, the political ideology of racial mixing as a solution to tension and antagonism in the colonial world proved at least equally important. In 1954, the French retreated from Indochina. In the period between 1954 and 1956, the Algerian revolution had entered into "total war," limiting the possibilities of a peaceful solution between France and its rebellious départements as Algeria's cause gained force in international opinion.[101]

Febvre's fear of an increasingly dichotomous relationship between colonizer and colonized, expressed in his preface to *Maîtres et esclaves*, took on new magnitude in the late 1950s. In this specific context, with a turn in the Algerian conflict that some people in France saw as a race war, a number of important French social scientists met in a castle in Normandy to discuss Freyre's work. Below is Bastide's description of the conference:

> What should we think of the "luso-tropical" solution to the racial question of which Gilberto Freyre has become the defender? Is the interpenetration of

civilizations the proof of the absence of prejudice? Can the affectionate paternalism of the Portuguese become a racist solution of the problem of exploitation of one race by another instead of a solution based on love?

How can we envision the disappearance of color prejudice and what is the best way to organize a fraternal community between races?[102]

Bastide, while keeping open the possibility of Freyre's thought as a "racist solution," in general praised it. Unfortunately, without minutes from the conference or other documents to know exactly what was discussed in Cerisy, the only traces remaining are those left by Freyre, who chronicled his experience for *O Cruzeiro* in Brazil. Freyre did not specifically mention the discussion of his racial theories, but he did insist that the conference was like a doctoral defense, with difficult questions being raised.[103]

It would be irresponsible to claim a direct relationship between the conference in Cerisy and the interest of intellectuals such as Braudel in maintaining the status quo in Algeria and the French Empire more generally. What is interesting, however, is the search by social scientists, in this specific moment of decolonization, for a peaceful solution to "racial problems." Freyre offered a solution of mixing, or *métissage*, but it was not the only solution. Lévi-Strauss, who was absent from the conference in Cerisy, offered another in *Race and History*.

For Lévi-Strauss, it was not one civilization that should be privileged, but many. The recognition and cultivation of human diversity, therefore, should be UNESCO's goal—and by extension, that of its member states. In his famous deconstruction of race, Lévi-Strauss insisted instead on culture. For him, "progress" (his own scare quotes) was neither necessary nor continuous.[104] While he shared the fears of Freyre and other humanists about the increasingly "mechanical" Western civilization "in its North American form," Lévi-Strauss approached the question of cultural mixture differently, at least in the short term.[105]

Seeing the drive for economic development and cultural homogenization as annihilating difference—and therefore reducing future cultural permutations much as a limited gene pool reduces promising genetic variation—Lévi-Strauss argued instead for its cultivation. He proposed "a world-wide coalition of cultures, each of which would preserve its own originality."[106] Although Lévi-Strauss never said so explicitly, such a preservation of difference had inherently conservative elements in regard to racial mixing. If "cultures" were to be preserved as separate, one might assume that races would be, too.[107]

Beyond Marxist critiques, Lévi-Strauss and Freyre offered two distinct positions from which to approach empire and its aftermath. Lévi-Strauss favored the cultivation of diversity (at its limit, in a kind of autarky), whereas

Freyre favored cultural and racial mixing; the former's natural conclusion was decolonization, the latter's a kind of dual assimilation. Freyre's *mestiçagem* demanded the incorporation of non-European elements into European culture as a way of mutual, if hierarchical, influence: "In Brazil," he wrote, "a Negro with a literary education finds no difficulty in considering himself not only a Brazilian, that is a full-fledged citizen of Brazil, but also a Latin, a member of the Latin race."[108]

Lévi-Strauss never had any personal relationship with Freyre, despite their shared interest in Brazil, claims to the legacy of Boas, and at times literary style. Part of this surely had to do with Lévi-Strauss's reluctance to enter professionally into any question having to do with African civilizations—the continent notably absent from Lévi-Strauss's doctoral dissertation, *The Elementary Structures of Kinship*. More recently, a heated debate between Lévi-Strauss and Caillois, Freyre's editor at Gallimard and present at Cerisy, had made their contact even less likely.[109] But the silence between Freyre and Lévi-Strauss is all the more striking with the knowledge of their shared intellectual network (notably Bastide and Braudel) and Lévi-Strauss's own participation at UNESCO, out of which *Race and History* emerged. The answer, at least in part, has to do with the politics of decolonization.

French social scientists were far from unanimous in their support of the French government in Algeria. Lévi-Strauss, Michel Leiris, and even Gurvitch were among the many signatories of a 1955 manifesto against the French government's use of force in quashing dissent.[110] Trained anthropologist Jacques Soustelle, then governor-general of Algeria, took their manifesto personally for obvious reasons.[111]

In a letter dated November 1955, Soustelle praised his "cher ami" (dear friend) Lévi-Strauss for the latter's "sympathetic comprehension of the people upon which you came to work." Soustelle was likely referring to the recently published *Tristes Tropiques*. But after extending his compliments, Soustelle continued, "I regret to have to send you, herewith, a less pleasant message, but you will understand without difficulty that, having found your name among the signatories of the manifesto . . . I thought I must take a clear and unequivocal position."[112]

In his response, Lévi-Strauss attempted to defuse Soustelle's anger, all while clarifying his own position—notably that the French government's policies vis-à-vis North Africa "are what they are," and that he, too, was "morally obliged" to take a position. Whatever Soustelle may have improved in day-to-day operations, it was unlikely to change the French government's extremism in the matter.[113] Lévi-Strauss, while justifying his own decision to speak out against the French colonial government, nonetheless excused himself for his "naivete" insofar as his friend Soustelle's actions were concerned. Concluding his letter, he wrote, "This proves that, when one stays out of 'public affairs,' it is best not to budge."[114]

Soustelle and Lévi-Strauss's correspondence, however, did not end there. Soustelle sent Lévi-Strauss his "Algérie," surely referring to *Aimée et souffrante Algérie*.[115] Lévi-Strauss thanked him for the book and reiterated that even if he and Soustelle at times had "divergent reactions" on certain subjects, "everything that you write interests me." Nonetheless, Lévi-Strauss insisted that he would be "more at ease" in commenting on one of Soustelle's "scientific" works, for in this case "my information is quite unequal to yours."[116] If, in the previous letter, Lévi-Strauss was apologetic about the unintended consequences of taking a position on "public affairs" of which he was not a specialist, in this letter he was much clearer to Soustelle. For Lévi-Strauss, France's policies in North Africa proved unjust in the long term, if not structurally.[117] Curiously enough, Lévi-Strauss's structural critique of colonialism was historical, no longer in any theoretical contradiction with Braudel's *longue durée* history. In any case, it should be clear that by 1956, Lévi-Strauss had broken definitely with his developmentalist language from the late 1920s.[118]

In the 1950s, anticolonial struggles in Algeria and in other places in the world radically brought into question Europe's political, economic, and cultural centrality. The strategies for French intellectuals to cope with these changes, of course, varied enormously. Some allied themselves with Third World revolutionaries.[119] Others embraced anthropology as a means of renewed intercultural dialogue. Many attempted to humanize colonialism and co-opt colonial populations, all while insisting on the intrinsically progressive value of European civilization—and, perhaps above all, of its economy.[120]

Freyre became a favorite of those in France who preferred the last solution. As he became discredited in his own country and in the international field of sociology, he increasingly referred to "Latin civilization" as a counterweight to the United States and the USSR. He maintained such a posture throughout Algerian and West African decolonization and all the way into the 1970s, when Portugal's African empire finally came undone.

In 1966, Freyre was offered an honorary doctorate at the Sorbonne but refused to accept it in a country that had overtly criticized Brazil's government (a military dictatorship as of 1964).[121] Politics aside, however, Freyre wrote of a shared civilization between Brazil and France, linked through Black Africa. Citing Senegal's first president, Léopold Sédar Senghor, and other leaders inspired by France, Freyre advocated for "a feeling of Latin solidarity." Latinity, the very concept that for him was "that which Europe has most universal to offer," would now emerge from outside Europe.[122] Senghor had indeed claimed that "all great civilizations were from cultural and biological mixture," but his *métissage* was part of an anticolonial project, regardless of what his critics—most notably Frantz Fanon—had to say.[123]

For Freyre and his acolytes, the goal was something else entirely: instead of advocating for decolonization, they sought to preserve hierarchical difference with the promise of mixture and harmony. France's Latinity, like that of the Portuguese, supposedly distinguished it from the racist Anglo-Saxon world, offering "universal" truths of a civilization largely bypassed national or imperial boundaries. Admittedly, France and Brazil were never quite like the United States or South Africa, where discrimination was enforced by law. So, were France and Brazil less racist than the United States? The more interesting question was how to realize the egalitarian elements of Brazilian racial democracy and French Republicanism all while recognizing the weight of the past and the right to difference.

Lévi-Strauss, it appears to me, seemed to ignore this question altogether, possibly because the very idea of racial democracy—even that proposed by people of color—largely neglected Brazil's indigenous inhabitants. Bastide, in his work and in his life, suggested that Afro-descended peoples in the Americas and Europe might embrace their rich heritage as a way of influencing dominant cultures, preserving their own, and integrating into late capitalist society on their own terms. In an homage, Senghor wrote of Bastide: "He was, among the white professors, one of the most authorized to speak of *nègres* and of negritude with pertinence, as he proved to us in Dakar several years ago."[124]

Florestan Fernandes, meanwhile, favored the incorporation of black workers into the class struggle against the bourgeoisie of all colors and staunchly opposed the Brazilian military dictatorship. His *Negro in Brazilian Society* and *Reflections on the Brazilian Counter-revolution* would later appear in English, but one is hard-pressed to find much more translated—into French or any other language, for that matter.[125] If Brazil is once again to become "an immense laboratory of experimental sociology" for the world, as Bastide thought it was in the 1930s,[126] Fernandes might be as good a place as any to start.

En Guise de Conclusion

In the 1950s and 1960s, Brazil and Latin America figured prominently in French social-scientific debates. Brazil's specific set of dichotomies allowed French social scientists to think through unresolved oppositions that structured their world: rural and urban, agricultural and industrial, European and non-European, and nature and culture, to name just a few. These "contrasts," to use a term employed by Roger Bastide, provided fertile ground for exploring questions both specific to academic fields and more broadly relevant to major themes in public life, such as decolonization, economic development, and race relations.[1] If the French brought Brazil back with them at an ideational or cognitive level, they did so based upon a long-standing collaboration with Brazilian intellectuals, dating back at least to the 1930s.

The "terms of exchange" between the two countries, at least in the social sciences, had become more equal in the postwar period. Long gone were the days when French intellectuals could pronounce on anything Brazil-related and be applauded for it. Fernand Braudel, who had given public lectures on Brazil's social flexibility in the 1930s, now refrained from publishing his monograph on Brazil, likely fearing a negative reception.[2] And even those Brazilians who had previously been most unconditional in their support of France's reputation and institutional significance began to question the demigods that they had helped to create. Paulo Duarte, by no means a model of anti-racism or anti-colonialism, ultimately repudiated Paul Rivet for his continuing support of French Algeria in his journal *Anhembi*.[3]

Brazilian universities, too, became increasingly autonomous from the French during and immediately following World War II. In the 1930s, European and North American scholars were recruited to teach because of their unique academic training. In the postwar period, Brazil granted its first doctoral degrees. Sociologists such as Florestan Fernandes, Maria Isaura Pereira de Quieroz, Gilda de Mello e Souza, and Antonio Candido, historians such as Alice Piffer Canabrava, Eurípides Simões de Paula, and Eduardo d'Oliveira França, geographers such as Maria Conceição Vicente de Carvalho, Ary França, and João Dias Silveira, and anthropologists Egon Schaden and Gioconda Mussolini earned their doctorates. Once *concursado* (having passed competitive public-service exams), they began to teach on their own terms. Henceforth, the French influence, even if still quite strong, would be mediated through Brazilians.

In certain disciplines more than others, the French presence remained firmly rooted. Philosophy was almost a caricature of itself—"a French overseas department," to use the words of Paulo Arantes.[4] In Brazilian historiography, *Annales* remained *the* methodological reference, because of Braudel and Febvre's efforts and the journal's international importance.[5] Frédéric Mauro, one of Braudel's first doctoral students, who taught in São Paulo after the war, claimed that his role was to maintain "the Braudelian tradition and what one could already call the spirit of the *Annales*." Mauro concluded that "the Brazilians do history, or rather write it, as the French do."[6]

Sociology was a different story. A significant part of this has to do with Florestan Fernandes, who emerged as the dominant figure at USP and in Brazil at large. Fernandes's training at the Escola Livre de Sociologia e Política, his commitment to empirical sociology, and his distaste for a certain Francophile elitism pushed him and his students toward other models, whether they be German, North American, or Marxist of different national variants. A growing literature on Fernandes and Paulista sociology helps us to understand these largely non-French references as well as how, through Fernandes, Brazilian sociology became increasingly autonomous.[7] Europeans such as the Portuguese historian Joaquim Barradas de Carvalho lamented this. Then teaching in Brazil, he wrote Braudel: "I have very good relations with the sociologists and philosophers, but I think that the sociologists are too often influenced by the American school—despite Bastide and Levy-Strauss [*sic*]—and despite history [and] time, even when they are Marxists!!!"[8] After philosophy, history may have been the most "French" of disciplines. Sociology, at least in the early 1960s, was arguably the least.

Barradas's claims are questionable on a number of counts, but his suggestion of American influence paints a much more complicated picture of the postwar Brazilian social sciences. The largely binational relationships between the universities in São Paulo, Rio de Janeiro, and even Porto Alegre with France had increasingly become trinational at the least, with French influence being nowhere near what it had been in the 1930s. Long gone were the days when the French scholars had exclusive responsibility for and control of the social sciences.

This decline in French influence was also brought about by the military dictatorship's alignment with the United States. The government that came to power in 1964 with the help of the United States quickly put together agreements with the United States Agency for International Development (USAID) that restructured university life in Brazil. Two fundamental changes were made to the nature of academic production: scholars deemed undesirable or treasonous toward the new regime were now persecuted, and disciplines and coursework were reorganized along American departmental lines, reducing the earlier practice of interdisciplinarity.[9] The French intellectual presence obviously did not disappear, but it did lose its institutional strength.[10]

Still, to see 1964 as a rupture would be overly simplistic. France remained—and perhaps will always remain—an important reference for Brazilian social scientists. The sociologist and future Brazilian president Fernando Henrique Cardoso, who had studied under Florestan Fernandes, was one of those exiled during the military dictatorship for his political opinions. He first went to Santiago, Chile, where he participated in the UN's Economic Commission for Latin America and the Caribbean, but ultimately made it to France. When sociologist Alain Touraine explained Cardoso's situation to Braudel, inquiring about the possibility of him teaching as a visiting professor at the École Pratique, Touraine wrote: "[Cardoso] let me know of his desire to come to Europe, and I would like to be able to reassure him quickly, because Europe in his mind can only mean France."[11] In Touraine's view—and likely Cardoso's— France signified Europe. If, in the nineteenth century, it had been a metonym for a continent and a certain idea of civilization, in the late twentieth century, it represented a social-scientific tradition. This is not to say that other places were invisible to Brazilian social scientists, but rather, that the strong bonds that connected them to France would persevere in the decades to come— through the dictatorship and into democratic reopening.

Caio Prado Jr.'s trajectory, perhaps more than that of anyone else, demonstrates Brazilian intellectuals' continuing engagement with France. When imprisoned in 1970, Prado could depend on the advocacy of French scholars to lobby for his release from prison. Upon the recommendations of geographers Pierre George, then teaching at USP, and Pierre Deffontaines, who had taught Prado in 1934 and founded the Associação dos Geógrafos Brasileiros with his help, Braudel arranged for a telegram to be sent to a certain Elvelrahia Deayrell. Paule Braudel remembered Deayrell as "one of the protagonists of the coup d'état" that "Braudel had by chance met" in Brazil.[12] The telegram read:

> We would be very grateful if you would support our efforts that will avoid, thanks to the benevolence of the [Brazilian] President toward our call, any public scandal in Paris, and which, in any case, could not improve the amical relations that exist between our country and yours.[13]

Beyond these French intellectuals, Prado, of course, had his own direct relationships with communist intellectuals elsewhere. Nonetheless, much of what he read was written in or translated into French. In other words, despite his criticisms of certain political, social, and intellectual developments in France, he could not dissociate himself from the country.

When what Prado called the "nouvelle vague" of French thought, notably Lévi-Straussian structuralism and Althusserian Marxism, had reached Brazil in the late 1960s, he wrote polemically to "shift the thinking of the least forewarned [*menos prevenidos*]."[14] He explicitly sought to counteract the acceptance of the structuralist "fashion," which he argued had "a false appearance of novelty . . . [and] scientific objectivity."[15] The irony of Prado's critique is that it was originally addressed to the French review *La Pensée*, but was ultimately never published outside Brazil.[16]

The 1920s Brazilian modernists' critique of their compatriots' European mimesis had in subsequent decades successfully influenced the institutionalization of the social sciences. Instead of passively and uncritically parroting foreign scholarship, Brazilians now studied Brazilian subjects on their own terms. Moreover, their work increasingly made it into internationally recognized centers of social-scientific thought. Bastide even imagined the modernists' most famous character romping the streets of Paris. In his homage to Mário de Andrade, Bastide depicted "Macunaíma with Gargantua, his Gallic brother, drinking wine and aguardiente, calling rum cachaça, cassoulet feijoada, screaming, laughing, [and] inveighing in Tupi terms."[17] To put it differently, this national "hero without character" had become somewhat of a cosmopolitan. Just as the Brazilian modernist project depended on a cannibalization of European influences rather than their outright rejection, the Brazilian social sciences would continue to appropriate European and particularly French sources in their own work. Since the French had laid the foundations for social-scientific research, teaching, and knowledge in Brazil, they would always be an inescapable presence to be digested and repurposed.

The ebbs and flows of French influence in Brazil were also reflected in Brazilianist research in France, both within the small group that made up the

FIG. 8 Monbeig with the CNRS delegation to Cuba. Archives Nationales, CNRS Direction Générale, 1960–1979. Côte 19850505/161.

French missions in the 1930s and in the broader social-scientific community. While Bastide and Monbeig continued to return to Brazil, Braudel, his students worried, seemed to have no time for his "South American friends."[18] Braudel assured them that he had not forgotten about them, and that the École Pratique would "make a very large effort in favor of Latin America"—with important faculty openings to boot.[19]

Bastide and Monbeig continued to write about Brazil, but other questions began to occupy them in the 1960s and 1970s. Bastide, for example, brought his interests in ethnic sociology to bear on black communities in France, helping to lead a collective inquiry into peoples of Haitian and Antillean descent in Paris.[20] Monbeig's time was increasingly consumed by bureaucratic and even diplomatic work with the Institut des Hautes Études de l'Amérique Latine, which he founded, and the Centre National de la Recherche Scientifique (CNRS). As director of the social sciences at the CNRS, he certainly helped to direct research interest and funding to South American projects, including those of anthropologists at the Collège de France, such as Pierre Clastres.[21] Pictured here is a photo of him in Havana in 1968, smoking a cigar, as the CNRS heightened scientific cooperation with Cuba.

The cluster that united these scholars with Braudel and Lévi-Strauss started to come apart for a number of reasons. For one, Brazil was no longer the country of hope and social mobility that they had previously perceived it to be. The dictatorship continued to harden throughout the late 1960s and 1970s, affecting not only social scientists but also the people on whom and with whom they worked. The *Journal de la Société des américanistes*, around which the Brazilianist network had been organized for so long, expressed indignation at the dictatorship's attacks on indigenous rights, property, and ways of life.[22]

Furthermore, the contact between these French and Brazilian intellectuals diminished as their trips there did, too. Beyond the political situation, personal factors such as family, the production of individual oeuvres, and professional responsibilities at newly founded institutions (École des Hautes Études en Sciences Sociales, Laboratoire d'Anthropologie Sociale, and Institut des Hautes Études de l'Amérique Latine) separated the French scholars from both one another and Brazilian scholars. These institutions consolidated relationships between the two countries and fostered important ties for younger generations of French and Brazilian scholars, but for the French scholars at the center of this book who were the architects of these institutions, the conviviality of the early period ceded to more settled and individualized activity. As Monbeig wrote Miguel Alvez de Lima, a colleague based at the Conselho Nacional de Geografia in Rio:

> It will not be very easy for me to get to Brazil soon, even though I have felt distant for too long. Be assured that I have forgotten neither Brazil nor my Brazilian friends. I have thought of them in updating my little book in the collection "Que sais-je?" ... In the actual state of things, an even slightly prolonged sojourn would be impossible.[23]

Monbeig fell out of touch with both his Brazilian colleagues and the likes of Bastide, Braudel, and Lévi-Strauss. After a period of coming of age and collective creative work, the group examined in this book was now at what sociologist Michael P. Farrell has called "the separation stage."[24] Lévi-Strauss's four volumes of *Mythologiques* are a perfect example of this. In contrast to the structuralist phase, which had been collective in genesis, the period following the 1962 publication of *Wild Thought* and through the *Mythologiques* (*The Raw and the Cooked, From Honey to Ashes, The Origin of Table Manners,* and *The Naked Man*) is one of increasing autonomy—an "oeuvre in the most traditional sense of the term."[25] It is also one of Lévi-Strauss's increasing dialogue and debate with philosophy.

These works lend themselves less to a sociological analysis, or at least to the network-based approach furthered in this study. Emerging more clearly out of Lévi-Strauss's previous work, and often times self-referential, they were also produced in isolation. In New York during the war, Lévi-Strauss saw demographic maps that identified Burgundy's Châtillonnais region as being the place of lowest population density in France;[26] his choice to spend most of his time not tied down at the Laboratoire d'Anthropologie Sociale there points to his desire for a removed, almost monkish approach to his mass of ethnological texts. To a lesser extent, we could say the same of Braudel's three-volume *Civilization and Capitalism, 15th–18th Centuries*.[27] Although much more synthetic of contemporary work than Lévi-Strauss was in *Mythologiques*, these volumes are less about proposing new frameworks than they are about building upon the foundational premises of *The Mediterranean*.

Nonetheless, even for Braudel and Lévi-Strauss, whose Brazilian pasts faded behind them, memories would continue to flicker. In old age, they waxed nostalgic about Brazil, where they knew it all began. Lévi-Strauss was the first of the two to be elected to the Académie Française, in 1973. He had taken longer than Braudel to enter into the Collège de France, but this time around, the order was reversed. In 1985, just over a decade after his own induction, Lévi-Strauss welcomed Braudel into the Académie. At the ceremony of Braudel's *remise de l'épée*—a knighting ceremony that Lévi-Strauss had rightly identified as a kind of tribal ritual—Lévi-Strauss introduced his colleague:

> Today's ceremony offers for me a more intimate coloring. A few days from now will mark the fiftieth anniversary of our first meeting, in São Paulo, where you arrived shortly following the large part of the French university mission, soon rejoined by Madame Braudel and your first child. This entry of your household into ours was an event that I have not forgotten.[28]

Just three years prior, in 1982, their mutual colleague Jean Maugüé had published his memoirs, *Les dents agacées*, in which he recounted his own experience teaching among such eminent social scientists.[29] Lévi-Strauss cited Maugüé in his speech and pointed to Braudel's strength in uniting them, characterized by "his eclecticism—in the best sense of the term." Here, as in a number of occasions throughout his life, Lévi-Strauss implicitly defined his formalist methodology against Braudel's more federative approach. Nonetheless, Lévi-Strauss claimed, Braudel's eclecticism is what allowed him to "draw up plans, floor by floor, of the monument" of work that he had constructed.[30]

In contrast to his peers who visited Brazil on numerous occasions in the postwar period, Lévi-Strauss only returned in 1985, with the end of the military dictatorship. It was his first time since 1939—accompanied by then president François Mitterrand, for a five-day state visit.[31] Rather than substantially reacquaint him with Brazil or the indigenous peoples he had worked with, the trip made him nostalgic for both his youth and the country he had known. In 1994, over half a century after his last prewar visit, Lévi-Strauss published *Saudades do Brasil*, a beautiful book of photos.[32] By that time, Monbeig, Bastide, and

Braudel had all passed away. Lévi-Strauss had outlived almost everyone, seeing his works bound in the Pléiade collection with authors the likes of Madame de Sévigné, Alexis de Tocqueville, and Proust. In 2009, when he finally passed away, J. M. G. Le Clézio called him "the most eminent and probably the last French philosopher."[33]

Neither Bastide nor Monbeig would attain such fame, but in some ways their influence is more durable. Because of their inspiring teaching and countless years in Brazil, Bastide and Monbeig helped to train some of Brazil's most important sociologists and geographers, in addition to scholars in France. Bastide's acolytes have contributed to a mini-renaissance of his work, publishing a fifty-six-volume journal, *Bastidiana*, that ran from 1993 to 2006.[34] Two of Monbeig's last students, both prominent geographers of Brazil, have also helped to make his work better known.[35] While it is true that Lévi-Strauss trained and inspired Americanist anthropologists such as Manuela Carneiro da Cunha, Eduardo Viveiros de Castro, and Philippe Descola, they came at a much later moment, when anthropology had largely been institutionalized in Brazil.

Unlike Braudel and Lévi-Strauss, whose audience was global in scope, Bastide and Monbeig were much more invested in Brazil itself. For them, Brazil was more than an object of a study that revealed the most elementary forms of kinship or the opening of the Mediterranean to transoceanic trade. It was a world in itself, with its own intellectual references, institutions, and phenomena that demanded significant dedication throughout the rest of their lives. Bastide's and Monbeig's total immersion in Brazil encouraged them to abandon previous understandings and excessive theorization. Especially during the war years, with no return on the horizon, they dedicated their time to Brazilian fieldwork and archives, reading Brazilian newspapers, discussing their research with Brazilian colleagues, and fully investing themselves in the intellectual culture of where they lived. This was not "central" or "peripheral"; it was simply where they found themselves.

The intellectual and personal geographies of Bastide, Braudel, Lévi-Strauss, and Monbeig are reflected in their archives—in terms of not only the nationalities of correspondents but also literally where they are housed. Both Monbeig and Bastide have archives in Brazil, at USP's Instituto de Estudos Brasileiros. Braudel's and Lévi-Strauss's archives, on the other hand, are entirely based in Paris—and in the center of Paris, at that. Bastide's correspondence, for the most part, is held in Normandy, at the Institut Mémoires de l'Édition Contemporaine, but much of his documentation remains in Brazil.

These archives served as an important basis for the story that I have told, but they did not suffice to give a full picture. In the archives in France, I discovered letters written by Brazilians such as Paulo Duarte and Florestan Fernandes, but ultimately had to go to Brazil, to their respective archives, to find the letters that Lévi-Strauss or Bastide had sent to them. In São Paulo, I found letters from Braudel to his student and assistant Eurípides Simões de Paula from the 1930s—a period that is largely absent in Braudel's own archive, at least in part because of the disruptions and dislocations caused by World War II. (Brazil never had occupying powers enter into its territory.) At times these letters were anecdotal, and at others they were fundamental for reconstructing the relations between the French and Brazilian social sciences, as was the case with Gilberto Freyre.

If the 1930s had been a moment of Brazilian dependency on French social-scientific models and teaching, by the 1950s the pendulum had shifted. Brazilian universities had trained their own professors, who were no longer students of the French, but free to choose between competing models. Scholars such as Freyre found a new audience for their work in France, too, aided by the preexisting networks of intellectual cooperation between the two countries.

Regardless of the directionality of relations, strong affinities and intellectual kinship remain between French and Brazilian social scientists. In some ways, today they are as connected as much as ever. At the École des Hautes Études en Sciences Sociales (EHESS) alone, there are two research groups focused on Brazil, and large conferences in France continue to make explicit connections between the two countries.[36] As far as broader intellectual networks, it is worth mentioning the Association pour la Recherche sur le Brésil en Europe, which came into existence during the research for this book. While massive cuts in higher education in Brazil are sure to diminish their numbers, Brazilian students in all disciplines continue to study in France, consistently making up the second-largest foreign national group at EHESS, following Italians.

The memory of these relationships, too, is constantly reactivated and institutionalized.[37] From the early twentieth century to today, Brazilians have been central to the conservation of the Maison d'Auguste Comte in Paris. After the fire that tragically burned down Brazil's Museu Nacional, in 2019, the Musée du Quai Branly (where a headdress from Lévi-Strauss's expeditions can be seen) dedicated one of its postdoctoral fellowships to the preservation of the Museu Nacional's cultural heritage. At USP, a research group on Brazilian-French relations meets periodically and has its own database.[38] And the Bibliothèque Nationale de France and the Biblioteca Nacional do Brasil have just launched a "France in Brazil" online database, with archives for future research.[39]

According to both a Lévi-Straussian kinship analysis (if we count professor-student relationships) and the Braudelian *longue durée*, the structures uniting these social-scientific communities remain intact. In certain fields, it would be problematic to speak of one country without the other. In others, especially anthropology, a working knowledge of both—at least at the level of theory—is indispensable.

There will always be those on either side of the Atlantic who favor stronger or weaker ties, but a few things are clear. For both national communities, the consolidation of the social sciences was an international project in which Brazilian universities played a significant role. They provided intellectual, institutional, and financial support for the training of French and Brazilian social scientists, many of whom became prominent practitioners in their respective fields. And the Franco-Brazilian cooperation in the social sciences helped to carve out an intellectual space that was at least partially autonomous from developments in the United States, methodologically, empirically, and even culturally.

This book has provided the English-speaking world with an introduction to some of the key thinkers, institutions, and debates within the intellectual space between France and Brazil. In it, I have attempted to show the agency of Brazilians in shaping the course of social-scientific history and conversations about themes as varied as the global economy, temporality, syncretism, race relations, and social structure. At a time when these themes are back on the table, my hope is that we might repurpose the thought of these Brazilian intellectuals in the present. At the very least, they should enrich our vocabularies of what Raewyn Connell calls "Southern Theory."[40] In an increasingly globalized academic world, they invite us to consider how "terms of exchange" operate. They also might help to reappraise other texts and concepts for which thinkers and places outside the North Atlantic, largely forgotten until recently, were equally foundational.

Acknowledgments

This project has accumulated financial, institutional, and properly intellectual debts in a number of countries. Since one of its major goals is the examination of the social construction of knowledge, I have attempted to be as thorough as possible in what follows, even if it is impossible to name all the librarians, archivists, administrators, and other professionals that made my research possible. I am particularly grateful to those who have read and commented on my work at its various stages, whether or not they see their names in what follows.

This project has been funded by a number of grants, large and small. NYU's Henry MacCracken Fellowship laid the basis for my studies and writing. A Fulbright-Hays Doctoral Dissertation Research Abroad grant funded a year-long stay in Brazil, and the Bourses Marandon of the Société des Professeurs Français et Francophones d'Amérique funded a semester in France. Additional research was made possible by the Alexander von Humboldt Foundation; the University of Miami; the University of Turin's Department of Cultures, Politics, and Society; the Research Travel Award from the Society for French Historical Studies and the Western Society for French History; the Jerrold Seigel Fellowship in Intellectual and Cultural History; a CIRHUS visiting research fellowship at the Laboratoire d'Anthropologie Sociale; NYU Provost's Global Research Initiative in Paris; the Andrew W. Mellon Pre-dissertation Fellowship; a Predoctoral Summer Fellowship from NYU's Graduate School of Arts and Science; a Tinker Grant from NYU's Center for Latin American and Caribbean Studies; and a Foreign Language and Area Studies Fellowship for Portuguese from the US Department of Education. This book was also awarded publishing support by the Société des Américanistes.

A special thanks goes to three mentors I have had the unusual privilege of working with closely on this project. Herrick Chapman, Barbara Weinstein, and Paulo Teixeira Iumatti have done more than anyone else to get this book off the ground, guide it intellectually, and make the result as polished as possible. Frédéric Viguier, Stefanos Geroulanos, and James Woodard have also intervened at critical stages to correct my mistakes, sharpen my insights, and broaden the relevance of this project.

Before widening the circle to include other conversations and exchanges, I want to thank everyone at the University of Chicago Press for getting the book into its current form. I could not have asked for better editors than

Darrin McMahon, Mary Al-Sayed, and Stephen Twilley. Thank you too to Tristan Bates, Elizabeth Ellingboe, Kristen Raddatz, Alan Thomas, the three anonymous readers, and June Sawyers for the index.

NYU's Institute of French Studies and Department of History provided a home for an otherwise wandering project. I thank Stéphane Gerson, Edward Berenson, and Isabelle Genest for their interest and support. Exchanges with professors such as Fred Cooper, Ada Ferrer, Greg Grandin, Stephen Gross, Molly Nolan, Guy Ortolano, and Andrew Sartori and peers that include Alexander Arnold, Scott Alves Barton, Muriam Haleh Davis, Liz Fink, Sarah Griswold, Rachel Kantrowitz, Sarah Kolopp, Allison Korinek, Gabriella Lindsay, Valerie McGuire, Erik Meddles, Tina Montenegro, Wendi Muse, Michelle Pinto, Samantha Presnal, John Raimo, Natasha Shivji, Matt Shutzer, Marcio Siwi, Evan Spritzer, Jonathan Michael Square, Christy Thornton, Nick Truesdale, Aro Velmet, and Natan Zeichner, among others, enriched this project.

Brazilian mentors, colleagues, and friends have been foundational for my work. In alphabetical order, I thank Larissa Alves de Lira, Cibele Barbosa, Iuri Bauler, Rafael Faraco Benthien, Angela de Castro Gomes, Felipe Charbel, Marcos Chor Maio, Marcia Consolim, Denilson Cordeiro, Luís Corrêa Lima, Antonio Dimas, Florestan Fernandes Jr., Luiz Paulo Ferraz, Ligia Ferreira, Claudia Damasceno Fonseca, Peter Fry, Afrânio Garcia, Luísa Girardi, Antonio Sérgio Alfredo Guimarães, Luiz Carlos Jackson, Renato Jacques, Elisa Klüger, Almir Leal de Oliveira, Tania Regina de Luca, Yvonne Maggie, Laura de Mello e Souza, Sergio Miceli, Carlos Guilherme Mota, Fernando Novais, Francisco Palomanes Martinho, Fernanda Peixoto, Gabriela Pellegrino Soares, Marcella Phubá, Maria Ligia Prado, Ana Rocha, Camila Gui Rosatti, Flávio dos Santos Gomes, Lilia Schwarcz, Lidiane Soares Rodrigues, Hugo Suppo, Hélgio Trindade, Luísa Valentini, Licia Valladares, Francini Venâncio de Oliveira, Carlos Zeron, and Bruno Zorek. I also thank archivists Maria Aparecida Ferreira, Flávia Carneiro Leão, Edmundo Oliveira Leite Junior, and especially Elisabete Ribas, at the Instituto de Estudos Brasileiros.

In France, I thank Emmanuelle Loyer and Maurice Aymard, respectively, for mediating my access to Lévi-Strauss's and Braudel's archives, and Monique Lévi-Strauss and the late Paule Braudel for granting me access to these rich sources. Further thanks go to those who made private collections available: Madile Gardet, daughter of Pierre Deffontaines; Jean-Claude Arbousse-Bastide, son of Paul Arbousse-Bastide; Daniel Métraux, son of Alfred Métraux; and above all the Monbeigs, Catherine Monbeig Goguel, Marianne (Hano), Laurent, and Geneviève. Archivists Sophie Assal at the Laboratoire d'Anthropologie Sociale, Brigitte Mazon at the EHESS, and Michèle Moulin at the Bibliothèque de l'Institut de France merit particular mention, as do scholars Elise Aurières, Howard Becker, Stefania Capone, Christophe

Charle, Vincent Debaene, Philippe Descola, Erwan Dianteill, Laurent Jean-pierre, Frédéric Keck, Benoît de L'Estoile, Isabelle Lostanlen, Jean-Christophe Marcel, Pap Ndiaye, Erato Paris, Jacques Revel, Carole Reynaud-Paligot, Gisèle Sapiro, Jean-Frédéric Schaub, Hervé Théry, and Blaise Wilfert.

Much of the revision process took place at Cornell University, where I benefited from exchanges with Ray Craib, Camille Robcis, Cristián Alarcón Ferrari, Nick Bujalski, Pedro Erber, Kyle Harvey, Susana Romero Sanchez, Daniela Samur, and Josh Savala. The same goes for the University of Miami, this time with Eduardo Elena, Scott Heerman, Mary Lindemann, Michael B. Miller, Martin Nesvig, and Dominique Reill. A number of people who do not fit either geographical or institutional categories also deserve mention: Paulina Alberto, Ulysse Baratin, Giuseppe Bianco, Dain Borges, Alice Conklin, Sebastian Conrad, Brandon County, Rosanna Dent, Elina Djebbari, Margarita Fajardo, Sebastián Gil-Riaño, Michael Goebel, Peter Gordon, Robert Howes, Timothy Scott Johnson, Chérif Keïta, John Marquez, Matthias Middell, Frank Mikus, Federica Morelli, Sam Moyn, Todd Shepard, and Edoardo Tortarolo.

None of this would have been possible without my family. I especially thank my parents, Timothy and Patricia, for their constant love and support. This book is dedicated to Mariella and Antonina, whom I love dearly. They came into my life alongside this project, making it all the more enjoyable and meaningful.

Abbreviations and Archives

AN. Archives Nationales de France. Pierrefitte-sur-Seine.

BN. Biblioteca Nacional do Brasil. Manuscritos. Rio de Janeiro.

BNF. Archive Lévi-Strauss. Bibliothèque Nationale de France, Richelieu. Manuscrits. Paris.

CAPH. Centro de Apoio ao Pesquisa em História Sérgio Buarque de Holanda. University of São Paulo.

CPDOC. Centro de Pesquisa e Documentação de História Contemporânea do Brasil. Rio de Janeiro.

FB. Archive Fernand Braudel. Bibliothèque de l'Institut de France. Paris.

GF. Fundo Gilberto Freyre. Fundação Gilberto Freyre. Apipucos.

IEB-USP. Instituto de Estudos Brasileiros. University of São Paulo.

IMEC. Archive Roger Bastide. Institut Mémoires de l'Édition Contemporaine. Caen.

LAS. Archives du Laboratoire d'Anthropologie Sociale. Paris.

MAE. Archive de la Ministère des Affaires Étrangères. La Courneuve.

MNHN. Archive Paul Rivet. Les Archives du Muséum National de l'Histoire Naturelle. Paris.

PD. Arquivo Paulo Duarte. Universidade Estadual de Campinas.

PMSP. Arquivo Municipal de São Paulo.

PROEDES. Arquivo do Programa de Estudos e Documentação da Educação e Sociedade. Universidade Federal do Rio de Janeiro.

SEF. Sociedade de Etnografia e Folclore, Centro Cultural São Paulo, Discoteca Oneyda Alvarenga. São Paulo.

UFSCAR-FF. Fundo Florestan Fernandes. Arquivos da Universidade Federal de São Carlos.

UNESCO. UNESCO Archives, Paris.

Archives de l'École Pratique des Hautes Études. Paris.

Arquivo Histórico do Itamaraty. Rio de Janeiro.

Arquivo João Cruz Costa. University of São Paulo.

Archive Lucien Febvre. Archives de l'École des Hautes Études en Sciences Sociales. Paris.

Archive Paul Arbousse-Bastide. Family Archive. Paris.

Archive Pierre Deffontaines. Family Archive. Paris.
Archive Pierre Monbeig. Family Archive. Paris.
Arquivo Público do Estado de S. Paulo. São Paulo.

Notes

INTRODUCTION

1. Roselyne de Ayala and Paule Braudel, eds., *L'histoire au quotidien: Les écrits de Fernand Braudel* (Paris: Éditions de Fallois, 2001), 35. Unless otherwise noted, all translations are my own.

2. Lévi-Strauss, interview by Antoine de Gaudemar, *Libération*, February 6, 1997, http://next.liberation.fr/livres/1997/02/06/levi-strauss-j-ai-fait-mes-premieres-armes-avec-lui_197779.

3. Luís Correia Lima, *Fernand Braudel e o Brasil: Vivência e brasilianismo (1935–1945)* (São Paulo: Edusp, 2009). For more on Braudel's importance within Latin America, see Carlos Antonio Aguirre Rojas, *Los Annales y la historiografía latinoamericana* (Mexico: UNAM, 1993).

4. For more on this early period, see Paulo Teixeira Iumatti, *Caio Prado Jr.: Uma trajetória intelectual* (São Paulo: Brasiliense, 2007). See also Iumatti, *História, dialética, e diálogo com as ciências: A gênese de Formação do Brasil contemporâneo, de Caio Prado Jr. (1933–1942)* (São Paulo: Intermeios, 2018), 145–213.

5. Undated letter from the president of the 4th section of the École Pratique des Hautes Études, Fonds Braudel, archives of the École Pratique des Hautes Études, Paris.

6. Paulo Teixeira Iumatti, "Historiographical and Conceptual Exchange between Fernand Braudel and Caio Prado Jr. in the 1930s and 1940s: A Case of Unequal Positions in the Intellectual Space between Brazil and France," trans. Ian Merkel, *Storia della storiografia* 71, no. 1 (2017): 89–110.

7. Caio Prado Jr., *Formação do Brasil contemporâneo* (1942; São Paulo: Companhia das Letras, 2011). Prado's book was translated into English by Suzette Macedo as *The Colonial Background of Modern Brazil* (Berkeley: University of California Press, 1971).

8. Joseph L. Love, "The Origins of Dependency Analysis," *Journal of Latin American Studies* 22, no. 1 (1990): 162–63.

9. Peter Burke, *The French Historical Revolution: The Annales School, 1929–2014*, 2nd. ed. (Stanford, CA: Stanford University Press, 2015).

10. Braudel to Prado, Paris, January 31, 1940, CPJ-CP-BRAU001, Caio Prado Jr. Archive, IEB-USP.

11. Fernand Braudel, "Au Brésil: Deux livres de Caio Prado," *Annales ESC* 3, no. 1 (1948): 99–103; Braudel, *La Méditerranée et le monde méditerranéen à l'époque de Philippe II* (Paris: Colin, 1949).

12. Educational reformer Fernando de Azevedo, who was at the heart of the creation of the University of São Paulo, defined his project for a new faculty as inherently different from previous university projects in Brazil. According to him, previous "universities" served simply as aggregates for law, medical, and engineering schools. *A Cultura Brasileira* (São Paulo: Edusp, 1971), 687. Brazil's "lack" of university has been questioned by scholars who have considered knowledge formation in Jesuit institutions, law schools, and other places of higher learning that preceded the federative idea of a university. That said, even the fiercest opponents to São Paulo's exceptionalist language admit that Brazilian universities were late, as if they were unexpectedly late children in a marriage. Luiz Antônio Cunha, *A universidade temporã: O ensino superior da colônia à era de Vargas* (Rio de Janeiro: Civilização Brasileira, 1980).

13. For a list, see Jean-Paul Lefebvre, "Les professeurs français des missions universitaires au Brésil (1934–44)," *Cahiers du Brésil Contemporain* 12 (1990): 22–33.

14. Sergio Miceli, *A desilusão americana: Relações acadêmicas entre Brasil e Estados Unidos* (São Paulo: Editora Sumaré, 1990).

15. This study builds on a large literature on the history of the Brazilian social sciences and USP's founding. See Sergio Miceli et al., *História das ciências sociais no Brasil*, vol. 1 (São Paulo: Vértice, 1989), and vol. 2 (São Paulo: Sumaré/Fapesp, 1995). Fernanda Arêas Peixoto's early work remains the fundamental reference for São Paulo. "Estrangeiros no Brasil: A missão francesa na Universidade de São Paulo" (master's thesis, Unicamp, 1991). See also Maria Helena Capelato and Maria Ligia Prado, "A l'origine de la collaboration universitaire franco-brésilienne: Une mission française à la faculté de philosophie de São Paulo," in *Préfaces* 14 (1989): 100–105. For more on the French missions to USP, see Patrick Petitjean, "As missões universitárias francesas na criação da Universidade de São Paulo (1934–1940)," in *A ciência nas relações Brasil-França (1850–1950)*, ed. Amélia Império Hamburger et al. (São Paulo: Edusp, 1996). See also the special edition of *Estudos Avançados* 8, no. 22 (1994). More recently, in English, see Hugo Rogelio Suppo, "French Intellectuals and Cultural Diplomacy in Brazil, 1934–1943," in *Oxford Research Encyclopedia of Latin American History*, article published April 26, 2019, https://doi.org/10.1093/acrefore/9780199366439.013.619.

16. For important precursors, see Thomas Skidmore, "Lévi-Strauss, Braudel, and Brazil: A Case of Mutual Influence," *Bulletin of Latin American Research* 22, no. 3 (2003); Fernanda Arêas Peixoto, *Diálogos brasileiros: Uma análise da obra de Roger Bastide* (São Paulo: Edusp, 2010). See also Luísa Valentini, *Um laboratório de antropologia: O encontro entre Mário de Andrade, Dina Dreyfus, e Claude Lévi-Strauss (1935–1939)* (São Paulo: Alameda, 2013).

17. The scholarship on each of these themes is immense and continues to grow. For a now-classic critique, see Carlos Guilherme Mota, *Ideologia da cultura brasileira (1933–1974): Pontos de partida para uma revisão histórica* (São Paulo: Editora 34, 2008).

18. Rodrigo Patto Sá Motta, *As universidades e o regime militar: Cultura política brasileira e modernização autoritária* (Rio de Janeiro: Zahar, 2014).

19. Ricardo D. Salvatore, *Disciplinary Conquest: U.S. Scholars in South America, 1900–1945* (Durham, NC: Duke University Press, 2016). For a critical engagement with the term "Americanization" from a European perspective, see Mary Nolan, *The Transatlantic Century: Europe and America, 1890–2010* (Cambridge: Cambridge University Press, 2012).

20. Guy Martinière, *Aspects de la coopération franco-brésilienne: Transplantation culturelle et stratégie de la modernité* (Grenoble: Presses universitaires de Grenoble / Éditions de la Maison des sciences de l'homme, 1984); Hugo Rogélio Suppo, "La politique culturelle française au Brésil entre les années 1920–1950" (PhD diss., Paris III-Sorbonne Nouvelle, 1999); Juliette Dumont, *L'Institut international de Coopération intellectuelle et le Brésil (1924–1946): Le pari de la diplomatie culturelle* (Paris: Éditions de l'IHEAL, 2009). See also Patrick Iber, *Neither Peace nor Freedom: The Cultural Cold War in Latin America* (Cambridge, MA: Harvard University Press, 2015).

21. Johan Heilbron, Nicolas Guilhot, and Laurent Jeanpierre, "Toward a Transnational History of the Social Sciences," *Journal of the History of the Behavioral Sciences* 44, no. 2 (2008). See also Mauricio Tenorio-Trillo, "Como escrever hoje a história das ideias e dos intelectuais de uma perspectiva comparativa, transnacional," in *Ateliê do pensamento social: Ideias em perspectiva global*, ed. J. M. Ehlert Maia, Claudio Costa Pinheiro, and Helena Bomeny (Rio de Janeiro: Fundação Getúlio Vargas, Editora CPDOC, 2014). For a useful model for the North Atlantic, see Christian Fleck, *A Transatlantic History of the Social Sciences: Robber Barons, the Third Reich, and the Invention of Empirical Social Research* (New York: Bloomsbury Academic, 2011).

22. For more on connected histories, see Sanjay Subrahmanyam, "Connected Histories: Notes Towards a Reconfiguration of Early Modern Eurasia," *Modern Asian Studies* 31, no. 3 (1997).

23. Lúcia G. Pallares-Burke and Peter Burke, *Gilberto Freyre: Social Theory in the Tropics* (Oxford: Peter Lang, 2008); Jeremy Adelman, *Worldly Philosopher: The Odyssey of Albert O. Hirschman* (Princeton, NJ: Princeton University Press, 2013); Federico Finchelstein, *Transatlantic Fascism: Ideology, Violence, and the Sacred in Argentina and Italy, 1919–1945* (Durham, NC: Duke University Press, 2010); Karin Alejandra Rosemblatt, *The Science and Politics of Race in Mexico and the United States, 1910–1950* (Chapel Hill: University of North Carolina Press, 2018); James P. Woodard, *Brazil's Revolution in Commerce: Creating Consumer Capitalism in the American Century* (Chapel Hill: University of North Carolina Press, 2020); Christy Thornton, *Revolution in Development: Mexico and the Governance of the Global Economy* (Oakland: University of California Press, 2021); Pablo Palomino, *The Invention of Latin American Music: A Transnational History* (Oxford: Oxford University Press, 2020); Margarita Fajardo, *The World That Latin America Created: The United Nations Economic Commission for Latin America in the Development Era* (Cambridge, MA: Harvard University Press, forthcoming); Michele Greet, *Transatlantic Encounters: Latin American Artists in Paris between the Wars* (New Haven, CT: Yale University Press, 2018), Barbara Haskell, ed.,

Vida Americana: Mexican Muralists Remake American Art, 1925–1945 (New Haven, CT: Yale University Press, 2020). See also Clara Ruvituso, "From the South to the North: The Circulation of Latin American Dependency Theories in the Federal Republic of Germany," *Current Sociology* 68, no. 1 (2020).

24. For a critical engagement with the term "Eurocentrism" in Brazilian and Latin American historiography, see Pedro Afonso Cristovão dos Santos, Thiago Lima Nicodemo, and Mateus Henrique de Faria Pereira, "Historiografias Periféricas em Perspectiva Global ou Transnacional: Eurocentrismo em Questão," *Estudos históricos* 30, no. 60 (2017). From a different regional perspective, see Alessandro Stanziani, *Eurocentrism and the Politics of Global History* (Cham, Switzerland: Palgrave Macmillan, 2018).

25. Steve J. Stern, "Feudalism, Capitalism, and the World-System in the Perspective of Latin America and the Caribbean," *American Historical Review* 93, no. 4 (1988): 872.

26. Samuel Moyn and Andrew Sartori, eds., *Global Intellectual History* (New York: Columbia University Press, 2013).

27. My approach in this regard has been heavily influenced by Fritz Ringer, *The Decline of the German Mandarins* (Middletown, CT: Wesleyan University Press, 1990); Christophe Charle, *La république des universitaires, 1870–1940* (Paris: Seuil, 1994); Laurent Jeanpierre, "Des hommes entre plusieurs mondes: Étude sur une situation d'exil; Intellectuels français réfugiés pendant la deuxième guerre mondiale" (PhD diss., École des Hautes Études en Sciences Sociales, 2004); Lidiane Soares Rodrigues, "A produção social do marxismo universitário em São Paulo: Mestres, discípulos, e 'um seminário' (1958–1978)" (PhD diss., University of São Paulo, 2011); Heloisa Pontes, *Destinos mistos: Os críticos do grupo Clima em São Paulo, 1940–1968* (São Paulo: Companhia das Letras, 1998); Michael P. Farrell, *Collaborative Circles: Friendship Dynamics and Creative Work* (Chicago: University of Chicago Press, 2001), 21–26. See also Michael Goebel, *Anti-imperial Metropolis: Interwar Paris and the Seeds of Third World Nationalism* (Cambridge: Cambridge University Press, 2015). More recently, see Mark Mazower, "Devenir Hobsbawm: Une internationalisation de la profession historienne," *Le mouvement social*, no. 259 (2017).

28. For more on this possibility, see Antoine Lilti, "Does Intellectual History Exist in France? The Chronicle of a Renaissance Foretold," in *Rethinking Modern European Intellectual History*, ed. Darrin M. McMahon and Samuel Moyn (Oxford: Oxford University Press, 2014), 67.

29. Pierre Bourdieu, *Manet: Une révolution symbolique* (Paris: Raisons d'agir / Le Seuil, 2013).

30. The term "cluster" is advanced by Terry Clark in *Prophets and Patrons: The French University and the Emergence of the Social Sciences* (Cambridge, MA: Harvard University Press, 1973), 67–84 passim. This study takes a slightly less hierarchical approach, focusing on the horizontal elements between members of a cluster. In its

analysis of ideas, it better resembles what some have called "constellations." See, e.g., Martin Mulsow, "Qu'est-ce qu'une constellation philosophique? Propositions pour une analyse des réseaux intellectuels," *Annales HSS* 64, no. 1 (2009).

31. In the postwar period, Braudel alone exchanged more than sixty letters each with Lévi-Strauss, Monbeig, and Bastide. MS 8510, Braudel Archive, Bibliothèque de l'Institut de France (henceforth FB).

32. Rafael Faraco Benthien, "Por uma história cruzada das disciplinas: Ponderações de ordens prática e epistemológica," *Revista de história*, no. 179 (2020). For a similar approach to the one advanced here focused on a single institution, see Camille Robcis, *Disalienation: Politics, Philosophy, and Radical Psychiatry in France* (Chicago: University of Chicago Press, 2021); for another, on a single concept, see Stefanos Geroulanos, *Transparency in Postwar France: A Critical History of the Present* (Stanford, CA: Stanford University Press, 2017).

33. Angela de Castro Gomes, "Nas malhas do feitiço: O historiador e os encantos dos arquivos privados," *Estudos históricos* 11, no. 21 (1998).

34. Claude Ravelet, *Etudes sur Roger Bastide* (Paris: L'Harmattan, 1996) and "Bibliographie de Roger Bastide," *Bastidiana: Cahiers d'études bastidiennes* 3 (1993); *Roger Bastide ou le réjouissement de l'abîme*, ed. Philippe Laburthe-Tolra (Paris: L'Harmattan, 1994); the journal *Bastidiana* in its entirety; Cibele Barbosa, "Le Brésil entre le mythe et l'idéal: La réception de l'oeuvre de Gilberto Freyre en France dans l'après-guerre" (PhD diss., Sorbonne, 2011); Christophe Brochier, *La naissance de la sociologie au Brésil* (Rennes: Presses Universitaires de Rennes, 2016); Giuliana Gemelli, *Fernand Braudel*, trans. Béatrice Propetto Marzi (Paris: Odile Jacob, 1995); Pierre Daix, *Braudel* (Paris: Flammarion, 1995); Patrick Wilcken, *Claude Lévi-Strauss: The Poet in the Laboratory* (London: Bloomsbury, 2010); Emmanuelle Loyer, *Claude Lévi-Strauss* (Paris: Flammarion, 2015); Martine Droulers and Hervé Théry, *Pierre Monbeig: Un géographe pionnier* (Paris: Éditions de l'IHEAL, 1999); Heliana Angotti Salgueiro, ed., *Pierre Monbeig e a geografia humana brasileira: A dinâmica da transformação* (Paris: EDUSC, 2006); Larissa Alves de Lira, *Pierre Monbeig e a formação da geografia no Brasil (1925–1956): Uma geo-história dos saberes* (São Paulo: Alameda, 2021); José Borzacchiello da Silva, *French-Brazilian Geography: The Influence of French Geography in Brazil* (Switzerland: Springer, 2016)—this list is far from exhaustive.

35. For an overview, see Suzanne Marchand, "Has the History of the Disciplines Had Its Day?," in McMahon and Moyn, *Rethinking Modern European Intellectual History*.

36. While focusing on Chicago sociology, Andrew Abbott's analysis is applicable to a variety of contexts. See *Department and Discipline: Chicago Sociology at One Hundred* (Chicago: University of Chicago Press, 1999). See also Jean-Louis Fabiani, "À quoi sert la notion de discipline?," in *Qu'est-ce qu'une discipline?*, ed. Jean Boutier, Jean-Claude Passeron, and Jacques Revel (Paris: EHESS, 2006).

37. The title makes explicit reference to Paulina Alberto's *Terms of Inclusion: Black Intellectuals in Twentieth-Century Brazil* (Chapel Hill: University of North Carolina Press, 2011).

38. Fernando Novais, "Braudel e a 'Missão Francesa,'" *Estudos Avançados* 8, no. 22 (1994): 161; Carlos Guilherme Mota, "Ecos da historiografia francesa no Brasil: Apontamentos e desapontamentos," in *Do positivismo à desconstrução: Idéias francesas na América*, ed. Leyla Perrone-Moisés (São Paulo: Edusp, 2004), 146–47.

39. Pascale Casanova's pioneering work sheds light on the inequalities of language and translation in literary markets. *The World Republic of Letters*, trans. M. B. DeBevoise (Cambridge, MA: Harvard University Press, 2007).

40. Dain Borges, "'Puffy, Ugly, Slothful, and Inert': Degeneration in Brazilian Social Thought, 1880–1940," *Journal of Latin American Studies* 25, no. 2 (1993): 239.

41. Dipesh Chakrabarty, *Provincializing Europe: Postcolonial Thought and Historical Difference* (Princeton, NJ: Princeton University Press, 2001), 39.

42. Here, I draw on Partha Chatterjee, *The Nation and Its Fragments: Colonial and Postcolonial Histories* (Princeton, NJ: Princeton University Press, 1993).

43. Kirsten Schultz, *Tropical Versailles: Empire, Monarchy, and the Portuguese Royal Court in Rio de Janeiro, 1808–1821* (New York: Routledge, 2001).

44. Jeffrey D. Needell, *A Tropical Belle Epoque: Elite Culture and Society in Turn-of-the-Century Rio de Janeiro* (Cambridge: Cambridge University Press, 2010); J. P. Daughton, "When Argentina Was 'French': Rethinking Cultural Politics and European Imperialism in Belle-Époque Buenos Aires," *Journal of Modern History* 80, no. 4 (2008).

45. For more on the First Republic and the importance of France in its imagination, see José Murilo de Carvalho, *The Formation of Souls: Imagery of the Republic in Brazil*, trans. Clifford E. Lander (Notre Dame: Notre Dame University Press, 2012). For Brazilian positivism in particular, see Alfredo Bosi, "O Positivismo no Brasil: Uma ideologia de longa duração," in Perrone-Moisés, *Do positivismo à desconstrução*. See also Paul Arbousse-Bastide, *Le positivisme politique et religieux au Brésil* (Turnhout: Brepols, 2010). The classic reference is João Cruz Costa, *A filosofia de Augusto Comte e as origens do positivism* (São Paulo: Ed. Companhia Nacional, 1959).

46. Oswald quoted in Barbara Weinstein, *The Color of Modernity: São Paulo and the Making of Race and Nation in Brazil* (Durham, NC: Duke University Press, 2015), 378n153.

47. Edith Wolfe, "Paris as Periphery: Vicente do Rego Monteiro and Brazil's Discrepant Cosmopolitanism," *Art Bulletin* 96, no. 1 (2014): 101.

48. Blaise Cendrars, *Etc. . . . etc. . . . : Um livro 100% brasileiro* (São Paulo: Perspectiva, 1976), 96.

49. Homi Bhabha, *The Location of Culture* (London: Routledge, 1994), 85–92.

50. Paulo Eduardo Arantes, *Um departamento francês de ultramar* (Rio de Janeiro: Paz e Terra, 1994).

51. Frantz Fanon, *Black Skin, White Masks*, trans. Richard Philcox (New York: Grove

Press, 2008). For an account of Aimé Césaire's project of departmentalization, see Gary Wilder, "Untimely Vision: Aimé Césaire, Decolonization, Utopia," *Public Culture* 21, no. 1 (2009).

52. For a broader historical discussion of mediators, see Angela de Castro Gomes and Patricia Santos Hansen, eds., *Intelectuais mediadores: Práticas culturais e ação política* (Rio de Janeiro: Civilização brasileira, 2016).

53. Hermano Vianna, *The Mystery of Samba: Popular Music and National Identity in Brazil* (Chapel Hill: University of North Carolina Press, 1999).

54. Hugh Raffles, *In Amazonia: A Natural History* (Princeton, NJ: Princeton University Press, 2002); Vanessa Smith, "Joseph Banks's Intermediaries: Rethinking Global Cultural Exchange," in Moyn and Sartori, *Global Intellectual History*; Richard Price, *Travels with Tooy: History, Memory, and the African American Imagination* (Chicago: University of Chicago Press, 2008); Amín Pérez, "Rendre le social plus politique: Guerre coloniale, immigration, et pratiques sociologiques d'Abdelmalek Sayed et de Pierre Bourdieu" (PhD dissertation, EHESS, 2015). See also Mariza Peirano, "The Anthropology of Anthropology: The Brazilian Case" (PhD dissertation, Harvard University, 1981).

55. Micol Seigel, *Uneven Encounters: Making Race and Nation in Brazil and the United States* (Durham, NC: Duke University Press, 2009), xvi.

56. Antonio Sérgio Alfredo Guimarães, "Intelectuais negros e formas de integração nacional," *Estudos avançados* 18, no. 50 (2004).

57. Andrew Sartori, *Bengal in Global Concept History: Culturalism in the Age of Capital* (Chicago: University of Chicago Press, 2008); Andrew Sartori, *Liberalism in Empire: An Alternative History* (Oakland: University of California Press, 2014).

58. Sebastian Conrad, *What Is Global History?* (Princeton, NJ: Princeton University Press, 2016).

59. Roberto Schwarz, *Misplaced Ideas: Essays on Brazilian Culture*, ed. John Gledson (New York: Verso, 1992), 6.

60. Sebastian Conrad, "Enlightenment in Global History: A Historiographical Critique," *American Historical Review* 117, no. 4 (2012): 1022.

61. To cite several prominent examples, see C. L. R. James, *The Black Jacobins: Toussaint l'Ouverture and the San Domingo Revolution* (New York: Vintage, 1989); Michel-Rolph Trouillot, *Silencing the Past: Power and the Production of History* (Boston: Beacon Press, 1997); Laurent Dubois, *Avengers of the New World: The Story of the Haitian Revolution* (New York: Belknap Press of Harvard University Press, 2005); Susan Buck-Morss, *Hegel, Haiti, and Universal History* (Pittsburgh: University of Pittsburgh Press, 2009); Ada Ferrer, *Freedom's Mirror: Cuba and Haiti in the Age of Revolution* (New York: Cambridge University Press, 2014).

62. As is common practice in Brazil with authors, the likes of Mário de Andrade, Oswald de Andrade, and Machado de Assis are often referred to by their first name in this book.

63. Gilberto Freyre, "Bastide: Francês Abrasileirado," *Afro-Ásia*, no. 12 (1976).

64. Peter Fry, "Gallus africanus est, ou como Roger Bastide se tornou africano no Brasil," in *Revisitando a terra de contrastes: A atualidade da obra de Roger Bastide*, ed. Olga Moraes Von Simon and Maria Isaura Pereira de Queiroz (São Paulo, USP-FFLCH-CERU, 1986).

65. Mário to Bastide, São Paulo, September 19, 1944, BST2.C1.01, Archive Roger Bastide, Institut Mémoires de l'Édition Contemporaine, Caen (henceforth IMEC).

66. Ibid.

67. Claude Lévi-Strauss, *Tristes Tropiques*, trans. John Weightman and Doreen Weightman (New York: Penguin, 1992), 101.

68. Ibid., 104.

69. Gilda de Mello e Souza, *O tupi e o alaúde: Uma interpretação de "Macunaíma"* (São Paulo: Duas Cidades/Editora 34, 2003): 9–10.

70. Gilda de Mello e Souza, *O espírito das roupas: A moda no século dezenove* (São Paulo: Companhia das Letras, 1987); Heloisa Pontes, "Modas e modos: Uma leitura enviesada de *O espírito das roupas*," *Cadernos Pagu*, no. 22 (2004).

71. Ian Merkel, "Fernand Braudel and the Empire of French Social Science: Newly Translated Sources from the 1930s," *French Historical Studies* 40, no. 1 (2017): 129–60. For a *longue durée* approach relevant to this question, see Mário Carelli, *Cultures croisées: Histoire des échanges culturels entre la France et le Brésil de la découverte aux temps modernes* (Paris: Nathan, 1993); Mário Carelli, *Culturas cruzadas: Intercâmbios culturais entre França e Brasil* (Campinas: Papirus, 1994). See also Leyla Perrone-Moisés, ed., *Cinco séculos de presença francesa no Brasil* (São Paulo: Edusp, 2013).

72. James Holston, *Insurgent Citizenship: Disjunctions of Democracy and Modernity in Brazil* (Princeton, NJ: Princeton University Press, 2007); Frederick Cooper, *Citizenship between Empire and Nation: Remaking France and French Africa, 1945–1960* (Princeton, NJ: Princeton University Press, 2016). See also Ann Laura Stoler and Frederick Cooper, "Between Metropole and Colony: Rethinking a Research Agenda," in *Tensions of Empire: Colonial Cultures in a Bourgeois World*, ed. Cooper and Stoler (Berkeley: University of California Press, 1997).

73. Jorge Cañizares-Esguerra, *How to Write the History of the New World: Histories, Epistemologies, and Identities in the Eighteenth-Century Atlantic World* (Stanford, CA: Stanford University Press, 2002); James Sweet, *Domingos Álvares, African Healing, and the Intellectual History of the Atlantic World* (Chapel Hill: University of North Carolina Press, 2011); Neil Safier, *Measuring the New World: Enlightenment Science and South America* (Chicago: University of Chicago Press, 2012); Pablo F. Goméz, *The Experimental Caribbean: Creating Knowledge and Healing in the Early Modern Atlantic* (Chapel Hill: University of North Carolina Press, 2017).

74. Durval Muniz de Albuquerque Jr., *A invenção do Nordeste e outras artes* (Recife: Fundação Joaquim Nabuco/Ed. Massangana, 2001), 45; translated by Jerry Dennis

Metz as *The Invention of the Brazilian Northeast* (Durham, NC: Duke University Press, 2014).

75. Weinstein, *Color of Modernity*, 9–10. Weinstein builds upon Jane Schneider, ed., *Italy's "Southern Question": Orientalism in One Country* (Oxford: Oxford University Press, 1998).

76. Nancy Appelbaum, *Muddied Waters: Race, Region, and Local History in Colombia, 1846–1948* (Durham, NC: Duke University Press, 2003), 40.

77. Mary Louise Pratt, *Imperial Eyes: Travel Writing and Transculturation*, 2nd ed. (New York: Routledge, 2007), 37.

78. Jose C. Moya, "Introduction: Latin America—the Limitations and Meaning of a Historical Category," in *The Oxford Handbook of Latin American History*, ed. Moya (Oxford: Oxford University Press, 2012), 14.

79. Weinstein, *Color of Modernity*, 7–9. For a now-classic Brazilian essay that criticizes the dualism of the dependency theorists based at CEPAL, see Francisco de Oliveira, "Crítica à razão dualista," in *Crítica à razão dualista / O Ornittorinco* (São Paulo: Boitempo, 2003).

80. Among others, see Herman Lebovics, *True France: The Wars over Cultural Identity, 1900–1945* (Ithaca, NY: Cornell University Press, 1994); Alice Conklin, *In the Museum of Man: Race, Anthropology, and Empire in France, 1850–1950* (Ithaca, NY: Cornell University Press, 2013); Emmanuelle Sibeud, *Une science coloniale pour l'Afrique? La construction des savoirs africanistes en France, 1878–1930* (Paris: École des Hautes Études en Sciences Sociales, 2002); Gary Wilder, *The French Imperial Nation-State: Negritude and Colonial Humanism between the Two World Wars* (Chicago: University of Chicago Press, 2005); Carole Reynaud-Paligot, "Les Annales de Lucien Febvre à Fernand Braudel entre épopée coloniale et opposition Orient/Occident," *French Historical Studies* 32, no. 1 (2009); Carole Reynaud Paligot, *La république raciale: Paradigme social et idéologie républicaine, 1860–1930* (Paris: Presses universitaires de France, 2006); Pierre Singaravélou, ed., *L'empire des géographes: Géographie, exploration et colonisation* (Paris: Belin, 2008). For a comparative study, see Benoît de L'Estoile, Federico Neiburg, and Lygia Sigaud, eds., *Empires, Nations, and Natives: Anthropology and State-Making* (Durham, NC: Duke University Press, 2005).

81. Alice Conklin, *A Mission to Civilize: The Republican Idea of Empire in France and West Africa, 1895–1930* (Stanford, CA: Stanford University Press, 1997).

82. Jeffrey D. Needell, "The Domestic Civilizing Mission: The Cultural Role of the State in Brazil, 1808–1930," *Luso-Brazilian Review* 36, no. 1 (1999).

83. Antonio Celso Ferreira, *A epopéia bandeirante: Letrados, instituições, invenção histórica (1870–1940)* (São Paulo: UNESP, 2001). For an introduction in English to this historiography, see Weinstein, *Color of Modernity*, 32–46. See also James Woodard, foreword to *Blacks of the Land: Indian Slavery, Settler Society, and the Portuguese Colonial Enterprise in South America*, by John Manuel Monteiro, ed. and trans. James Woodard and Barbara Weinstein (Cambridge: Cambridge University Press, 2019).

84. Tania Regina de Luca, *A "Revista do Brasil": Um diagnóstico para a (N)ação* (São Paulo: Editora Unesp, 1998).

85. Thomas Skidmore, *Black into White: Race and Nationality in Brazilian Thought* (Durham, NC: Duke University Press, 1992).

86. Mariza Corrêa, *Ilusões da liberdade: A escola Nina Rodrigues e a antropologia no Brasil* (Rio de Janeiro: Fundação Oswaldo Cruz, 2013).

87. Lucien Lévy-Bruhl, *Primitive Mentality* (1923; Boston: Beacon Press, 1966).

88. For exciting new work on Freyre and luso-tropicalism, see *Luso-tropicalism and Its Discontents: The Making and Unmaking of Racial Exceptionalism*, ed. Warwick Anderson, Ricardo Roque, and Ricardo Ventura Santos (New York: Berghahn Books, 2019).

89. It is worth noting here that Freyre's critiques of the imposed categories of others began by emphasizing the plurality of modernism and modernity writ large in opposition to the Paulistas' presumed monopoly of them. See his *Manifesto Regionalista de 1926* (Rio de Janeiro: Ministério de Educação e Cultura, Serviço de Documentação, 1955).

90. Pierre Bourdieu and Loïc Wacquant, "On the Cunning of Imperialist Reason," *Theory, Culture, and Society* 16, no. 1 (1999).

91. For a reading of US social science in Latin America even prior to this period, see Salvatore, *Disciplinary Conquest*. For France, see Brigitte Mazon, "La Fondation Rockefeller et les sciences sociales en France, 1925–1940," *Revue française de sociologie* 26, no. 2 (1985); Ludovic Tournès, "La fondation Rockefeller et la construction d'une politique des sciences sociales en France (1918–1940)," *Annales HSS* 6, no. 63 (2008). See also Licia do Prado Valladares, *A escola de Chicago: Impacto de uma tradição no Brasil e na França* (Belo Horizonte: Editora UFMG, 2005). For a comparative perspective, it is also worth noting here recent work by Álvaro Morcillo Laiz, including "La Gran Dama: Science Patronage, the Rockefeller Foundation, and the Mexican Social Sciences in the 1940s," *Journal of Latin American Studies* 51, no. 4 (2019).

92. Mário de Andrade, "Decadência da influência francesa no Brasil: Respostas a um inquérito," *Diário de Manhã*. Recife, April 16, 1936. Reproduced in Mário de Andrade, *Vida literária* (São Paulo: Edusp, 1993), 3.

93. Ibid.

94. Ibid., 5.

95. Ibid.

96. Ibid.

97. Dreyfus quoted in Suppo, "La politique culturelle française au Brésil," 705.

98. Antonio Pedro Tota, *The Seduction of Brazil: The Americanization of Brazil during World War II* (Austin: University of Texas Press, 2009). For a broader cultural history, see Gilbert Joseph, Catherine Legrand, and Ricardo Salvatore, eds., *Close Encounters of Empire: Writing the Cultural History of U.S. Latin American Relations* (Durham, NC: Duke University Press, 1998).

99. Michel Gobat, "The Invention of Latin America: A Transnational History of Anti-Imperialism, Democracy, and Race," *American Historical Review* 118, no. 5 (2013).

100. Greg Grandin, "The Liberal Traditions in the Americas: Rights, Sovereignty, and the Origins of Liberal Multilateralism," *American Historical Review* 117, no. 1 (2012).

101. For a classic exploration of these dichotomies, see Octavio Paz, *The Labyrinth of Solitude* (New York: Penguin, 2008). Of course, for working-class and revolutionary intellectuals, the problem of authenticity is a bit different. See, for example, Raymond Craib, *The Cry of the Renegade: Politics and Poetry in Interwar Chile* (Oxford: Oxford University Press, 2016).

102. Gabriela Ramos and Yanna Yannakakis, eds., *Indigenous Intellectuals: Knowledge, Power, and Colonial Culture in Mexico and the Andes* (Durham, NC: Duke University Press, 2014).

103. Pratt, *Imperial Eyes*, 5.

104. Walter Mignolo, *Local Histories / Global Designs: Coloniality, Subaltern Knowledges, and Border Thinking* (Princeton, NJ: Princeton University Press, 2000), 5.

105. Freud to Ramos, Vienna, May 20, 1927, Manuscritos, CF-49,02,01 n.002, Biblioteca Nacional (henceforth BN).

106. Alice Leonardos da Silva Lima to "Dr Rivet," Rio de Janeiro, September 20, 1928, 2AP1C LEON, Archives Paul Rivet, Archives du Muséum de l'Histoire Naturelle (henceforth MnHn).

107. Schwarz, *Misplaced Ideas*, 6.

CHAPTER ONE

1. USP's statutes, however, were only approved by federal decree on September 3, 1934, by Getúlio Vargas and his minister of Education and Health, Gustavo Capanema.

2. GC g 1938.05.30 Arquivo Capanema, Centro de Pesquisa e Documentação de História Contemporânea do Brasil (henceforth CPDOC).

3. Ibid. For more on the politics behind social science in Brazil and the use of different national traditions, see Patrick Petitjean, "As missões universitárias francesas na criação da Universidade de São Paulo (1934–1940)," in *A ciência nas relações Brasil-França (1850–1950)*, ed. Amélia Império Hamburger et al. (São Paulo: Edusp, 1996). See also Fernanda Arêas Peixoto, "Franceses e norte-americanos nas ciências sociais brasileiras (1930–1960)," in *História das ciências sociais no Brasil*, vol. 1, ed. Sergio Miceli et al. (São Paulo: Vértice, 1989).

4. "Paulista" refers to someone or something from the state of São Paulo.

5. Andrew J. Kirkendall, *Class Mates: Male Student Culture and the Making of a Political Class in Nineteenth-Century Brazil* (Lincoln: University of Nebraska Press, 2002), 179.

6. Joseph L. Love, *São Paulo in the Brazilian Federation, 1889–1937* (Stanford, CA:

Stanford University Press, 1980), 91. For more on the relationship between the newspaper and the Partido Democrático, see Maria Lígia Coelho Prado and Helena Rolim Capelato, *O bravo matutino: Imprensa e ideologia no jornal "O Estado de S. Paulo"* (São Paulo: Alfa-Ômega, 1980).

7. Irene Cardoso, *A universidade de comunhão paulista* (São Paulo: Autores Associados/Cortez, 1982), 52. Throughout this text, I use the terms "liberalism" and "liberal" in ways that are uncommon in the English language. In Brazil and elsewhere liberalism and liberals were defined by a desire to preserve the market economy and access to labor and an elite preoccupation with the excesses of popular participation.

8. Joaquim A. Sampaio Vidal, *Synthese do pensamento politico de Armando de Salles Oliveira* (São Paulo: Empreza Graphica da "Revista dos Tribunaes," 1937), 34.

9. Júlio de Mesquita Filho, *A Crise nacional: Reflexões em torno de uma data* (São Paulo: Secção de Obras d'"O Estado de São Paulo," 1925), 89–90. For more specific educational writings, see, in the same volume, "As Universidades" and "O Ensino das Humanidades."

10. *Interventores* were federally appointed governors during the Vargas years. Oliveira, exceptionally, despite being part of the opposition to Vargas, was allowed to occupy this important position. Duarte, while largely absent from official documents, claimed to have been an important part of USP's founding. Duarte, *Memórias*, vol. 3, *Selva Escura* (São Paulo: Hucitec, 1979), 69–73, 200–3.

11. Cardoso, *A universidade de comunhão paulista*, 153, 157; John W. F. Dulles, *A Faculdade de Direito de São Paulo e a resistência anti-Vargas, 1938–1945* (São Paulo: Edusp, 1984), 72. Mesquita, like Duarte, would be exiled once again by Vargas during the Estado Novo in 1937, this time in Paris.

12. GC g 1938.05.27, p. 14, Arquivo Capanema, CPDOC.

13. Fernando Limongi, "A Escola Livre de Sociologia e Política," in *História das ciências sociais no Brasil*, vol. 1.

14. Milliet quoted in Barbara Weinstein, *The Color of Modernity: São Paulo and the Making of Race and Nation in Brazil* (Durham, NC: Duke University Press, 2015), 381.

15. Coffman quoted in Armando de Salles Oliveira, *Para que o Brasil continue (Discursos Políticos)* (Rio de Janeiro: José Olympio, 1937), 73.

16. Caio Prado Jr., *A cidade de São Paulo: Geografia e história* (São Paulo: Brasiliense, 1993), 60.

17. Richard Morse, *De comunidade à metrópole: A biografia de São Paulo* (São Paulo: Comissão do IV Centenário da Cidade de São Paulo, 1954), 293.

18. In colonial times, a chronicler, Frei Vicente, lamented the Portuguese tendency to "scuttle along the shore like crabs." Vicente quoted in Raymundo Faoro and Sylvania Franco, eds., *Modos de ver a produção do Brasil* (São Paulo: Educ, 2004), 449.

19. Sérgio Milliet, *Roteiro do café e outros ensaios* (São Paulo: Hucitec, 1982), 23. For more on the growth of industry, see Warren Dean, *The Industrialization of São Paulo, 1880–1945* (Austin: University of Texas Press, 2012).

20. Antonio Candido de Mello e Souza (henceforth Antonio Candido), "Um homem, duas cidades," Instituto de Estudos Brasileiros, lecture delivered in September 2011, YouTube video, 27:26, https://www.youtube.com/watch?v=wXgG0GR7CYg. See also Antonio Candido, "A revolução de 1930 e a cultura," *Novos Estudos* 2, no. 4 (1984).

21. Morse, *From Community to Metropolis*.

22. Love, *São Paulo in the Brazilian Federation*, 90.

23. Sergio Miceli, *Intelectuais e classe dirigente no Brasil (1920–1945)* (São Paulo: Difel, 1979). For more on "autonomy" in the intellectual field, see Gisèle Sapiro, "Rethinking the Concept of Autonomy for the Sociology of Symbolic Goods," trans. Jean-Yves Bart, *Bien symboliques / Symbolic Goods*, no. 4 (2019), http://journals .openedition.org/bssg/334.

24. Marisa Midori Deaecto, "Anatole Louis Garraux e o comercio de livros franceses em São Paulo (1860–1890)," *Revista Brasileira de História* 28, no. 55 (2008): 87–88.

25. The most emblematic figure in this was a Paulista, Monteiro Lobato. For more on his Editora Revista do Brazil, see Alice Mitika Koshikyama, *Monteiro Lobato: Intelectual, empresário, editor* (São Paulo: T. A. A Queiroz Editor, 1982), esp. chap. 4.

26. Sergio Miceli, *Intelectuais à brasileira* (São Paulo: Companhia das Letras, 2001), 4.

27. Miceli, 148.

28. For an excellent introduction, see Daryle Williams, *Culture Wars in Brazil: The First Vargas Regime, 1930–45* (Durham, NC: Duke University Press, 2001), 36–48. For an important historical—as opposed to aesthetic or literary—interpretation, see Mônica Pimenta Velloso, "A brasilidade verde-amarela: Nacionalismo e regionalismo paulista," *Estudos Históricos* 6, no. 11 (1993).

29. Mário to Bandeira, São Paulo, 1924, quoted in Angela de Castro Gomes, *Essa gente do Rio . . . : Modernismo e nacionalismo* (Rio: Editora Fundação Getúlio Vargas, 1999), 7.

30. For more on Brazil's Northeast and its importance for the Brazilian editorial market, see Gustavo Sorá, *Brasilianas: José Olympio e a gênese do mercado editorial brasileiro* (São Paulo: Edusp, 2010), esp. 180–97.

31. Mário's diaries of his travels were published as Mário de Andrade, *O turista aprendiz* (Belo Horizonte: Editora Itatiaia, 2002).

32. Luísa Valentini's analysis of Mário's library confirms the presence of several of Lévy-Bruhl's books in French. *Um laboratório de antropologia: O encontro entre Mário de Andrade, Dina Dreyfus, e Claude Lévi-Strauss (1935–1939)* (São Paulo: Alameda, 2013), 114. For a useful rereading of Lévy-Bruhl and his interwar importance, see Thomas Hirsch, "Un 'Flammarion' pour l'anthropologie? Lévy-Bruhl, le terrain, l'ethnologie," *Genèses* 90, no. 1 (2013). See also Frédéric Keck, *Lucien Lévy-Bruhl: Entre philosophie et anthropologie; Contradiction et participation* (Paris: CNRS Éditions, 2008).

33. Oswald de Andrade, "Manifesto of Anthropophagy," *Tarsila do Amaral: Invent-*

ing Modern Art in Brazil, ed. Stephanie D'Alessandro and Luis Pérez-Omaras (Chicago: Art Institute of Chicago, 2017), 176. Other Brazilians took Lévy-Bruhl's assumptions about "primitive" irrationality to the letter. Mesquita was asked if he believed in the supernatural. He responded, "How could I not, if I belong to the last generation that nursed from former slaves? This means that I am their product, and that I inherited an affinity with cultural vices of mystical origin, as my *mestre* Lévy would say. Many residuals of the law of participation remain alive in my spirit, even if today they appear with much less intensity than when I was a child or even an adolescent." "Como Vivem e Trabalham nossos escritores."

34. Weinstein, *Color of Modernity*, 57. For a useful definition of the *pau-brasil* group, see ibid., 90. Paulista intellectuals such as Mário and Monteiro Lobato, editor of the *Revista do Brasil,* may have anticipated the "nationalization" of Brazilian culture that would take place in the 1930s but were by no means the only ones to deal with Brazilian subjects and "realities." For more on the *Revista do Brasil,* see Tania Regina de Luca, *A "Revista do Brasil."*

35. For more on educational reform and the social sciences in São Paulo during this transitional period, see Love, *São Paulo in the Brazilian Federation,* esp. 93–96.

36. Fernando de Azevedo, *A educação pública em São Paulo: Problemas e discussões; Inquérito para "O Estado de S. Paulo," em 1926* (São Paulo: Companhia Editora Nacional, 1937).

37. Maria Luiza Penna, *Fernando de Azevedo: Educação e transformação* (São Paulo: Editora Perspectiva, 1987), xix–xx.

38. Despite Azevedo's insistence on technical education alongside "general knowledge," his choice of interviewees for his survey privileged industrial over vocational training. See Barbara Weinstein, *For Social Peace in Brazil: Industrialists and the Remaking of the Working Class in São Paulo, 1920–1964* (Chapel Hill: University of North Carolina Press, 1997), 36–37.

39. Azevedo quoted in Penna, *Fernando de Azevedo,* 196.

40. Valentini, *Um laboratório de antropologia,* 17. Mário de Andrade headed the Departamento from 1935 to 1938. Among the many publications about his role there, of particular interest are "Mário de Andrade," special edition of *Revista do Arquivo Municipal,* no. 206 (São Paulo: Arquivo Histórico de São Paulo, 2015), and Carlos Augusto Calil, *Mário de Andrade, Diretor do Departamento de Cultura de São Paulo* (São Paulo: Imprensa Oficial, 2003).

41. For more on the *Revista,* see Silene Ferreira Claro, "Revista do Arquivo Municipal de São Paulo: Um espaço científico e cultural esquecido" (PhD diss., University of São Paulo, 2008).

42. Weinstein, *Color of Modernity,* 37–38.

43. For more on this political conjuncture, see James P. Woodard, *A Place in Politics: São Paulo, Brazil, from Seigneurial Republicanism to Regionalist Revolt* (Durham, NC: Duke University Press, 2009), 143–87.

44. For an extended analysis of the party and its politics, see Maria Lígia Coelho Prado, *A democracia ilustrada (O Partido Democrático de São Paulo, 1926–1934)* (São Paulo: Atica, 1986).

45. The Old Republic was called the *cafe com leche* alliance, based on the alternating presidencies between São Paulo and Minas Gerais. The latter is synonymous with dairy products and is thus the "milk" to São Paulo's coffee. When Luís, a Paulista, appointed Prestes as his successor, Minas Gerais and other states rose up.

46. Weinstein, *Color of Modernity*, esp. 65–68.

47. Ibid., chaps. 3 and 4. It was the "Constitutionalist Revolution" for many Paulistas; for the rest of the Brazilians, it was a revolt or a civil war. To this day, it is commemorated statewide as a holiday in São Paulo.

48. Carolina S. Bandeira de Melo and Regina Helena de Freitas Campos, "Scientific Exchanges between France and Brazil in the History of Psychology: The Role of Georges Dumas between 1908 and 1946," *Universitas Psychologica* 13, no. 5 (2014).

49. "Prof Georges Dumas," *O Estado de São Paulo*, August 30, 1912; Georges Dumas, "A sociologia de Durkheim," *Correio Paulistano*, October 5, 1912. For an engaging study of Dumas's intellectual contributions and relationship to the Durkheimians, see Marcia Consolim, "Georges Dumas et Marcel Mauss: Rapports réels et pratiques entre la psychologie et la sociologie," *Durkheimian Studies* 24, no. 1 (2020).

50. Hugo Rogélio Suppo, "La politique culturelle française au Brésil entre les années 1920–1950," (PhD diss., Paris III-Sorbonne Nouvelle, 1999), 91; Marcel Fournier, *Marcel Mauss* (Paris: Fayard, 1994), 298, 726. Mentions of Marx's relationships with Durkheimian Henri Hubert also appear in recent scholarly literature: see, e.g., Jean-François Bert, "Hubert, Durkheim, Mauss: Amizades e filiações," in Henri Hubert, *Estudo sumário da representação do tempo na religião e na magia* (São Paulo: Edusp, 2016), 109.

51. For South America specifically, see Gilles Matthieu, *Une ambition sud-américaine: Politique culturelle de la France, 1914–1940* (Paris: L'Harmattan, 1991). For a North American comparison, see Robert Young, *Marketing Marianne: French Propaganda in America, 1900–1940* (New Brunswick, NJ: Rutgers University Press, 2003).

52. "A decimal conferência de Paul Fauconnet na Escola Normal," *O Estado de S. Paulo*, September 10, 1927. Fauconnet's relationships with Brazilian intellectuals merits a more thorough study. One of these intellectuals is João Cruz Costa, who claimed to serve as Fauconnet's "interpreter" at the "Société de Philosophie et Lettres de São Paulo." Fauconnet to Cruz Costa, Paris, May 6, 1931, Arquivo João Cruz Costa. I thank Francini de Oliveira for sharing many of João Cruz Costa's letters with me.

53. Ian Merkel, "Terms of Exchange: Brazilian Intellectuals and the Remaking of the French Social Sciences" (PhD diss., New York University / University of São Paulo, 2018), 46–48.

54. Johan Heilbron, *French Sociology* (Ithaca, NY: Cornell University Press, 2015), 101–2.

55. Mesquita to Marina, Ibirapuera, São Paulo, n.d., quoted in in Ruy Mesquita

Filho, ed., *Cartas do exílio: A troca de correspondência entre Marina e Júlio de Mesquita Filho* (São Paulo: Editora Albatroz, 2006), 33. Chiquinho was Mesquita's younger brother, Francisco.

56. See, for example, chap. 4, "A obra metodologica de E. Durkheim," which deals with Durkheim and the Durkheimians, including Fauconnet. In *Princípios da sociologia: Pequena introdução ao estudo de sociologia geral* (Rio: Companhia Editora Nacional, 1939).

57. Fernando Salla and Marcos César Alvarez, "Paulo Egídio e a sociologia criminal em São Paulo," *Tempo Social* 12, no. 1 (2000): 102–6. For more on Durkheim's Brazilian reception in general, see Vamireh Chacon, *História das ideias sociológicas no Brasil* (São Paulo: Edusp, 1977), 61–71. See also José Benevides Queiroz, "La réception de la sociologie d'Émile Durkheim au Brésil," *Incursions*, no. 8 (2014).

58. Émile Durkheim, *De la division du travail social* (Paris: Félix Alcan, 1893); Durkheim, "L'élite intellectuelle et la démocratie," *Revue bleue* 5, no. l (1904)

59. Mesquita Filho, *Cartas do exílio*, 11–13. For more on Durkheim and the Third Republic's project of organic solidarity through education, see Renato Ortiz, "Durkheim: Arquiteto e herói fundador," *Revista Brasileira de Ciências Sociais* 4, no. 11 (1989): 6–7.

60. Paulo Duarte, *Júlio Mesquita* (São Paulo: Hucitec, 1977), 138–39, 192–93.

61. Jean-Louis Fabiani writes of the editor Félix Alcan, the primary philosophical editor in Paris, as being the product of a "South American vision of French philosophy." *Les philosophes de la République* (Paris: Les Éditions de Minuit, 1988), 109.

62. Mr. Hermite, ambassador of France in Brazil, to Mr. Barthou, minister of foreign affairs, Rio de Janeiro, February 16, 1934, AJ 16 6964, Archives Nationales, File Brésil 1909–1957. This is also cited by Petitjean, "As missões universitárias," 262.

63. Louis Baudin, "L'effort realisé par la France en Amérique du Sud depuis la guerre: Conférence du 6 mars 1935," Livro Miscelânea 191.3.6 N. 5, p. 16, Instituto Histórico e Geográfico Brasileiro, Rio de Janeiro.

64. For more on American influence during this period see, among others, Moniz Bandeira, *Presença dos Estados Unidos no Brasil* (Rio: Civilização Brasileira, 1978); Nicolau Sevcenko, *Orfeu extático na metrópole: São Paulo, sociedade, e cultura nos fre-mentes anos 20* (São Paulo: Brasiliense, 1983).

65. Manoel Tosta Berlinck, "Depoimento: Criação da ELSP," in *A Escola Livre de Sociologia e Política: Anos de formação, 1933–1953*, ed. Íris Kantor, Débora A. Maciel, and Júlio A. Simões (São Paulo: Escuta, 2004), 101–2.

66. Roberto Simonsen, *Rumo à verdade* (São Paulo: São Paulo Editora Limitada, 1933), 7.

67. This might also have something to do with the *O Estado de S. Paulo* group's stance against Italian immigrants and their "materialism" as infiltrating the higher culture of "native" Brazilians. Fernando Limongi, "Mentores e clientelas da Universidade de São Paulo," *História das ciências sociais*, 1:148.

68. Paulina Alberto, *Terms of Inclusion: Black Intellectuals in Twentieth-Century Brazil* (Chapel Hill: University of North Carolina Press, 2011), 77.

69. "A Função Cultural do Ensino: Discurso de abertura dos cursos da Faculdade em 11-III-1935, pelo Prof. A. de Almeida Prado, Diretor da Faculdade de Filosofia, Ciências e Letras," *Anuário 1934–1935 FFCL-FFLCH/USP* (São Paulo: FFLCH/USP, 2009), 32.

70. Gustavo Capanema, however, seems to have been an exception. Although his French readings were often of a Catholic persuasion (Barrès, Mauriac, etc.), his interest in France in general is apparent in his archive (Cocteau, André Honnorat, President of the Cité Universitaire, the French economy). GC pi Capanema, G. 0000.00.00/21; GC pi Cocteau, J. 1945.06.15/27; GC pi Honnorat, A. 1928.03.09; Arquivo Capanema, CPDOC.

71. Mesquita to Dumas, São Paulo, February 26, 1934, carton 443 (Côte 417QO/443), Archive de la Ministère des Affaires Étrangères in La Courneuve (henceforth MAE).

72. Ambassade de la République Française au Brésil to Monsieur le Docteur Rostaing Lisboa, Directeur du Protocole au Ministère des Relations Extérieures, Rio de Janeiro, September 11, 1931, França, Notas Recebidas, 1931–1932 (June), 84/3/16, Arquivo Histórico do Itamaraty, Rio de Janeiro.

73. Souza Dantas, ambassador, to Minister of Foreign Relations, Paris, July 18, 1931, Telegramas Recebidas (from Paris to Rio), 1931–1933, 39/2/15, Arquivo Histórico do Itamaraty, Rio de Janeiro.

74. Dumas to "Monsieur le Sécretaire" João Cruz Costa, Paris, June 7, 1931, Arquivo João Cruz Costa.

75. Patrick Petitjean, "Entre ciência e diplomacia: A organização da influência científica francesa na América Latina, 1900–1940," in *A ciência nas relações Brasil-França (1850–1950)*.

76. Duarte, *Memórias* 3:71.

77. Petitjean, "As missões universitárias," 263.

78. Georges Dumas to Pierre Deffontaines, Telegram, Paris, n.d., Archive Deffontaines. The immediacy and informality of the recruitment is confirmed by various testimonies, including Pierre Monbeig, "Les années de formation," interview by Claude Bataillon, in *Pierre Monbeig: Un géographe pionnier*, ed. Martine Droulers and Hervé Théry (Paris: Éditions de l'IHEAL, 1991), http://books.openedition.org/iheal/1496, and Claude Lévi-Strauss, *Tristes Tropiques*, trans. John Weightman and Doreen Weightman (New York: Penguin, 1992), 47.

79. Petitjean, "As missões universitárias," 276–77.

80. Petitjean, "As missões universitárias," 267. This was significantly different from the quality of professors sent to the Institute of High Culture in Rio de Janeiro and, later, to the Universidade do Distrito Federal.

81. Émile Coornaert, "Notes sur une mission à la Faculté de São Paulo" (June-December 1934), carton 443 (Côte 417QO/443), MAE.

82. Ibid.

83. Ibid.

84. Deffontaines's role in the AGB has been thoroughly analyzed in a collected volume: Paulo Iumatti, Manoel Seabra, and Heinz Dieter Heidemann, eds., *Caio Prado Jr. e a Associação dos Geógrafos Brasileiros* (São Paulo: Edusp, 2008). See also, more recently, Federico Ferretti, "Pierre Deffontaines et les missions universitaires françaises au Brésil: Enjeux politiques et pédagogiques d'une société savante outremer (1934–1938)," *Cybergeo: European Journal of Geography*, document 703 (2014), http:// cybergeo.revues.org/26645?lang=en.

85. Geneviève Deffontaines's "livre de nos jours" was shared with me by Pierre Deffontaines's daughter, Madile Gardet, at her home in Paris. Entries of July 12 and 13, 1934, p. 72, Archives Deffontaines.

86. G. Deffontaines, "Livre de nos jours," entry of September 14, 1934, p. 82, Archives Deffontaines.

87. For more on Deffontaines, see Antoine Huerta, "La géographie, ça sert aussi les relations culturelles internationales: Le cas de Pierre Deffontaines, un géographe français aux Amériques (1934–1967)" (PhD diss., Université de la Rochelle, 2016). For more on Henri Hauser in Brazil, see José Adil Blanco de Lima, "A obra de Henri Hauser e sua trajetória intelectual no Brasil (1866–1946)" (PhD diss., University of São Paulo, 2017).

88. This can be seen in comparing "Lições Inaugurais da Missão Francesa" (PROEDES), BR.UFRJ.FE PROEDES UDF Public, book 1/01., with USP's *Anuário*, or course directory. *Anuário da Faculdade de Filosofia, Ciências, e Letras (1934–1935)* (São Paulo: Seção de Publicações da USP, 1937). USP, from its beginnings, had courses in Brazilian history and Tupi-Guarani languages.

89. For a brief description of these divergences, see Jean-Paul Lefebvre, "Les professeurs français des missions universitaires au Brésil (1934–44)," *Cahiers du Brésil Contemporain* 12 (1990), esp. 28–30; Lúcia Lippi de Oliveira, "As ciências sociais em Rio de Janeiro," in *História das ciências sociais*, 2:234–307; Maria de Lourdes de A. Fávero and Sonia de Castro Lopes, eds., *A Universidade do Distrito Federal (1935–1939): Um projeto além du seu tempo* (Rio de Janeiro: CnPQ, 2009). For Hauser, see Marieta Moraes Ferreira, "A trajetória de Henri Hauser," in *Estudos de historiografia brasileira*, ed. Lúcia Bastos et al. (Rio de Janeiro: FGV, 2011).

90. G. Deffontaines, "Livre de nos jours," entry of "Début janvier 1935," p. 87, Archives Deffontaines.

91. Duarte, *Memórias*, 3:70; *Memórias*, vol. 4, *Os mortos de Seabrook* (São Paulo: Hucitec, 1976), 207.

92. Pascal Bousseyroux, "Robert Garric, les Équipes sociales et le travail social," *Vie sociale* 2, no. 2 (2021); Suppo, "La politique culturelle française au Brésil," 118.

93. G. Deffontaines, "Livre de nos jours," entry of June 8, 1934, p. 68, Archives

Deffontaines. Tristain d'Athaïde, pseudonym for Alceu Amoroso Lima, ultimately became dean of UDF in 1938.

94. G. Deffontaines, "Livre de nos jours," entry of June 14, 1936, p. 98, Archives Deffontaines. Deffontaines, for example, took a horseback tour of the mountains and forests of Rio with the family of the Prince d'Orléans, picnicking at the summit.

95. G. Deffontaines, "Livre de nos jours," entries of September 25, 1936, p. 105; August 25, 1938, p. 193; October 21, 1938, p. 206, Archives Deffontaines.

96. G. Deffontaines, "Livre de nos jours," entry of May 2, 1938, p. 174, Archives Deffontaines. For more on Bernanos's reception among Brazilian Catholic intellectuals, see Teresa de Almeida, "Bernanos no Brasil: O rastro de uma permanência," in *Aquém e além mar: Relações culturais; Brasil e França,* ed. Sandra Nitrini (São Paulo: Editora Hucitec, 2000).

97. Sorá, *Brasilianas,* 114–31.

98. Between July 1935 and October 1937, Dumas sent Capanema at least twelve letters, mostly in response to inquiries. Capanema's two long letters, "Aboard the Campana," July 1, 1935, and "Aboard the Mendoza," September 1935, are particularly informative about the project around UDF. GC/DUMAS, G., b, CPDOC.

99. Angela de Castro Gomes, ed., *Capanema: O ministro e seu ministério* (Rio: Editora FGV, 2000). For more on Capanema and modernism, see Williams, *Culture Wars in Brazil,* esp. chap. 3. Concerning his alliance with Catholics, see Simon Schwartzman, Helena Maria Bousquet Bomeny, and Vanda Maria Ribeiro Costa, eds., *Tempos de Capanema* (São Paulo: Edusp, 1984), esp. 61–64.

100. Gilberto Freyre, *Sociologia: Introdução ao Estudo dos seus princípios* (Rio de Janeiro: José Olympio, 1957), 100–101.

101. Lippi de Oliveira, "As ciências sociais em Rio de Janeiro," 246.

102. Henri Hauser, *Ouvriers du temps passé, XVe–XVIe siècles* (Paris: Alcan, 1899).

103. Hauser quoted in Ferretti, "Pierre Deffontaines et les missions universitaires françaises au Brésil."

104. Suppo, "La politique culturelle française au Brésil," 267–68.

105. Secretary of state for foreign affairs to the Brazilian embassy in Paris, May 10, 1939, Rio de Janeiro, telegram no. 51-41440, Telegramas Expedidas (Rio to Paris) 39/3/14, Arquivo Histórico do Itamaraty, Rio de Janeiro.

106. Gisèle Sapiro, *La guerre des écrivains, 1940–53* (Paris: Fayard, 1999), esp. part 2, chap. 1, for a sociological understanding of the Académie Française and its inherent conservatism.

107. Fortunat Strowski, *Une crise de l'intelligence* (Paris: Imprimeurs de l'Institut de France, 1937). Dedicated to Gustavo Capanema, Rio de Janeiro, July 10, 1939, GC 1199, CPDOC.

108. Ibid., 4, 7.

109. Ibid., 5.

110. Fortunat Strowski, *France endormie, 1920–1940* (Rio de Janeiro: Livraria Geral Franco-Brasileira Ltda, 1941), 91–92. Strowski's title, *France endormie* (literally "sleeping France"), suggests that France was dormant during this period.

111. Suppo, "La politique culturelle française au Brésil," 277.

112. The term "faculdadezinha" comes from João Cruz Costa, "Os antigos cursos de conferências," *Filosofia, ciências, e letras*, no. 9 (1945): 13.

CHAPTER TWO

1. Georges Canguilhem, "La décadence de l'idée du progrès," *Revue de métaphysique et de morale* 92, no. 4 (1987).

2. Olivier Compagnon, *L'adieu l'Europe: L'Amérique latine et la Grande Guerre (Argentine et Brésil, 1914–1939)* (Paris: Fayard, 2013).

3. See Johan Heilbron, *French Sociology* (Ithaca, NY: Cornell University Press, 2015), 112.

4. Paul Nizan, *Les chiens de garde* (Paris: Maspero, 1969).

5. Albert Demangeon, *Le déclin de l'Europe* (Paris: Payot, 1920), 145–55.

6. Lucien Febvre, "Un champ privilegié d'études: L'Amérique du Sud," *Annales d'histoire économique et sociale* 1, no. 2 (1929): 258.

7. Ibid., 277, 259.

8. Fernand Braudel, "The Concept of a New Country," in Merkel, "Fernand Braudel and the Empire of French Social Science: Newly Translated Sources from the 1930s," *French Historical Studies* 40, no. 1 (2017).

9. Mário de Andrade, "Dia de São Paulo," *Revista do Arquivo Municipal*, no. 206 (2015): 13, repr. of *Revista do Arquivo Municipal* 19 (1936).

10. Sérgio Buarque de Holanda, *Raízes do Brasil* (1936; São Paulo: Companhia das Letras, 1995), 59.

11. Lévi-Strauss, "Os mais vastos horizontes do mundo," *Filosofia, ciências, e letras* 1, no. 1 (1936).

12. Stefan Zweig, *Brazil: A Land of the Future*, trans. Lowell A. Bangerter (Riverside, CA: Ariadne Press, 2000).

13. Roger Bastide, "Chronique des livres de sociologie brésilienne," *Revue internationale de sociologie* 47, no. 1–2 (1939): 91. The language of Brazil as a "laboratory" goes back to at least 1929; see Rüdiger Bilden, "Brazil: Laboratory of Civilization," *The Nation*, January 16, 1929, 73–74.

14. For a convincing analysis of the overlaps between ethnology and geography, see Marie-Claire Robic, "Rencontres et voisinages de deux disciplines," *Ethnologie française* 34, no. 4 (2004). For history and geography, see Olivier Dumoulin, "Les noces de l'histoire et de la géographie," *Espaces temps*, no. 66–67 (1998).

15. Lefebvre, "Les professeurs français," 26–27.

16. François Sirinelli, *Génération intellectuelle: Khâgneux et normaliens dans l'entre-*

deux-guerres (Paris: Fayard, 1988). Bastide, the only one of the four to participate in WWI, did so indirectly, as "more a student than a soldier," according to Paul Arbousse-Bastide. "Mon ami Roger Bastide," *Communauté*, no. 40 (1976): 42.

17. Antonio Candido, "A importância de não ser filósofo," *Discurso* 37 (2007); Denilson Cordeiro, "A formação do discernimento: Jean Maugüé e a gênese de uma experiência filosófica no Brasil" (PhD diss., University of São Paulo, 2008).

18. Pierre Monbeig, "La réforme agraire en Espagne," *Annales d'histoire économique et sociale* 5, no. 24 (1933).

19. Paul Claval, "The Historical Dimension of French Geography," *Journal of Historical Geography*, 10, no. 3 (1984): 232–33. See also Vincent Berdoulay, *La formation de l'école française de géographie (1870–1914)* (Paris: Bibliothèque Nationale, 1981). From a historian's perspective, see Roger Chartier, "L'histoire entre géographie et sociologie," in *Au bord de la falaise, L'histoire entre certitudes et inquietude* (Paris: Albin Michel, 2009), 269–70, 273.

20. Pierre Monbeig, "Les années de formation," interview by Claude Bataillon, in *Pierre Monbeig: Un géographe pionnier*, ed. Martine Droulers and Hervé Théry (Paris: Éditions de l'IHEAL, 1991), 27–34, http://books.openedition.org/iheal/1496.

21. Pierre Denis, *Le Brésil au XXᵉ siècle* (Paris: Armand Colin, 1928); Denis, "Uma nova geographia do Brasil," *O Estado de S. Paulo*, January 12, 1928. For the previous generation, see Jacques Élisée Reclus, *Amérique du Sud: L'Amazonie et La Plata (Guyanes, Brésil, Paraguay, Uruguay, République argentine)* (Paris, Hachette, 1894).

22. Luís Donisete Benzi Grupioni, "Claude Lévi-Strauss parmi les Amérindiens: Deux expeditions ethnographiques dans l'intérieur du Brésil," in *Brésil Indien: Les arts des amerindiens du Brésil* (Paris: Réunion des Musées Nationaux, 2005), 316–17.

23. Jean-François Bert, *L'atelier de Marcel Mauss: Un anthropologue paradoxale* (Paris: CNRS Éditions, 2012).

24. Christine Laurière, *Paul Rivet: Le savant et le politique* (Paris: Publications scientifiques du Muséum national d'histoire naturelle, 2008). For his institutional legacy at the Musée de l'Homme, see Claude Blanckaert, ed., *Le Musée de l'Homme: Histoire d'un musée laboratoire* (Paris: Éditions Artlys, 2015).

25. Christine Laurière, "La Société des Américanistes de Paris: Une société savante au service de l'américanisme," *Journal de la Société des américanistes* 95, no. 2 (2009).

26. Lévi-Strauss to Marcel Mauss, Paris (no month), 15, 1934, NAF 28150 (181), folder 2, transcribed by Hugo Suppo, BnF; Lévi-Strauss to Rivet, Paris, December 22 (no year), NAF 28150 (181), transcribed by Hugo Suppo (1996), BnF.

27. Fernand Braudel, "Les espagnols et l'Afrique du Nord de 1492 à 1577," *Revue africaine* 69, nos. 335–37 (1928).

28. Hauser to Braudel, [Rio?], April 7, 1935, FB.

29. Important precedents for my efforts include Erato Paris, "L'époque brésiliene de Fernand Braudel (1935–1937) et les origines intellectuelles de La Méditerranée et le méditerranéen à l'époque de Philippe II," *Storia della Storiografia* 30 (1996): 31–56.

See also Carlos A. Aguirre Rojas's pioneering work on the subject; for just one article, refer to Aguirre Rojas, "Braudel in Latin America and the U.S.: A Different Reception," *Review* (Fernand Braudel Center) 24, no. 1 (2001): 26–32.

30. Hugo Rogélio Suppo, "La politique culturelle française au Brésil entre les années 1920–1950," (PhD diss., Paris III-Sorbonne Nouvelle, 1999), 174–76. For Pierre Bourdieu's definition of symbolic capital, see Bourdieu and Loïc Wacquant, "Symbolic Capital and Social Classes," *Journal of Classical Sociology* 13, no. 2 (May 2013).

31. For more on this, see Patrick Petitjean, "As missões universitárias francesas na criação da Universidade de São Paulo (1934–1940)," in *A ciência nas relações Brasil-França (1850–1950)*, ed. Amélia Império Hamburger et al. (São Paulo: Edusp, 1996), 277–78, 295–301.

32. Jean Maugüé, *Les dents agacées* (Paris: Buchet-Chastel, 1982), 94.

33. Ibid.

34. Claude Lévi-Strauss folder, p. 1, FB.

35. My analysis here is indebted to Pierre Bourdieu's *Manet: Une révolution symbolique* (Paris: Raisons d'agir / Seuil, 2013), esp. 262–310. Manet's "symbolic revolution" in painting depended on the new kinds of critics such as Zola and Mallarmé that emerged alongside him.

36. Fernando Devoto, "Itinerario de un problema: 'Annales' y la historiografía argentina (1929–1965)," *Anuario del IEHS*, no. 10 (1995): 157.

37. Febvre, "Un champ privilegié d'études."

38. See Luís Correia Lima, *Fernand Braudel e o Brasil: Vivência e brasilianismo (1935–1945)* (São Paulo: Edusp, 2009), 155.

39. Roger Bastide, "Les Arméniens de Valence," *Revue Internationale de Sociologie* 39, no. 1–2 (1931).

40. Some of this correspondence is published in Françoise Morin, "Les inédits et la correspondance de Roger Bastide," in *Roger Bastide, ou, Le réjouissement de l'abîme*, ed. Philippe Laburthe-Tolra (Paris: L'Harmattan, 1994).

41. Halbwachs to Bastide, Strasbourg, April 16, 1935, BST2.C1.02., IMEC. Unfortunately, I did not have access to Bastide's letters to Halbwachs.

42. Halbwachs to Bastide, Les Houches (Haute Savoie), July 21, 1936, BST2.C1.02, IMEC.

43. Bastide to Mauss, Valence, October 20, 1936, box 11, 57 CdF 54-7, Fonds Mauss, Collège de France. This letter is also reproduced in Marcel Fournier, *Marcel Mauss* (Paris: Fayard, 1994), 650n2.

44. Mauss to Bastide, Paris, November 3, 1936, BST2.C1.03, IMEC.

45. Ibid.

46. Arbousse-Bastide to Bastide, La Rochelle, October 29, 1922, BST2.C1-01, IMEC. See also Arbousse-Bastide, "Mon ami Roger Bastide."

47. Heloisa Pontes, *Destinos mistos: Os críticos do grupo Clima em São Paulo, 1940–1968* (São Paulo: Companhia das Letras, 1998), 30.

48. Arbousse-Bastide to Bastide, Paris, January 18, 1937, BST2.C1-01, IMEC.

49. Considering the date of publication and the content, the article in question was likely Roger Bastide, "L'enseignement et la sociologie en France," *Revue internationale de sociologie* 44, no. 7–8 (1936).

50. Arbousse-Bastide to Bastide, São Paulo, January 18, 1937, BST2.C1-01, IMEC.

51. Pierre to Juliette Monbeig, aboard the *Campana*, February 26, [1938?], Archive Pierre Monbeig, Paris.

52. Pierre to Juliette Monbeig, n.d., Archive Pierre Monbeig, Paris.

53. Petit-Nègre was originally a simplified French used for communication in the army, where colonial troops served. It was then used as a stereotype for how Africans spoke French.

54. Micol Seigel, *Uneven Encounters: Making Race and Nation in Brazil and the United States* (Durham, NC: Duke University Press, 2009), 120, 113. See also Anaïs Fléchet, *"Si tu vas à Rio . . .": La musique populaire brésilienne en France au XXᵉ siècle* (Paris: Armand Colin, 2013).

55. Manoel Corrêa do Lago, ed., *Uma outra missão francesa 1917–1918: Paul Claudel e Darius Milhaud no Brasil* (Rio de Janeiro: Éstudio Andrea Jakobsson, 2017).

56. Livro de Registro de Contratos de Professores para a Universidade de São Paulo (1934–1936), p. 37, Arquivo Público do Estado de S. Paulo, E 01145A-, consulted at the Arquivo Geral da USP.

57. Claude Lévi-Strauss, *Tristes Tropiques*, trans. John Weightman and Doreen Weightman (New York: Penguin, 1992), 22.

58. Fernand Braudel, interview in *Jornal da Tarde*, January 28, 1984.

59. It is worth noting Eric Jennings's recent book, which makes a similar point, although in an entirely different context: *Escape from Vichy: The Refugee Exodus to the French Caribbean* (Cambridge, MA: Harvard University Press, 2018).

60. Pierre to Juliette Monbeig, "Monday evening," February 12, [1935?], Archive Pierre Monbeig, Paris.

61. "Chegada de Professores Franceses," *O Estado de S. Paulo*, March 25, 1936; "A Realisação da 'Semana de Criança' em Campinas," *O Estado de S. Paulo*, August 27, 1936.

62. Lilia Moritz Schwarcz, *O Sol do Brasil: Nicolas-Antoine Taunay e as desventuras dos artistas franceses na corte de d. João* (São Paulo: Companhia das Letras, 2008). See also Kirsten Schultz, *Tropical Versailles: Empire, Monarchy, and the Portuguese Royal Court in Rio de Janeiro, 1808–1821* (New York: Routledge, 2001).

63. Lévi-Strauss, *Tristes Tropiques*, 21.

64. Ibid.

65. Hourcade quoted in Suppo, "La politique culturelle française," 188.

66. Maugüé, *Les dents agacées*, 94.

67. Fernanda Peixoto, "Lévi-Strauss no Brasil: a formação do etnólogo," *Mana* 4, no. 1 (1998): 88.

68. Pierre to Juliette Monbeig, São Paulo, "Saturday the 9th," [1935?], Archive Pierre Monbeig, Paris.

69. Gagé to Simões de Paula, Strasbourg, December 25, 1937, Arquivo Eurípides Simões de Paula, Centro de Apoio ao Pesquisa Sérgio Buarque de Holanda (henceforth CAPH).

70. Arbousse-Bastide to "tres chers," São Paulo, February 12, 1938, p. 169, Archive Paul Arbousse-Bastide, Paris.

71. Emmanuelle Loyer, *Claude Lévi-Strauss* (Paris: Flammarion, 2015), 51; Pierre to Juliette Monbeig, São Paulo, March 16, [1935?], Archive Pierre Monbeig, Paris.

72. *Pied-noirs* are white French citizens born in Algeria.

73. Livro de Registro de Contratos de Professores para a Universidade de São Paulo (1934–1936), p. 69, Arquivo Público do Estado de S. Paulo, E 01145A-, consulted at the Arquivo Geral da USP.

74. Aziz Ab'Saber, "Pierre Monbeig: A herança intelectual de um geógrafo," *Estudos Avançados* 8, no. 22 (1994): 222.

75. Simões de Paula to Osorio de Oliveira, São Paulo, January 9, 1937, box 20, doc. 2032, p. 1., CAPH.

76. Maugüé, *Les dents agacées*, 131. For more on Cruz Costa, see Francini Venâncio de Oliveira, *Fantasmas da tradição: João Cruz Costa e a cultura filosófica uspiana em formação* (PhD diss., University of São Paulo, 2012).

77. Braudel quoted in Lidiane Soares Rodrigues, "A produção social do marxismo universitário em São Paulo: Mestres, discípulos, e 'um seminário' (1958–1978)" (PhD diss., University of São Paulo, 2011), 265.

78. Braudel to Cruz Costa, aboard the "société des transports maritimes à vapeur," November 8, 1935, Archive João Cruz Costa, São Paulo.

79. "Homage aos professores Deffontaines, Arbousse Bastide e Coornaert" (1934), CPJ, AGB056, Caio Prado Jr. Archive, IEB-USP.

80. Couto de Barros was a lawyer, landowner, entrepreneur, and journalist. Paula Souza was a medical doctor who had studied at Johns Hopkins and the founder of the school of public health at USP.

81. Pierre to Juliette Monbeig, São Paulo, April 2, 1935, Archive Pierre Monbeig, Paris.

82. Duarte, *Memórias*, 3:202–3.

83. Pierre to Juliette Monbeig, São Paulo, March 16, [1935?], Archive Pierre Monbeig, Paris.

84. Julio de Mesquita to Braudel, São Paulo, July 17, 1950, Gilles Lapouge folder, FB. I thank Lidiane Soares Rodrigues for bringing this quotation to my attention.

85. Claude Lévi-Strauss, *Saudades de São Paulo* (São Paulo: Instituto Moreira Salles / Companhia das Letras, 1996), 10; Claude Lévi-Strauss and Didier Eribon, *De près et de loin* (Paris: Odile Jacob, 1988), 33. This version—and others—are widely cited. See, for example, Luís Donisete Benzi Grupioni, *Coleções e expedições vigiadas:*

Os etnólogos no conselho de fiscalização das expedições artísticas e científicas no Brasil (São Paulo: Editora Hucitec / Anpocs, 1998), 139.

86. Júlio de Mesquita Filho, *A crise nacional: Reflexões em torno de uma data* (São Paulo: Secção de Obras d'"O Estado de S. Paulo," 1925), 23.

87. Patrick Wilcken, *Claude Lévi-Strauss: The Poet in the Laboratory* (London: Bloomsbury, 2010), 29–31; Loyer, *Lévi-Strauss*, 197; Roberto Salone, *Irredutivelmente liberal: Política e cultura na trajetória de Júlio de Mesquita Filho* (São Paulo: Albatroz Editora, 2009).

88. For a list of the members of the Departamento de Cultura, see Luísa Valentini, *Um laboratório de antropologia: O encontro entre Mário de Andrade, Dina Dreyfus, e Claude Lévi-Strauss (1935–1939)* (São Paulo: Alameda, 2013), 199–200.

89. For more on palacetes, see Maria Cecilia Naclério Homem, *O palacete paulistano e outras formas urbanas de morar da elite cafeeira* (São Paulo: Martins Fontes, 2010).

90. For more on modernism's institutionalization, see Daryle Williams, *Culture Wars in Brazil: The First Vargas Regime, 1930–45* (Durham, NC: Duke University Press, 2001), and Randal Johnson, "The Institutionalization of Brazilian Modernism," *Brasil/Brazil: A Journal of Brazilian Literature*, 3, no. 4 (1990).

91. Lévi-Strauss's text, unlike many others, can be consulted in its original French version at the Archive de la Ministère des Affaires Étrangères (MAE).

92. Pierre Monbeig, "Orientação didática," in *Anuário da Faculdade de Filosofia, Ciências, e Letras (1934–1935)* (São Paulo: Revista dos Tribunais, 1937).

93. Ibid., 115.

94. Pierre Monbeig, "A geographia: Sciencia de utilidade pública," *O Estado de S. Paulo*, April 4, 1935.

95. Monbeig, "Orientação didática," 116.

96. Ibid., 119.

97. Monbeig, "Orientação didática," 144. Several of these studies would be published in the journal *Geografia*, including Branca da Cunha Caldeira's "A indústria textile paulista" *Geografia* 1, no. 4 (1935), and Caio Prado Jr.'s "O fator geográfico na formação e desenvolvimento da cidade de São Paulo," *Geografia* 1, no. 3 (1935).

98. Ruy Coelho quoted in Pontes, *Destinos mistos*, 173.

99. For more on the *Associação dos Geógrafos* during this period, see Paulo Iumatti, Manoel Seabra, and Heinz Dieter Heidemann, *Caio Prado Jr. e a Associação dos Geógrafos Brasileiros* (São Paulo: Edusp, 2008).

100. Olivier Dumoulin, "À l'aune de Vichy? La naissance de l'agrégation de géographie," in *Les Facs sous Vichy* (Clermont Ferrand: L'Institut des Études du Massif Central, 1993).

101. Marie-Claire Robic, "La crise des années trente et la tension vers l'expertise géographique: Expériences françaises et internationales; Une nouvelle frontière?," *Confins*, no. 5 (2009), https://journals.openedition.org/confins/5652.

102. Monbeig, "Orientação didática," 120.

103. Ibid.

104. My understanding of porosity or "openness" and "disciplinarity" comes from Heilbron, *French Sociology*, 174.

105. Claude Lévi-Strauss, "A sociologia cultural e o seu ensino," in *Anuário da Faculdade de Filosofia, Ciências, e Letras (1934–1935)* (São Paulo: Revista dos Tribunais, 1937); original French version in box 417QO/443, MAE.

106. Bourdieu, *Manet*, 25.

107. Johan Heilbron emphasizes how Durkheim presented sociology as "an essentially French science." *French Sociology*, 77.

108. Claude Lévi-Strauss, "Em prol de um Instituto de Antropologia Física e Cultural," *Revista do Arquivo Municipal* 2, no. 18 (1935). For more on French "anthropologie," as opposed to Rivet's "ethnologie," see Alice Conklin, *In the Museum of Man: Race, Anthropology, and Empire in France, 1850–1950* (Ithaca, NY: Cornell University Press, 2013), chap. 1.

109. Lévi-Strauss to Fernando de Azevedo, São Paulo, May 17 (no year), FA, Cp, Cx 17, 36, Arquivo Fernando de Azevedo, IEB-USP.

110. Fauconnet to Lévi-Strauss, Paris, December 29, 1935; November 2, 1936; December 12, 1936, NAF 28150 (184), Correspondance, BnF.

111. Lévi-Strauss to Mauss, São Paulo, November 10, 1935, NAF 28150 (181), Correspondance, BnF.

112. For example, letter 9, São Paulo, February 5 (no year); see also letter 96, both Archive Paul Arbousse-Bastide, Paris.

113. Unlike Monbeig's and Braudel's essays in the *Anuário*, whose translation from French into Portuguese is the only text available, Lévi-Strauss's original French text, "La sociologie culturelle et son enseignement," is in box 417QO/443, MAE.

114. Ibid.

115. Ibid., 2.

116. Ibid., 3.

117. For a discussion of Mauss's relationship to American anthropologists, see Fournier, *Marcel Mauss*, 315.

118. Lévi-Strauss, "La sociologie culturelle," 5.

119. For more on Freyre's identification with Boas in his own words, see Freyre, *Casa-grande e senzala: Introdução à história da sociedade patriarcal no Brasil* (1933; Rio de Janeiro: Editora Record, 2001), 45.

120. For more on Freyre's impact during this period, see Antonio Candido, "O significado de *Raízes do Brasil*," in Sérgio Buarque de Holanda, *Raízes do Brasil*, 9. As for social-scientific methodology, see Lúcia G. Pallares-Burke and Peter Burke, *Gilberto Freyre: Social Theory in the Tropics* (Oxford: Peter Lang, 2008).

121. Lévi-Strauss, "La sociologie culturelle," 10.

122. Ibid., 12.

123. See Paulo Teixeira Iumatti's analysis of Prado's unpublished manuscript "Sociologia e antropologia" from 1936, in *História, dialética, e diálogo com as ciências: A gênese de Formação do Brasil contemporâneo, de Caio Prado Jr. (1933–1942)* (São Paulo: Intermeios, 2018), 320–33.

124. Fernand Braudel, "The Teaching of History and Its Guidelines," trans. Ian Merkel, *French Historical Studies*, 40, no. 1 (2017): 151–57. For more on Braudel's teaching, see Paulo Henrique Martinez, "Fernand Braudel e a primeira geração de historiadores universitários da USP (1935–1956)," *Revista de história* 146 (2002).

125. Ibid., 151.

126. Braudel, "The Concept of a New Country."

127. Braudel, "The Teaching of History," 151.

128. Ibid., 153.

129. Ibid.

130. Pierre Bourdieu, *Homo Academicus*, trans. Peter Collier (Stanford, CA: Stanford University Press, 1988), 113. For anthropology, see Vincent Debaene, *Far Afield: French Anthropology between Science and Literature* (Chicago: University of Chicago Press, 2014).

131. For more on these differences, see Fernanda Arêas Peixoto, "Franceses e norte-americanos nas ciências sociais brasileiras (1930–1960)," in *História das ciências sociais no Brasil*, vol. 1, ed. Sergio Miceli et al. (São Paulo: Vértice, 1989).

132. Braudel, "The Teaching of History," 152.

133. Henri Hauser, for example, deliberately undercut the Durkheimians in *L'enseignement des sciences sociales: État actuel de cet enseignement dans les divers pays du monde* (Paris: Chevalier Marescq, 1903), 221–39.

134. This struggle is amply explored in Thomas Hirsch, *Le temps des sociétés* (Paris: Éditions de l'EHESS, 2016). For more on historians' reading of the Durkheimians, see Jacques Revel, "Histoire et sciences sociales: Les paradigmes des Annales," *Annales ESC* 34, no. 6 (1979): 1360–76, esp. 1362–63 and 1366.

135. Braudel, "The Teaching of History," 151.

136. Ibid., 152; my italics.

137. André Burguière, *L'école des Annales: Une histoire intellectuelle* (Paris: Odile Jacob, 2006), esp. 71–98.

138. Larissa Alves de Lira, "Fernand Braudel e Vidal de La Blache: Geohistória e história da geografia," *Confins* 2, no. 2 (2008): 2–15; Pierre Daix, *Braudel* (Paris: Flammarion, 1995), 49–78.

139. Braudel, "The Teaching of History," 154.

140. At the newly founded university, history and geography overlapped, sharing professors and students. See the testimony of Alice Piffer Canabrava, in Eva Alterman Blay and Alice Beatriz da Silva Gordo Lang, *Mulheres na USP: Horizontes que se abrem* (São Paulo: Editora Humanitas, 2004), 85–106.

141. Nizan, *Les chiens de garde*.

142. Arbousse-Bastide to his parents, São Paulo, February 23, 1935, Archive Paul Arbousse-Bastide, Paris.

143. Lévi-Strauss and Eribon, *De près et de loin*, 33.

144. Arbousse-Bastide to his parents, São Paulo, February 5, 1937, Archive Paul Arbousse-Bastide, Paris.

145. For more on the Popular Front see Pascal Ory, *La belle illusion: Culture et politique sous le signe du Front populaire, 1935–1938* (Paris: Plon, 1994).

146. For more on the politics of the Musée de l'Homme, see Laurière, *Paul Rivet*. See also Conklin, *In the Museum of Man*, esp. chap. 3, "Ethnology for the Masses."

147. Arbousse-Bastide to his parents. São Paulo, February 5, 1937, Archive Paul Arbousse-Bastide, Paris.

148. Suppo, "La politique culturelle française," 195; Braudel to Simões, Paris, February 4, 1937, doc. 2416, p. 1, CAPH.

149. Livro de Registro de Contratos de Professores para a Universidade de São Paulo (1936–1939), p. 57, Arquivo Público do Estado de S. Paulo, E01145B-, consulted at the Arquivo Geral da USP.

150. Paul Arbousse-Bastide, introduction to Émile Durkheim, *As regras do método sociológico* (São Paulo: Ed. Nacional, 1937).

151. Paul Arbousse-Bastide, "Condições e organização da sociologia," in *Anuário da Faculdade de Filosofia, Ciências, e Letras (1934–1935)* (São Paulo: Revista dos Tribunais, 1937).

152. Valentini, *Um laboratório de antropologia*, 129.

153. Claude Lévi-Strauss, "Entre os Bororos em Matto Grosso," *Geografia* 2, nos. 2–3 (1936): 68; Dina Lévi-Strauss, "Indios da Bolivia," *Geografia* 2, nos. 2–3 (1936): 63–67.

154. Many of these courses can be consulted in Dina Lévi-Strauss's published manual, *Instruções práticas para pesquisas de antropologia física e cultural* (São Paulo: Departamento de Cultura, 1936).

155. Valentini, *Um laboratório de antropologia*. More recently, see Fernanda Azevedo de Moraes, "Les cahiers de Dina Dreyfus," June 14, 2021, https://nambikwara.hypotheses.org/1024.

156. Carlos Sandroni, "Mário, Oneida, Dina, e Claude," *Revista do patrimônio histórico e artístico nacional* 30 (2002): 234–46. For more on Mário's method, see Antonio Gilberto Ramos Nogueira, *Por um inventário dos sentidos: Mário de Andrade e a concepção de patrimônio e inventário* (São Paulo: Editora Hucitec, 2005).

157. For Monbeig, see Iumatti, Seabra, and Heidemann, *Caio Prado Jr. e a Associação dos Geógrafos Brasileiros*, 55–62, 78; for Lévi-Strauss, see Grupioni, "Claude Lévi-Strauss parmi les Amérindiens," 314.

158. Pierre Monbeig to Juliette Monbeig, Londrina, June 25, 1935, Archive Pierre Monbeig, Paris. Juliette Monbeig published, for example, "Regiões jovens do Mediterraneo," *Geografia* 2, no. 4 (1935): 55–59.

159. For more on this, see Hélène Charron, *Les formes de l'illégitimité intellectuelle: Les femmes dans les sciences sociales françaises, 1890–1940* (Paris: CNRS Éditions, 2013).

160. Pierre Monbeig to Juliette Monbeig, Londrina, June 25, 1935, Archive Pierre Monbeig, Paris.

161. Arbousse-Bastide to his parents, São Paulo, February 12, 1938, Archive Paul Arbousse-Bastide, Paris.

162. Livro de Registro de Contratos de Professores para a Universidade de São Paulo (1936–1939), p. 44, Arquivo Público do Estado de S. Paulo, E01145B-, consulted at the Arquivo Geral da USP.

163. Prior to going to Brazil, Bastide must have spoken of Durkheim's dogmatism, as evidenced by Maurice Halbwachs's response to a letter of his. Halbwachs to Bastide, Paris, October 14, [1936?], IMEC.

164. Bastide to Rivet, São Paulo, June 22, 1939, "São Paulo" folder, Musée de l'Homme.

165. "Circular de Antonio Rubbo Muller," June 7, 1939, box 3, doc. 119, Sociedade de Etnografia e Folclore Archive, Discoteca Oneyda Alvarenga, Centro Cultural São Paulo.

166. For a similar argument in a completely different context, see Carl Schorske, *Fin-de-Siècle Vienna: Politics and Culture* (New York: Vintage Books, 1981)

CHAPTER THREE

1. Pierre Denis, *Le Brésil au XXᵉ siècle* (Paris: Armand Colin, 1909); translated by Bernard Miall as *Brazil* (New York: Charles Scribner's Sons, 1911).

2. Claude Lévi-Strauss, *Tristes Tropiques*, trans. John Weightman and Doreen Weightman (New York: Penguin, 1992), 81, 83–84, 326, 335, 351, 353; Jean de Léry, "Histoire d'un voyage faict en la terre du Brésil" (1574). For parallels between Léry's and Lévi-Strauss's travels to Brazil, see Frank Lestringant, "De Jean de Léry a Claude Lévi-Strauss: Por uma arqueologia de *Tristes trópicos*," *Revista de antropologia* 43, no. 2 (2000): 81–103.

3. Pierre Singaravélou, ed., *L'empire des géographes: Géographie, exploration et colonisation* (Paris: Belin, 2008); Alice Conklin, *In the Museum of Man: Race, Anthropology, and Empire in France, 1850–1950* (Ithaca, NY: Cornell University Press, 2013), 189–235.

4. Muriam Haleh Davis, "Restaging *Mise en Valeur*: 'Postwar Imperialism' and the Plan de Constantine," *Review of Middle East Studies* 44, no. 2 (2010): 182. For our purposes here, an article by Lévi-Strauss best represents the collective belief in humanizing empire, rather than in decolonization: "Le socialisme et la colonisation," *L'étudiant socialiste* 1 (1929): 7–8, cited in Emmanuelle Loyer, *Claude Lévi-Strauss* (Paris: Flammarion, 2015), 114. For a broader analysis of what reformist colonialism entailed, see Catherine Coquery-Vidrovitch, "The Popular Front and the Colonial Question. French West Africa: An Example of Reformist Colonialism," in *French Colo-*

nial Empire and the Popular Front: Hope and Disillusion, ed. Tony Chafer and Amanda Sackur (New York: St. Martin's Press, 1999), 155–69.

5. For a similar argument, see Stefanie Gänger, "Disjunctive Circles: Modern Intellectual Culture in Cuzco and the Journeys of Incan Antiquities, c. 1877–1921," *Modern Intellectual History* 10, no. 2 (2013): 399–414.

6. Fernanda Peixoto's *A viagem como vocação: Itinerários, parcerias et formas de conhecimento* (São Paulo: Edusp, 2015) is particularly attentive to these questions.

7. Mário quoted in Roger Bastide, *Poetas do Brasil* (1946; São Paulo: Editora da Universidade de São Paulo / Duas Cidades, 1997), 75. A guariba is a brown howler monkey common to Brazil.

8. Lévi-Strauss to Mauss, São Paulo, November 10, 1935, NAF 28150 (181), BnF.

9. Caio Prado Jr., *Formação do Brasil contemporâneo* (São Paulo: Companhia das Letras, 2011), 1–2. Other authors from this period directly criticized "feudalism" as an explanation of Latin American agrarian society and economy.

10. Aziz Ab'Saber, "Pierre Monbeig: A herança intelectual de um geógrafo," *Estudos Avançados* 8, no. 22 (1994): 224.

11. This "discovery" of Brazil was almost simultaneous with that of the Paulistas, who, in 1938, more or less exhibited the Carajá in São Paulo. Folder CFE.F.003, Arquivo Museu de Astronomia e Ciências Afins, Rio de Janeiro.

12. Patrick Wilcken, *Claude Lévi-Strauss: The Poet in the Laboratory* (London: Bloomsbury, 2010), 74.

13. Claude Lévi-Strauss, "Les Français et le Panaméricanisme," *Pour la Victoire*, January 24, 1942.

14. Lévi-Strauss to Mauss, São Paulo, November 10, 1935, BnF.

15. Lidiane Soares Rodrigues, "A produção social do marxismo universitário em São Paulo: Mestres, discípulos, e 'um seminário' (1958–1978)" (PhD diss., University of São Paulo, 2011), 255.

16. Pierre Singaravélou, "Géographie et colonisation: Approches historiographiques," in *L'empire des Géographes: Géographie, exploration et colonisation*, ed. Singaravélou (Paris: Belin, 2008), 48–49.

17. René Courtin to parents, São Paulo, early September 1937, private archive, Paris.

18. Lévi-Strauss quoted in Loyer, *Lévi-Strauss*, 164–65.

19. Caio Prado Jr., "Distribuição da propriedade fundiária rural no estado de São Paulo," *Geografia* 1, no.1 (1935): 52–68; Prado, "Contribuição para o estudo das influencias étnicas no Estado do Paraná," *Geografia* 1, no. 2 (1935): 217–18.

20. Pierre Monbeig, "A zona pioneira do Norte Paraná," *Geografia* 1, no. 3 (1935): 221–36.

21. Ibid., 229.

22. For a convincing argument that juxtaposes Lévi-Strauss's structuralism with Monbeig's geography, see Hervé Théry, "Claude Lévi-Strauss, Pierre Monbeig et Roger Brunet," EchoGéo, no. 7 (2008), http://echogeo.revues.org/9503.

23. Pierre to Juliette Monbeig, São Paulo, Saturday the 9th, (no month or year), Archive Pierre Monbeig, Paris.

24. Lévi-Strauss to Monbeig, Utiarity, June 27, 1938, NAF 28150 (181), BnF. Two undated letters from Lévi-Strauss to Mário in the same folder mention the news he received via Monbeig from Mário.

25. Monbeig's letters to his wife, mostly from 1935, attest to him frequenting and even dining with Lévi-Strauss's parents (e.g., on Tuesday, March 9). Raymond Lévi-Strauss painted a portrait of Marianne Monbeig (now Hano), which she has to this day. Archive Pierre Monbeig, Paris.

26. Pierre Monbeig, "La population de l'état de São Paulo," *Annales de géographie* 46, no. 259 (1937): 91.

27. Ibid.

28. Pierre Monbeig, "Goyania," *O Estado de S. Paulo*, October 5, 1938.

29. Barbara Weinstein, *The Color of Modernity: São Paulo and the Making of Race and Nation in Brazil* (Durham, NC: Duke University Press, 2015), 32–46; Antonio Celso Ferreira, *A epopéia bandeirante: Letrados, instituições, invenção histórica (1870–1940)* (São Paulo: UNESP, 2001). Braudel also inscribed himself in the tradition of "bandeirologists" in "The Concept of a New Country," in Ian Merkel, "Fernand Braudel and the Empire of French Social Science: Newly Translated Sources from the 1930s," *French Historical Studies* 40, no. 1 (2017): 146.

30. Monbeig, "Goyania."

31. Ibid.

32. Ibid.

33. Pierre Monbeig, "Colonisation, peuplement et plantations de cacao dans l'état de Bahia," *Annales de géographie* 46, no. 261 (1937): 281.

34. Ibid., 291.

35. Ibid., 296.

36. Ibid., 299.

37. Albert Demangeon, *L'empire brittanique: Étude de géographie coloniale* (Paris: Armand Colin, 1923) and "Pionniers et fronts de colonisation," *Annales de géographie* 41, no. 234 (1932): 631–36.

38. Monbeig's interest in North African demographics, particularly of white settlers, can be seen in his article "Dados estatísticos: África Franceza do Norte," *Geografia* 2, no. 4 (1936): 65.

39. Pierre Monbeig, "Les zones pionnières de l'état de São Paulo," *Annales d'histoire économique et sociale* 9, no. 46 (1937): 345.

40. Ibid., 350.

41. Ibid., 362.

42. Robert H. Block, "Frederick Jackson Turner and American Geography," *Annals of the Association of American Geographers* 70, no. 1 (1980): 31–42.

43. Monbeig, "Les zones pionnières," 364.

44. Ibid., 364.

45. Pierre Monbeig, review of *White Settlements in the Tropics*, by A. Grenfell Price, *Annales d'histoire sociale* 1, no. 4 (1939): 463.

46. Monbeig, "Les zones pionnières," 365.

47. Luiz de Castro Faria, *Another Look: A Diary of the Serra do Norte Expedition*, trans. David Rodgers (Rio de Janeiro: Ouro Sobre Azul, 2001). The contrast with Malinowski is inspired by Wilcken, *Lévi-Strauss*, 84.

48. Lévi-Strauss to Mauss, São Paulo, November 10, 1935, NAF 28150 (181), BnF. Part of this and the following letter are reproduced in Loyer, *Lévi-Strauss*, 179.

49. Mauss to Lévi-Strauss, Paris, February 20, 1936, NAF 28150 (181), BnF.

50. Vincent Debaene and Frédéric Keck, *Claude Lévi-Strauss: L'homme au regard éloigné* (Paris: Gallimard, 2009), 34–37.

51. Claude Lévi-Strauss, "Contributions sur l'organisation sociale des Indiens Bororo," *Journal de la Société des américanistes* 28, no. 2 (1936): 269–304.

52. Lévi-Strauss to Mário, Corumba, January 15, 1936, MA-C-CPL3997, Arquivo Mário de Andrade, IEB-USP; reproduced in "Lettres à Mário de Andrade," *Les temps modernes*, no. 628 (2004): 257.

53. Lévi-Strauss to Mauss, São Paulo, March 14, 1936 (photocopied), folder 1, NAF 28150 (181), BnF.

54. Ibid.

55. Until the 1940s, the Indians of Marajó Island were seen as possible descendants of "Andean, Meso-American, or possibly, Asiatic civilizations." Daryle Williams, *Culture Wars in Brazil: The First Vargas Regime, 1930–45* (Durham, NC: Duke University Press, 2001), 242.

56. Lévi-Strauss to Mauss, São Paulo, March 14, 1936 (photocopied), folder 1, NAF 28150 (181), BnF.

57. Ibid.

58. Marcel Mauss, *The Gift*, expanded ed., trans. Jane I. Guyer (Chicago: Hau Books, 2016). Here and throughout the book, I refer to the "dissertations" of the four figures at the heart of the book (Bastide, Braudel, Lévi-Strauss, Monbeig), as the published books they would become.

59. Luís Donisete Benzi Grupioni, *Coleções e expedições vigiadas: Os etnólogos no conselho de fiscalização das expedições artísticas e científicas no Brasil* (São Paulo: Editora Hucitec / Anpocs, 1998), 135.

60. "Clube de Geografos Brasileiros: Interessante comunicação do professor Lévi-Strauss sobre os indios bororo," *O Estado de S. Paulo*, June 2, 1936. Correct spelling: Karl von den Steinen.

61. These include "A crise do evolucionismo" (August 1935), "Há diferenças entre os povos e as raças?," (September 1935), and "A caminho de uma nova filosofia do progresso" (September 1935), all published in *O Estado de S. Paulo*.

62. Nimuendajú quoted in Marcela Coelho de Souza and Carlos Fausto, "Reconquistando o campo perdido: O que Lévi-Strauss deve aos ameríndios," *Revista de antropologia* 47, no. 1 (2004): 87–88.

63. Baldus quoted in Elena Welper, "Interwar Anthropology from the Global Periphery: Curt Nimuendajú's Correspondence with Robert Lowie and Claude Lévi-Strauss," *HAU: Journal of Ethnographic Theory* 10, no. 2 (2020): 676.

64. Fauconnet to Lévi-Strauss, Paris, November 29, 1936, NAF 28150 (184), BnF.

65. Lévy-Bruhl to Lévi-Strauss, Paris, n.d., 1936, NAF 28150 (195), BnF.

66. Métraux to Lévi-Strauss, Honolulu, November 15, 1936, NAF 28150 (196), BnF.

67. Alfred Métraux, *La religion des Tupinambá et ses rapports avec celle des autres tribus Tupi-Guarani* (Paris: Librairie Ernest Leroux, 1928); Métraux, *La civilisation matérielle des tribus Tupi-Guarani* (Paris: Librairie Orientaliste Paul Geutner, 1928). For more on Métraux in Argentina, see, among others, Edgardo C. Krebs, "Jorge Luis Borges and Alfred Métraux: Disagreements, Affinities," *HAU: Journal of Ethnographic Theory* 6, no. 2 (2016): 297–321.

68. Métraux to Lévi-Strauss, Honolulu, May 12, 1937, NAF 28150 (196), BnF.

69. Later, Lévi-Strauss returned to São Paulo with a monkey from Mato Grosso, a gift from the Nambicuara.

70. Vincent Debaene and Frédéric Keck, "Chronologie," in Claude Lévi-Strauss, *Œuvres* (Paris: Gallimard, Bibliothèque de la Pléiade, 2008), xlv.

71. Paul Rivet to Paulo Duarte, Paris, February 12, 1937, "São Paulo" folder, MnHn.

72. Lévi-Strauss to Mauss, São Paulo, September 25, 1937, NAF 28150 (181), BnF.

73. See Germaine Dieterlen, "Les résultats des Missions Griaule au Soudan français (1931–1956)," *Archives de sociologie des religions*, no. 3 (1957): 137–42. See also Conklin, *In the Museum of Man*, esp. 199–220.

74. Luís Donisete Benzi Grupioni, "Claude Lévi-Strauss parmi les Amérindiens: Deux expeditions ethnographiques dans l'intérieur du Brésil," in *Brésil Indien: Les arts des amerindiens du Brésil* (Paris: Réunion des Musées Nationaux, 2005), 318.

75. Todd Diacon, *Rondon: O marechel da floresta* (São Paulo: Companhia das Letras, 2006), esp. 31–64.

76. Loyer, *Lévi-Strauss*, 207.

77. Grupioni, "Claude Lévi-Strauss parmi les Amérindiens," 327.

78. Ibid., 318–19.

79. Embassy of the French Republic in Brazil to the Brazilian Ministry of Foreign Affairs, Rio de Janeiro, March 9, 1939, França, Notas Recebidas, 1938–41 (April), 84/4/2, Arquivo Histórico do Itamaraty, Rio de Janeiro.

80. Ian Merkel, "Terms of Exchange: Brazilian Intellectuals and the Remaking of the French Social Sciences" (PhD diss., New York University / University of São Paulo, 2018), 50–53.

81. See Mariza Corrêa, "Dona Heloïsa e a pesquisa de campo," *Revista de Antropo-*

logia 40, no. 1 (1997): 11–54. See also Mariza Corrêa and Januária Mello, eds., *Querida Heloïsa/Dear Heloïsa*: *Cartas de campo para Heloïsa Alberto Torres* (Campinas: PAGU/Unicamp, 2008).

82. Lévi-Strauss to Rivet, São Paulo, April 10, 1937, 2AP1C, MS1/4848B, Archive Paul Rivet, MnHn.

83. Loyer, *Lévi-Strauss*, 205.

84. Lévi-Strauss to Rivet, São Paulo, April 10, 1937, 2AP1C, MS1/4848B, Archive Paul Rivet, MnHn.

85. Hugo Rogélio Suppo, "La politique culturelle française au Brésil entre les années 1920–1950" (PhD diss., Paris III-Sorbonne Nouvelle, 1999), 190.

86. Bruno Rodolfer to the Head of the Division of Historical and Social Documentation, Departamento de Cultura, São Paulo, March 19, 1936, box 73, Arquivo Municipal de São Paulo (henceforth PMSP). These films can be watched in their entirety at the Discoteca Oneyda Alvarenga, Centro Cultural São Paulo. Selected portions can be viewed on YouTube, here: https://www.youtube.com/playlist?list =PLM3Gpc3IS79r9jEq13Qw3OVDI5e25qA_V. For more, consult Emmanuel Leclercq, "Quelques fragments de vie primitive: Claude Lévi-Strauss cinéaste au Brésil," *Les temps modernes* 1, no. 639 (2005): 327–32.

87. "Sociedade de Etnographia e Folklore: Uma communicação do professor Claude Lévi-Strauss, na sessão de hontem, sobre 'Algumas bonecas carajá,'" *O Estado de S. Paulo*, October 7, 1937. For more on this presentation see *Boletim da Sociedade de Etnografia e Folclore* 1, no. 2 (1937): 4–6, in box 4, doc. 287, Sociedade de Etnografia e Folclore Archive, Centro Cultural São Paulo, Discoteca Oneyda Alvarenga, São Paulo (henceforth SEF).

88. Adhemar Pereira de Barros to José Cardoso de Melo Neto, São Paulo, April 29, 1938, cover no. 034.996/1938, case no. 2003,0.094.295-4, 19/4/1938, PMSP.

89. Wilcken, *Lévi-Strauss*, 84.

90. Lévi-Strauss to Mário, Utiariti, January 17, 1938; reproduced in *Les temps modernes* 1, no. 628 (2004): 260.

91. Lévi-Strauss to Monbeig, Utiariti, June 27, 1938; copy in NAF 28150 (181), BnF.

92. Pierre Monbeig, "Récentes recherches ethnographiques en Amérique latine," *Annales de Géographie* 48, no. 274 (1939): 443–45. This of course, was but the culmination of recognition, began by Paul Rivet's note "Mission au Brésil" in the *Journal de la Société des américanistes* (1935) and Jacques Soustelle's "Nouvelles recherches au Brésil" in 1936.

93. Fernand Braudel, "Ma formation d'historien," in *L'histoire au quotidien: Les écrits de Fernand Braudel*, ed. Roselyne de Ayala and Paule Braudel (Paris: Éditions de Fallois, 2001), 16.

94. Caio Prado Jr., *Formação do Brasil contemporâneo* (1942; São Paulo: Companhia das Letras, 2011), 11.

95. I refer here to an article "Bahia," published in two parts in *O Estado de S. Paulo*,

October 24 and 27, 1937. It was retranslated into French by Paule Braudel for *L'histoire au quotidien* as "Bahia." For the firefly reference, see Paulo Miceli, "Sobre história, Braudel e os vaga-lumes: A escola dos Annales e o Brasil (ou vice-versa)," in *Historiografia brasileira em perspectiva*, ed. M. C. de. Freitas (São Paulo: Contexto, 1998), 265.

96. Fernand Braudel, "Bahia," in *L'histoire au quotidien*, 42.

97. Ibid., 43.

98. Ibid.

99. Ibid.

100. Fernand Braudel, review of [Spanish translation] *Los sertones*, by Euclides da Cunha, *Revue historique* 186 (1939): 329. For an English translation, see Euclides da Cunha, *Rebellion in the Backlands*, trans. Samuel Putnam (Chicago: University of Chicago Press, 1944).

101. It is likely that Braudel's reading of Chicago was informed by Maurice Halbwachs's article "Chicago, expérience ethnique," *Annales d'histoire économique et sociale* 4, no. 13 (1932): 11–49.

102. Braudel, "Bahia," 47.

103. Ibid.

104. Ian Merkel, "Fernand Braudel and the Empire of French Social Science: Newly Translated Sources from the 1930s," *French Historical Studies* 40, no. 1 (2017): 129–60. See also Omar Carlier, "Braudel avant Braudel? Les années algériennes (1923–1932)," *Insaniyat* 19–20 (2003): 143–76.

105. Braudel, "Bahia," 48.

106. Ibid.

107. Ibid.

108. Luís Corrêa Lima analyzes this text, which he received from Paule Braudel personally—it has been withheld from his archive. *Fernand Braudel e o Brasil: Vivência e brasilianismo (1935–1945)* (São Paulo: Edusp, 2009), 192.

109. While the *Annales'* editors Lucien Febvre and Marc Bloch often consecrated as much as a third (and sometimes half) of an issue's articles to contemporary issues, their historical interests aligned more closely with their work on archaic societies. See André Burguière, "Histoire d'une histoire: La naissance des Annales," *Annales ESC* 34, no. 6 (1979): 1354.

110. Braudel, *L'histoire au quotidien*, 44. Karl Friedrich Philipp von Martius was an early nineteenth-century German botanist whose principal interest was the flora of Brazil.

111. Braudel, *L'histoire au quotidien*, 45.

112. Carole Reynaud-Paligot, "Les *Annales* de Lucien Febvre à Fernand Braudel entre épopée coloniale et opposition Orient/Occident," *French Historical Studies* 32, no. 1 (2009).

113. Thomas Hirsch, *Le temps des sociétés* (Paris: Éditions de l'EHESS, 2016), 373.

114. Braudel, *L'histoire au quotidien*, 46.

115. Ibid., 48.

116. Braudel, "Ma formation d'historien," 16.

117. Suppo, "La politique culturelle française," 212.

118. See Mário to Bastide, Rio de Janeiro, May 3, 1939, BST2.C1.01, IMEC.

119. Amurabi Oliveira, "Afro-Brazilian Studies in the 1930s: Intellectual Networks between Brazil and the USA," *Brasiliana: Journal for Brazilian Studies* 8, no. 1–2 (2019): 32–49; Yvonne Maggie, "No Underskirts in Africa: Edison Carneiro and the 'Lineages' of Afro-Brazilian Religious Anthropology," *Sociologia e Antropologia*, 5, no. 1 (2015): 101–27. See also Livio Sansone, "'No Sun Helmets!' Melville and Frances Herskovits in Brazil," in *Bérose: Encyclopédie internationale des histoires de l'anthropologie* (Paris: Bérose, 2021), https://www.berose.fr/article2357.html, and Richard and Sally Price, *The Roots of Roots, or How Afro-American Anthropology Got its Start* (Chicago: Prickly Paradigm Press, 2003).

120. Bastide quoted in Thomas Hirsch, "Un 'Flammarion' pour l'anthropologie? Lévy-Bruhl, le terrain, l'ethnologie," *Genèses* 90, no. 1 (2013): 109.

121. Roger Bastide, "Commemorações do cincoentenario da abolição da escravatura no Brasil," *Folha da Noite*, May 10, 1938; Bastide, "A data do cincoentenario da Abolição sera festivamente commemorada nesta Capital," *Folha da Manhã*, May 12, 1938.

122. Roger Bastide, "A sociologia da escravidão," *O Estado de S. Paulo*, May 13, 1938.

123. Ibid.

124. Bastide, "Commemorações do cincoentenario da abolição."

125. Roger Bastide, "Pretos e brancos," *O Estado de S. Paulo*, July 17, 1938.

126. Roger Bastide, "Méditations brésiliennes sur un marché de São Paulo," *Dom Casmurro*, July 2, 1938; republished in *Bastidiana*, no. 6 (1994): 113–14. *Dom Casmurro* published articles in their original language, primarily in Portuguese and in French.

127. Bastide, "Méditations brésiliennes sur un marché de São Paulo."

128. Bastide, "A sociologia da escravidão."

129. Ricardo Benzaquen de Araújo, *Guerra e paz: Casa-grande e senzala e a obra de Gilberto Freyre nos anos 30* (São Paulo: Editora 34, 1994).

130. Bastide, "A sociologia da escravidão."

131. Stefania Capone, "Roger Bastide or the 'Darkness of Alterity,'" chap. 7 in *Out of the Study and Into the Field: Ethnographic Theory and Practice in French Anthropology*, ed. Robert Parkin and Anne de Sales (New York: Berghahn Books, 2010).

132. Roger Bastide, "Hommage à Machado de Assis," *Dom Casmurro*, May 20, 1939.

133. Ibid.

134. For more on Machado de Assis and the Academia de Letras Brasileiras, see K. David Jackson, *Machado de Assis: A Literary Life* (New Haven, CT: Yale University Press, 2015).

135. Bastide, "Hommage."

136. Roger Bastide, "L'esthétique positiviste et la poésie de Martins Fontes," *Dom Casmurro*, December 23, 1939.

137. Ibid.

138. Sérgio Buarque de Holanda, *Raízes do Brasil* (1936; São Paulo: Companhia das Letras, 1995), 79, 160.

139. Bastide, "L'esthétique positiviste."

140. Ibid.

141. Ibid.

142. Roger Bastide, "État actuel des études afro-brésiliennes," *Revue internationale de sociologie* 47, no. 1–2 (1939): 77–89; republished in *Revista do Arquivo Municipal* 5, no. 57 (1939): 108–11. The version cited here is from Herbert Baldus, ed. *Anais do XXXI Congresso das Americanistas* (São Paulo: Anhembi, 1954), 534.

143. "Circular de Antonio Rubbo Muller, Secretário da SEF, aos [sócios], convidando para a reunião de 08 de junho de 1939 e comunicação 'Metodologia Afro-Brasileiro' por Roger Bastide," São Paulo, June 1, 1939, box 3, doc. 119, SEF. This lecture was published as Roger Bastide, "Ensaios de metodologia afro-brasileira," *Revista do Arquivo Municipal* 5, no. 59 (1939): 31.

144. Future research would analyze Bastide's relationship with American anthropologist Melville Herskovits, with whom he corresponded since 1939. These letters can be found in BSTD2-C1.02, IMEC.

145. Marcel Mauss, "L'animisme fétichiste des nègres de Bahia," *L'année sociologique* 5 (1900–1901): 224–25.

146. Bastide to Ramos, São Paulo, July 20, 1938, Fundo Arthur Ramos, I-35, 22, 638, BN.

147. Bastide to Ramos, São Paulo, May 26, 1939, Fundo Arthur Ramos, I-35, 22, 622, BN.

148. Bastide to Ramos, São Paulo, n.d., 1939, Fundo Arthur Ramos, I-35, 22, 621, BN.

149. Peter Schöttler, "Marc Bloch et le XIVᵉ Congrès international de sociologie, Bucarest, août 1939," *Genèses* 20, no. 1 (1995): 143–54.

150. Bastide to Ramos, São Paulo, September 20, 1938, Fundo Arthur Ramos, I-35, 22, 617, BN.

151. Bastide to Ramos, São Paulo, September 28, 1938, Fundo Arthur Ramos, I-35, 22, 618, BN.

152. Bastide to Freyre, São Paulo, March 4, 1939, Fundo Gilberto Freyre, Fundação Gilberto Freyre, Apipucos, Brazil (henceforth GF). For additional documentation related to the conference, see RB-P32-026, Arquivo Roger Bastide, IEB-USP.

153. Roger Bastide, "La sociologie brésilienne et le Congrès international de Bucarest," *Journal des nations américaines*, no. 60 (1939): 558.

154. Freyre to Bastide, May 7, 1939, BST1.C1.02, IMEC.

155. Roger Bastide, "Chronique des livres de sociologie brésilienne," *Revue internationale de sociologie* 47, no. 1–2 (1939): 91.

156. Ibid. Calmon was a law professor in Rio de Janeiro, an active member of the Instituto Histórico e Geográfico Brasileiro, and was elected to the Academia Brasileira de Letras. Calmon's three-volume *História social do Brasil* (1935–39) is probably what Bastide was referring to.

157. Bastide to Rivet, June 22, 1939, 2AP1C1f, MnHn. For more on the Northeast in Brazilian popular culture during this period, see Bryan McCann, *Hello, Hello Brazil: Popular Music in the Making of Modern Brazil* (Durham, NC: Duke University Press, 2004), esp. 96–128. For a critical perspective of this production of the Northeast by the sugar elite, see Thomas D. Rogers, "Laboring Landscapes: The Environmental, Racial, and Class Worldview of the Brazilian Northeast's Sugar Elite, 1880s–1930s," *Luso-Brazilian Review* 46/2 (2009): 22–53.

158. Senghor to Bastide, Paris, May 2, 1939, BST2.C2-01, IMEC.

159. Ibid.

160. Undated letter from the president of the 4th section of the École Pratique des Hautes Études, Fonds Braudel, archives of the École Pratique des Hautes Études.

161. Braudel to Simões, Paris, February 1938, doc. 2435, p. 2, CAPH.

162. Braudel to Simões, Paris, April 18, 1939, doc. 2461, p. 2., CAPH.

163. Braudel to Simões, Paris, February 1938, doc. 2435, p. 2., CAPH.

164. These include, but are not limited to, a review of *Les origines de Buenos Aires et le sens de son evolution historique*, by Ricard Levene, *Revue historique* 186, no. 1 (1939): 188; a "Bibliographie sur l'Amérique latine," *Annales d'histoire sociale* 1 (1939): 73–75; notes on immigration to São Paulo and specifically the *Boletim da directoria de terras, colonização e immigração* (São Paulo, Brazil), *Annales d'histoire sociale* 4 (1939): 464; notes on the first two volumes of *Revista de economia e estatística* (Brazil), the new Mexican journal *Revista de historia de America* under the direction of M. Silvio Zavala, and *Annales d'histoire sociale* 4 (1939): 464; and, finally, a review of the new Spanish translations of works by Pedro Calmon (*História de la civilización brasileña*), Francisco José de Oliveira Vianna (*Evolución del pueblo brasileño*), and Euclides da Cunha (*Los sertones*), *Revue historique* 186 (1939): 329.

165. Fernand Braudel, "En Algérie: Problèmes généraux et problèmes d'Oranie," *Annales d'histoire économique et sociale* 10, no. 54 (1938): 509–12.

166. Almeida Prado quoted in *O Estado de S. Paulo*, May 1, 1938.

167. *O Estado de S. Paulo*, April 28, 1938.

168. "Expedição à Serra do Norte: Regresso do Professor Lévi-Strauss," *O Estado de S. Paulo*, January 13, 1939.

169. "Sociedade de Etnografia e Folklore: Homenagem ao professor Lévi-Strauss," *O Estado de S. Paulo*, January 28, 1939.

170. "Sociedade de Etnographia e Folklore," *O Estado de S. Paulo*, February 23, 1939.

171. Loyer, *Lévi-Strauss*, 236.

172. Azevedo to Freyre, São Paulo, July 9, 1938, FA CR114p2doc18, GF.

173. Alfred Bonzon, Jean Gagé, Jean Maugüé, and Arbousse-Bastide also found themselves in this predicament. See Lefebvre, "Les professeurs français," 33.

CHAPTER FOUR

1. Pierre Daix, *Braudel* (Paris: Flammarion, 1995), 179.

2. The New School was known as the university in exile, first hosting refugees from the Nazis and then other refugees. See Claus-Dieter Krohn and Rita Kimber, *Intellectuals in Exile: Refugee Scholars and the New School for Social Research* (Amherst: University of Massachusetts Press, 1994); François Chaubet and Emmanuelle Loyer, "L'École Libre des Hautes Études de New York: Exil et resistance intellectuelle (1942–1946)," *Revue historique* 302, no. 4 (616) (2000): 939–72. See also, more recently, Judith Friedlander, *A Light in Dark Times: The New School for Social Research and Its University in Exile* (New York: Columbia University Press, 2019), esp. chap. 10.

3. For more on this, see Ian Merkel, "Terms of Exchange: Brazilian Intellectuals and the Remaking of the French Social Sciences" (PhD diss., New York University / University of São Paulo, 2018), 181–221.

4. Monbeig to Febvre, São Paulo, January 27, 1940, Archives Lucien Febvre, Archives de l'École des Hautes Études en Sciences Sociales (henceforth EHESS-LF).

5. Lévi-Strauss quoted in Jeanpierre, "Des hommes entre plusieurs mondes: Étude sur une situation d'exil; Intellectuels français réfugiés pendant la deuxième guerre mondiale" (PhD diss., École des Hautes Études en Sciences Sociales, 2004), 513.

6. French scholars exiled in the Americas offer an interesting counterpoint to Germans such as Hannah Arendt, Theodor Adorno, or Max Horkheimer in the United States. The French migrated later and in smaller numbers. Emmanuelle Loyer, "La débâcle, les universitaires et la Fondation Rockefeller: France/États-Unis, 1940–1941," *Revue d'histoire moderne et contemporaine* 48, no. 1 (2001): 138–59. See also Jeffrey Mehlman, *French Intellectuals in Wartime Manhattan, 1940–1944* (Baltimore: Johns Hopkins University Press, 2000). For more on German academics in the US, see, most recently, Christian Fleck, *A Transatlantic History of the Social Sciences: Robber Barons, the Third Reich, and the Invention of Empirical Social Research* (New York: Bloomsbury Academic, 2011).

7. Martin Jay, *Permanent Exiles: Essays on the Intellectual Migration from Germany to America* (New York: Columbia University Press, 1985).

8. Pierre Monbeig, *La crise des sciences de l'homme* (Rio de Janeiro: Casa do Estudante do Brasil, 1943).

9. Christophe Charle, *La république des universitaires, 1870–1940* (Paris: Seuil, 1994), esp. 343–96.

10. Pierre Monbeig, *Pionniers et planteurs de São Paulo* (Paris: Armand Colin, 1952); Monbeig, *La croissance de la ville de São Paulo* (Grenoble: Institut et revue de géogra-

phie alpine, 1953). Writing a secondary dissertation, or "thèse complémentaire," was part of the requirements for a doctorate in France during this period.

11. Roger Bastide, *Imagens do Nordeste místico em branco e preto* (Rio: Cruzeiro, 1945); Bastide, *Poetas do Brasil* (1946; São Paulo: Editora da Universidade de São Paulo / Duas Cidades, 1997); Bastide, *Le candomblé de Bahia* (Paris: Mouton, 1958); Bastide, *Les religions africaines au Brésil* (Paris: Presses universitaires de France, 1960).

12. Lévi-Strauss to Rivet, New York, December 16, 1943, NAF 28150 (181), BnF.

13. Claude Lévi-Strauss, *Le totemisme aujourd'hui* (Paris: Presses universitaires de France, 1962), 132.

14. For field-specific criticism of each of the scholars work during this period, I would suggest looking at, for Braudel, John A. Marino, ed., *Early Modern History and the Social Sciences: Testing the Limits of Braudel's "Mediterranean"* (Kirksville, MO: Truman State University Press, 2002), and Stanley Stein and Barbara Stein, *Silver, Trade, and War: Spain and America in the Making of Early Modern Europe* (Baltimore: Johns Hopkins University Press, 2000); for Bastide, Stefania Capone, "Transatlantic Dialogue: Roger Bastide and the African American Religions," *Journal of Religion in Africa* 37, no. 2 (2007): 336–70, and Marcio Goldman, "Cavalo dos deuses: Roger Bastide e as transformações das religiões de matriz africana no Brasil," *Revista de Antropologia* 54, no. 1 (2011); for Monbeig, Larissa Alves de Lira, *Pierre Monbeig e a formação da geografia no Brasil (1925–1956): Uma geo-história dos saberes* (São Paulo: Alameda, 2021); and, for Lévi-Strauss, Francis Korn, *Elementary Structures Reconsidered: Lévi-Strauss on Kinship* (Abingdon, UK: Routledge, 2004), and François Héran, *Figures de la Parenté: Une histoire critique de la raison structurale* (Paris: Presses universitaires de France, 2009).

15. Pierre Monbeig, "The Colonial Nucleus of Barão de Antonina, São Paulo," *Geographical Review* 30, no. 2 (1940): 260–71.

16. Ibid., 260.

17. Demangeon and Jean Brunhes emphasized the human aspects of geography to a much greater extent than the other Vidalians. For a brief introduction to their work, situated alongside their peers, see Paul Claval, "The Historical Dimension of French Geography," *Journal of the History of Geography*, 10, no. 3 (1984): 234.

18. Monbeig, "Colonial Nucleus," 261.

19. Ibid., 262.

20. Ibid.

21. Monbeig generally preferred to leave his terms in Portuguese italicized rather than to translate them. In the shortened French version of the article in question, he simply leaves *caboclo* as is. Monbeig, "Un centre de colonisation officielle dans l'Etat de São Paulo," *Annales de Géographie* 50, no. 283 (1941): 208–11. In the English text, he—or more likely, the editors of *Geographical Review*—provided the following definition: "The term *caboclo* originally designated a white-Indian half-breed; but as such half-breeds form the majority of the Brazilian peasantry, the word has commonly lost

its strict ethnic meaning and acquired a geographical connotation, i.e. any man who leads the life of a true caboclo." Monbeig, "Colonial Nucleus," 261n3.

22. Hervé Théry, "Claude Lévi-Strauss, Pierre Monbeig et Roger Brunet," *EchoGéo*, no. 7 (2008): 1–8.

23. Monbeig, "Colonial Nucleus," 264–65.

24. Ibid., 268.

25. Ibid., 271.

26. Monbeig, "Un centre de colonisation," 211.

27. See Carlo Eugênio Nogueira, "O lugar da fronteira na geografia de Pierre Monbeig" (PhD diss., University of São Paulo, 2013). For a useful historiographical synthesis on different immigrant experiences, contrasting it with intra-Brazilian migration, see Jeffrey Lesser, *Immigration, Ethnicity, and National Identity in Brazil, 1808 to the Present* (Cambridge: Cambridge University Press, 2013).

28. For more on this, see Barbara Weinstein, *The Color of Modernity: São Paulo and the Making of Race and Nation in Brazil* (Durham, NC: Duke University Press, 2015).

29. Monbeig, "Un centre de colonisation," 211.

30. Ibid.

31. Pierre Monbeig, "Algumas observações sobre Marília, cidade pioneira," *Revista do Arquivo Municipal* 7, no. 78 (1941): 221.

32. Ibid., 222.

33. "*Espigão*: Designates the ridge beam of a roof. The word is used very precisely to describe the tight plateaus that descend slowly toward the Paraná river, to the West, as well as the lateral spurs that detach off of it." Monbeig, *Pionniers et planteurs*, 367.

34. Monbeig, "Algumas observações sobre Marília," 224.

35. The high-water mark in this discussion remains Euclides da Cunha's masterpiece *Os sertões* (1902), which posited the *sertão* as the antithesis of civilization and progress. For an extended analysis of the term, see Nísia Trindade Lima, *Um sertão chamado Brasil: Intelectuais e representação geográfica da identidade nacional* (Rio de Janeiro: Revan, 1999).

36. Monbeig, *Pionniers et planteurs*, 369.

37. Pierre Deffontaines, "Le réseau des villes: Comment il s'est constitué au Brésil," *Bulletin de la Société de Géographie de Lille* 82, no. 9 (1938): 321–48. Monbeig cites this article as a privileged source in his article "O estudo geográfico das cidades," *Revista do Arquivo Municipal* 78, no. 7 (1941): 5–38, to which we will return shortly.

38. Deffontaines, "Le réseau des villes," 332.

39. Monbeig, "Algumas observações sobre Marília," 226.

40. Ibid., 226–27.

41. Ibid., 225.

42. Ibid., 227.

43. Pierre Monbeig, "Comentário em torno do mapa de evolução da população

do Estado de São Paulo entre 1934 e 1940 (por municipio)," *Boletim da Associação dos Geógrafos Brasileiros* 3, no. 3 (1943):48.

44. Nogueira, "O lugar da fronteira," 139.

45. Monbeig, "The Colonial Nucleus," 260.

46. Monbeig, "O estudo geográfico das cidades."

47. For more on this text, see Martine Droulers, "L'étude géographique des villes," in *Pierre Monbeig: Un géographe pionnier*, ed. Droulers and Hervé Théry (Paris: Éditions de l'IHEAL, 1991), http://books.openedition.org/iheal/1496. See also Maurício de Almeida Abreu, "Pierre Monbeig e os primórdios da geografia urbana no Brasil," in *Pierre Monbeig e a geografia humana brasileira: A dinâmica da transformação*, ed. Heliana Angotti Salgueiro (Paris: EDUSC, 2006), 134–39.

48. For more on the influence of the Chicago school and Robert Park in Brazil, see, e.g., Lícia do Prado Valladares, "A visita do Robert Park ao Brasil, o 'homem marginal' e a Bahia como laboratório," *Caderno CRH* 23, no. 58 (2010): 35–49.

49. Ibid., 38. For a complete list of Monbeig's students and their work, see Almeida Abreu, "Pierre Monbeig e os primórdios," 133–34.

50. Caio Prado Jr., "Nova contribuição para o estudo geográfico da cidade de São Paulo," *Estudos brasileiros* 3, no. 7 (1941): 195–122.

51. Monbeig, "O estudo geográfico das cidades," 6.

52. Ibid., 36.

53. Ibid., 8.

54. Ibid.

55. Ibid., 16.

56. Ibid., 18–19.

57. Ibid., 21.

58. Ibid., 35.

59. Ibid., 23.

60. Ibid.

61. This pamphlet was printed after being read out in the conference room of the Ministry of Foreign Affairs Library in Rio de Janeiro, on July 13, 1943.

62. Arthur Ramos, *As ciências sociais e os problemas de após-guerra* (Rio de Janeiro: Casa do Estudante do Brasil, 1944).

63. Monbeig, *La crise des sciences de l'homme*, 27.

64. Ibid., 29.

65. Ibid., 32.

66. Ibid., 33.

67. Ibid., 37–38.

68. Ibid., 39.

69. Ibid., 43–44.

70. Ibid., 47.

71. Ibid., 48.

72. Brigitte Mazon, "La Fondation Rockefeller et les sciences sociales en France, 1925–1940," *Revue française de sociologie* 26, no. 2 (1985).

73. Monbeig, *La crise des sciences de l'homme*, 54–55.

74. Étienne Anheim, "Le rêve de l'histoire totale," in *Une autre histoire: Jacques le Goff*, ed. Jacques Revel and Jean-Claude Schmitt, 79–86 (Paris: Éditions de l'École des hautes études en sciences sociales, 2015).

75. Monbeig, *La crise des sciences de l'homme*, 59–60.

76. Ibid., 60.

77. Pierre Monbeig, Antonieta de Paula Souza, and Maria Conceição Vicente de Carvalho, *Geografia de hoje* (Rio de Janeiro: Livraria José Olympio, 1944).

78. For an engagement with and critique of a similar method in the work of Michel Leiris, see Paul Christopher Johnson, "Scholars Possessed! On Writing Africana Religions with the Left Hand," *Journal of Africana Religions* 4, no. 2 (2016): 154–85.

79. Roger Bastide, "Contribution à l'étude du syncrétisme catholico-fétichiste," in *Poètes et dieux: Études afro-brésiliennes*, trans. Luiz Ferraz (Paris: L'Harmattan, 2002), 183–221; for the Portuguese version, first published in 1946, consult Bastide, "Contribuição ao estudo do sincretismo católico-fetichista," in *Estudos Afro-brasileiros* (São Paulo: Perspectiva, 1973).

80. See, for example, Roger Bastide, *Arte e sociedade*, trans. Gilda de Mello e Souza (São Paulo: Companhia Editora Nacional, 1979).

81. Bastide to Ramos, São Paulo, September 5, 1940, I-35, 22, 624, Manuscritos, Fundo Arthur Ramos, BN.

82. Roger Bastide, "Psicanálise do cafuné," *Revista do Arquivo Municipal* 6, no. 70 (1940): 118–30; Bastide, "Introdução ao estudo de alguns complexos afro-brasileiros," *Revista do Arquivo Municipal* 8, no. 90 (1943): 7–54.

83. Roger Bastide, *Sociologie et psychanalyse* (Paris: Presses universitaires de France, 1950).

84. Bastide, "Psicanálise do cafuné," 118.

85. Rimbaud paraphrased in ibid., 120.

86. Ibid., 126.

87. Ibid., 130.

88. Bastide, "Introdução ao estudo," 11.

89. Ibid., 15.

90. Bastide, *Poètes et dieux*, 51–57, 81–112; originally published in Bastide, *A poesia afro-brasileira* (São Paulo: Editora Martins, 1943).

91. For a recent analysis of the question of class and caste in the work of Pierson, who concluded his thesis "Negros in Brazil" in 1942, see Marcos Chor Maio and Thiago da Costa Lopes, "Entre Chicago e Salvador: Donald Pierson e o estudo das relações raciais," *Estudos históricos* 30, no. 60 (2017): 123. See also Isabela Oliveira Pereira da Silva, "De Chicago à São Paulo: Donald Pierson no mapa das ciências sociais (1930–1950)" (PhD diss., University of São Paulo, 2012), esp. 147–207.

92. Bastide, "Introdução ao estudo," 14.

93. Ibid., 13.

94. Ibid., 26.

95. Bastide to Ramos, São Paulo, August 18, 1941, I-35, 22, 625, Manuscritos, Fundo Arthur Ramos, BN.

96. Câmara Cascudo to Bastide, Natal, December 16, 1942, BST2.C1-01, IMEC.

97. Bastide to Freyre, São Paulo, June 10, 1941, GF. The article in question is "Aspectos de um século de transição do Nordeste," in *Região e tradição* (Rio de Janeiro: José Olympio, 1941).

98. Ibid.

99. See Maria Isaura Pereira de Queiroz, "Nostalgia do outro e do alhures: A obra sociológica de Roger Bastide," in *Roger Bastide* (São Paulo: Editora Ática, 1983), 7.

100. Gisèle Sapiro, *La guerre des écrivains, 1940–53* (Paris: Fayard, 1999), 533.

101. Bastide to Freyre, São Paulo, June 10, 1941, GF.

102. Bastide to Freyre, São Paulo, November 6, 1942, GF.

103. Freyre to Bastide, Santo Antonio de Apipucos, Recife, December 14, 1942, BST1.C1.02, IMEC.

104. Freyre to Bastide, Santo Antonio de Apipucos, Recife, January 19, 1943, BST1.C1.02, IMEC.

105. For more on Bastide's literary criticism, see Gloria Carneiro do Amaral, ed., *Navette literária França-Brasil*, vol. 1, *A crítica de Roger Bastide* (São Paulo: Edusp, 2010); Amaral, ed., *Navette literária França-Brasil*, vol. 2, *Textos de crítica literária de Roger Bastide* (São Paulo: Edusp, 2010).

106. Roger Bastide, "Incorporação da poesia africana à poesia brasileira," in *Poetas do Brasil* (1946; São Paulo: Editora da Universidade de São Paulo / Duas Cidades, 1997), 17–55; originally in *O Estado de S. Paulo*, October 22 and 29, 1942, November 5, 1942, July 8, 15, and 22, 1943; Bastide, "Machado de Assis, paisagista," *Revista USP*, no. 56 (2002–3): 192–202; originally published in *Revista do Brasil* 3, no. 29 (1940): 1–14.

107. Bastide, "Incorporação da poesia africana," 23.

108. Ibid., 25.

109. Ibid., 32.

110. For more on this period, see Thomas Skidmore, *Black into White: Race and Nationality in Brazilian Thought* (Durham, NC: Duke University Press, 1992), esp. chap. 3.

111. Bastide, "Incorporação da poesia africana," 36.

112. Ibid., 41.

113. Ibid., 51.

114. Ibid., 55.

115. Mário de Andrade to Bastide, Araraquara, July 3, 1943, BST2.C1.01, IMEC; Carlos Drummond de Andrade to Bastide, Rio de Janeiro, September 13, 1943, BST2.C1.01, IMEC.

116. Alberto Schneider and Richard Correll, "The Brazil of Sílvio Romero and Machado de Assis: History of a 'Polemic,' or the Writer as Critic of the Critic," *Portuguese Studies* 26, no. 2 (2010): 205–31.

117. Bastide, "Machado de Assis paisagista," 195. Sidney Chalhoub's work on Machado, which examines his role as a functionary in the abolition of slavery, provides further evidence for Machado's engagement with the fate of his country and its people. *Machado de Assis, historiador* (São Paulo: Companhia das Letras, 2003), esp. chap. 4.

118. Bastide, "Machado de Assis paisagista," 198.

119. Ibid.

120. Ibid., 199.

121. See Antonio Candido, *Recortes* (São Paulo: Companhia das Letras, 1996), 103–9.

122. Ferreira to Bastide, Recife, July 26, 1944, BST2.C1-02, IMEC.

123. Ibid.

124. Bastide to Ramos, Recife, February 20, 1944, I-35, 22, 626, Manuscritos, Fundo Arthur Ramos, BN.

125. Roberto Motta, preface to Roger Bastide, *Poètes et dieux*, xiii.

126. Bastide's book was first published, in Portuguese, as *Imagens do Nordeste místico em branco e preto*. Here, I use Bastide, *Images du Nordeste mystique en noir et blanc* (Paris: Actes Sud, 1995). The original articles appeared as Bastide, "O carnaval de Recife," *Revista do Brasil*, no. 1 (1944): 49–52, and Bastide, "Nordeste brasileiro, impressões de viagem," *Revista franco-brasileira*, no. 123 (1944): 14–18. On the macumba of São Paulo, see Bastide, "La macumba pauliste," in *Poètes et dieux*, 223–77.

127. Roger Bastide, "Monografia do candomblé. O Cerimonial da polidez. O Lundum do Padre," *Revista do Arquivo Municipal* 10, no. 98 (1944): 81–103.

128. Bastide to Ramos, Recife, February 20, 1944, I-35, 22, 626, Manuscritos, Fundo Arthur Ramos, BN.

129. Bastide, *Images du Nordeste mystique*, 157.

130. Bastide, *Images du Nordeste mystique*, 113.

131. Bastide, "Contribution à l'étude du syncrétisme catholico-fétichiste," 210.

132. Ibid., 53.

133. Ibid., 73. *Terreiros* are religious grounds, almost always with a house in which most ceremonies take place.

134. J. Lorand Matory, *Black Atlantic Religion: Tradition, Transnationalism, and Matriarchy in Afro-Brazilian Candomblé* (Princeton, NJ: Princeton University Press, 2005), chap. 4.

135. Bastide, "Contribution à l'étude," 91–92.

136. Bastide to Freyre, São Paulo, n.d., [1943?], GF.

137. Bastide, *Images du Nordeste mystique*, 188.

138. Gilberto Freyre, *Sobrados e mucambos: Decadência do patriarcado rural e desenvolvimento do urbano*, vol. 1 (Rio de Janeiro: José Olympio, 1951), 23.

139. Bastide, *Images du Nordeste mystique*, 189.

140. Ibid., 277.

141. Bastide, "Monografia do candomblé."

142. Abreu to Bastide, Bahia, October 31, 1945, BAST2.C1-01, IMEC.

143. Mário to Bastide, São Paulo, September 19, 1944, BST2.C1.01, IMEC.

144. Ibid.

145. Roger Bastide, "Stéréotypes des noirs dans la littérature brésilienne," in *Poètes et dieux*, 133.

146. Febvre to Braudel, Paris, May 16, 1942; quoted by Giuliana Gemelli, *Fernand Braudel*, trans. Béatrice Propetto Marzi (Paris: Odile Jacob, 1995), 72.

147. Gemelli, *Fernand Braudel*, 78–82; Daix, *Braudel*, 163–83; Howard Caygill, "Braudel's Prison Notebooks," *History Workshop Journal*, no. 57 (2004): 151–60.

148. Fernand Braudel, "Ma formation d'historien," in *L'histoire au quotidien: Les écrits de Fernand Braudel*, ed. Roselyne de Ayala and Paule Braudel (Paris: Éditions de Fallois, 2001), 17.

149. Peter Schöttler, "Fernand Braudel, prisonnier en Allemagne: Face à la longue durée et au temps présent," *Sozial.Geschichte Online*, no. 10 (2013): 11–15.

150. Daix, *Braudel*, 179.

151. Fernand Braudel, *Les ambitions de l'histoire*, ed. Roselyne de Ayala and Paule Braudel (Paris: Flammarion, 1997), 12.

152. Ibid.

153. Ibid. The word that I have rendered as "bombarded" (*deverser*) is closer in meaning to "flooded"; however, for the structure of the sentence I have opted for the present solution.

154. This section has attempted to maintain the chronology of the war years. I have consulted Braudel's dissertation held at the Sorbonne and the first edition of *The Mediterranean*, published by Armand Colin, in 1949. Citations are from the most recent edition of the book: Braudel, *La méditerranée et le monde méditerranéen à l'époque de Philippe II*, 3 vols. (Paris: Armand Colin, 1990). At times, I use the English translation: Braudel, *The Mediterranean and the Mediterranean World in the Age of Philip II*, 2 vols., trans. Siân Reynolds (New York: Harper Colophon Books, 1972). The notebooks and conferences cited can be found edited as Braudel, "L'histoire, mesure du monde," in *Les ambitions de l'histoire*, 11–83.

155. Braudel's review of Freyre's work appeared as "À travers un continent d'histoire: Le Brésil et l'oeuvre de Gilberto Freyre," *Mélanges d'histoire sociale* 4 (1943): 3–20. For an extended analysis of Braudel's review, see Andrew Dausch, "The French University Mission to Brazil, Racial Theory, and the Formation of a New Social Science Paradigm," in *Cultural Exchanges between Brazil and France*, ed. Regina R. Félix and Scott D. Juall (West Lafayette, IN: Purdue University Press, 2016), 127–30.

156. Braudel, *L'histoire au quotidien*, 45.

157. For more, see Giuliana Gemelli, *Fernand Braudel e l'Europa universale* (Venice: Marsilio Editori, 1990); in my own analysis, I will use the French translation, Gemelli, *Fernand Braudel*. Although critiquing Braudel's temporal fragmentation, Bernard Bailyn cites both *The Mediterranean* and the work of French historians inspired by Braudel on several occasions. Bailyn, *Atlantic History: Concepts and Contours* (Cambridge, MA: Harvard University Press, 2005).

158. Earl J. Hamilton, "Imports of American Gold and Silver into Spain, 1503–1660," *Quarterly Journal of Economics* 43, no. 3 (1929): 436.

159. Ibid.

160. Braudel, *La méditerranée*, 206.

161. Ibid., 261.

162. Ibid., 351.

163. The gold and silver was coming, precisely, from the Viceroyalty of Peru (Bolivia) and New Spain (Mexico).

164. Earl Hamilton was a Keynesian whose now-classic book served as one of the foundations of economic-history research. Hamilton, *American Treasure and the Price Revolution in Spain, 1501–1650* (Cambridge, MA: Harvard University Press, 1934). For an evocative article, see Hamilton, "American Treasure and the Rise of Capitalism (1500–1700)," *Economica*, no. 27 (1929): 338–57. For an economist's review of this "classic" and its contributions, see John Munro, review of *American Treasure and the Price Revolution in Spain, 1501–1650*, by Earl J. Hamilton, accessed January 20, 2017, https://eh.net/book_reviews/american-treasure-and-the-price-revolution-in-spain-1501-1650/.

165. Lucien Febvre, "Le problème historique des prix," *Annales d'histoire économique et sociale* 2, no. 7 (1930): 384.

166. Febvre, "Le problème historique des prix"; Henri Hauser, "Un comité international d'enquête sur l'histoire des prix," *Annales d'histoire économique et sociale* 2, no. 7 (1930): 384–85. For more on these subjects, see Arthur H. Cole and Ruth Crandall, "The International Scientific Committee on Price History," *Journal of Economic History* 24, no. 3 (1964): 381–88; Olivier Dumoulin, "Aux origines de l'histoire des prix," *Annales HSS* 45, no. 2 (1990): 507–22.

167. Lucien Febvre, "Or d'Amérique et capitalisme," *Annales d'histoire économique et sociale* 3, no. 9 (1931): 160.

168. See John A. Marino, "The Exile and His Kingdom: The Reception of Braudel's *Mediterranean*," *Journal of Modern History* 76, no. 3 (2004): 634.

169. Fernand Braudel, review of "Monetary Inflation in Castile (1598–1660)," by Earl A. Hamilton, *Revue Historique* 168, no. 2 (1931): 387–89.

170. For exciting new work on the Genoese and the history of capitalism, see Padraic Rohan, "Outsourcing the Colonial Project: The Genoese Role in Iberian Expansion," *World History Bulletin* 35, no. 2 (2019): 15–28.

171. See Max Weber, *The Protestant Ethic and the "Spirit" of Capitalism*, ed. and trans.

Peter Baehr and Gordon C. Wells (New York: Penguin, 2002). Braudel later took on Weber in his three-volume *Civilization and Capitalism, 15th–18th Century*. Braudel cites these debates in the fourth edition of *La méditerranée*, 353.

172. Braudel, *The Mediterranean*, 321.

173. Braudel, *La méditerranée*, 444.

174. Braudel, *La méditerranée*, 192.

175. Ibid., 178, 183.

176. Henri Hauser, and surely others, made this point well before Braudel. Hauser, "Réflexions sur l'histoire des banques à l'époque moderne de la fin du XVᵉ à la fin du XVIIIᵉ siècle," *Annales d'histoire économique et sociale* 1, no. 3 (1929): 340.

177. Braudel, *La méditerranée*, 47; *The Mediterranean*, 319.

178. Braudel, *La méditerranée*, 275.

179. Braudel, "Histoire, mesure du monde," 77.

180. Braudel, *La méditerranée*, 382.

181. Ibid., 190.

182. Caio Prado Jr., *Formação do Brasil contemporâneo* (São Paulo: Companhia das Letras, 2011), 18. For a convincing analysis of the parallels between Braudel's and Prado's works, particularly *The Mediterranean* and *Formação do Brasil contemporâneo*, see Paulo Teixeira Iumatti, "Historiographical and Conceptual Exchange between Fernand Braudel and Caio Prado Jr. in the 1930s and 1940s: A Case of Unequal Positions in the Intellectual Space between Brazil and France," trans. Ian Merkel, *Storia della storiografia* 71, no. 1 (2017): 89–110. Braudel's correspondence with Prado leading up to the war and immediately following it indicate a rich exchange of ideas, but it is likely that Braudel had not read *Formação do Brasil contemporâneo* much before 1948, when he reviewed it for *Annales*: Braudel, "Au Brésil: Deux livres de Caio Prado," *Annales ESC* 3, no. 1 (1948): 99–103.

183. Braudel, *La méditerranée*, 148. Whether or not Braudel had known Simonsen from his time in São Paulo, he surely would have known of him by 1939, when Hauser reviewed his work. Henri Hauser, "Compte rendu de Roberto Simonsen, *História economica do Brasil, 1500–1830*," *Revue historique* 185, no. 1 (1939): 168–70.

184. Braudel, *La méditerranée*, 230.

185. Ibid., 539.

186. For more on the Moriscos, see Mayte Green-Mercado, *Visions of Deliverance: Moriscos and the Politics of Prophecy in the Early Modern Mediterranean* (Ithaca, NY: Cornell University Press, 2020).

187. See, for example, Braudel, *La méditerranée*, 484, 531.

188. Braudel, *The Mediterranean*, 117.

189. Braudel, *La méditerranée*, 533. Braudel's citations of Freyre on other aspects, from banditry (475) to Iberian Catholicism (496) are abundant throughout the text, as well.

190. For more on this, see Peter Schöttler, "La continuation des Annales sous

l'occupation—une 'solution élégante'?," in *Les intellectuels et l'occupation, 1940–1944: Collaborer, partir, résister,* ed. Albrecht Betz and Stefan Martens, 243–61 (Paris: Autrement, 2004).

191. Monbeig to Febvre, São Paulo, January 27, 1940, EHESS-LF.

192. Peter Burke, "Gilberto Freyre e a nova história," *Tempo social* 9, no. 2 (1997): 1–12.

193. Braudel, "À travers un continent," 11.

194. Ibid., 8.

195. Gilberto Freyre, *Casa-grande e senzala* (Rio de Janeiro: Record, 2000), 343.

196. Braudel, "À travers un continent," 10.

197. Braudel's 1937 lecture "Concept of a New Country" distinguished Algeria from places such as Brazil or Argentina where he saw the indigenous question as less of an impediment. Braudel, "Concept of a New Country," in Ian Merkel, "Fernand Braudel and the Empire of French Social Science: Newly Translated Sources from the 1930s," *French Historical Studies* 40, no. 1 (2017): 147.

198. Braudel, "À travers un continent," 13.

199. For perhaps his most seething criticism, see Edmund Leach, "Claude Lévi-Strauss: Anthropologist and Philosopher," *New Left Review,* 1st ser., no. 34 (1965): 12–27; specifically about *The Elementary Structures,* see Leach, *Claude Lévi-Strauss* (Chicago: University of Chicago Press, 1989), 105–24.

200. Simone de Beauvoir, review of *Les structures élémentaires de la parenté,* by Claude Lévi-Strauss, *Les temps modernes* 5, no. 45 (1949): 943–44. For an extended analysis of de Beauvoir's reading of Lévi-Strauss, see Frédéric Keck, "Beauvoir lectrice de Lévi-Strauss: Les relations hommes/femmes entre existentialisme et structuralisme," *Les temps modernes* 1, no. 647–648 (2008): 242–55.

201. For more on structuralism's early years and Lévi-Strauss's pioneering role, see François Dosse, *History of Structuralism,* vol. 1, *The Rising Sign, 1945–1966,* trans. Deborah Glassman (Minneapolis: University of Minnesota Press, 1997), esp. 5–58.

202. Kinship, which is one of the traditional pillars of social and cultural anthropology, has for some decades been supplanted by other themes, questions, and subfields; see Paulo Sousa, "The Fall of Kinship: Towards an Epidemiological Explanation," *Journal of Cognition and Culture* 3, no. 4 (2003): 265–303. For an approach that analyzes Lévi-Strauss within kinship studies alongside his critics, see Maurice Godelier, *The Metamorphoses of Kinship,* trans. Nora Scott (New York: Verso, 2011), 14–22.

203. Métraux to Steward, New Haven, June 7, 1941, NAF 28150 (196), BnF.

204. Claude Lévi-Strauss, "Tribes of the Right Bank of the Guaporé River," in *The Tropical Forest Tribes,* vol. 3 of *Handbook of South American Indians,* ed. Julian Steward (Washington, DC: Government Printing Office, 1948); Lévi-Strauss, "The Social Use of Kinship Terms among Brazilian Indians," *American Anthropologist* 45, no. 3 (1943): 398–409; Lévi-Strauss, "On Dual Organization in South America," *America Indígena* 4, no. 1 (1944): 37–47; Lévi-Strauss, "Guerre et commerce chez les Indiens de

l'Amérique du Sud," *Renaissance. Revue trimestrielle publiée par l'École libre des hautes études* 1, no. 1–2 (1943): 122–39; Lévi-Strauss, "The Social and Psychological Aspects of Chieftainship in a Primitive Tribe: The Nambikuara of Northwestern Mato Grosso," *Transactions of the New York Academy of Sciences*, 2nd ser., 7, no. 1 (1944): 16–32.

205. Patrick Wilcken, *Claude Lévi-Strauss: The Poet in the Laboratory* (London: Bloomsbury, 2010), 159.

206. Lévi-Strauss recounts his presence at Boas's death in Lévi-Strauss and Didier Eribon, *De près et de loin* (Paris: Odile Jacob, 1988), 58.

207. Vincent Debaene, "'Like Alice through the Looking Glass': Claude Lévi-Strauss in New York," *French Politics, Culture, and Society* 28, no. 1 (2010): 48. For more on Benedict and Mead, see, for example, Peter Mandler, *Return from the Natives: How Margaret Mead Won the Second World War and Lost the Cold War* (New Haven, CT: Yale University Press, 2013).

208. Lévi-Strauss to Rivet, New York, December 6, 1943, NAF 28150 (181), BnF.

209. Ibid.

210. Lévi-Strauss to Jakobson, New York, April 20, [1942?], NAF 28150 (181), BnF. Lévi-Strauss's contribution to Jakobson's journal was "L'analyse structurale en linguistique et en anthropologie," *Word* 1, no. 1 (1945): 1–12.

211. Unfortunately, this letter was lost or misplaced, as it is not present at Lévi-Strauss's archive.

212. Lévi-Strauss to Rivet, New York, December 16, 1943, NAF 28150 (181), BnF.

213. Ibid.

214. Lévi-Strauss to Rivet, New York, September 21, 1943, NAF 28150 (181), BnF.

215. For more, see François Héran, "De Granet à Lévi-Strauss: 1. L'échange à sense unique," *Social Anthropology* 6, no. 1 (1998): 1–60; "De Granet à Lévi-Strauss: 2. Le doute et le double," *Social Anthropology* 6, no. 2 (1998): 169–201; "De Granet à Lévi-Strauss: 3. La légende du Hollandais volé," *Social Anthropology* 6, no. 3 (1998): 309–30.

216. Claude Lévi-Strauss, *The Elementary Structures of Kinship*, trans. James Harle Bell and John Richard von Sturmer (Oxford: Beacon Press, 1969), xxiii.

217. The importance of such marriage preferences for Lévi-Strauss's thought is dutifully explained, in layman's terms, in Dosse, *History of Structuralism*, 1:20.

218. Lévi-Strauss, *Elementary Structures of Kinship*, xxiv.

219. Lévi-Strauss, *Elementary Structures of Kinship*, xxiii.

220. See Godelier, *Metamorphoses of Kinship*, 10–13.

221. Thomas Trautmann, *Lewis Henry Morgan and the Invention of Kinship* (Berkeley: University of California Press, 1987).

222. Lévi-Strauss, "The Social and Psychological Aspects of Chieftainship," 17.

223. Ibid., 19.

224. Lévi-Strauss, *Elementary Structures of Kinship*, xxiii.

225. For an extended discussion of these distinctions for both Lévi-Strauss and

Durkheim, see Raymond Jamous, "Élémentaire, complexe: De certaines formes d'explication en anthropologie," *European Journal of Sociology* 40, no. 2 (1999): 279–303.

226. Lévi-Strauss to Rivet, New York, August 3, 1945, NAF 28150 (181), BnF.

227. Lévi-Strauss, *Les structures élémentaires*, 279–86; Lévi-Strauss, *Elementary Structures*, 221–29.

228. Embassy of the French Republic in Brazil to the Brazilian Ministry of Foreign Affairs, Rio de Janeiro, March 28, 1944, França, Notas Recebidas, 1943–44, 84/4/4, Arquivo Histórico do Itamaraty, Rio de Janeiro.

229. "The moiety system is a more unusual form of unilineal descent and involves the occurrence of descent groups in linked pairs which assume complementary positions and functions. Each moiety (or half) of a pair will almost always be exogamous and take its husbands and wives exclusively from the matched group." Brian Schwimmer, "Moieties," University of Manitoba tutorial, accessed March 20, 2018, https://www.umanitoba.ca/faculties/arts/anthropology/tutor/descent/unilineal/moiety.html.

230. Lévi-Strauss, *Elementary Structures of Kinship*, 75.

231. Ibid., 459.

232. Marcel Mauss, "Essai sur le don," in *Sociologie et anthropologie* (Paris: Presses universitaires de France, 1985), 228.

233. Claude Lévi-Strauss, "Introduction à l'oeuvre de Marcel Mauss," in Mauss, *Sociologie et anthropologie*, xxxiii.

234. Maurice Godelier analyzes Freud's arguments, especially those of *Totem and Taboo*, alongside those of *The Elementary Structures*. Godelier, *Metamorphoses of Kinship*, 391–430. Although Lévi-Strauss does not cite her, it is worth noting Leslie White's article "The Definition and Prohibition of Incest," *American Anthropologist* 50 (1948): 416–34.

235. Translation used from Godelier, *Metamorphoses of Kinship*, 408.

236. Lévi-Strauss, *The Elementary Structures*, 136.

237. Godelier, *Metamorphoses of Kinship*, 404.

238. See Camille Robcis, *The Law of Kinship: Anthropology, Psychoanalysis, and the Family in France* (Ithaca, NY: Cornell University Press, 2013), esp. 62.

239. Godelier, *Metamorphoses of Kinship*, 410.

240. Claude Lévi-Strauss, "New York post- et préfiguratif," in Lévi-Strauss, *Le regard éloigné* (Paris: Plon, 1983); Emmanuelle Loyer, *Paris à New York: Intellectuels et artistes français en exil (1940–1947)* (Paris: Éditions Grasset et Fasquelle, 2005), 134–35, 161–62; Claude Imbert, "Les itinéraires urbains de Claude Lévi-Strauss," *Les temps modernes* 3 no. 628 (2004): 24–36; Debaene, "Like Alice through the Looking Glass."

241. Laurent Jeanpierre, "Les Structures d'une Pensée d'Éxilé: La formation du structuralisme de Claude Lévi-Strauss," *French Politics, Culture, and Society* 28, no.1 (2010): 58–76.

242. For a definition of "habitus," see Pierre Bourdieu, *Outline of a Theory of Practice*, trans. Richard Nice (Cambridge: Cambridge University Press, 1977), 72–95.

243. Rivet to Lévi-Strauss, Bogotá, October 25, 1941, NAF 28150 (200), BnF.

244. Alice Conklin, *In the Museum of Man: Race, Anthropology, and Empire in France, 1850–1950* (Ithaca, NY: Cornell University Press, 2013), 282–326. See also Daniel Fabre, "L'ethnologie française à la croisée des engagements (1940–1945)," in *Résistants et résistance*, ed. Jean-Yves Boursier (Paris: L'Harmattan, 1997), and Marc Knobel, "L'ethnologue à la dérive: Montandon et l'ethnoracisme," *Ethnologie française* 18, no. 2 (1988): 107–13.

245. Claude Lévi-Strauss, *Structural Anthropology*, trans. Claire Jacobsen and Brooke Grundfest Schoepf (Garden City, NY: Anchor Books, 1967), 354–56; Philippe Descola, "Claude Lévi-Strauss, une présentation," *La lettre du Collège de France*, hors-série 2 (2008): 4–8, http://lettre-cdf.revues.org/210.

246. Leach, "Claude Lévi-Strauss," 14.

247. Lévi-Strauss to Mauss, New York, October 2, 1944, transcribed by Hugo Suppo, NAF 28150 (181), BnF.

248. Ibid. This would be published as Lévi-Strauss, *La vie familiale et sociale des Indiens Nambikwara* (Paris: Société des Américanistes, 1948).

249. Lévi-Strauss to Mauss, New York, October 2, 1944. The same letter is cited in Emmanuelle Loyer, *Claude Lévi-Strauss* (Paris: Flammarion, 2015), 306.

250. Loyer, *Lévi-Strauss*, 341. For more on Georges Gurvitch and his relations with Durkheimian thought, see Jean-Christophe Marcel, "Georges Gurvitch: Les raisons d'un succès," *Cahiers internationaux de sociologie* 1, no. 110 (2001): 97–119. For more on Lévi-Strauss's conflicts with Gurvitch, see Laurent Jeanpierre, "Une opposition structurante pour l'anthropologie structurale: Lévi-Strauss contre Gurvitch, la guerre de deux exilés français aux États-Unis," *Revue d'histoire des sciences humaines* 2, no. 11 (2004): 13–44.

CHAPTER FIVE

1. For an anthropologist's perspective, see Lilia Schwarcz, "História e etnologia: Lévi-Strauss e os embates em região de fronteira," *Revista de antropologia* 42, no. 1–2 (1999): 199–222. For a historian's, see François Hartog, "Le regard éloigné: Lévi-Strauss et l'histoire," in *Claude Lévi-Strauss*, ed. Michel Izard (Paris: Éditions de l'Herne, 2004), 313–19.

2. For more on this period in São Paulo, see Maria Arminda do Nascimento Arruda, *Metrópole e cultura: São Paulo no meio século XX* (São Paulo: Edusp, 2015).

3. FB; Archive Roger Bastide, IMEC.

4. Herrick Chapman refers to the period 1944–62 as the "long reconstruction." Chapman, *France's Long Reconstruction: In Search of the Modern Republic* (Cambridge, MA: Harvard University Press, 2018).

5. For the development of empirical sociology in France, mostly based out of the CNRS, see Johan Heilbron, *French Sociology* (Ithaca, NY: Cornell University Press, 2015), 135–48. Heilbron argues that for most empirical sociologists in this period, travel and study in the United States served as a kind of rite of passage. This, too, was the case for François Perroux, whose Institut des Sciences Économiques et Mathématiques Appliquées (ISEMA) depended on American foundations; see Giuliana Gemelli, "U.S. Foundations and Braudel's Institution Building," *Review* (Fernand Braudel Center) 24, no. 1 (2001): 63. This, of course, did not prevent Perroux from developing his own kind of economic analysis, centered on lesser-developed countries, and even serving as a mentor for the Brazilian economist Celso Furtado. See, for example, Alain Alcouffe, "Furtado, le Brésil et les économistes français: Influences croisées" (2008), https://hal.archives-ouvertes.fr/hal-01154453/document.

6. Angela Lühning, ed., *Verger/Bastide: Dimensões de uma amizade* (Rio de Janeiro: Bertrand Brasil, 2002). See also Roger Bastide and Pierre Verger, *Diálogo entre Filhos de Xangô: Correspondência, 1947–1974*, ed. Françoise Morin (São Paulo: Edusp, 2017).

7. Bastide to Braudel, São Paulo, May 13, 1950, FB.

8. For more on the *épuration*, see François Rouquet, *Une épuration ordinaire (1944–1949): Petits et grands collaborateurs de l'administration française* (Paris: CNRS Éditions, 2011); Claude Singer, *L'université libérée, l'université épurée (1943–1947)* (Paris: Belles Lettres, 1997); Henri Rousso, "L'épuration en France: Une histoire inachevée," *Vingtième siècle* 33 (1992): 78–105; Peter Novick, *The Resistance versus Vichy: The Purge of Collaborators in Liberated France* (London: Chatto & Windus, 1968).

9. Hugo Rogélio Suppo, "La politique culturelle française au Brésil entre les années 1920–1950" (PhD diss., Paris III-Sorbonne Nouvelle, 1999), 817.

10. "Musée de l'Homme, Institut Français des Hautes Études Brésiliennes, Séance Inaugurale et Status," pamphlet, Arquivo Paulo Duarte, Universidade Estadual de Campinas, Campinas (henceforth PD).

11. Lucien Febvre, "Un champ privilegié d'études: L'Amérique du Sud," *Annales d'histoire économique et sociale* 1, no. 2 (1929).

12. This section is largely indebted to Guy Martinière, "L'école des *Annales* et les Amériques Latines (1929–1949)," in *Aspects de la coopération franco-brésilienne: Transplantation culturelle et stratégie de la modernité* (Grenoble: Presses universitaires de Grenoble / Éditions de la Maison des sciences de l'homme, 1984). For Braudel's review of Freyre's work, see "À travers un continent d'histoire: Le Brésil et l'oeuvre de Gilberto Freyre," *Mélanges d'histoire sociale* 4 (1943): 3–20.

13. Fernand Braudel, "Au Brésil: Deux livres de Caio Prado," *Annales ESC* 3, no. 1 (1948): 99–103; Braudel, "Monnaies et civilisations: De l'or du Soudan à l'argent d'Amérique; Un drame méditerranéen," *Annales ESC* 1, no. 1 (1946): 9–22; "L'Amérique du Sud devant l'histoire," special issue, *Annales ESC* 3, no. 4 (1948).

14. Braudel quoted in Paulo Teixeira Iumatti, "Historiographical and Conceptual Exchange between Fernand Braudel and Caio Prado Jr. in the 1930s and 1940s: A Case

of Unequal Positions in the Intellectual Space between Brazil and France," trans. Ian Merkel, *Storia della storiografia* 71, no. 1 (2017): 99.

15. Braudel to Prado, Paris, November 8, 1945, CPJ-CP-BRAU002a, IEB-USP.

16. Ibid.

17. Braudel to Prado, Paris, May 6, 1946, CPJ-CP-BRAU003a, IEB-USP.

18. Prado to Freyre, São Paulo, March 2, 1940, GF; Freyre to Prado, Recife, April 3, 1940, IEB-USP, CPJ-CP-FREY001.

19. Braudel to Prado, Paris, May 6, 1946, CPJ-CP-BRAU003a, IEB-USP.

20. Braudel to Prado, Paris, August 6, 1946, CPJ-CP-BRAU004, IEB-USP.

21. For more, see Iumatti, "Historiographical and Conceptual Exchange."

22. Braudel to Freyre, Paris, November 8, 1945, GF; Braudel to Prado, Paris, August 6, 1946, CPJ-CP-BRAU004, IEB-USP.

23. Pierre Monbeig, "Économie ou économies brésiliennes," *Annales ESC* 2, no. 2 (1947): 171.

24. Ibid.

25. Ibid., 173.

26. Ibid., 174.

27. Ibid., 175.

28. One should also note the presence of Argentine and Mexican authors such as Fernando Marquez Miranda and Silvio Zavala in the issue. With regard to the Argentines, see, for example, Fernando Devoto, "Itinerario de un problema: 'Annales' y la historiografia argentina (1929–1965)," *Anuario del IEHS*, no. 10 (1995); for the Mexicans, see Carlos Antonio Aguirre Rojas, *Los Annales y la historiografia latinoamericana* (Mexico: UNAM, 1993).

29. Lucien Febvre, "Introduction: L'Amérique du Sud devant l'histoire," *Annales ESC* 3, no. 4 (1948): 385–92.

30. Ibid., 388.

31. Paul Rivet, "Sur l'Amérique latine: Propos d'un ami," *Annales ESC* 3, no. 4 (1948): 393–400.

32. Ibid., 394–95.

33. Ibid., 396.

34. José Vasconcelos, *La raza cósmica* (Mexico City: Espasa Calpe SA, 1948).

35. Rivet, "Sur l'Amérique latine," 398.

36. Ibid.

37. Ibid., 400.

38. Roger Bastide, "Dans les Amériques noires: Afrique ou Europe?," *Annales ESC* 3, no. 4 (1948): 409–26.

39. Ibid., 410.

40. Febvre in ibid., 409.

41. Ibid., 410.

42. Ibid., 417. The article in which Frazier made the cited argument is "The Negro Family in Bahia, Brazil," *American Sociological Review* 7, no. 4 (1942): 465–78.

43. Bastide, "Dans les Amériques noires," 418.

44. Ibid., 426.

45. Ibid. For more on the correspondences between Christianity and candomblé, see Bastide, "Contribuição ao estudo do sincretismo católico-fetichista."

46. Fernand Braudel, "Le jeu des portraits: La règle du jeu," *Annales ESC* 3, no. 4 (1948): 437–38. The cited article is Roger Bastide, "La psychologie ethnique en Amérique du Sud," *Revue de psychologie des peuples*, no. 1 (1948): 27–38.

47. Fernand Braudel, "Antilles et Amérique," *Annales ESC* 3, no. 4 (1948): 537.

48. Fernand Braudel, "L'Amérique latine noyée dans l'unité américaine?," *Annales ESC* 3, no. 4 (1948): 460.

49. Émile Coornaert and Fernand Braudel, "Aux origines du Brésil du Nord et du centre," *Annales ESC*, 3, no. 4 (1948): 529, 530.

50. Ibid., 530.

51. Ibid.

52. Fernand Braudel, "Du Potosí à Buenos Aires: Une route clandestine de l'argent," *Annales ESC* 3, no. 4 (1948): 550.

53. See, e.g., Pierre Chaunu, "Une île continentale: La Colombie," 447–49, and Frédéric Mauro, "À Saint-Domingue au XVIIIᵉ siècle," 532–36, both in *Annales ESC* 3, no. 4 (1948).

54. Brigitte Mazon, *Aux origines de l'EHESS: Le role du mécénat américain (1920–1960)* (Paris: Cerf, 1988). Gemelli, "U.S. Foundations and Braudel's Institution Building."

55. Devoto, "Itinerario de un problema," 162.

56. Gurvitch was so singularly important in this period that Francis Farrugia's book almost reads as an intellectual biography. Farrugia, *La reconstruction de la sociologie française (1945–1965)* (Paris: L'Harmattan, 2000).

57. Simões to Braudel, São Paulo, September 10, 1949, FB.

58. Ibid.

59. It is likely that Febvre and Camus met at "Causeries du mardi" (Tuesday talks), promoted by the French foreign service (Suppo, "La politique culturelle française," 767). Febvre's private archive contains a photo of him and Camus, in Rio or the vicinity thereof (Brazil Folder, EHESS-LF).

60. Lucien Febvre, "Vers une autre histoire," *Revue de métaphysique et de morale* 54, no. 3/4 (1949): 225–47.

61. Ibid., 246.

62. Bastide to Braudel, São Paulo, June 19, 1949, FB.

63. "Carnet Brésil" (Brazil notebook), pp. 82–83, EHESS-LF.

64. Febvre to Freyre, São Paulo, September 16, 1949, GF.

65. Simões to Braudel, São Paulo, September 10, 1949, FB.

66. Lucien Febvre, "O homem do século XVI," *Revista de história* 1, no. 1 (1950): 3–17.

67. Ibid., 3.

68. This is according to Lévi-Strauss's memory of Célestin Bouglé. Claude Lévi-Strauss, *Tristes Tropiques*, trans. John Weightman and Doreen Weightman (New York: Penguin, 1992), 47.

69. Charles Morazé, *Un historien engagé: Mémoires* (Paris: Fayard, 2007), esp. 208–22; Morazé, *Les trois âges du Brésil* (Paris: Armand Colin, 1954).

70. Bastide to Miguel Reale, São Paulo, March 7, 1950, BST2.C5-01, IMEC.

71. Bastide to Braudel, São Paulo, May 13, 1950, FB.

72. Febvre to Bastide, Paris, August 10, 1950, BST1.C1.02, IMEC.

73. Febvre to Bastide, Paris, November 16, 1951, BST1.C1.02, IMEC.

74. Braudel to Bastide, Paris, October 22, 1951, FB.

75. Febvre to Bastide, Paris, November 16, 1951, BST1.C1.02, IMEC.

76. Braudel to Bastide, Paris, October 22, 1951, FB.

77. Braudel to Bastide, Paris, February 14, 1951, FB.

78. Lévi-Strauss to Braudel, Paris, November 1, 1948, FB.

79. Emmanuelle Loyer, *Claude Lévi-Strauss* (Paris: Flammarion, 2015), 361.

80. Lévi-Strauss to Braudel, Paris, June 20 and 21, 1949, FB.

81. Lévi-Strauss to Braudel, Paris, June 9, 1951, FB.

82. Lévi-Strauss to Braudel, Paris, October 25, 1948, FB; Claude Lévi-Strauss, "Histoire et ethnologie," *Revue de métaphysique et de morale* 54, no. 3/4 (1949): 363–91.

83. Gurvitch to Braudel, Antibes, September 23, 1949, FB.

84. Braudel to Cruz Costa, Paris, March 20, 1952, FB.

85. Braudel to Simões, Paris, n.d., FB.

86. Fernanda Arêas Peixoto, "Franceses e norte-americanos nas ciências sociais brasileiras (1930–1960)," in *História das ciências sociais no Brasil*, vol. 1, ed. Sergio Miceli et al. (São Paulo: Vértice, 1989), 458.

87. Georges Gurvitch, "Continuité et discontinuité en histoire et en sociologie," *Annales ESC* 12, no. 1 (1957): 73–84.

88. Braudel to Simões, Paris, May 28, 1952, FB.

89. Simões to Braudel, São Paulo, June 9, 1952, FB.

90. Pierre Monbeig, *Pionniers et planteurs* (Paris: Armand Colin, 1952); Monbeig, "La croissance de la ville de São Paulo," *Revue de géographie alpine* 41, no. 1 (1953): 59–97; Monbeig, "La croissance de la ville de São Paulo (suite et fin)," *Revue de géographie alpine* 41, no. 2 (1953): 261–309; Lucien Febvre, "Pierre Monbeig, 'La croissance de la ville de São Paulo,'" *Annales ESC* 10, no. 3 (1955): 463–64; Monbeig, *Le Brésil* (Paris: Presses Universitaires, 1954).

91. Jacques Lambert, *Le Brésil: Structure sociale et institutions politiques* (Paris:

Armand Colin, 1953); Roger Bastide, "Trois livres sur le Brésil," *Revue française de science politique* 5, no. 1 (1955): 110–18.

92. Roger Bastide, "A. Carneiro Leão, panorama sociologique du Brésil," *Annales ESC* 8, no. 3 (1953): 410.

93. For more on Amado's French reception, see Jean-Yves Mérian, "Jorge Amado dans la collection 'La Croix du Sud' de Roger Caillois," *Amerika* 10 (2014), http:// amerika.revues.org/4992.

94. See Patrick Wilcken, *Claude Lévi-Strauss: The Poet in the Laboratory* (London: Bloomsbury, 2010), 205–8; Loyer, *Lévi-Strauss*, 424–28. Vincent Debaene's work remains the deepest literary analysis of *Tristes Tropiques*, making parallels with other "second books" by French ethnologists, especially Michel Leiris's *Afrique fantôme*. Debaene, *Far Afield: French Anthropology between Science and Literature* (Chicago: University of Chicago Press, 2014).

95. Nathan Wachtel, "*Saudade.* De la sensibilité lévi-straussienne," in *Claude Lévi-Strauss,* ed. Michel Izard, Cahiers de L'Herne 82, (Paris: Éditions de L'Herne, 2004), 442–55. See also Lévi-Strauss, *Saudades do Brasil* (Paris: Plon, 1994).

96. Claude Lévi-Strauss, *Structural Anthropology,* trans. Claire Jacobsen and Brooke Grundfest Schoepf (Garden City, NY: Anchor Books, 1967).

97. Monbeig, "La croissance de la ville de São Paulo," 59. See, among others, Warren Dean, *The Industrialization of São Paulo, 1880–1945* (Austin: University of Texas Press, 2012), and, recently, Bruno de Macedo Zorek, "O futuro de São Paulo na década de 1950" (PhD diss., University of Campinas, 2019).

98. Braudel to Cruz Costa, Paris, March 20, 1952, FB.

99. I thank Marianne Hano (Monbeig) for access to this book. Archive Pierre Monbeig, Paris.

100. Lévi-Strauss, *Tristes Tropiques*, 325–26.

101. Ibid., 38.

102. Ibid.

103. Ibid., 95–126.

104. Ibid., 326.

105. Bastide to Fernandes, Paris, January 7, 1950, Fundo Florestan Fernandes, Arquivos da Universidade Federal de São Carlos (henceforth UFSCar-FF); Florestan Fernandes, *A função social da guerra na sociedade Tupinambá* (São Paulo: Universidade de São Paulo, 1951).

106. Jean Cazeneuve, "Tristes tropiques: les leçons d'un voyage philosophique," *Annales ESC* 13, no. 4 (1958): 781–86.

107. Lévi-Strauss, *Tristes Tropiques*, 314–16. For a discussion of Lévi-Strauss's reading of Rousseau, see Stefanos Geroulanos, *Transparency in Postwar France: A Critical History of the Present* (Stanford, CA: Stanford University Press, 2017), 267–81.

108. Lévi-Strauss, *Tristes Tropiques*, 317.

109. Ibid., 17.

110. Ibid., 23.

111. Theodor Adorno, "Cultural Criticism and Society," in *Prisms*, trans. Samuel and Shierry Weber (Cambridge, MA: Mit Press, 1983), 34.

112. Lévi-Strauss, *Tristes Tropiques*, 321.

113. Ibid.

114. Ibid., 20. In the years leading up to the publication of *Tristes Tropiques*, a number of students of the École Normale Supérieure, including Foucault, visited Sainte-Anne. Foucault even held an "internship" there. Dider Eribon, *Michel Foucault* (Paris: Champs, 2011), 75–88.

115. Lévi-Strauss, *Tristes Tropiques*, 415.

116. Lévi-Strauss, *La vie familiale et sociale des Indiens Nambikwara* (Paris: Société des Américanistes, 1948).

117. Pierre Monbeig, "Les Indiens Nambikwara du Mato Grosso d'après M. Claude Lévi-Strauss," *Annales de géographie* 60 (1951): 379.

118. Marie-Vic Ozouf-Marignier, "Un domínio contestado: A geografia psicológica no tempo de Pierre Monbeig," in *Pierre Monbeig e a geografia humana brasileira: A dinâmica da transformação*, ed. Heliana Angotti Salgueiro (Paris: EDUSC, 2006).

119. Sérgio Buarque de Holanda, *Raízes do Brasil* (1936; São Paulo: Companhia das Letras, 1995), 43.

120. Lévi-Strauss to Braudel, December 22, 1948, FB; Sérgio Buarque de Holanda, "Au Brésil colonial: Les civilisations du miel," *Annales ESC* 5, no. 1 (1950): 78–81.

121. Lévi-Strauss, *Tristes Tropiques*, 351–52.

122. Roger Bastide, "Lévi-Strauss ou l'ethnographe 'à la recherché du temps perdu,'" *Présence africaine*, no. 7 (1956): 150.

123. Ibid.

124. Ibid., 152.

125. Ibid.

126. Lévi-Strauss to Bastide, June 30, 1956, BST2. C1-03, IMEC.

127. Febvre to Lévi-Strauss, Paris, October 29, 1955, NAF 28150 (190), BnF.

128. See Robert Mandrou's note in Cazeneuve, "Tristes tropiques," 781n1.

129. Fernand Braudel, "Histoire et sciences sociales: La longue durée," *Annales ESC* 13, no. 4 (1958): 725–53; translated by Immanuel Wallerstein as "History and the Social Sciences: The *Longue Durée*," *Review* (Fernand Braudel Center) 32, no. 2 (2009): 171–203.

130. Braudel to Lévi-Strauss, Paris, January 10, 1956, FB.

131. Roger Bastide, "Colloque sur le mot 'Structure,'" *Annales ESC* 14, no. 2 (1959): 351–52. The conference took place January 10–12, 1958, at the 6th section of the École Pratique des Hautes Études.

132. Roger Bastide, ed., *Sens et usages du terme structure* (La Haye: Mouton, 1962), 139.

133. Braudel, "Histoire et sciences sociales," 730–31.

134. Claude Lévi-Strauss, "Introduction: History and Anthropology," chap. 1 in Lévi-Strauss, *Structural Anthropology*; Lévi-Strauss, "Histoire et ethnologie," *Revue de métaphysique et de morale* 54, no. 3/4 (1949): 363–91.

135. Lévi-Strauss, *Structural Anthropology*, 6.

136. Ibid., 18.

137. Ibid., 19.

138. Ibid., 22.

139. For an extended discussion of Lévi-Strauss and history, see Francine Iegelski, *Astronomia das constelações humanas: Reflexões sobre Claude Lévi-Strauss e a história* (São Paulo: Humanitas, 2016).

140. Lévi-Strauss, *Structural Anthropology*, 24.

141. Lucien Febvre, *The Problem of Unbelief in the Sixteenth Century: The Religion of Rabelais*, trans. Beatrice Gottlieb (Cambridge, MA: Harvard University Press, 1985).

142. Lévi-Strauss, *Structural Anthropology*, 24, 26.

143. Schwarcz, "História e etnologia," 209–12.

144. Braudel, "Histoire et sciences sociales," 725.

145. Ibid., 725–26.

146. Lévi-Strauss's cited response to Caillois was Lévi-Strauss, "Diogène couché," *Les temps modernes* 110 (1955): 1217. For more on the Lévi-Strauss–Caillois debate, see Loyer, *Lévi-Strauss*, 404–8.

147. Braudel, "Histoire et sciences sociales," 737. For more on Lévi-Strauss's efforts at UNESCO to advance mathematical models in the social sciences, see Lévi-Strauss, "Les mathématiques de l'homme," in *Bulletin international des sciences sociales* 6, no. 4, 643–53.

148. Braudel, "Histoire et sciences sociales," 736.

149. Ibid., 746.

150. Tiré à part de Lévi-Strauss (Lévi-Strauss's complementary copies), TLS.3609, Archives du Laboratoire d'anthropologie sociale (henceforth LAS).

151. Lévi-Strauss to Braudel, Paris, October 26, 1958, FB.

152. Lévi-Strauss to Braudel, Paris, February 1, 1959, NAF 28150 (181), BnF.

153. Braudel to Lévi-Strauss, Paris, February 9, 1959, NAF 28150 (185), BnF.

154. Lévi-Strauss, "Leçon inaugurale au Collège de France 5 janvier 1960," *La lettre du Collège de France*, hors-série 2 (2008): 56–57, http://journals.openedition.org/lettre-cdf/232.

155. Bastide to Duarte, Paris, December 25, 1959, Documentos Especiais de Pessoas, Pasta (DEP. 18), PD.

156. Lévi-Strauss, "Leçon inaugurale au Collège de France."

157. Roger Bastide, *The African Religions of Brazil. Toward a Sociology of the Interpenetration of Cultures*, trans. Helen Sebba (Baltimore: Johns Hopkins University Press, 2007).

158. Ibid., 28. For more on Bastide's choice to go native or at least claim to, see Peter Fry, "Gallus africanus est, ou como Roger Bastide se tornou africano no Brasil," in *Revisitando a terra de contrastes: A atualidade da obra de Roger Bastide*, ed. Olga Moraes Von Simon and Maria Isaura Pereira de Queiroz (São Paulo, USP-FFLCH-CERU, 1986).

159. Claude Lévi-Strauss, *Wild Thought: A New Translation of "La pensée sauvage"*, trans. Jeffrey Mehlman and John Leavitte (Chicago: University of Chicago Press, 2020).

CHAPTER SIX

1. This chapter is a slightly modified version of an article that appeared as "Brazilian Race Relations, French Social Scientists, and African Decolonization: A Transatlantic History of the Idea of Miscegenation," *Modern Intellectual History* 17, no. 3 (2020): 801–32.

2. Fernand Braudel, "À travers un continent d'histoire: Le Brésil et l'oeuvre de Gilberto Freyre," *Mélanges d'histoire sociale* 4 (1943): 3.

3. Roland Barthes, "Maîtres et esclaves de Gilberto Freyre," *Lettres nouvelles* 1 (1953): 107.

4. This chapter builds on growing historiography on France's twentieth century that has emphasized the openings and closings of imperial politics during the postwar period as well as the noninevitability of decolonization in the form of the nation-state. See, among others, Todd Shepard, *The Invention of Decolonization: The Algerian War and the Remaking of France* (Ithaca, NY: Cornell University Press, 2008); Gary Wilder, *Freedom Time: Negritude, Decolonization, and the Future of the World* (Durham, NC, 2015); Frederick Cooper, *Citizenship between Empire and Nation: Remaking France and French Africa, 1945–1960* (Princeton, NJ: Princeton University Press, 2016). While I tend to agree with Michael Goebel that we should not overemphasize these possibilities, it is clear that for those who sought to preserve European empires in the postwar period, new combinations of assimilation and association proved quite appealing. Goebel, "'The Capital of Men without a Country': Migrants and Anticolonialism in Interwar Paris," *American Historical Review* 121, no. 5 (2016): 1466.

5. Luiz Felipe de Alencastro was among the first to critically analyze the ideological and geopolitical uses of *mestiçagem* (*métissage*) in his article "Geopolítica da mestiçagem," *Novos estudos* 11 (1985): 49–63. Freyre's particular version of luso-tropicalism and his relation to Salazarist intellectuals have been analyzed by Omar Ribeiro Thomaz, "Do saber colonial ao lusotropicalismo: 'Raça' e 'nação' nas primeiras décadas do Salazarismo," in *Raça, ciência e sociedade*, ed. Marco Chor Maio and Ricardo Ventura Santos (Rio de Janeiro, 1996), 101–4. See also Lorenzo Macagno, "Um antropólogo norte-americano no 'mundo que o português criou': Relações raciais no Brasil e Moçambique segundo Marvin Harris," *Lusotopie* 6 (1999): 143–61. For a more state-centered history of Brazil's relation to African decolonization, see Jerry Dávila, *Hotel*

Trópico: Brazil and the Challenge of African Decolonization, 1950–1980 (Durham, NC: Duke University Press, 2010), esp. 11–26 and 108–10.

6. For the most up-to-date literature, see the special issue "New Perspectives on Luso-tropicalism / Novas Perspetivas sobre o Luso-tropicalismo" of the *Portuguese Studies Review* 26, no. 1 (2018), and the edited volume *Luso-tropicalism and Its Discontents: The Making and Unmaking of Racial Exceptionalism*, ed. Warwick Anderson, Ricardo Roque, and Ricardo Ventura Santos (New York: Berghahn Books, 2019).

7. Colóquio de Cerisy, Pasta FR 1956, GF. For a pioneering article on this theme, see Cibele Barbosa, "*Casa grande e senzala*: A questão racial e o 'colonialismo esclarecido' na França do Pós-Segunda Guerra Mundial," *Revista brasileira de ciências sociais* 33, no. 96 (2018): 1–16.

8. In the following paragraphs, *mestiçagem* will be used as a noun for racial mixing, *mestiço* as its product (i.e., a mixed-race person), and *mestiçamente* as a created adverb that means similar to or by way of *mestiçagem*.

9. Gilberto Freyre, *O mundo que o Português criou* (Rio de Janeiro: José Olympio, 1940), 45–46. This book is a set of published lectures delivered by Freyre in England and in Portugal, patronized by the Brazilian government.

10. Gilberto Freyre, *Tempo morto e outros tempos* (Rio de Janeiro: José Olympio, 1975), 32–33. For more on Freyre's time in Texas, see Lúcia G. Pallares-Burke and Peter Burke, *Gilberto Freyre: Social Theory in the Tropics* (Oxford: Peter Lang, 2008), 24–25.

11. Joan W. Scott, "The Evidence of Experience," *Critical Inquiry* 17, no. 4 (1991): 794. One might wonder, for example, if Freyre's "memories" are, more than his own, those of American writers whom he likely read around the time, especially considering his well-known tendency for exaggeration and self-aggrandizement. See, e.g., Elizabeth Freeman, "The Waco Horror," supplement to the *Crisis* (July 1916), reprinted in *Witnessing Lynching: American Writers Respond*, ed. Anne P. Rice (New Brunswick, NJ: Rutgers University Press, 2003), 141–50.

12. For a history of black intellectuals' formulations of racial democracy prior to and concomitant with those of Freyre, see Paulina Alberto, *Terms of Inclusion: Black Intellectuals in Twentieth-Century Brazil* (Chapel Hill: University of North Carolina Press, 2011), esp. 178–81. For the *Estado Novo* and international representations, see Jessica Graham, "Question raciale, production culturelle et image démocratique du Brésil pendant la Seconde Guerre mondiale," *Brésil(s)* 13 (2018), http://journals.openedition.org/bresils/2569.

13. "Mestre Metraux em Salvador da Bahia," *O Cruzeiro*, September 8, 1951, article 161, GF.

14. The word "Latindade" or "Latinité" (English: Latinity) is frequent in both Freyre's discourse and that of his French interlocutors with strong connections to the Right. See Chelsea Stieber, "Gérard de Catalogne, passeur transatlantique du maurrassisme entre Haïti et la France," in *Doctrinaires, vulgarisateurs et passeurs des droits radicales au XXe siècle*, ed. Olivier Dard (Bern, Peter Lang, 2012), 233–54. Here and

perhaps more generally in the postwar period, the word seems to be used as a proxy for anything anti-"Anglo-Saxon."

15. Barthes, "Maîtres et esclaves de Gilberto Freyre," 108.

16. For more on this question, see, among others, Emmanuelle Saada, *Les enfants de la colonie: Les métis de l'émpire français entre sujétion et citoyenneté* (Paris: La Découverte, 2007). Based on the period and geography, Owen White's *Children of the French Empire: Miscegenation and Colonial Society in French West Africa, 1895–1960* (Oxford: Oxford University Press, 1999) and Hilary Jones's *The Métis of Senegal: Urban Life and Politics in French West Africa* (Bloomington: Indiana University Press, 2013) are most relevant here.

17. Brazilian historians and sociologists have emphasized the tense, and often conflicting, relationship that Freyre had with USP. In particular, see Joaquim Falcão, "A luta pelo trono: Gilberto Freyre versus USP," in *O imperador das idéias: Gilberto Freyre em questão*, ed. Joaquim Falcão and Rosa Maria Barboza de Araújo (Rio de Janeiro: Topbooks, 2001), 131–67. See also Carlos Guilherme Mota, *História e contra-história: Perfis e contrapontos* (São Paulo: Globo, 2010), 167–84.

18. Paul Arbousse-Bastide, preface to *Um engenheiro francês no Brasil*, by Gilberto Freyre (Rio de Janeiro: José Olympio, 1940), 2.

19. Cibele Barbosa, "Le Brésil entre le mythe et l'idéal: La réception de l'oeuvre de Gilberto Freyre en France dans l'après-guerre" (PhD diss., Sorbonne, 2011), esp. 138.

20. "Carnet Brésil" (Brazil notebook), p. 3, EHESS-LF.

21. Gilberto Freyre, "O professor Febvre no Brasil," *O Cruzeiro*, September 10, 1949, article 56, GF.

22. Febvre to Freyre, São Paulo, September 16, 1949, GF.

23. A detailed itinerary can be found in the "Carnet Brésil" (Brazil notebook), EHESS-LF. Febvre's trip seems to have lasted from mid-July through early October of 1949. In Rio, Febvre had on his agenda "Ministre de l'Éducation," "Itamaraty," and lectures at the "École de Guerre" and the "Faculté de Lettres"; among his more informal commitments were meetings with the conservative editor Augusto Frederico Schmidt and the scientists Carlos Chagas and Olympio da Fonseca Filho. Febvre also attended Albert Camus's lecture in Rio and met with Gabrielle Mineur from the French foreign service. Febvre, "Carnet Brésil," 3–4.

24. Febvre to Freyre, Paris, September 18, 1949, GF. "Pernambucan" means from the state of Pernambuco, of which Recife is the capital.

25. I thank Thomas Rogers for this clarification.

26. *Bumba-meu-boi* is a folk theatrical tradition most associated with Brazil's North and Northeast, especially the state of Maranhão. The religious and cultural content vary regionally, but all *bumba-meu-boi* are based around the figure of the *boi*, or cow, and share *brincantes*—music, dance, song, and theater as fundamental aspects. "Bumba-meu-boi," Centro Nacional de Folclore et Cultura Popular, accessed March 16, 2018, http://www.cnfcp.gov.br/interna.php?ID_Secao=103.

27. Febvre to Freyre, Rio de Janeiro, September 18, 1949, GF.

28. Febvre to Bastide, Paris, October 10, 1950, BST1.C1.02, IMEC.

29. For more on the intellectual currents shared between Freyre and the *Annales*, see Peter Burke, "Gilberto Freyre e a *nova história*," *Tempo social* 9, no. 2 (1997): 1–12.

30. Gurvitch to "Mon Cher Ami" [Freyre], Paris, June 1, 1952, GF.

31. Lucien Febvre, "Brésil, terre d'histoire," preface to *Maîtres et esclaves: La formation de la société brésilienne*, trans. Roger Bastide (Paris: Gallimard, 1952), 13–14.

32. Febvre, "Brésil, terre d'histoire," 15.

33. Ibid., 17.

34. Ibid.

35. Ibid.

36. Ibid., 18.

37. Ibid.

38. Ibid., 19–20.

39. Lucien Febvre and François Crouzet, *Nous sommes des sang-mêlés: Manuel d'histoire de la civilization française* (Paris: Albin Michel, 2012).

40. Gurvitch to Bastide, Paris, November 16, 1948, BST2.C1.02, IMEC; Gurvitch to Freyre, Paris, January 19, 1952, GF.

41. Gurvitch to Freyre, Paris, April 4, 1952, GF. The book was Gilberto Freyre, *Um brasileiro em terras portuguêsas: Introdução a uma possível luso-tropicologia, acompanhada de conferências e discursos proferidos em Portugal e em terras lusitanas e ex-lusitanas da Ásia, da África e do Atlântico* (Rio de Janeiro: José Olympio, 1953).

42. Gurvitch to "Chers Amis" [the Freyres], Paris, January 2, 1953, GF.

43. For more on these reviews, see Jacques Leenhardt, "A consagração na França de um pensamento heterodoxo," in *Reinventar o Brasil: Gilberto Freyre entre história e ficção*, ed. Antônio Dimas, Jacques Leenhardt, Sandra Jatahy Pesavento (Porto Alegre: Editora da UFRGS / Editora da USP, 2006), 25–40.

44. Georges Balandier, review of *Maîtres et esclaves*, by Gilberto Freyre, *Cahiers internationaux de sociologie* 16 (1954): 183–85.

45. Bastide to "Cher Monsieur" [Freyre], São Paulo, September 7, 1953, GF.

46. Ibid.

47. Febvre to Freyre, Paris, November 6, 1952, GF. The other non-French member was historian Armando Sapori. I thank Brigitte Mazon for clarifying this point.

48. Marco Chor Maio's dissertation is by far the most comprehensive source on this topic. Maio, "A História do projeto UNESCO: Estudos raciais e ciências sociais no Brasil" (PhD diss., Instituto Universitário de Pesquisas do Rio de Janeiro, 1997). A more recent conference on the project's fifty-year anniversary updated and expanded upon Maio's findings. Cláudio Pereira and Livio Sansone, eds., *Projeto UNESCO no Brasil: Textos Críticos* (Salvador: EDUFBA, 2007).

49. For more on these statements and their internal tensions, see Marco Chor Maio and Ricardo Ventura Santos, "Antiracism and the Uses of Science in the Post-World

War II: An Analysis of UNESCO'S First Statements on Race (1950 and 1951)," *Vibrant* 12, no. 2 (2015): 1–26. See also Sebastián Gil-Riaño, "Relocating Anti-Racist Science: The 1950 UNESCO Statement on Race and Economic Development in the Global South," *British Journal for the History of Science* 51, no. 2 (2008): 281–303.

50. Ramos's posthumously published book *Le métissage au Brésil* largely confirmed the first race statement, which suggested that there were no fundamental biological differences between peoples. "The experience of 'racial mixing' in the tropics," he wrote, "did not reveal any disadvantage as far as the mixture of races." *Le métissage au Brésil*, trans. M. L. Modiano (Paris: Hermann, 1952), 4.

51. Marco Chor Maio, "O projeto UNESCO e a agenda das ciências sociais no Brasil dos anos 40 e 50," *Revista brasileira de ciências sociais* 41, no. 14 (2000): 156.

52. For Métraux's initials statement on the "racial problem," see Alfred Métraux, "UNESCO and the Racial Problem," *International Social Science Bulletin* 2, no. 3 (1950): 384–90. For more on Métraux's relationships that informed some of this research, see Angela Lühning, "Verger, Bastide e Métraux: Três trajetórias entrelaçadas," *Revista USP*, no 95 (2012): 133–35.

53. Alfred Métraux, "An Inquiry into Race Relations in Brazil," *UNESCO Courier* 5, no. 8–9 (1952): 6.

54. Alfred Métraux, "Brazil: A Land of Harmony for All Races?," *UNESCO Courier* 4, no. 4 (1951). Lorenzo Macagno analyzes the "luso-tropicalist" aspects of Métraux in his article "Alfred Métraux: Antropologia aplicada e lusotropicalismo," *Etnográfica* 17, no. 2 (2013), esp. 225–31.

55. Métraux, "Brazil: A Land of Harmony for All Races?," 3. Métraux offered to have Freyre's *Casa-grande e senzala* translated into English while he was working at Yale University, but does not seem to have found a satisfactory translator (Métraux to Freyre, New Haven, June 3, 1941, GF). Métraux's archive, which holds his lecture notes for his courses on Latin American history and culture, demonstrate that he understood Brazil to have a "lack of racial prejudice . . . as we understand them in the United States. Mulattoes were and are more than ever slowly absorbed into the white groups and the Negroes into the mulatto population" ("Notes de cours sur les discriminations selon les critères de race et de classe sociale dans divers pays de l'Amérique du sud," p. 1, FAM.AS.E.01.01.03, LAS).

56. Gilberto Freyre, "Mestre Metraux confirma," *O Cruzeiro*, April 5, 1952, article 191, GF.

57. Métraux, "An Inquiry into Race Relations in Brazil," 6.

58. Métraux, "Carnet n. 87," Thursday, November 30, 1950, FAM.H.MT.01.23, LAS.

59. Métraux to Freyre, Paris, August 22, 1951, GF.

60. Gilberto Freyre, *Sobrados e mucambos: Decadência do patriarcado rural e desenvolvimento do urbano*, vol. 1 (Rio de Janeiro: José Olympio, 1951), 1075.

61. Métraux to Freyre, Paris, March 31, 1952, GF.

62. Métraux to Freyre, Paris, April 11, 1952, GF.

63. Dávila, *Hotel Trópico*, 11–26.

64. Gilberto Freyre, "The Negro's Role in Brazilian History," *UNESCO Courier* 5, no. 8–9 (1952): 7–8.

65. Ibid., 8.

66. Here I appropriate Simone Meucci's term to express the increasing distance between Freyre and the Paulista school of sociology. Meucci, *Artesania da Sociologia no Brasil: Contribuições e intepretações de Gilberto Freyre* (Curitiba: Editora Appris, 2015).

67. Roger Bastide, "São Paulo: The Octopus Town," *UNESCO Courier* 5, no. 8–9 (1952): 9.

68. Ibid.

69. The criticisms in question appear in Gilberto Freyre, "Uma interpretação de São Paulo," *Diário de São Paulo*, January 25, 1954.

70. This study has become a classic in Brazilian social-scientific literature. First published in parts in 1953 in the journal *Anhembi*, it was published as a book in 1955 as Roger Bastide and Florestan Fernandes, *Relações raciais entre negros e brancos em São Paulo* (São Paulo: UNESCO/Anhembi, 1955), only to become *Brancos e negros em São Paulo* in subsequent editions. Whether in texts about Fernandes, the UNESCO project, or the book specifically, analyses of it abound. For a recent example, see Eliane Veras Soares, Maria Lúcia de Santana Braga, and Diogo Valença de A. Costa, "O dilema racial brasileiro: De Roger Bastide a Florestan Fernandes ou da explicação teórica à proposição política," *Sociedade e cultura* 5, no. 1 (2002): 35–52. Here I use the original, serialized version and limit myself to the study's direct criticisms of Freyre and of claims about "racial democracy." For a historical and empirical critique of Fernandes, see George Reid Andrews, *Blacks and Whites in São Paulo, Brazil, 1888–1988* (Madison: University of Wisconsin Press, 1991), esp. 71–81.

71. Antonio Sérgio Alfredo Guimarães, "O projeto UNESCO na Bahia," in *Projeto UNESCO no Brasil: Textos Críticos*, ed. Cláudio Pereira and Livio Sansone (Salvador: EDUFBA, 2007), 32–33.

72. Florestan Fernandes, "Do escravo ao cidadão," *Anhembi* 10, no. 30 (1953): 440, 484.

73. Ibid., 473.

74. Ibid., 476.

75. Ibid., 480.

76. For an excellent essay by Flávio dos Santos Gomes that speaks to the inherent problem of agency in the work of historical sociologists like Fernandes who deal with slavery, see "Em torno da herança: Do escravo-coisa ao negro massa," in *Ideias de modernidade e sociologia no Brasil: Ensaios sobre Luiz Aguiar Costa Pinto*, ed. Marcos Chor Maio and Gláucia Villas Bôas (Porto Alegre: UFRGS, 1999).

77. Florestan Fernandes, "Cor e estrutura social em mudança," *Anhembi* 11, no. 31

(1953): 14. For more on class versus race in Fernandes, see Marcos Chor Maio and Rosemary Galli, "Florestan Fernandes, Oracy Nogueira, and the UNESCO Project on Race Relations in São Paulo," *Latin American Perspectives* 3 (2011): 140.

78. Fernandes, "Cor e estrutura social em mudança," 18.

79. Ibid., 20.

80. Ibid., 48.

81. Ibid., 62.

82. Roger Bastide, "Manifestações do preconceito de cor," *Anhembi* 11, no. 32 (1953): 242–77. Bastide's lengthy correspondence with Fernandes is found at UFSCar-FF. Unfortunately, at Bastide's archive in France (IMEC), there is only one letter from Fernandes, from 1971.

83. Bastide, "Manifestações do preconceito de cor," 243.

84. Ibid., 251.

85. Bastide to Fernandes, Paris, March 4, 1952, p. 1, 002654.02.09.2016, UFSCar-FF.

86. Ibid., p. 2.

87. Ibid.

88. Bastide to Fernandes, Paris, March 18, 1952, 00265302.09.2015, UFSCar-FF.

89. Bastide, "Manifestações do preconceito de cor," 253.

90. Ibid., 257.

91. Ibid., 242. This often-cited occurrence is analyzed in Andrews, *Blacks and Whites in São Paulo*, 184, and Alberto, *Terms of Inclusion*, 175–76.

92. Bastide, "Manifestações do preconceito de cor," 260. For a comparison on the research conducted in Bahia and São Paulo, the two principal centers of UNESCO's work, see Guimarães, "Baianos e paulistas 'duas escolas' de relações raciais?" *Tempo social* 11, no. 1 (1999): 75–95.

93. For more on this, see Alberto, *Terms of Inclusion*, esp. chap. 1.

94. For Bastide's analysis of the *Teatro Experimental do Negro*, see Roger Bastide, "A propósito do Teatro Experimental do Negro," *Anhembi* 3, no. 9 (1951): 541–44.

95. See, for example, Arthur Ramos, "Foreign Research on Brazilian Blacks," *Vibrant* 7, no. 1 (2010), http://www.vibrant.org.br/issues/v7n1/artur-ramos-foreign-research-on-brazilian-blacks/. For an eloquent questioning of the "problem," even if two decades later, see Paulina L. Alberto, "When Rio Was *Black*: Soul Music, National Culture, and the Politics of Racial Comparison in 1970s Brazil," *Hispanic American Historical Review* 89, no. 1 (2009): 3–39.

96. Bastide, "Manifestações do preconceito de cor," 269. "Morena" is an inherently untranslatable word, particularly because it is regionally specific. It can be read as referring to either a brunet(te) or "a person with tan or light brown skin" (Andrews, *Blacks and Whites in São Paulo*, 264).

97. For more on this, see Florestan Fernandes, *A integração do negro na sociedade de classes*, vol. 1 (Rio de Janeiro: Globo Editora, 2008). For an English version, see

Fernandes, *The Negro in Brazilian Society*, trans. Jacqueline D. Skiles, A. Brunel, and Arthur Rothwell (New York: Columbia University Press, 1969).

98. By this point, Freyre increasingly defined himself as a writer rather than as a pure sociologist, partially as a way of distinguishing himself from the younger generation of university-trained and -affiliated sociologists, such as Fernandes. See Gilberto Freyre, *Como e por que sou e não sou sociológo* (Brasília: Editora da Universidade, 1968).

99. That said, these criticisms did not prevent Freyre and Fernandes from maintaining a collegial and even friendly relationship. After Freyre hosted Fernandes at his home in Recife, however, the latter sent a thank-you letter that demonstrates the tension between the two. Fernandes wrote of their *entendimento franco* (frank understanding)—in Brazil, where arguments often take the form of accommodation rather than direct challenge, this language is strong. Fernandes to Freyre, São Paulo, April 7, 1961, GF.

100. *Nordeste* was translated by Jean Orecchioni as *Terres du sucre* (Paris: Gallimard, 1956). Freyre later claimed to have preferred Orecchioni's translation to Bastide's, because of his attentiveness to Freyre's style. This question has been analyzed by Ria LeMaire ("Amores inteligentes," in Dimas, Leenhardt, and Pesavento, *Reinventar o Brasil*, 91–95).

101. Matthew Connelly, *A Diplomatic Revolution: Algeria's Fight for Independence and the Origins of the Post–Cold War Era* (Oxford: Oxford University Press, 2002), 69–116.

102. Colóquio de Cerisy, Pasta FR 1956, GF.

103. Gilberto Freyre, "Ainda sobre o Seminário de Cerisy," *O Cruzeiro*, March 16, 1957, article 444, GF.

104. Claude Lévi-Strauss, *Race and History* (Paris: UNESCO, 1952), 21. Later in this book, he noted that "the historical concomitant of technical progress has been the development of the exploitation of man by man" (ibid., 47).

105. Ibid., 26–27.

106. Ibid., 45.

107. My goal here is not to denigrate Lévi-Strauss as a racial purist, which he never was. It is instead to suggest another possible reason why he and Freyre may have disagreed.

108. Freyre, "The Negro's Role in Brazilian History," 8.

109. Caillois's criticism of *Race et histoire*, and Lévi-Strauss's response, have been thoroughly analyzed in the secondary literature. Patrick Wilcken, *Claude Lévi-Strauss: The Poet in the Laboratory* (London: Bloomsbury, 2010), 191–93. The original citations are Roger Caillois, "Illusion à rebours," *Nouvelle revue française* 24 (1954): 1010–24; 25 (1955): 58–70; and Claude Lévi-Strauss, "Diogène couché," *Les temps modernes* 10, no. 110 (1955): 1218–19.

110. Among the original signatories were, in addition to Lévi-Strauss, Gurvitch, and

Leiris, Paul Ricoeur, François Mauriac, André Breton, Jean-Paul Sartre, Marguerite Duras, Henri Lefebvre, and Jean Cocteau. For more on this, see James D. Le Sueur, "Decolonizing 'French Universalism': Reconsidering the Impact of the Algerian War on French intellectuals," in *The Decolonization Reader*, ed. Le Sueur (New York: Routledge, 2003), 107–9, 115. Gurvitch's presence is, to a certain extent, a mystery, but suffice it to say that, being naturalized rather than born French, his loyalties toward empire were less visceral.

111. See Emmanuelle Loyer, *Claude Lévi-Strauss* Loyer (Paris: Flammarion, 2015), 593–94. For a more extended analysis, see Christine Laurière, "Jacques Soustelle, de Mexique terre indienne à l'Algérie, terre française," in *Ethnologues en situations coloniales*, ed. Laurière and André Mary, Les carnets de Bérose 11 (Paris: Bérose, 2019), http://www.berose.fr/article1706.html.

112. Soustelle to "Mon Cher Ami" [Lévi-Strauss], Algiers, November 14, 1955, Manuscrits, NAF 28150 (202), BnF.

113. Lévi-Strauss to "Mon cher Soustelle," Paris, November 21, 1955, Manuscrits, NAF 28150 (202), BnF.

114. Ibid.

115. Lévi-Strauss to "Mon cher Soustelle," Paris, December 1, 1956, Manuscrits, NAF 28150 (202), BnF; Jacques Soustelle, *Aimée et souffrante Algérie* (Paris: Plon, 1956).

116. Lévi-Strauss to "Mon cher Soustelle," Paris, December 1, 1956, Manuscrits, NAF 28150 (202), BnF.

117. Ibid.

118. Claude Lévi-Strauss, "Le socialisme et la colonisation" (1929), cited in Loyer, *Lévi-Strauss*, 114.

119. For more on this project, see Jeffrey James Byrne, *Mecca of Revolution: Algeria, Decolonization, and the Third World Order* (Oxford: Oxford University Press, 2016).

120. For two poignant analyses, see Todd Shepard, "Thinking between Metropole and Colony: The French Republic, 'Exceptional Promotion,' and the 'Integration' of Algerians, 1955–1962," in *The French Colonial Mind*, ed. Martin Thomas (Lincoln: University of Nebraska Press, 2011), 298–323; Muriam Haleh Davis, "'The Transformation of Man' in French Algeria: Economic Planning and the Postwar Social Sciences, 1958–62," *Journal of Contemporary History* 52, no. 1 (2017): 73–94.

121. It may have been the case that he was requested not to go by the Brazilian government.

122. Gilberto Freyre, "Nós e a França," *O Cruzeiro*, November 19, 1966, article 837, GF.

123. Senghor quoted in Cooper, *Citizenship between Empire and Nation*, 262. For more on Fanon and negritude, see Wilder, *Freedom Time*, 134–35.

124. Léopold Sédar Senghor, "Roger Bastide, sourcier et sorcier de la négritude," in *L'autre et l'ailleurs: Hommage à Roger Bastide*, ed. Jean Poirier and François Raveau (Nice: Institut d'études et de recherches interethniques et interculturelles, 1976): 97.

125. Fernandes, *Negro in Brazilian Society*; Fernandes, *Reflections on the Brazilian Counter-revolution*, ed. Warren Dean (New York: Routledge, 1981).

126. Roger Bastide, "Chronique des livres de sociologie brésilienne," *Revue internationale de sociologie* 47, no. 1–2 (1939): 91.

EN GUISE DE CONCLUSION

1. Roger Bastide, *Brésil, terre de contrastes* (Paris: Hachette, 1957).

2. For more, see Luís Correia Lima, *Fernand Braudel e o Brasil: Vivência e brasilianismo (1935–1945)* (São Paulo: Edusp, 2009), 188–93.

3. Paulo Duarte, "Solidariedade democrática," *Anhembi* 27, no. 81 (1957): 450.

4. Paulo Eduardo Arantes, *Um departamento francês de ultramar* (Rio de Janeiro: Paz e Terra, 1994).

5. For the most comprehensive study on the subject, see Diogo da Silva Roiz and Jonas Rafael Santos, *As transferências culturais na historiografia brasileira: Leituras e apropriações do movimento dos Annales no Brasil* (Jundiaí: Paco Editorial, 2012).

6. Mauro quoted in Hugo Rogélio Suppo, "La politique culturelle française au Brésil entre les années 1920–1950" (PhD diss., Paris III-Sorbonne Nouvelle, 1999), 864.

7. Sylvia Gemignani Garcia, *Destino ímpar: Sobre a formação de Florestan Fernandes* (São Paulo: Editora 34, 2002); Garcia and Maria Arminda do Nascimento, *Florestan Fernandes: Mestre de sociologia moderna* (Brasília: Paralelo 15/CAPES, 2003). See also Luiz Carlos Jackson, "Tensões e disputas na sociologia paulista (1940–1970)," *Revista brasileira de ciências sociais* 22, no. 65 (2007): 33–49.

8. Barradas to Braudel, São Paulo, December 31, 1964, FB.

9. The most comprehensive work on this period to date is Rodrigo Patto Sá Motta, *As universidades e o regime militar: Cultura política brasileira e modernização autoritária* (Rio de Janeiro: Zahar, 2014), esp. 110–48.

10. A sociological study using geometric data analysis to relate variables such as class, previous overseas experience, politics (in favor of, openly resistant to, or accommodating of the military regime), and kinds of disciplines would certainly provide an interesting point of departure for an analysis of "French" versus "American" models for social science in authoritarian Brazil. For the field of economics, see Elisa Klüger, "Meritocracia dos laços: Gênese e reconfigurações do espaço dos economistas no Brasil" (PhD diss., University of São Paulo, 2017).

11. Touraine to Braudel, Paris, June 17, 1964, FB.

12. Note by Paule Braudel, Paris, 2001, FB.

13. Braudel to Deayrell, telegram, March 5, 1970, FB.

14. Caio Prado Jr., *Estruturalismo de Lévi-Strauss: Marxismo de Althusser* (São Paulo: Brasiliense, 1971), 13.

15. Ibid.

16. Ibid., 9.

17. Roger Bastide, "Macunaíma em Paris," *O Estado de S. Paulo*, February 3, 1946; reproduced in *Navette literária França-Brasil*, vol. 2, *Textos de crítica literária de Roger Bastide*, ed. Gloria Carneiro do Amaral (São Paulo: Edusp, 2010), 532.

18. Eduardo d'Oliveira França to Braudel, Salvador, September 28, 1962, FB.

19. Braudel to França, Paris, June 13, 1963, FB.

20. Roger Bastide, Françoise Morin, and François Raveau, eds., *Les haïtiens en France* (Paris: Mouton, 1974).

21. For the Clastres fieldwork of 1966–77 among the Guarani and Chaco, see Correspondence personnelle du Directeur Général du CNRS, 1953–1979, Cote (finding number) 19850505/10, "Laboratoire d'anthropologie sociale. Rapport d'activité, 1966–1967," p. 3, Archives Nationales de France, Pierrefitte-sur-Seine (henceforth AN). More generally, the CNRS archives suggest that Monbeig was a useful contact for Braudel, Lévi-Strauss, and other Latin Americanists as they built up their institutions.

22. "Lettre ouverte à Son Excellence le général Arthur Costa e Silva Président de la République du Brésil," *Journal de la Société des américanistes* 56, no. 2 (1967): 612–17.

23. Monbeig to Miguel Alvez de Lima, Paris, May 2, 1968, Cote (finding number) 19850505/1, AN. The pedagogical and popularizing collection Que sais-je? published Monbeig's *Le Brésil* (Paris: Presses Universitaires de France, 1968).

24. Michael P. Farrell, *Collaborative Circles: Friendship Dynamics and Creative Work* (Chicago: University of Chicago Press, 2001), 25–26.

25. Loyer, *Lévi-Strauss*, 532; Claude Lévi-Strauss, *Wild Thought: A New Translation of "La pensée sauvage"*, trans. Jeffrey Mehlman and John Leavitte (Chicago: University of Chicago Press, 2020); Lévi-Strauss, *The Raw and the Cooked* (Chicago: University of Chicago Press, 1969), *From Honey to Ashes* (New York: Harper & Row, 1973), *The Origin of Table Manners* (Chicago: University of Chicago Press, 1978), *The Naked Man* (Chicago: University of Chicago Press, 1981). These last four were translated into English by John and Doreen Weightman.

26. Loyer, *Lévi-Strauss*, 538.

27. Fernand Braudel, *Civilization and Capitalism, 15th–18th Centuries*, 3 vols., trans. Sian Reynolds, vol 1, *The Structures of Everyday Life* (New York: Harper & Row, 1982), vol. 2, *The Wheels of Commerce* (New York: Harper & Row, 1982), vol. 3, *The Perspective of the World* (New York: Harper & Row, 1984). For more on this period in Braudel's oeuvre, see, for example, Pierre Daix, *Braudel* (Paris: Flammarion, 1995), 383–97, 465–90.

28. Claude Lévi-Strauss, "Discours pour remise de l'épée d'académicien à F. Braudel" (unpublished notes), March 18, 1985, FB.

29. Jean Maugüé, *Les dents agacées* (Paris: Buchet-Chastel, 1982).

30. Lévi-Strauss, "Discours pour remise de l'épée."

31. Wilcken, *Lévi-Strauss*, 315.

32. Lévi-Strauss, *Saudades do Brasil* (Paris: Plon, 1994).

33. J. M. G. Le Clézio, "The Savage Detective," *New York Times*, November 7, 2009, http://www.nytimes.com/2009/11/08/opinion/08le-clezio.html.

34. *Bastidiana* (website), accessed March 23, 2018, http://claude.ravelet.pagesperso -orange.fr/revue.html.

35. Martine Droulers and Hervé Théry, eds., *Pierre Monbeig: Un géographe pionnier* (Paris: Éditions de l'IHEAL, 1991).

36. One such conference was France-Brésil en miroir: Reflets et réflexions d'une anthropologie contemporaine, Laboratoire d'Anthropologie Sociale, Paris, October 26 and 27, 2017, http://las.ehess.fr/index.php?2575.

37. An interesting documentary on USP, for example, was created by Marcello G. Tassara: *O Brasil, os Índios, e Finalmente, a USP* (1988), available at http://www.iea.usp .br/midiateca/video/videos-1988/o-brasil-os-indios-e-finalmente-a-usp.

38. Banco de Dados França-Brasil / Banque de Données France-Brésil Português (website), created by Mario Carelli, accessed July 28, 2021, http://bfb.iea.usp.br/.

39. A França no Brasil (website), Biblioteca Nacional do Brasil and Biblio- thèque Nationale de France, accessed July 28, 2021, http://bndigital.bn.br/francebr/ apresentacao.htm.

40. Raewyn Connell, *Southern Theory: Social Science and the Global Dynamics of Knowledge* (Cambridge: Polity Press, 2007). See also Jean Comaroff and John L. Comaroff, *Theory from the South, or How Euro-America Is Evolving toward Africa* (New York: Routledge, 2012).

Index

Abbott, Andrew, 203n36
Abreu, Askhelão de, 114
Academia Brasileira de Letras, 22–23, 87
Académie Française, 33, 42, 189
Action Française, 109
Adorno, Theodor, 109, 152, 237n6
Africa, 12–13, 44, 66, 77–78, 104, 106–7, 110, 113, 126–27, 135, 142, 151, 167, 170, 180
African Americans, 175
Africanness, 110
African Religions of Brazil, The (Bastide), 159
Afro-Brazilian studies, 84, 88
agregé, 76, 85
Alcan, Félix, 214n61
Alcântara, José de, 25
Algeria, 1, 12, 48, 81, 90, 121–22, 163, 178–80, 183, 247n197; Algerian revolution, as race war, 177; as "failed Brazil," 82
Aliança Nacional Libertadora, 2, 49; backlash against, 33
Almeida Prado, Antônio de, 28–29
Almeida Prado, Décio de, 90
Almeida Prado, João Fernando de, 143
Alves, Castro, 110
Alvez de Lima, Miguel, 188
Amado, Jorge, 72, 150
Amaral, Tarsila do, 8, 23
Americanization, 3
American Treasure and the Price Revolution in Spain, 1501–1650 (Hamilton), 118

Amoroso Lima, Alceu, 33
Andaman Islands, 102
Andes, 74–75
Andrada, Raul de, 100
Andrade, Mário de, 1–2, 9–10, 13–14, 16, 23, 38, 62, 67, 75, 79, 111, 114–15, 186, 211n32, 212n40
Andrade, Oswald de, 7–8, 23, 111
Angola, 170
Annales (journal), 17, 38, 41, 56–57, 59, 72, 90, 94, 104, 116, 121, 134, 136–39, 144–45, 147, 154–55, 157, 159, 163, 165, 168, 177, 184, 233n109; Latin America, special issue on, 142–43, 153; *mentalités*, use of, 82–83
Annales school, 1, 4
anthropology, 6, 8, 12, 39, 54–55, 96, 123–24, 129, 131, 150, 156–57, 190, 192; Afro-Brazilian studies, as subfield of, 84; Brazilian, 76; cultural, 43, 52; ethnology, antagonism between, 130; fascism and anti-Semitism, association with, 130; and history, 157; indigenous, 16, 66; intercultural dialogue, 180; physical, 40, 62, 125; social, 148, 158; structural, 1, 17; United States, as established field in, 77
Antilles, 88, 141–42
anti-Semitism, 130
Antwerp (Belgium), 119
Appelbaum, Nancy, 12
Arantes, Paulo, 8, 184
Arbos, Philippe, 100

Made in United States
North Haven, CT
19 September 2023

41731051R00163